333.24
581c

The author of THE CHILD SEDUCERS traces the steps that Dewey and his followers have taken in converting the tax supported schools of America into one huge vehicle for transporting Marxist revolution.

Steinbacher makes the charge, substantiated within the pages of this book, that conscientious educators and teachers have been brainwashed by behaviorists and Third Force Psychologists in a massive attempt to convert America's classrooms into extensions of mental health wards, with teachers serving as parapsychologists or clinicians and *students openly identified as PATIENTS.*

"There has been enough probing to reveal that within a broad, humanistic framework, your children are being *manipulated as experimental animals,"* Steinbacher writes.

He continues, "Parental values are the target. Attitudes can be changed and behavior altered, but only by strenuous indoctrination, or the use of behavior modification drugs or psychological techniques carefully designed to inculcate differing attitudes and behaviors . . . and the manipulation of the young is predetermined by a handful of people who say, 'There are absolutely no moral absolutes, and we know that, absolutely.' "

Steinbacher spells out the final outcome of all this planned subversion, unless America's parents reverse the trends in education.

"In Germany, the silent majority elected Adolph Hitler. The silent majority in America, when their TV is finally interrupted and their security utterly shattered, will also scream for a dictator—*a police state to protect them from the revolutionaries now being spawned by the hundreds of thousands in our so-called schools of knowledge . . . "*

One of Steinbacher's bitterest enemies, Dixon Gayer (leftist professor at Cal State, Long Beach, Calif.), reviewed the book as follows:

"It would be good to be able to dismiss 'The Child Seducers' as the irresponsible garbage it is, but to do so would be foolish. In two short years John Steinbacher, through his School and Family column in the Anaheim Bulletin, has become a national champion for decency in the schools.

"Mr. Steinbacher's book will be a million-seller and it will be quoted in school meetings from California to Maine. It is a vicious, devastating book, but in the present climate of fear and suspicion, it will be read and accepted as gospel."

THE CHILD SEDUCERS

by JOHN STEINBACHER

"For evil men and seducers shall wax worse and worse, deceiving and being deceived . . . " 2nd Timothy 3:13

Educator Publications Inc.

DEDICATION

Dedicated to the thousands of mothers and fathers all over America who cared enough about their children to form committees to fight the depredations of the Child Seducers and to many teachers in hundreds of school districts who kept the committees informed.

Many thanks to Eleanor Howe, for checking the manuscript and to the following people for their encouragement: Douglas Sewell, Lucille Townsend, Sam Campbell, and to Vic McLeod, my editor at Educator Publications.

— **John Steinbacher**

1st Printing — Dec. 1970
2nd Printing — Jan. 1971
3rd Printing — March 1971
4th Printing — April 1971

AUTHOR'S NOTE

This book is in response to literally hundreds of requests from parents and teachers around the nation who have looked to the author and to the Anaheim Bulletin for guidance in the controversy over sex instruction and sensitivity training in the schools.

Readers of the author's daily newspaper column realize that the problem they face is multi-faceted and deals with much more than a few dirty words used in a classroom or the imparting of clinical knowledge to children before they are old enough to absorb it.

Sex instruction is only one small part of a massive bulldozer operation to convert America's public school system into a series of behavioral science clinics for reshaping and restructuring the children into the International Child of Orwell's 1984.

For a new alien strain has crept into our culture – humanism, a religion that denies the very existence of all the eternal verities.

The charge—we believe substantiated within the pages of this book—is that the giant tax supported school system (and increasingly, the Parochial schools, as well) has become the vehicle through which Humanism will be made the new religious cult in America.

Religions of all kinds claim that their sole purpose for existence is to "change" people, to restructure their lives around a set of values or beliefs they call a creed. In the West, it has traditionally been that of Judeo-Christianity.

Family life and sex instruction courses are, by and large, written and designed by Humanists, a small, fanatical band of extremists who seek to impose their immoral cult upon millions of American children.

JOHN STEINBACHER
Anaheim, California

iii

FOREWORD

In writing the foreword for "The Child Seducers" my initial impulse was to enthuse over the completeness of John Steinbacher's chilling expository. My considered opinion is, however – this book needs no endorsement, for Mr. Steinbacher has so precisely presented a vast amount of research that the book stands superbly on its own merits. The author graphically demonstrates the fact that the children of America are being gripped in the vise of either an unwise or unscrupulous education system, and are being forcefully made accessories to the incomes of huge publishing empires, and others. This factually presented information is sufficient to unsettle even the most complacent or indifferent reader.

Parents are faced with the problem of trying to protect their children against vast educational experiments, euphemistically described as 'pilot programs,' wherein carefully indoctrinated puppeteers are completely mesmerizing the youth of America. However, these poseurs do not identify their program as hypnotism – rather their functions are completely disguised as 'developing good interpersonal relations,' as operant conditioning, as family life-sex education, as sensitivity training-role playing, as teaching ABOUT morality through teaching immorality, as teaching ABOUT learning through the medium of non-teaching. These are the monstrously intertwined educational speciations which have been spawned by permissive-progressive educationists and are being tolerated by rubber stamp school boards. These educationists, and others, are inducing behavioral changes in millions of victims through the misuse of the psychological-theoretical constructs of Skinner

v

(operant conditioning), and Sullivan and Timothy Leary (interpersonal relations), and Freud (in the heathenish family life-sex education programs), and Moreno's psychodrama (role playing and sensitivity training), as well as the atheistic philosophies of Humanism, and by the wholly inane philosophy of schools having no failures, and most startling, they are altering minds through the use of drugs.

Students have become captive participants in vast pseudo-psycho-therapeutic, and/or drug directed experiments wherein educationists, and others, are utilizing or promoting various psycho-biological techniques which are perfectly valid when used in a carefully controlled, ethically governed psychotherapeutic setting, for the purpose of stabilizing the emotionally disturbed, but which have no validity when misused in a 'normal' school setting, upon normally adjusted students. All of this is thoroughly discussed in The Child Seducers.

Operant conditioning is finely delineated in Chapter XV of The Child Seducers in the discussion of Taxonomy, and the 3M Family Life Programs, originally developed as the federally funded SHES program, and which, when introduced into many school districts, is being carefully described as "a grass roots approach for solving the 'problem' of sex education." When the author of 'Taxonomy of Educational Objectives' states that the *intended* behavior of students is being classified, the reader must understand that such classification can only come about *if* a student has been programmed by a trainer either through operant conditioning, or some other form of sensitivity training. These are separately defined methods for achieving a singular result: a robotized, group-dependent human being. Succinctly, a trainer carefully arranges conditions in ways specified by the laws of a system, and in this manner, the trainer not only can predict − he controls. In Skinner's words, "The hypothesis that man is NOT FREE is essential to the application of scientific method (operant conditioning) to the study (and control) of human behavior." For in his Designing a Culture, Skinner envisages the ultimate possibilities of con-

vi

trolling the larger political and ethical aspects of society to be boundless. And what better point of beginning than the nation's schools.

Even though the idea that any EXPERT in conditioning techniques may set out *deliberately* to shape behavior to conform to some individually pre-conceived particular pattern is repugnant to all thinking Americans, this in no manner dissuades the zealots dedicated to the cause of reshaping human behavior. Even though operant conditioning carries such accurately derogatory labels as 'mind-bending' and 'brain washing' you will find this technique being implemented with great speed in many of the schools of our land. Operant conditioning is such a highly controversial psychological technique that its ethical, and other ramifications, of *scientifically* controlling human behavior, has long been debated.

Under normal circumstances of day to day living, each individual is relatively free to select that behavior which is meaningful to him as an individual. Under operant conditioning, individual behavior patterns can be drastically altered, for here behavior patterns are selected FOR the individual BY a trainer, or an experimentalist, or eventually by the State. This is a frightening form of human intervention, and manipulation, being promoted in our government controlled schools. However, the anthill society is the dream of every man of power. And the crucial question must be asked . . . "Who will be in control?"

The rationale under which sex education has been introduced into the schools may be found in the following statements. According to Sigmund Freud (Social Medicine and Hygiene, 1907) "I should prefer that parents NOT concern themselves at all with any explanations regarding matters of sexuality. Above all, schools should not evade the task of mentioning sexual matters. Schools should present lessons about the animal kingdom which should include the great facts of reproduction. These facts should be given their due significance, and emphasis should be laid on the fact that man shares with the higher animals EVERYTHING essential to his own organization." And "In those countries which leave the education of children either wholly or in part in the hands of religious the above method urged, would of course, NOT be practicable. For NO religion will ever admit the IDENTITY in NATURE of MAN and BEAST, since to the religious person the IMMORTALITY of the soul is an absolute foundation for MORAL training, which they cannot forego."

Freud cites as the authority for these views the writings of the self-avowed atheistic Dutch dramatist 'Multatuli' who separated from his family, led a Bohemian life in Amsterdam, Brussels and elsewhere, finally settling in Germany. Multatuli particularly opposed the influence of the church, and religion, on individual freedom of thought. The simple fact, is family life-sex education courses are vehicles of this philosophy, for they expound absolute permissiveness, designed to encourage atavistic behavior; the films invigorate the labile fantasies of even the dullest, not-yet-self-controlled child, and no child, so titillated, can learn the basics of education which properly should be the only material presented in a classroom setting. This can only be defined as an absolute usurpation of the child's right to be properly educated.

Sensitivity training, a technique employing 'psychological uppers and downers,' is a slough of Esalen, and National Training Laboratories (NTL) of the National Education Association (NEA). Initially, sensitivity training was eulogized as a promoter of "good interpersonal relations" and group cohesiveness. However, trainers insist that each individual must submerge his own integrity to that of the group, leaving the participant subject to the machinations of the trainer and/or the group.

In recent years, countless numbers of individuals have reported that depravity has become the epoxy of sensitivity training. And now word comes in from widely differing parts of the country that participation in sensitivity training courses is becoming increasingly demanded of school administrators and of those who teach family life-sex education courses, those who are involved in physical education, the various branches of the social studies programs, home economics, etc.

It is as Dr. Charlotte Crabtree recently enthused to those attending a Social Studies Symposium in Portland, Oregon, "You are pioneers; you are right out on the frontier when you teach this very dangerous material. To date, NO analyses of our programs are possible . . . analyses are still very primitive . . . but we HOPE for some changes when *Taxonomy* is committed to PPBS (Planning, Programming, Budgeting System - data processing procedures)."

From variously designed sensitivity training sessions, most resembling nothing more than a witches' Sabbath, 'newly trained trainers' are spewed forth to spread their heresies, and to effect various forms of behavioral and attitudinal changes throughout the land and especially throughout the whole educational system of America, for in the words of Lester Kirkendall, "We have too many youth indoctrinated with the provincial attitudes of their families." (Basic Issues in Sex Education, California School Health, Vol. 3, No. 1, January, 1967).

And from NEA's Issues in Training comes this word, "Training, even though it has NOT reached professional status, and ill-defined as it is, has had good acceptance in many organizations. (Note: Notably in the field of education.)

"There is NO clear-cut set of standards for trainers" . . . (therefore no ethical absolutes) . . . "professionally, knowledge in the fields of sociology, psychology, social work, educational psychology, psychiatry, personnel or administration, whether gained from an academic situation OR whether self-taught, is considered to be helpful," and " 'Getting to know you, Getting to feel, free and easy' is more than just a line from a popular song. It is BASIC to success in interpersonal relations."

Through the mediums of education in sexuality, of sensitivity training, and of operant conditioning, trainers have learned that it is all too easy to manipulate a child by denigrat-

ix

ing parents. By extolling amorality, they have also learned how to preclude the formation of individual conscience and individual integrity in a child, and how to effectively alienate a child from his parents through the changing of moral norms. When sufficient downgrading of parental values has occurred, a child will not identify with the appropriate, or like-sex parent. An ongoing study of child-parent identification has revealed fairly serious, to severe maladjustment in 92% of those children not making the proper identification with his or her parent(s). This is a frightening statistic.

Professor George Odiorne of the University of Michigan summed up the whole problem when he stated "Many trainers are 'amateur head shrinkers' that lack the proper psychological training, psychiatric damage may result, and it's experimental, and an invasion of privacy."

All of which Mr. Steinbacher has researched so thoroughly, and explains so clearly in The Child Seducers.

M. Royer, M.S.

PUBLISHER'S NOTE

In her letter to us that accompanied her foreword to this book, Mary Royer said: "Thank you for inviting me to write the foreword to this thoroughly researched and beautifully written book. Isn't it a shame that it has been necessary to write such a book about a decadent educational system in a country as great as our own United States . . . but necessary it is. No one could have done the job half as well as John Steinbacher. His tenacity as a good journalist shows clearly in every line. You asked that my foreword be a genuine critique, and I hope that you find it so. At no point in the book could I find any point on which the author and I are not in complete agreement. His findings are sound, his conclusions are well drawn."

MARY ROYER, M.S., received her BA degree from the University of Portland in 1961. She majored in psychology, with minors in sociology and philosophy. In 1963 she received her graduate degree from St. Louis University in psychology, with heavy emphasis on research.

In addition to her graduate coursework at St. Louis, Mrs. Royer devoted 30 hours per week to work in the University Clinic.

Her personal duties included clinical therapy, in-service training of school counselors, specialized and industrial testing. Two assistants and a secretary were under her direct supervision.

Administering and evaluating projectives and other individual tests was her responsibility.

In 1963, Mrs. Royer served on the President's Committee on Delinquency and Crime, a pilot program in St. Louis.

A studious and devoted researcher, she developed and perfected the objectively scored Royer Identification Scale which is diagnostic of maladjustment at an early age. Identification Scale test results, as well as a vast body of ad hoc research, have repeatedly demonstrated that whenever individual and appropriate primary identification is deviated, and/or substantially altered, by intervening others (whether these are some powerful social institution, rejecting parents or a peer group), the individual so affected is easily and successfully destroyed.

Mrs. Royer studied for one year at Northwestern School of Law and is a guest lecturer at Portland State University in the graduate division. Her course title is "Psychopathic Personality."

She has been a real estate broker for 16 years and much of her work in drawing up contracts, advertising copy and listing contracts has been adopted by other realtors.

Earlier she served as credit manager for Sears, in Decatur, Ill. and El Paso, Texas.

In that capacity she developed the New Employee's Training Guide, which was adopted for use by the Chicago District Office.

For four years she was employed as claims clerk/interim deputy for the Illinois State Department of Labor.

While attending the University of Portland, Mrs. Royer was associated with Oregon Physician's Service (Blue Shield), where she inaugurated and was director of the Testing and Placement Division. She developed the Index for the Physician's Medical Fee Schedule, a pioneer project, and designed the Interview and Rating Sheets for use by department heads.

Concurrently with her real estate practice, Mrs. Royer was an instructor at Central Business College, Denver, in the fields of real estate principles, real estate law and appraising.

Under the sponsorship of Judge Ballard Coldwell of the El Paso Juvenile Court, Mrs. Royer served as Committee Chairman to establish and develop recreational facilities for adolescents in deprived and underdeveloped areas.

She was assistant to the general manager of United Funds

in Denver, with supervisorial responsibilities and at present is co-owner of Harned Inc., manufacturers and distributors of electrical and electronic components.

She works actively with citizen groups throughout Oregon to promote sanity in education and speaks widely on the subject, "Hedonism, Humanism and Family Life-Sex Education."

In her talks, Mrs. Royer shows the absolute parallels of those philosophies with those of Utilitarianism and Dialectical Materialism, the basis of Marxism.

(The following Editorial appeared in the West Seattle Herald on September 3, 1970.)

COMMENTARY: A SUBCULTURE
by Beth Gilligan

The silent majority. The societal sleepers vaguely aware of snowballing chaos within the system, but loathe to become sufficiently aware and involved to cope with the symptoms. Homer described this legion 2000 years ago as "those who are dead and asleep in the graveyard."

John Steinbacher last Thursday cited simple apathy as America's greatest enemy in a time of national crisis during his West Seattle lecture on "progressive education."

"In Germany, the silent majority elected Adolph Hitler. The silent majority in America, when their TV is finally interrupted and their security utterly shattered, will also scream for a dictator. A Police State to protect them from the revolutionaries spawned by our own progressive education . . . the so-called 'liberal left,' " he said.

It seems the kids are playing their roles to the hilt. The steps are strictly predictable. All of it planned.

Steinbacher, veteran reporter, author, lecturer and one-time educator and social worker, is currently on a Northwest lecture tour with a view to rousing that silent majority into action before the final chapter, state control, intercedes permanently, to remove the final freedom of choice.

Steinbacher presents a strong case for individual freedom and the protection of civil rights in his crusade to protect the children of America from what he outlines as programmed "indoctrination into humanism" through the "new morality" adopted by our state-supported institutions; namely the public school system.

"The swift acceleration of America's new, permissive philosophy, aided and abetted by people in high places throughout our country, is about to sink us. As the war heats up and the

xv

revolution gets ever closer to our living rooms, unfortunately, the resistance will become less apparent," Steinbacher warned West Seattleites.

He stated: "There is present in our land a growing subculture dedicated to the promotion of the new morality, and to this group even the suggestion that there exists a concept of moral absolutes appears to be total anathema.

"In the past few years, we're had to come to the conclusion that many of today's educators not only endorse the philosophy of permissiveness, but they're actively engaged in promoting it in every way they can."

Steinbacher mentioned an Elysium Institute publication that contains countless photographs of nude, adult humans in a wide variety of sexual postures, promotes drugs and promiscuity, and lists SIECUS (Sex Information and Education Council of the U.S.) in its official directory of contacts.

But the SIECUS-styled sex education is just one small aspect of the overall planned change coming through public school education, according to Steinbacher:

"There has been enough probing by enough people to reveal that, within this broad, humanistic framework, your sons and daughters are being manipulated as experimental animals. Children are being trained in giant pilot school research projects designed by educators promoting various differentiated staff and research projects whose stated purpose is to alter attitudes, or bring about various forms of behavioral modification and changes.

"Parental values are the target," Steinbacher declared. "Attitudes can be changed, and behavior altered, but only by strenuous indoctrination, or the use of behavior modification drugs or psychological techniques which have been carefully designed to inculcate differing attitudes and behaviors. No basic research has been done for the purpose of determining the beneficial or detrimental aspects of these programs."

Steinbacher sees the current educational trend lapsing into a pattern of mass sit-in psychouts, while the traditional academic skills wither on the vine.

"The manipulations of the young, tragically determined by only a small handful of people,' told the packed audience. "They say, 'There is a moral absolute, and we know that, absolutely!' I ⎣ ... ᴜᴀᴄ line from Mary Calderone herself," Steinbacher grinned.

How was it that Anaheim became the "SIECUS Showcase" of America? Mainly because Anaheim is Mickey Mouseland, according to the star reporter of the Anaheim Daily Bulletin.

He said: "Sex education came into Anaheim unheralded and unnoticed. Once the program was entrenched, the people awoke to discover that they had literally been had. They'd paid a million and a half dollars for a program that not very many people wanted, and that even fewer understood. When they discovered the nature of the thing, they decided it wasn't for them."

The unvarnished facts were often too far out, sometimes, for even Steinbacher to believe, from actual "Sex Knowledge Inventory Tests" used in the school to secret meetings with sexologists charting courses in "how to deal with the opposition to sex education in the schools."

Parents were shocked, administrators outraged. Citizens became involved, checked for themselves, got to work, and within a year, were finally rid of the amazing sex instruction program.

Steinbacher has found nearly identical experimental curricula throughout the U.S. Much of the established social studies courses might astonish the average uninvolved citizen. But the majority of people are still unaware and bewildered as to why their youngsters are coming home from school remolded, antagonistic, and super-sophisticated.

He declared, "In this country, you can attack the church, God, motherhood, or spit on the flag, but the minute you suggest openly that there might be any question about how your tax-supported state schools are run, the whole roof falls in on you. Why? Because apparently everyone involved in the schools

xvii

a vested interest."

Steinbacher last year predicted that America would soon see the federal government take over sex education programs because the individual states would begin to vote in checks.

Last Sunday's Oakland Tribune (Aug. 23) read: "FEDERAL GOVERNMENT TO TAKE OVER SEX EDUCATION." Steinbacher appears to have more savvy than schmaltz.

Steinbacher's lecture pointed up indications that this country is already so far along the road to complete control under the guise of "liberalism" that freedom may already be out of reach for the individual.

Despite the expected accusation of being "right-wing," Steinbacher apparently shares his denouncers' dread of exactly that — the ultimate national outcry for federal police control, unless American's quickly and properly awaken to their personal responsibilities. But, how to awaken them?

TABLE OF CONTENTS

"I HATE TO STEP ON ANY TOES, BUT YOU PARENTS

HAVE NO RIGHTS AT ALL!"

The ELLIS BROWN TRUST
ADMINISTRATOR

I

"MICKEY MOUSELAND"

Where once only orange groves and palm trees grew, a bustling city now sprawls horizontally across the Southern California landscape, its flat monotony broken by the vertical thrust of a man made Matterhorn that lifts its dingy gray head into skies frequently grayer with smog.

Anaheim—where tourists from a thousand American sounding names like Toledo or Kansas or Flatbush or Chicago crowd into garish, neon lighted hotels on the strip along Harbor Boulevard and jostle each other's elbows while gawking their way through the magic wonders of the Happiest Little Kingdom.

Anaheim—where once the oranges grew golden and fat on glossy green leaved branches and a great adventure was an all day outing at the beach.

Anaheim—meaning, simply, the home of Anna—or home on the Santa Ana River, the precise origin lost in contradictory legend—for this town was settled by Germans, who picked that unlikely name from a half dozen even more unlikely names — and then they built a wall around their village, with four gates, North, East, South and West—and a hundred years later another village, Disneyland (which IS Anaheim to most people in America), built a wall around *itself.*

Meanwhile, the walls of Anaheim could not hold the bustling town for long, and the population spilled beyond the walls, and the walls came down—without the aid of Jericho's trumpet —though the Gate Streets remained, still called North, East, South, and West to this day.

Something happened, then, in the middle of the frantic Fifties, and a lot of Orange growers suddenly found they were millionaires overnight when Walt Disney brought his hoopla and his razz matazz to Anaheim—despite the skeptics who predicted instant financial ruin for him and his studio kingdom

1

built by the likes of Mickey Mouse and Donald Duck.

Overnight, Anaheim was a city—with growing pains—and it grew, and it grew and it kept right on growing until it ran into the cities of Buena Park and Fullerton and Santa Ana and bumped smack up against the Santa Ana River, where it had to stop because the city of Orange already owned all the territory, or most of it, east of there.

Population? 171,000 or so, give or take a few depending on the fortunes of government contracts delivered to the city's biggest industry, Autonetics.

Because, while Anaheim was making tourists happy on this earth—it was also producing the means for those tourists to fly out of it—and not on those toy rockets at Disneyland, but rather on rockets engineered at Autonetics, a sprawling monstrosity of a plant that spends a million dollars a day just to keep its doors open.

Jim Townsend knows all that. He should, since he was living there when Anaheim was little more than a wide spot on the famous Red Car line from Los Angeles to *San Berdoo.*

And he's lived there ever since—more or less—between stints as an enlisted man in World War II and as an officer in the Korean police action and a little while spent working in Yuma.

But he always came back to Anaheim — and it is there his two children went to school, at Anaheim High, and it was there they were confirmed in the Catholic Church — though Jim is not, himself, a member of that faith.

Still, he respects it — if only because his wife, Lucille, also a product of Anaheim's schools, is a devout and rather exemplary example for him to look up to and admire, though his admiration doesn't quite extend to the big plunge of becoming a communicant.

A holder of the Silver Star for bravery in Korea, Townsend is the last one to ever let anyone know about it.

It was sometime in the early 1960's that Townsend first became involved in local and state political issues. From that

2

initial beginning came membership in various Republican groups and top leadership posts statewide in the Goldwater for President campaign and in the abortive passage of Proposition 14, the freedom of choice housing initiative.

Somewhere along the line Townsend awoke to the obvious truism that good government begins at home, in your own back yard. He began to watchdog the local city council — to their outrageous howls of protest.

Once again, one thing leading to another, Townsend ended up the head of an organization called the Telephone Taxpayer's Committee.

Originally the name was to be the Taxpayer's Telephone Committee, implying that campaigns would be conducted by phone. But somehow the Anaheim Bulletin transposed the first two words — and the name stuck.

Over the years the committee became the bane and scourge of local petty politicians, especially those who were out to feather their own nests at the expense of the taxpayer's badly drained pocketbook or those who went berserk in attempts to build a bonded indebtedness empire.

The batting score for the committee is phenomenal — although Townsend is the first to cheerfully admit that he has also lost his share of important fights.

Sometime in January, 1963, Townsend and some of his Anaheim friends started an organization they called Citizen's Committee of California, Inc.

It was this committee, made up originally of some of the most active citizens of Orange County, that played major roles in some of the biggest political battles ever fought in the state of California.

But no battle was bigger than the battle over the Anaheim Union High School District sex instruction program — and no battle seemed so hopeless at the beginning.

****

3

Eleanor Howe sat on the edge of her chair, stunned disbelief reflecting in her eyes.

"Are you sure?" she said, lighting a cigarette and promptly forgetting about it as the blue smoke curled up toward the lofty, beamed ceiling.

Her son nodded his head, angry lines tight around his eyes. "That's exactly what the teacher said in that sex class – and I want out of it."

"Suits me," she said, "but no teacher is getting off quite that easy. I'm going to get to the bottom of it if it takes the rest of the year."

Not only was it to take the rest of *that* year. It was to take more than two years of titanic struggle before she finally got *some* satisfaction.

But let Eleanor tell it in her own words.

"One of my twins came home and told me something I never expected to hear. To say it upset me is putting it mildly. I was just plain mad. Without spelling it out, the teacher was asking students in the sex instruction classes some amazingly personal – and embarrassing – questions that were way out of the scope of public school education. I didn't like it, and I decided to do something about it."

Eleanor Howe, wife of a retired Marine major and working mother of three boys and a girl, was typical of millions of American women.

She had never been particularly concerned about politics, especially in the years when her husband was flying for Uncle Sam and she was frequently left alone to handle her growing family.

Military base after military base was her home during those many years – and now, in her beautiful poolside home in Anaheim she felt she had at last found security and peace.

All that changed on the day her son came home from school with his story about the sex class. Eleanor Howe overnight became interested in what was going on around her – especially in the school district.

4

It was only natural that she would go to Jim Townsend with her problem, and it was only natural that Jim would tell her he wasn't interested in getting involved in any battle over sex instruction in the local school district.

Sex, he thought, was a rather private affair. He didn't see why the school district was even involved in the matter.

It wasn't until Eleanor had briefed him on some of the materials being used in the school district that Jim suddenly came awake — and interested.

"My God," he said, an expletive that probably summed up his feelings as well as anything could.

Jim Townsend was in the fray — along with his powerful statewide organization he called the CCC.

The die was cast — and the battle had begun.

****

Paul Cook was a confident man. Drawing $30,000 as superintendent of the high school district, and known nationally as an innovative superintendent who would try almost anything that promised to be of value — or even of questionable value — in the classrooms, Cook could look to the future with buoyancy and arrogant self confidence.

Many years before, he had come to the small city of Anaheim as superintendent of its rapidly growing elementary district. Then, when he had proved himself socially, professionally and politically, he moved up the ladder and became the powerful head of one of the largest school districts in the nation.

From the pinnacle of educational power, Cook surveyed his broad domain stretching from the hills on the east almost to the ocean on the west.

It hadn't been easy, reaching that rather heady zenith — though it must have given him considerable satisfaction to know that he had done so without a major mishap.

Cook, red haired and brawny, was a man of persuasive

5

energy — and even a heart attack failed to slow him down for long.

Still, despite that power, Cook remained an obscure, unknown school superintendent, nationally, until his innovative ideas about sex instruction grabbed the fancy of some of the more widely read journals.

Overnight he became famous — and the Anaheim Union High School District, heretofore known only for being next door to Mickey Mouse land, was a national cause celebre.

The program he initiated, with the aid of the school board and Sally Williams, was to become a historical watershed in the area of school-parent relations.

Sally Williams, overweight, square-jawed and a brilliant foil for Cook's ideas, became the first coordinator of the Anaheim Union High School District Family Life and Sex Education program.

Those were happy days — in the beginning, in 1965, when Mrs. Williams seemed to know exactly where she was going and she was all set to take all the youngsters in Anaheim along with her.

An effective and persuasive speaker, Mrs. Williams had only recently been elected to the board of a nationally based organization called the Sex Information and Education Council of the United States, better known to millions as SIECUS.

Mrs. Williams must have felt downright euphoric. She and fellow SIECUS board member Esther Schulz had coauthored the district's sex curriculum, and it embodied much of what was later to become infamous as the SIECUS program. That program of too much, too soon became a raging, controversial issue throughout America by the middle of 1968.

Just a school nurse a year or two before, Mrs. Williams, too, found herself in the airy reaches of national recognition among certain groups and among certain organizations.

It was during those first three or four happy years that she flew hither and yon, all over America, presenting seminars on the great success she and Paul Cook had achieved in the city of

6

Anaheim.

But there were many who emphatically disagreed — angrily and loudly!

It was that disagreement that led to the biggest crisis in Anaheim's educational history, and it was that disagreement which nearly destroyed the school system.

Let us turn back the clock now, to the frightening years of the Great Depression.

Columbia University in 1932 was famous for one thing; for its Teacher's College and for the man who headed that school, John Dewey.

Together, John Dewey and his coterie of sycophantic followers were to reshape American public school education, and many a child was to suffer because of those changes.

The philosophy of Dewey was not new, in the strictest sense of that word, for he merely followed the destroyers who have appeared and reappeared throughout history.

"There is no God," Dewey cried, "and there is no soul. Hence, there are no needs for the props of traditional religion. With dogma and creed excluded," he continued, "then immutable truth is also dead and buried. There is no room for fixed, natural law or permanent moral absolutes."

There is, in that philosophy, an attitude toward social reform that leads inevitably to Socialism—or Communism— or perhaps the Fascism of an Adolph Hitler.

It didn't matter. We only know that Dewey's philosophy finds its fulfillment in totalitarian systems, as you shall discover in these pages.

But 1932 was a weathervane year for several reasons. Not only did Dewey burst upon the scene like a scarlet rocket in a dark night; he was echoed by the fledgling National Education Association (NEA) when, in their yearbook, the teacher's national organization called for the abolition of free enterprise and capitalism, demanding that a Soviet system replace it. Lambasting traditional moral precepts found in Judeo-Christian

7

truths, the yearbook called for a new morality that would no longer be based upon traditions that molded Western thought for a thousand and more years.

One year later, in 1933, the American Humanist Association was to echo that same sentiment — and on the board of that Association were John Dewey, and such Dewey disciples as Harry Elmer Barnes, Robert Lovett, editor of the New Republic, Joseph Weinstein, Jewish student advisor at Columbia and Charles Potter of the First Humanist Society, New York.

Also on the board were a dozen other prominent editors, teachers, Jewish and Unitarian clergymen, attorneys and writers.

In that Humanist Manifesto, the writers and leaders in the field of religion and education were saying the following things:

"Humanism is a way of life which relies on human capacities and natural and social resources. Humanists see man as a product of this world — of evolution and human history — and acknowledge no cosmic mind or super-natural purposes or forces. Humanism expresses an attitude or conviction which requires the acceptance of responsibility for human life in this world, emphasizing mutual respect and recognizing human interdependence."

Thirty years and more later, the United States Supreme Court was to give Humanism the sanction of a Religion in two notable cases. One is the Torcaso case, 1961, and the other is the Seeger case, 1964.

Further, in the case, "The Fellowship of Humanists vs the County of Alameda," September 17, 1957, a California court agreed that the fellowship was a *church* in the sense that their facilities were used as a church and therefore, tax exempt.

Humanism, then, is by court definition a "Religion."

Humanists meet in churches.

Humanists claim pacifism as a church tenet, and it has so been conceded by the courts of this land.

Further, since the Humanist religion is purely materialistic, then the goals of the Humanists are also solely materialistic.

8

This means that the "things of this world" dominate all aspects of Humanist thought.

And what has all this to do with Paul Cook and the debacle in Anaheim?

Simple. Paul Cook, you see, was a typical product of the Progressive Education philosophy rampant in America's institutions of higher learning in his college days. It should, then, come as no surprise that the program he initiated in Anaheim would have as its primary base the philosophy of Humanism, the philosophy wholeheartedly endorsed and promoted by John Dewey.

One of the men closely involved in the Anaheim program was Dr. Lester Kirkendall, sociology professor from Oregon State University and the past president of the American Humanist Association.

Skip ahead now, around three decades, and come with me to a mass meeting at Anaheim High School in the Fall of 1969. A family life teacher is standing before the school board, telling them about a meeting he had with Paul Cook some five or six years earlier.

After informing the board that he had met with leading sexologist, Dr. Lester Kirkendall, in an Anaheim motel room, he added that he had gone straight to Cook's office after that meeting.

According to the Anaheim Bulletin's account of that teacher's recitation before the board, he "had warned Cook that if he introduced Humanism into the Anaheim school system, he would have a war on his hands."

Not only did Cook ignore him, but that same man was later to become one of the teachers in that Humanistic program.

Again, it should come as no surprise that the godless ideas of Humanism would supplant prayer and Bible reading in the public school system in Anaheim.

Also, it should come as no shock to realize that the Family Life course was deliberately designed and implemented to

9

make "good little Humanists out of the kids," as one parent charged before the school board.

Without being classified as a Religion, the doctrine of Humanism penetrated and permeated the entire Family Life course, as described in the May 9, 1969 publication of the California State Department of Education booklet called Guidelines for Moral Instruction in California Schools.

"The controversy over sex education in California's public schools has been shown to be closely associated with the recent affirmation of a New Morality. Both of these movements are in turn connected with the sex revolution which has been a planned program of indoctrination underway on many college campuses for years. Any cursory examination will reveal all three movements to be connected with leading personalities in Humanist or allied organizations of one type or another. Often the sex education programs for the K - 12 years follow upon the heels of these well planned sex revolution programs, such as that conducted in Sacramento the week of February 26 through March 1, 1968 and sponsored by the colleges of the community. Entitled 'The Sexual Revolution, 1968,' the program featured a number of well established sexologists: Ira Reiss; James Elias, an associate of Kinsey; *Anson Mount,* public affairs manager of Playboy Magazine; plus the grandaddy of all sexologists, Albert Ellis, a man who has devoted his life and fortune to 'urge young Americans to perpetrate almost any sexual act their cunning little minds can devise.' "

All these people have been heavily involved in promoting sex education in countless school districts all over the United States.

The kind of sex education they are capable of producing — and the kind used in Anaheim — is described further in the State Department of Education report.

Throughout his address (to students at American River College) Anson Mount referred to 'situation ethics,' that right and wrong in the old sense is dead. Medicine and modern science have made 'sex relatively safe.' The idea that pre-

10

marital sex is dangerous is old hat, and guilt feelings about 'illicit sex' are ridiculous, he said.

"The new measure for right and wrong (according to Mount) is whether 'it affects the human happiness of others.' Intercourse is OK among students if it doesn't violate their own moral standards. It is immoral only when it interferes with human welfare or happiness. The only evil in life is lack of love for our fellow men. Nothing is wrong except as it affects other people. The older generation is unqualified to judge since they have actually rejected Christian morality and are sick, inhuman, unchristian, boobs and babbits. The New Morality," he said, "is a rebellion against this phoney parental authority."

He also told the impressionable and (we presume) normally sexed young people that adults are to be deprecated for being shocked at "one little dirty deed of a boy and a girl out in the woods."

All through his speech he referred to Humanisn as a *great good . . .*

"The Highest Good is Human Welfare and Happiness," he insisted, "The religion of your parents is fossilized . . . better to join the Peace Corps or the Southern Christian Leadership Conference.

"Our Religion is our love affair with life."

Is it any wonder, then, that the parents of Anaheim, when alerted to the fact that this was basically the philosophy of the "family life" program in their schools, would demand that it be abolished?

Hundreds, even thousands of parents besieged the school board, demanding that their children be protected from the ravages of the child seducers.

They took Paul Cook at his word when he said at Chapman College, in a speech to some of the students: "The trouble with the American people is that they are sex threatened because of their Christian hangups."

Paul Cook also told a gathering of teachers in a town in

11

California, "A few years ago I would have been hung for what I am doing today."

Among those who helped fashion the scaffold for the hangman's noose were — in addition to Townsend and Mrs. Howe — Jan Pippenger, a vivacious blond who once had serious problems of her own until God straightened her out; Blanche Kelly, irrepressible wife of an Anaheim fireman; Dr. Melvin Anchell, a Physician's physician; Evelyn Burns, a housewife who wasn't fooled by all the false rhetoric and — Sam Campbell, editor of the Anaheim Bulletin.

Sam Campbell, short, balding, and tough as a tiger in a quiet kind of way, was fed up. He didn't like the sex instruction program on religious grounds and he didn't like it on any other grounds either.

It took him about five minutes to figure out that the Anaheim Bulletin was going to fight it, editorially. And so he did — risking everything in the process.

Sam had made up his mind when he discovered to his astonishment and dismay, some of the materials that were being used in the sex classes at the local Anaheim High School.

Or perhaps it was just on general principles, since his basic philosophy is that the State has very little right to intrude into the everyday lives of people. As a matter of fact, he believes emphatically that the state has no such right — period.

A crusading editor of the old school, Sam is something of a throwback — yet his ideas are as timely as today, because he seems to be always about five hours ahead of everyone else in understanding trends and in evaluating those trends.

It wasn't surprising, then, that he decided the sex instruction program — not just in Anaheim, but nationally — was thoroughly evil.

He turned your author loose on the story, with carte blanche privileges. We were only to get the story — the BIG story of the 1968-69 school year throughout America.

It turned out to be even bigger than he thought.

12

As for Townsend, he was furious. He pounded his fist on his desk and roared his rage for anyone within earshot.

"This program is one of the most evil, vile and filthy things ever foisted on any community," he thundered, "and those in charge are nothing but a bunch of subversive montebanks using public funds to further their own ungodly aims."

"They portray themselves as Messiahs," he said scornfully, blue eyes flashing, "as if they are the first people on earth to discover sex. For their information, sex has been around since creation and I expect it'll keep right on being here. Teaching these kids all about sex is like trying to teach a salmon to find its way through a lot of streams to its spawning ground."

"Sex instruction? Hogwash!" he roared. "We have to abolish it once and for all here in Anaheim — where the mess started, apparently — so the rest of the country will learn a lesson. The program started here and it's going to end here."

Paul Cook, sitting in his ivory tower at the administration building didn't seem to care — or perhaps he did not know — what was in store for him in the tumultous months ahead.

13

II

SEX PROBLEMS

Jan Pippenger stepped into her car to drive the few miles to the Anaheim Union High School District board room.

It was a cold Thursday night. Threatening rain clouds loomed toward the west where the sun was just sinking beyond the rim of the sea.

Alone in the car, Jan thought about the meeting ahead of her and shivered.

For weeks, now, she had been attending the school board meetings – and each time the meetings had grown more hectic, more crowded and more impassioned as the Citizen's Committee pressed its battle against the sexologists, the board and Paul Cook.

Perhaps to get all that out of her mind, she flipped on the car radio and ran the needle back and forth across the dial until she found what she was looking for, a station that specialized almost exclusively in religious music.

The sound of an organ wafted out of the speakers, wrapped itself around the car interior and fled into the gathering darkness outside.

"Rock of Ages, cleft for me," she hummed under her breath, "let me hide myself in Thee."

Not a bad idea, she thought, and softly whispered a prayer under her breath that the confusion and discord in the district would finally lead to something constructive and worthwhile.

The words of the song whirling in her head sent her reeling back through time – to an earlier day when there was another problem to worry about.

She was a bit younger then, a stunning blond who seemed to have everything: an attractive husband, a beautiful home, security.

But none of that had mattered at the time – because Jan had a problem she could not handle. That problem was alcohol.

14

There was a time when she wouldn't even admit she had a problem — but the courage and strength to admit that a problem did exist had finally come to her when she had turned her back on sin and had looked on the face of Jesus Christ for the first time, with understanding and a prayer of penitence on her lips.

Life, for her, changed — miraculously — and Jan found herself all turned around, heading upward instead of downward, working for constructive things instead of yielding to destructive impulses.

She became a member of the Nazarene church and one by one she saw her children accept the things of Christ.

The last few years, she thought, had been very rewarding.

But now she had another problem, and she was frustrated. She had prayed about it, a rather instinctive thing for her at this stage of her spiritual development, but somehow no answers came through.

Jan didn't know it then, but God was to use her in a mighty way in the months ahead.

The song had ended. An announcer was tolling the hour of 7:30 as Jan eased her new Cadillac into the parking lot at the district office on La Palma Avenue, noting as she did that the lot was nearly full.

There was going to be another full house, just as there had been for meeting after meeting for the past two months.

Jan had met some of the members of the Citizen's Committee, and she had discovered that she wasn't the only one who was concerned about certain trends in the school district.

She was relieved to learn that her son, Gary, wasn't the only young man who had been embarrassed by some of the activities in the district's sex class.

So, for the past several board meetings she had made herself very much a part of the agenda, demanding to speak to the board in a soft, sweet voice that was frequently in marked incongruity with some of the things she was saying.

Her appearances before the board were marked by quota-

15

tions from the Bible, personal testimonies to the saving grace of Christ and a sharp and incisive intellect that frequently left both trustees and audience agape with astonishment.

In the words of Jim Townsend, "Jan Pippenger has more old-fashioned guts than any two people in the district."

But let Townsend describe Jan's appearances before the board.

"There she stood," he said, with a wry grin, "a goodlooking blond in an expensive dress, looking like she stepped out of the pages of Harper's Bazaar. She says about four words and the board president politely tells her to shut up and sit down. Pretty soon he isn't so polite. But none of it bothers Jan. When they try to shut her up, that's when they make their first mistake, because she keeps right on talking in that little voice, cutting right through, naming names and reading things out of textbooks that would make a stevedore turn red."

At least once during every board meeting, some trustee or another would have enough, and he would demand that she be forcibly removed from the podium.

But it was all in vain. Jan would stand her ground, daring them to attack her — and of course, none did.

Still, despite the humor that she managed to inject into board meetings, Jan was deadly serious and the "enemy" knew it. She had her facts and she always came well prepared.

Since the board meetings had grown from around four or five district patrons to a regular attendance of over a hundred, it was inevitable that Jan would finally have her day in court — the court of public opinion.

At least 150 district patrons stood outside this night, trying to listen to the speakers over a public address system that wasn't working very well.

Jan started her speech, reading from a prepared script. Everything went swimmingly until she mentioned the name of Paul Cook, district superintendent.

"Paul Cook" she said, "is not telling the truth."

Board president Royal Marten came alive in a hurry.

16

"You can't talk like that," he said, "I suggest you meet in executive session with the board if you want to talk about a personnel matter."

Jan paused in mid sentence, tossing back her head. She leveled her baby blue eyes at Marten.

"Well, where is he?" she demanded. "When I call a man a liar, I want to look him in the eye. What's the matter? Is he afraid to come to his own board meetings?"

By that time the whole audience was wide awake — even though it was nearly midnight. Friends and enemies alike were grinning, collectively wondering if the chairman of the board would have her removed from the room.

Jan stood her ground waiting for an answer.

How the board got out of that particular situation is lost in the records of innumerable memorable meetings that followed. Needless to say, Jan had made her point.

She took her seat to a spontaneous burst of applause.

Sex education in Anaheim, involving as it did the inner probing of the mind of the student, recalls the words of Dr. Herbert Carroll, one of the best known psychology professors in the United States.

He was for 20 years the professor of clinical psychology and the chief counselor at the University of New Hampshire.

Recently Carroll said, "Most of us are disturbed by reports of voluntary disrobing in so-called sensitivity training classes elected by some students. Far more disturbing is the forced disrobing of the emotions and inner selves of adolescents and younger children through the general use of probing personality tests in grade and high schools which they are required to attend."*

*Statement of Dr. Herbert Carroll submitted to the Senate Committee by California State Senator John G. Schmitz in support of SB 669 and SB 670 in 1969.

17

He then quoted from a 1965 Columbia Law Review article written by Oscar Reubhauser, then president of the Russell Sage Foundation.

"Private personality," he read, "is as complex and many-faceted as human beings themselves, but two principle aspects of the claim to privacy are clear. The one most frequently expressed is the 'right to be left alone' . . . but there is an even more obvious facet of the claim to privacy, the 'right to share and communicate.'

"We all need to withhold for a variety of reasons."

Carroll adds, "There are a great many things men cannot reveal for a variety of reasons, and therefore they suppress them — things other men neither want to know or discuss.

"Then too, there are ideas of beliefs or behavior that we are not sure we understand, or even if we do, we fear the world may not. So, to protect ourselves, all of us seek to withhold at least certain things from certain persons at certain times."

"The essence of freedom," Carroll maintains, "is the right to pick and choose for himself the time and place when a person's attitudes, beliefs, behavior and opinions are to be withheld from others."

"The right to privacy," states Carroll, "is a positive claim to a status of personal dignity . . . a claim for freedom."

Parents in Anaheim opposing the sex program were saying essentially the same thing.

They objected to their children being forced to strip themselves psychologically naked before other young people. They objected to the debasement that comes when the sensibilities become dulled through programmed and repetitious use of four letter Anglo-Saxonisms in a classroom.

And then along came Kelly — Blanche Kelly, that is.

Catholic wife and mother, Blanche was one of the first to get involved in the Anaheim controversy.

With a face like a pixie, she has a rapier-like wit and a unique ability to slice away all the layers of phoney pretensions, especially when it comes to political types like school board members.

Her standing joke, and one that became kind of a slogan before the controversy finally waned, revolved around the fact that she is very much Italian.

"You got a problem?" she roars, laughing all the while. "Don't worry — I'll call the Mafia!"

But she didn't need the Mafia or the Cosa Nostra or anything else when it came to terror tactics against the school trustees.

Blanche worked like a busy beaver against the sex instruction program in the early months of 1968, at the very time when we were all trying to collect information on the program.

The first to take the trouble to sit in on classes, she could always be expected to brief the Anaheim Bulletin on whatever she had learned.

However, it was one of her little forays into the forbidden halls of Ivy that first exposed a counter plot within the Anaheim Bulletin building.

Hank Davis, a former public relations specialist with the Army, had come to work for the Anaheim Bulletin some time before the sex instruction battle broke out.

A thin, wiry fellow with a mustache, it might have been that latter fact that made us somewhat suspicious of his motives at the outset — a la the villain in an Alfred Hitchcock movie.

Still, he seemed to be pretty much of a run-of-the-mill kind of reporter — although the city editor seemed to have a rather hard time making much sense out of some of his articles. There were constant battles back and forth between the editor, Jerry Chaney — who has some pretty definite ideas about how an article should be written — and Davis, who managed to do the wrong things, apparently.

19

...sn't until I wrote an article that exposed the secret, ...onally coordinated effort to inject sex into every classroom in the country that Davis' true colors manifested themselves.

A secret meeting of sexologists took place at the Charter House Hotel. Sponsored by the IBM Corporation, the three day seminar was headed by professional sexologist, Dr. Lester Kirkendall, from Oregon State University.

Fortunately, I had a spy on the inside, and copious quantities of materials soon came into my hands along with some of the most sensational testimony on the subject from such people as Kirkendall and Anaheim's Sally Williams.

The gist of the story was, according to Kirkendall, that sex instruction was to be sneaked into every school district in the country, the idea being that once the program was installed, little could be done to rid the district of it. On the other hand, if the conspirators were discovered in the act by outraged parents, they were to pretend that the program was merely an "improvement" on an already existing health program — nothing to become alarmed about.

When I handed the material over to Sam Campbell, he promptly called a staff meeting, realizing that this was one of the BIG stories of the year. Out of that staff meeting came a series of assignments, with various reporters assigned to write articles on various facets of the conspiracy.

I had already prepared what later came to be known as the Charter House series, and Davis — after many painful rewrites by a disgusted Jerry Chaney — finally produced a series of his own that brought the wrath of some of the more informed readers down on our heads.

Davis, it seemed, was all on the side of those who were involved in the sex program.

That was upsetting enough, but there were a number of other things that added fuel to the fires of discontent among the top echelon staff at the newspaper.

For one thing, my Charter House series took off like a jet,

reprinted by the hundreds across the nation, and almost overnight we were inundated with phone calls, letters and visitors who turned the paper into a three-ring circus.

Meanwhile, the rest of the staff painfully tried to put out a newspaper every day — while my phone rang incessantly and the letters arrived on my desk by the thousands.

Thanks to the understanding patience of most of the staff, we weathered the storm — until the day when Blanche Kelly came bouncing into the editorial offices and announced she was going to visit the sex class at a local school.

Hank Davis happened to be sitting very close to me at the time — and he soon disappeared, while we proceeded to discuss the matter with Blanche.

Blanche left shortly, but minutes later called to say that Davis was on the phone downstairs, talking to someone at the school district office.

"He's cluing them in," she said excitedly.

Sure enough.

As it turned out, Davis admitted to being the culprit and was promptly relieved of his duties. Actually, he *resigned,* shall we say, *under pressure.*

A few weeks later he went to work for the school district as the public relations specialist, at just about twice the salary he had been making at the Anaheim Bulletin — or any other newspaper for that matter.

Davis, with a gleam in his eye, proceeded to make the defense of the sex program his number one priority, bird-dogging my every step and writing letters to the editor of the Bulletin decrying my attempts to expose what was happening.

He was particularly upset about reports I was carrying in my daily "School and Family" column of sex instruction problems in other districts around the state and nation.

Shortly thereafter Davis was editing a newsletter for the school district that became nothing more than a defense of the sex program and a defense of Paul Cook.

21

Somewhere along the line, Blanche Kelly had a brilliant idea — one that caused a major uproar in the city of Anaheim.

Enlisting the aid of a dozen or so concerned women, she went from door to door, dropping leaflets entitled ADULT BULLETIN on doorsteps that spelled out in explicit terms exactly what was happening under the name of sex instruction.

That did it. Thousands of parents began reading those leaflets, aghast, over their morning coffee, their newspapers forgotten momentarily.

To put it bluntly — all hell broke loose!!

Blanche had hit upon a good old fashioned American technique, one as old as the Revolutionary War.

Sam Campbell had often stated the old adage that the quickest way to spread news was by telephone, television and telewoman. He also believes a most effective way to communicate is with the old mimeograph machine and a direct, door to door campaign on behalf of whatever cause the person might be espousing. Now his theory was put to the test, and it worked in an astonishing fashion.

The Citizen's Committee had learned that a few people could be very effective if their forces are properly deployed.

What was upsetting Blanche Kelly? Well, it was something like the following assignment that was given to the students in a Sacramento High School.

ENGLISH THREE AUTOBIOGRAPHY

The wise man guards against the future as if it were the present — Publius Syrus, Sentertial

Our lives are always influenced by other people. Usually when we are quite young, the people who influence us most are members of the family. Now, in senior high school, a person outside your immediate family may be quite influential.

In a theme of at least five (5) paragraphs, each of which

22

contains not fewer than ten sentences, write an analysis and explanation of several elements of your life's history.

Your autobiography, needless to say, should be the best writing you have done so far. Not only should the material reflect your deeper thoughts and feelings, and some of the fundamental changes in your life; it should reflect also all the progress you have made in your everyday living.

Your theme must be selective. By careful examination of your life material, one can select a subject about which he feels most deeply and can write most vividly.

Below appear some suggestions that may help you to choose a central thread of thought upon which to base your theme.

1. Get down to important incidents of your life with which you associate your mother or father. Could you weave your story around one of them, relating in detail five or six incidents, and showing what feeling about your mother or father each of them produced in you? The important thing is, of course, the shifts and changes in your personality, and how your parents were in part responsible for them.

2. Name five or six teachers whom you have liked or disliked. What important lessons did you learn from each one? How did each of them affect your thinking and philosophy on life? Relate one important incident to illustrate this, or choose one teacher and show by relating a series of incidents how he or she influenced your personality and educational progress.

3. Have you known over a period of years or more recently one friend who has shared your thoughts and daily experiences? Show five or six ways in which you have befriended each other, or shared each other's good times, or reached certain convictions.

4. What do you consider the most important year in the formation of your ideas and personality? What things happened in that year that produced a curve or a shift in your life? Show how you changed, or what important things happened to you, in the space of one year.

23

5. How has your father's employment, or lack of employment, affected you? When did you begin to think most seriously about the necessities of life for your family and you? Do you or did you help the family by earning money? How has prosperity or the lack of prosperity changed your thoughts and actions through the years?

6. Can you trace any changes in some element of your personality, such as bad temper and inclination to disobedience or disrespect for authority, a lack of self-confidence, or a tendency to be too friendly?

7. Has any activity such as athletics, music, painting, camping or religion made any significance in your personality or attitude toward life?

Needless to say, Blanche Kelly and her friends took umbrage with this kind of prying into the private lives of students.

III

THE DOCTOR PRESCRIBES

Sometime in 1968 the Citizen's Committee discovered Dr. Melvin Anchell — or perhaps he discovered them. In any case, the association turned out to be an interesting one.

Anchell, who had once worked with Dr. Alfred Kinsey, was dead set against the kind of sex programs that were being introduced into such districts as Anaheim.

A handsome man of humble demeanor, something happens to Anchell when he gets in front of an audience. He becomes a persuasive and eloquent speaker — one who made even Paul Cook wince on many an occasion.

It isn't the religious aspect that bothers Anchell apparently, but rather the psychological damage that can be done to children who are exposed to clinical sex facts that would boggle the mind of the gynecologist — and all at a tender age when the child, normally, would be more interested in just being a child and not a frustrated sex machine.

"The sex instruction program," Anchell told the Anaheim school board, "fails to comprehend the psychological forces operating in regard to the sexual needs of children."

"The teachers," said Anchell, his resonant voice booming around the auditorium, "are seducing the young and causing psycho-sexual trauma from which the young will never recover."

"In fact," he added, after ticking off a long list of alleged abuses in the classroom, "there will not be enough psychologists and psychiatrists in the whole country to take care of the matter."

Somewhere along the line, a newspaper or two got the false impression that Anchell was a practicing psychiatrist — or at least that he claimed to be one.

That, as it turned out, was false - since he never made such a claim — but it got him temporarily into hot water with a certain division of the Los Angeles County Medical Association.

It seemed that certain doctors on that board of ethics were all in favor of sex instruction — and they were eagerly looking for a chance to back Anchell into a corner.

However, since the charges were baseless and totally false, they really didn't have much to go on — and after a hearing, the whole matter was quietly dropped.

We suspect there were some red faces, especially when the good doctors realized they had been used — unconsciously, by the powerful sexologist lobby. They had been used to attack one of the most eloquent spokesmen for those millions of parents who objected to the sexual exploitation of their own children in the tax supported school system.

But Anchell was cheerful and charitable about the whole affair. After all, he said later, the doctors were only doing their duty — and he wasn't about to fault them for being concerned and conscientious.

The thing that teed off the sexologists was the formation of an organization called the Sex Information and Education Council of Physicians (SIECOP), an organization of doctors, nationwide, headed at that time by Anchell and a couple of other physicians, Dr. Donald Cortum and Dr. James Parsons.

The members of SIECUS were outraged. How dare this group of doctors assume they knew as much about sex as they did. After all, such people as Dr. Mary Calderone — the head of SIECUS and past head of the Planned Parenthood Association — had some kind of special Messianic mission to make sex machines out of the whole population.

Yet here they were — this silly group of medical men — actually assuming they knew something about the mechanics of mating and the psychological and spiritual aspects of sexuality. It was absolutely revolting. Besides, it was a distinct threat to SIECUS, the organization that had a corner on the potentially lucrative sex instruction materials market.

Something would have to be done about it — and they did. They promptly demanded, through their attorneys, that the SIECOP name be dropped — getting, in effect, the reply from

26

Anchell to "drop dead."

He wasn't about to knuckle under to the totalitarian gambits of the SIECUS crowd.

It was shortly after that controversy erupted that Anchell was cordially hauled before the medical association – and it was shortly after that he was cleared of the phoney charges.

One year later he was to receive an award from the Medical Association for his outstanding contributions to the field of medical education.

It was a strange ending to a strange interlude in the sex education war.

But why did Anchell become involved in the first place? He had it made, after all, and there was little reason, seemingly, for him to get embroiled in the sex instruction battle.

It was then that another of those strange things happened, for as it turned out, Anchell was the logical one to take on the SIECUS forces. Not only had he worked with Kinsey, he had also authored books on sexual adjustment and had authored many articles on the subject of sex and psychological problems resulting from sexual maladjustments.

When the Citizen's Committee called on him to drive to Anaheim from Los Angeles and address the school board, he was primed and ready for the confrontation.

It was a full house that buzzed and hummed in eager expectation as Anchell strode down the center aisle of the auditorium and approached the microphone.

None of the audience had ever heard him speak before, but the word had gotten around that he was a formidable foe of the kind of program Anaheim school administrators boasted of so proudly.

He stood there for a minute, his iron grey hair glistening in the dim light that filtered down from the lofty ceiling, while the hum of voices behind him rose and then fell away into a strained silence.

His voice echoed out over the auditorium in impassioned tones.

27

"Thank you, gentlemen," he said, "for having me down here this evening to speak to you. As you know, I am a general practitioner in Los Angeles . . . "

He began to give his medical background, ending with a description of his "psychiatric" work while a medical officer in the Army — though, he hastened to add, that did not make him a practicing psychiatrist in civilian life.

"I am here to tell you," he stated, "that some of your teachers are seducing their own students . . . psychologically . . . and causing psychological sexual trauma from which many will never recover . . . causing sexual distortion . . . "

Anchell was particularly upset because "sex educators were concerned about teaching children the mechanics of mating."

He thought that to be comparable to teaching geese how to fly south in the winter.

"In fact," he added, "the sexologists would teach the geese how to fly south in the summer — before there was any need to do so."

Anchell told the Anaheim school board, who listened to him with mixed feelings, since most of them didn't seem to want to hear what he had to say, that teaching children about breathing, digestion, and the use of muscles is natural.

"However," he said, "teaching about genital sex is not."

"After all," he insisted in a cultured and compelling voice, "human sexuality has evolved from an instinct having primarily animalistic qualities to one in which the physical is inseparably fused with mental and cultural needs."

Anchell mocked those who said that third or fourth grade children should learn all about sex and then forget it as far as experimentation is concerned.

"You might as well give the children a gun and a cache of ammunition with the warning not to use them," was his answer.

Anchell added that trying to tell children about sex without arousing sensuous feelings is about as hypocritical or naive as trying to describe the nature of fire without acknowledging the heat.

There were no answers to his argument.

They could only squirm and refuse to accept w to say, denying the truth without any answers of th

Of course, Anchell is no fool. He knows full well that the sex education promoters are not working in a vacuum, but they are, in fact, working on a national level under orders.

In his address to the school board, he used some simple terminology to describe the very complex psychological damage that is done to children in sex instruction classes.

There have probably never been profounder words spoken during the nationwide battle, and we set them down here as a living and vital refutation from one spokesman from the medical professions. The argument has never been answered by the sexologists and it never will be, because it is simply unanswerable.

"Analysis reveals that these drives," he said, "are a stage of sexual development in which the child's fantasies and imaginations are involved."

Anchell was talking about curiosity and desire to learn on the part of children.

"These mental activities," he said, "gratify the young individual's lust for knowledge and give pleasure. Resolving this stage in a natural way is essential for proper sexual growth.

"Undue meddling on the part of educators, catapulting children into a world of authoritative, factual sexual information stunts normal development. Sterile facts, devoid of mystery and fancy, do not sate children's sexual needs. Their unrequited minds build up tension and find it difficult to determine which is truth, fact or fancy. Some adults, experiencing no doubts about their own sexual awareness, and others, feeling the child is obligated, expect children to express admiration and joy about learning sexual matters. These adults cannot conceive that shattering the fantasies and doubts of children without proper aging can act as a premature seduction, causing irreparable psychological harm, including perversions."

After that broadside, Anchell followed it up with something

29

onger.

"The sex educators report that through observing schools having sex education, sex experimentation is less likely to occur. The programs, they claim, are not to stimulate but to educate, not to provoke injudicious behavior but to encourage good judgment."

Anchell made it clear that as a physician he disagreed with the beliefs of the sexologists.

"The observed lack of sexual curiosity on the part of the child," he told the board, "is no commendation for sex education. Much the opposite. It attests to the harm that is done in these classes. Children, you see, have a conscience regarding matters sexual. They are aware of sexual desires, but natural mental phenomenon, reaching down into their unconscious, causes them to avoid convictions too early in life. The child senses that the wish for sexual understanding should not be so abruptly fulfilled. It subconsciously seems to the child that the sexual pleasures, though desirable, are too difficult and too good to be true."

Needless to say, by this time the board members were blinking and swallowing hard and the audience was listening with bated breath. Anchell was mercilessly slashing away at all the false pretensions of the sexologists.

"The child who has sex education early," continued Anchell, "develops a feeling of disbelief, with accompanying depression. Initially he disbelieves that he could be beholding sexual reality, which in normally paced growth would be regarded as only a possibility. The disbelief is the child's attempt to repudiate the reality to which he is exposed, and which is out of focus with his or her sexual needs and conscience."

"Even worse," he said, "the accompanying depression is a form of regret, and other emotional disorders result. The child is literally wrecked by success. When the teacher removes the opposition of the environment to sexual urges, the child's struggle for expression is turned inward instead of outward.

That distortion leads to antisocial behavio
sion and schizophrenia, readily observed in
so-called beatniks."

"The child is seduced," he added, "by
eventually the child tries to relieve the incre
things really exist as they were learned. He   ....s the
quality of what has been heard, read or been taught. Testing
out these explicit sex instructions leads to depersonalized relationships between young people. The boy learns to masturbate intravaginally and the pill protected girl acts as a receptacle
for sperm."

By that time the audience was on its feet, cheering Anchell,
because he had managed to verbalize all their feelings.

A disgruntled member of the school board complained
loudly about the unseemly behavior of the cheering parents,
but Anchell had made his point, just as Jan Pippenger had
made her point when she questioned Paul Cook's veracity.

Anchell sits in his medical office in Los Angeles and talks
about the tragic waste of youthful lives.

"There are around 100,000 young people who get venereal
disease between the ages of 11 to 17," he says, "and the use
of hallucinatory drugs induce sensuous trips in impotent, sexually informed youths."

"Virginal girls," he continues, "find it increasingly difficult
to compete with non-virgin contemporaries for dates and professional prostitutes are put out of business by high school
amateurs."

"In some localities," Anchell goes on, "the mothers of 40
out of 100 babies are unmarried, and some states have legalized
abortion in order to reduce hardships created by illegitimacies.
On top of all that, the masochism and sadism of perverted
young people are apparent in their delinquency and crimi-
nality."

All that social disorientation worries Anchell. A man of in-
finite compassion, his faith has given him a deep and abiding
respect for human life.

31

passion for our fellow man," he says over and over, a relatively new instinct. It is the farthest removed from hat of the beast, and it marks the greatest advancement in instinctual force. It is a newly created need, and has not yet had much time to develop. Only a few centuries separate our civilization from that which fed humans to lions for sport."

And outside of his office there is the sound of civilization – the roar of cars, a voice drifting off into the distance, the sound of a faraway siren. Yet, with civilization all around – you somehow know that Anchell is right.

Eleanor Howe admired Dr. Anchell greatly, but she didn't wait around for grass to grow under her feet. She worked night and day, tirelessly, to inform other people about her concerns.

One night, at a packed board meeting, she blasted the Anaheim trustees with the following words:

"It would appear you are convinced that the Anaheim program originated before the formation of SIECUS. Gentlemen, you are wrong."

Fixing the board members with an insistent and compelling glare, she didn't wait for interruptions, but plowed straight ahead.

"Anaheim began its sex course in February, 1965 and SIECUS received its charter in May, 1964," she said, thereupon putting the lie to one of Paul Cook's staunchest claims. She then ticked off a long list of objections to the sex education program.

First, she blasted the program for costing too much. Next, she insisted the program drew in students against their will, because they did not want to feel like freaks.

Clergymen of unknown background, she said, from outside the district, came into the classrooms to give the so-called spiritual side of the program. She wondered if the board knew

32

what beliefs the clergymen held.

Parent and child relationships are being systematically destroyed, she maintained, and the entire sex program is an attack upon modesty and morality.

Board members were becoming rather restive at this point, but she wasn't about to let them off the hook.

"We are aware that outside influences, organization and cults of suspect character," she continued, "are involved in the concepts of the Family Life and Sex Education programs. Are you board members aware of that?"

If they were, the board members weren't about to tell her.

Sam Campbell, a legend in his own time, doesn't look like the kind of man who would take on the forces of evil in their own lair — but he is one in a million.

There is something about his quiet, frequently obstinate approach to problems that sets him apart from other men.

Sam is a religious man, a genuine Christian soul in an age of counterfeits.

His prayers, eloquently understated, have enlivened many a meeting of the Anaheim Chamber of Commerce, and his constant references to the Bible, though upsetting to chronic sinners, have often punctured many an inflated ego.

Possibly nobody in the country can write an editorial like Sam, when he is in a mood to take on the Establishment. He was writing against the draft before the peaceniks ever heard of it. He was attacking the evils of the public school system before those evils became popular points for politicians to run on. He was speaking out against corrupt lawmakers when the rest of the American people thought that if you are a Senator, it automatically means you are respectable.

Sam Campbell, in a word, has guts — a rare commodity in an age when most people are trying to prove that black is white and up is down.

Around Christmas, 1968, he decided that he would not print any more articles on sex education, since, he reasoned,

33

the subject of sex instruction was hardly edifying during the season when people wanted to think about Christ's birth.

To his surprise, the public disagreed. The mail and phone calls increased, and the Bulletin was literally inundated with material opposing sex education from all over the nation.

Nothing would do but that he put out a special four page insert that, he hoped, would answer many of the questions and get them off the backs of the Bulletin staff.

It didn't work. In fact, it merely increased the interest of the general public.

The nationwide controversy continues to this day and the mail and phone calls still keep coming to the Bulletin from people and places so distant that Bulletin staffers are continually amazed.

One such letter came from an angry parent in Anaheim and Sam printed it on the editorial page.

"I was one of the complacent ones, one of the trusting ones," the letter read. "I was one of those who thought the local paper was causing a tempest in a teapot by bringing up the family life program."

"I was working during the time the orientation classes were held," she continued, "so I did not attend. But I had great faith in the judgement of our school leaders."

"Yesterday I learned my 14-year old daughter had been instructed in all the details of sexual intercourse by a junior high school teacher in a mixed class of boys and girls.

"The entire process, even to the emotions, physical reactions and the results was completely explained to the children. A film was recently shown that described stimulation and reactions to this same mixed group.

"Even if sexual details were deemed necessary and mandatory, I still question the disclosures of all to a mixed class at this age. The teacher rationalized it by saying that statistics showed marital problems were due to a lack of communication.

"Well, lack of communication might be MY generation's problem, but not to the kids, since they shout sex every

34

other word.

"The mystery is gone, and our school is helping in a Socialistic fashion to treat sex as a simple body function. True, the teacher did say the spiritual was stressed, but it seems most of the children never heard the word God, since they were too busy observing their neighbor's reactions to such words as penis, erection and ejaculation.

"Can't we please lock the bedroom door and remove ourselves from the level of animals? Like a fool, I left it up to that doggone PTA again, and they approved the teachers playing God, as usual."

About the same time, a woman in Cypress was exclaiming, "What in the name of God is going on!" and Jim Townsend was having the following exchange before the Anaheim school board.

Former board chairman, Royal Marten, who served on the board from 1955 through 1969, normally presided over the meeting in a relaxed style, quipping and joking while puffing languidly on a fat cigar.

A man who loves children, Marten was perhaps the most tragic figure in the whole controversy, and was one of the first to admit that he might be wrong as 1969 drew to a close. He resigned his position, using the excuse that he had served too long on the board, and other more pressing questions and problems faced him, both as a teacher at Santa Ana City College and with his real estate holdings.

Marten's patience wore thin on many an occasion, and numerous times he simply gaveled down his opponents who either ignored a time limit or spoke out of order.

In the words of Herman Wong, a staff writer for the Los Angeles Times, "A vocal donnybrook usually followed, with other opponents popping up and down in their chairs like soloists in a choir."

Wong described one typical interchange between Marten and Townsend, who, by the way, was one of Marten's pupils at Anaheim High School and who still considers Marten a great teacher and close friend. His wife, Lucille, was also a Marten pupil.

"The exchanges between Marten, who has a machine-gun-like voice," writes Wong, "and Townsend, who has a slightly reedy voice, frequently went something like this:"

"Marten: Jim, now I don't have to tell you that you're way out of line. We are listening to another discussion right now that has nothing to do with the program you want to talk about.

"Townsend: That's your whole trouble. You trustees never listen . . . You just . . .

"Marten: Jim, we're tired and its a very long agenda. We've heard and considered your views very carefully (at a board-called forum). Now please be seated.

"Townsend: I won't until you people realize what's going on. We're sick and damn tired of you and that program. We don't . . .

"Marten: Sit down, Jim.

"Townsend: Make me.

"Marten: Jim, I'm not going to get into a hassle with you over this. Now sit . . .

"Townsend: None of you are big enough to make me.

"Marten: (turning to other trustees) What's the next item?

"Townsend: (grumbling as he takes his front row seat) You can't shut us up. You can't. (Applause from his delegation.)"

Wong's description of Jan Pippenger is almost as colorful. He refers to her as a "saucer eyed woman with a sweet, almost tiny voice."

"At one meeting," he writes, "she handed out to the trustees excerpts from a book co-authored by the then Family Life coordinator Sally Williams, that described sexual intercourse.

"And this is what our children are reading," said Mrs. Pippenger. "Read it. Go on. There's nothing but filth!"

But the board members took one look at the contents and decided the material should not be read aloud to the adults

36

who were present.

"At the marathon August 21 meeting," Wong adds, "when trustees voted 3 to 2 to continue the sex program (a new board was to reverse that later) in some form in 1969-70, Mrs. Pippenger rose from a front row seat like a prophet in wrath and cast the program guidebook to the floor.

" 'God is on our side,' she shouted, 'We're right. What you're doing is a godless, shameful thing.' "

Sam Campbell agreed with her.

"I would feel guilty not to oppose the program," he says, "especially when our taxes are being used to promote beliefs contrary to our religious convictions. That is unbearable."

Paul Dearth, handsome Anaheim High School sex instruction teacher agreed with Sam that it was unbearable, but in a different fashion.

"They had a blueprint of harassment designed to get this district down on its knees over this program," he complained bitterly.

Dearth, who was one of those who hitched his wagon to Cook's rising star, found himself in the situation of defending the impossible, and is now a teacher at Long Beach State College, teaching the sex teachers.

Long Beach State, of course, is a school that is known principally for two events, the showing of lewd and lascivious statues on campus, for which a student received a master's degree in art, and for a class conducted in the area of "myths" that involved naked male and female "models" and so-called "skin flicks" in the classroom.

Evelyn Burns, housewife and sweet faced mother appeared more or less regularly before the board during the early days of the Anaheim battle.

Generally dressed in a print, her hair held back with a scarf, she stood before the men of the board and calmly addressed them in a professional manner that belied her appearance.

Mrs. Burns had reason to dislike Paul Cook.

On October 24, 1968, Cook tongue-lashed her at a meeting of the board. She was, he said, "a hostile parent."

She didn't disagree with him, since she probably was feeling rather hostile at that point. But she particularly disliked being "maligned," as she put it, by Lowell Butler Jones, Cook's assistant. The attack took place in a Rotary Club newsletter edited by Jones.

Jones, she said in wounded tones, referred to her as an "old pro."

Actually Jones, who is a professional social club gadabout in Anaheim, had the following to say about her:

"Who is Mrs. Burns? She does her thing about sex at every meeting held anywhere in Orange County and perhaps nationwide, wherever the subject is mentioned. She's a real 'old Pro.' She attends every meeting of the Board of Trustees and demands to be heard and she says the same thing over and over. Enough of Mrs. Burns."

That ungallant and ungentlemanly attack on a lovely little lady, printed in the Anaheim Bulletin for all to see, brought the wrath of district patrons down upon the head of LBJ, as he is known, an acronym for Lowell Butler Jones.

During all this time, Paul Cook was fit to be tied. He was roaring like a wounded bull and demanding redress of grievances from everyone and sundry, especially the Bulletin.

"The charges are baseless," he roared, "and they are the most unremitting and scandalous attacks. We do not teach sex techniques."

The attacks were certainly unremitting, but they were far from baseless and sex techniques were most certainly taught in the classes, including methods of performing oral copulation.

William Daly was another district employee who found himself up to his armpits in the sex instruction controversy.

Noted around the district for his socializing, Daly was an instructor and president of the Anaheim High School PTA.

When things got hottest for the old school board (prior to

38

the election shake up of the Spring, 1969), D
their defense.

"Involvement is our theme for the year,"
intend to carry it out . . . it is our intention t
board, and the superintendent support in any other area, designed for our common good, which may come under attack
from a vocal minority. We don't think that you should have
to stand alone every time some program in the district is
challenged, and from now on you won't."

That sticky bit of doggerel didn't exactly endear Daly to
the patrons who were battling the board. No doubt, the time
was to come when he wished he had kept his mouth shut . . .
when he ran for city council a year later and was defeated.

Many ministers in Anaheim were involved in the battle
over sex education, not the least of whom was the Rev. William Auld, a Presbyterian pastor who prides himself on having
some of the hippiest looking bunch of young people in Orange
County in his church.

Auld noisily defended the sex program at every opportunity,
insisting it was everything one could want. He was, in fact,
one of the ministers who worked hardest to see that it was installed in the first place.

How could he, an alleged minister of the gospel, now admit
he had made a mistake?

He never did admit it, but he became unusually silent after
the new board was elected in the spring of 1969.

Auld, like all the ministers supporting the sex classes across
the country, is a man whose basic philosophy could be
described as that of Situation Ethics. Under that philosophy,
school sex instruction becomes the greatest thing since Eve
gave Adam the apple.

"Old beliefs and faith are under severe attack," editorialized the Sacramento Union recently. "Concepts of beauty,
truth and morality are being driven from the minds of our
young people, who, by a peculiar kind of pressure, are now
infecting their elders. They dare us to remain loyal to our

39

...ent truths.

The writer continued, "The 19th Century philosopher, John Locke, advanced the theory of Tabula Rosa, in which he conceived the mind of a newborn baby as being like a slate, upon which memories would be inscribed as experiences transpire. We know it is now possible to achieve this effect upon many, regardless of their age. It is required only that the values we have given to our experience be undermined and given substitute values of opposite effect. Commonly, we refer to this as brainwashing. When these minds have had their value judgment weakened and reversed, it is as if the slate were washed clean. Thereupon, those who would, may write in what they please to accomplish their objectives."

"Frightening," the editorialist comments, and adds, "We seriously wonder if this is not precisely what is happening. Diabolical as it may seem, it has been a common tool of Communists for years . . . on every side we see ample evidence of mass ideological movement. The direction of this movement has been toward collectivism and socialistic destruction of individualism and personal responsibility. The attributes for which we all once strived are now forgotten. We have traded them for qualities we once despised . . . we have reached the point where we are confronted with our own image . . . for some of us the confrontation will be the final burial of all our expectations."

One generation turned into amoral Androyds will suffice to enslave us all.

Townsend was not about to let that happen; Anaheim would not be a breeding ground for the Child Seducers.

Armed with affidavits citing four letter sex words, pornographic school pamphlets and subversive textbooks, Jim was ready for the battle.

As allies he had thousands of irate citizens.

One year later, his brainchild dead at his feet, Paul Cook was to declare on a CBS-TV news broadcast that the Citizen's Committee of California, Inc. was "totally to blame" for his dilemma. Later he was to change that story and blame the John Birch Society and the Christian Crusade.

"We freely admit blame," Townsend said on the same newscast. "We told them (Cook and his supporters) the parents of Anaheim would not tolerate their shenanigans, and we made it stick."

Townsend, it seemed, was a better gauge of the character of the good people of Anaheim, than was Cook.

How did it happen? How did an expensive program, touted in the Liberal press as the greatest innovation in education since the invention of the blackboard end up demolished one year after Townsend and Mrs. Howe first talked about it?

It was a masterstroke of strategy and timing. On top of all that, it was a masterpiece of salesmanship on the part of Sam Campbell, editor of the city's daily newspaper.

The Citizen's Committee didn't plan it that way. In fact, around two years ago, they had worked very hard to elect Edward Hartnell to the school board, trusting that Hartnell had Conservative leanings even though he was a Democrat.

Hartnell, a good-looking, curly headed ex-policeman with a large family, spent about two dollars of his own money in the campaign. The Citizen's Committee did much of the rest, and he became the fifth man on the school board.

Members of the Committee had reasons to believe that Hartnell would be opposed to the Humanist sex education program. After all, he was an ex-policeman who sang in the St. Boniface Catholic church choir. He had even signed a petition against the sex instruction program right on the steps of St. Boniface about six years or so before his election to the board.

However, the committee members were in for a rude shock.

Hartnell's colors changed rapidly once he was ensconced safely on the board.

There are those who say he did not change at all, that he was always a Liberal at heart. Chances are that no one will ever know for sure. Suffice to say that he became the number

41

one champion of Cook's program.

The hotter the heat became, the more he spoke out in favor of sex instruction. Finally, after two opponents of the program were elected in the Spring of 1969, Hartnell took to the airwaves, talking on the radio and on TV, defending the program to anyone who would listen.

Finally, when the new board members dumped Sally Williams and temporarily shelved the whole program, Hartnell, in September, 1969, turned to the students for help.

He wrote a letter to the student body presidents of the various district high schools, on district stationery, calling on them to come to the aid of Cook and the sex program. He urged them to convince their parents that the program was wanted and to urge their parents to get into the battle.

But if Hartnell was frustrated, board president Royal C. Marten seemed to be simply confused.

He was widely liked in the city and had been, for years, a teacher at Anaheim High School. Now he is an instructor at neighboring Santa Ana City College and is much loved by his former students.

Poor Marten!

During those chaotic days of 1968 and 1969, when he was being assailed on all sides by irate parents, it would have been quite an experience to get into Marten's mind and find out what he was really thinking.

Stocky, with an ever-present cigar clamped in his teeth, between twinkling eyes that crinkled at the corners, he looks like a happy grandfather.

One thing seems obvious at this point. Marten suddenly regretted that he had allowed Paul Cook free rein to run the district with practically no board interference.

Marten awoke to discover that he had created a situation he could no longer control.

Cook was literally stripped of all responsibility in the Spring of 1969 and his duties were turned over to his deputy assistant superintendent, Ken Wines, who was later appointed

42

superintendent.

Enraged by this public humiliation, Cook apparently went on a rampage. He traveled throughout the state, promoting his sex program to anyone who would give him a forum. He called a meeting of businessmen at the Disneyland Hotel, desperately trying to convince them that what he was doing was right.

Cook found, instead, a hostile audience, convinced by the local newspaper that the program was detrimental to the well-being of the youngsters in Anaheim.

One such businessman, at the hotel, faced with Cook's desscription of what went on in the classroom, was heard to say, "Frankly, the thought of girls and boys sitting around in a classroom and talking about those things just makes me want to vomit."

Cook visibly cringed at the man's remark. Perhaps it was then that he realized he was beaten.

If his own explanation of his own program got that kind of reaction out of prominent Anaheim businessmen, then there seemed to be little hope that he could sell the program to the rest of the city.

In the midst of the furor in Anaheim, the clandestine meeting of sexologists was held at the Charter House Hotel, sponsored by the Science Research Associates, affiliate of the IBM Corporation.

The speaker at that meeting was Dr. Lester Kirkendall, and that meeting turned out to be a major blunder on the part of the sexologists.

Kirkendall's theme was "How to Cope with the Growing Resistance to the Sex Instruction in the Schools."

The Anaheim Bulletin had an informant in the ranks of the sexology teachers who were present for that two-day meeting, and from that informer came material that was printed on the

43

front page in a three part series that came to be known as the Hush Hush Series.

Kirkendall, unaware that he was walking into a trap, came to the meeting well prepared for his role as leading traveling salesman of school sex instruction. He had been involved in spreading the gospel according to Humanism for years, especially through his connection with a lurid magazine called Sexology, and through his membership on the board of the Sex Information and Education Council of the United States (SIECUS).

Little publicity was given the affair in advance, and the participants were invited to attend through invitations sent to their places of employment.

As it turned out, it is no wonder the meeting was a hush-hush affair, because the talks given by Kirkendall only added a lot of coals to the already blazing fire of dissent.

Labeling all dissidents as "fringe groups who don't think rationally," Kirkendall is reported to have said that all those who oppose the radicalizing of America's sexual attitudes have "hangups about sex."

That phrase is a recurrent one throughout the whole tight little world of the sexologists. Anyone who questions their motives or their program is labeled as an oddball who has sexual maladjustments with which to contend.

That accusation was not one to soothe the ruffled feelings of the millions of Americans who thought they were fairly normal until Kirkendall and his cohorts came along to assure them that they were not properly adjusted and therefore they could not possibly be expected to pass on sane and sensible information to their children.

"Society is changing," said Kirkendall at the Charter House, "and has shifted from the religious to the secular."

Kirkendall handed out a number of position papers dealing with the subject at hand, sex. One of the papers vividly described a sex meeting at Oregon State University, sponsored by Kirkendall, in which seven college boys talked about their

44

alleged sexual prowess before an audience consisting, in part, of 15 junior and senior high school boys and girls.

Stressing that the boys' sexual proclivities must be kept from the folks back home, Kirkendall said that arrangements were made to protect them from being embarrassed by word of their vivid descriptions leaking back to the old home town.

Apparently it was not too embarrassing to the 15 youngsters in the audience who must have learned a great deal that they didn't know before.

Kirkendall was delighted that an Anaheim anti-nudity ordinance – put through the City Council when the local legit theatre, Melodyland, had started staging shows in the buff – had been overthrown by the courts.

It was to be expected that he would praise nudity, since his organization, SIECUS, is listed approvingly in *NUDE LIVING* magazine which is published by an outfit in Los Angeles called, in bizarre fashion, ELYSIUM, for the fields of orgy and antiquity. (The publisher of this magazine was arrested on several counts of publishing lewd material in June, 1970.)

Sally Williams, coordinator of sex education for the Anaheim High Schools, showed up at the meeting, irate because the local daily had been bird-dogging her steps around the country and reporting on her activities to the local taxpayers.

"Lies," she moaned, "nothing but lies" were being printed about her.

Of course, she didn't mention that she was also a board member of SIECUS, and that her fellow board member, ISADORE RUBIN, was identified before the House Committee on Un-American Activities (HCUA) as a Communist, and that he was the editor of the much criticized Sexology magazine. (Rubin died in an auto accident in July, 1970.)

But Kirkendall didn't forget dear old Isadore. He decried those who linked his buddy with the Reds by saying that it was patently ridiculous. After all, Rubin had only written a paper for the Communist DAILY WORKER one time.

45

SIECUS, said the sex guru, was going to meet in New York City on January first to discuss the growing opposition to sex instruction in the schools and would take steps to stop the actions of their opponents.

One other thing came out of the Charter House meeting and that was the sneaky nature of the whole enterprise.

"Sneak the program into the schools," said Kirkendall. "Never say you are going to start a program . . . Say you are going to improve it or make it better . . . Once the program is begun, the opponents cannot stop it." Later he weakly denied that he had really meant that or that he had said it exactly that way.

The people of Anaheim soon found out that Kirkendall's predictions were only too true. Despite violent opposition to the program, the district board members did little to mollify their constituents.

They were looking into the program, they said, and eventually would give their opinions about it.

Meanwhile, they reappointed Cook, who had been the very center of the hurricane, to two more years as superintendent at $30,000 per year, and continued with the sex instruction program that was costing nearly $300,000 per year.*

All right, so there was an argument, pro and con. What was all the fuss about, and why was the battle raging all across the land?

Perhaps a quote from the Sacramento News of July 24, 1968, will give the reader a clue.

In an article entitled *City Schools to Begin Sex Education Program,* Reinhart Knudsen said: "The film (for third graders) on Fertilization and Birth showed how fish do it, and how chickens do it and how giraffes do it, with precise drawings of the act of copulation. But, when it comes to human beings, a drawing descreetly showed the uniting partners covered by a

---

*It depends on who quotes the figures. The administration claims $267,000, and the critics claim $375,000.

46

blanket, but the general idea was quite clear."

Clear to whom? To kids in the third grade? Dr. Melvin Anchell replies (to this kind of sexual education for third graders) that people are not animals and you cannot learn from animals, and furthermore, that kind of film could cause "sexual trauma" in the young.

Maybe *that is* the idea.

IV

PARENTS STRIKE BACK

In a parent law suit filed recently in the City of Sacramento, the complaint alleged, and not without substance, that the sex instruction program in the school district fostered immorality by advocating, among other things, sexual license.

One teacher was quoted as saying that "sexual relations should be explored before marriage to determine compatability."

The parents should not have been too amazed at this remark by the teacher. After all, that instructor is a product of his own education in California's higher immorality dens known as colleges. A perfect case in point is the recent matter involving the statues created by one William Spater, for which he received a master's degree from Long Beach State College. The statues showed nude individuals engaged in various and sundry acts, mostly perverted.

On Monday, January 5, 1970, an incredible performance took place at Long Beach State, involving naked male and female models and large screen versions of various sexual acts including lesbians "performing" and heterosexual couples engaging in the sex act.

The "show" was put on by two so-called professors who were allegedly as much interested in publicity as they were in conducting a college class. They went to great pains to inform the press, and then went on the air to complain that the press had written them up.

Over 400 "relevant and responsible" students took part in the class that day, and when the two "professors" were promptly suspended by an administration that should have known beforehand what was going on, the students started their usual sophomoric sit-ins, etc., ad nauseum.

The class was promptly transferred to the Long Beach Unitarian "church," which came as no surprise to people in

48

Long Beach who have had to sniff the obnoxious philosophical fumes from that place for years.

Did teachers who are teaching sex acts to children in local grade schools get their own education from the same kind of teachers who awarded the degree to Spater?

San Francisco school board members were "terribly shaken up and appalled" when they got a look at material proposed for their fourth grade classes — including material describing intercourse, step by step, in the kind of language that is to be found in books purchased in dingy pornographic bookstores.

Dr. Rhoda Lorand, a prominent New York psychologist, doesn't think much of the sexologist's approach to sex education that was being used in Anaheim.

The material, she said, "is overwhelming, disturbing and embarrassing, upsetting and exciting and very likely to lead to sex difficulties later in life."

Ah ha. Is that what they are up to, you wonder? Well, if you are wondering that, then you are guilty of what Paul Cook and Sally Williams referred to as "hangups about sex."

Never mind that you might have five kids and a perfect sexual relationship with your spouse. If you question the motives of the sexologists, you are all hung up and probably have secret and hidden sex desires.

Sweden has had sex instruction for the past 13 years, and yet venereal disease is rampant in their schools, the suicide rate among the young is at epidemic proportions and 100 of the most famous doctors in the country petitioned the government to do something about it, since the sex classes had created "sexual hysteria in the young, which was a direct result of the school sex program."

Not too surprising. Whatsoever you sow, that shall you also reap — or maybe it should be RAPE? Like the 13 year old who tried to rape his little sister, to find out what it was all about after getting his curiosity awakened in a sex class, according to his parents.

A choice bit of erotica presented to the fourth graders in

49

Redwood City, in a film entitled "Time of Your Life" included the following words spoken by a woman in the film.

"One very important way that a husband and wife have of showing their love for each other is by their physical contact and having what is called 'sexual intercourse.' When a couple has sexual intercourse, this is physically the closest they can ever be. This is a beautiful way of showing and sharing the love that they have for each other. When a couple has sexual intercourse, they are usually lying down very close to each other and usually in a bed. They usually start by kissing and holding each other. Each person, the husband and wife, gets a very strong feeling of love for the other and excitement in being together. The man's penis has an erection and the woman's vagina becomes moist or wet. At this point, as the couple is lying very close together and because the penis of the man is designed by nature to fit into the vagina of the woman, the man, gently but firmly, pushes his penis into his wife's vagina. His penis has an ejaculation, and this is when the sperm are released. They are released into the vagina, and they begin traveling into the uterus and up into the tubes. They do not know where they are going nor which direction to go. Their tiny tails propel them, and they move quickly, considering their microscopic size. At the time that a man's penis has an ejaculation, or when the sperm comes out, he gets a very strong but very good feeling, and this is called an orgasm or a climax. At about this same time, the woman, too, may get a very strong but good feeling, and this also is called an orgasm or a climax. After this happens the couple usually lie, still very close together, very quietly and still. They experience a very peaceful, warm and loving feeling about each other."

---

*Time Of Your Life, Teachers Guide, programs 10-15, page 20.

50

Now, if that wouldn't arouse a normal youngster, that youngster isn't very normal. Any adult who wants this presented to a youngster by a stranger in a film in a darkened room, in a mixed class, is ready for the psychiatrist's couch himself.

That same film tells the youngster how he can entertain himself on cold nights, namely by masturbating, and any child who doesn't become an afficionado after hearing the following is probably suffering from a hormone imbalance.

" . . . *having sperm when he is awake; this is called masturbation. During this time he will have an erection, say, at some time or another, and he will handle his penis so as to cause the sperm to come out. He will usually do this in private, where he is away from other people. The average would, I suppose, be every week and two or three times a week. But it varies. It may be every day for some boys and every other week for other boys.*

"There are religions that have raised some questions that this was something that was wrong. We know as doctors that physically it does not hurt boys, and we know as psychiatrists that it does not hurt people emotionally to masturbate. (Editor's note: There is some dispute among physicians about these last two points.) *But certainly people who think that it is wrong might talk to their parents or their minister, priest or rabbi, and I think they should check about this. It does not hurt you not to masturbate. There is a problem that is raised. People say, well, what would be too much? Is it possible to do it too much? Can you hurt yourself? No. Physically you cannot. But there are times when boys have problems. Maybe a boy isn't doing well in school. Maybe he has troubles, with his father or with his mother, brothers, sisters, or friends. Because he gets tense, he gets upset and unhappy. He may masturbate more frequently as a way to get rid of tensions. Now, this does not solve the*

51

problem. So, since it does not solve the problem, he has to do it over again. And he may do it more often than once a day. Since it does not solve the problem, it in itself can be an indicator that there are difficulties. Now, once the problems get straightened around, the boy gets along better with his parents or something like this. Then the whole problem disappears and his frequency of masturbation, how often he does it, returns to about an average amount. I would like to mention one thing, and that is there are two words that are frequently confused. One is menstruation. Menstruation, as we talked about a couple weeks ago, occurs in a girl when the lining of the uterus comes off and is shed, coming down in the vagina. The other word is masturbation, and that is what we have been talking about just now when a boy or girl stimulates himself, causing sexual excitement. Now actually, almost all boys masturbate, but we do not know how many girls do."

If an adult male used this kind of language in talking with a young boy or girl in the neighborhood, the parents of that child would probably call the police and have the adult arrested for contributing to the delinquency of a minor or for making sexual approaches to a child. Yet, those same parents are eager to have strangers in a classroom talk to their children in this manner and that is supposed to be education.

Evidence is mounting rapidly that much of the explicit sexual information given in classrooms is causing serious psychological and social disorientation among the young.

The following is just one of countless documented cases that have come to the attention of child analysts in recent days as a result of sex education in schools. It could be repeated time and again, but space will not allow an endless repetition of case histories.

52

"I would like to share with you the experience we have had with our six year old daughter. It's rather touching to hold a six year old girl in your arms and try to comfort her when she is crying, 'Mommy, I've tried to forget, but I can't.'

"As you can guess, I am writing about sex education in our schools. As a parent, I am opposed to these kinds of programs because there are no evaluations to show they are needed or that they have any helpful role to play or that they are harmful. We, as parents, do believe the programs are harmful because of our own experience.

"We were not aware of any such program at the school our daughter attended. For seven whole months we went through a living hell, with no idea what was upsetting our first grader.

"I was expecting our fifth baby at the time, and during my pregnancy I talked with my daughter about her fears of the baby dying before he was born. We finally withdrew her from school at the suggestion of a school principal and two psychologists at the nearby medical school.

"In the fall we started her at another school, one that had been highly recommended. We still had no idea of what had taken place, since we did not know they had sex classes at her previous school.

"At this new school they had a course called Human Development and Interpersonal Relationships. However, the parents were not informed of it until the year was nearly over, and that was when a local newspaper printed an article about the two pilot programs going on in our school district.

"My daughter was attending one of those programs.

"By this time I had read a little bit about sex education and had heard some wild rumors. I decided to go to the school the next day to see what was really going on.

"I had, then, full confidence in the principal and teacher. She told me nothing was going on and that they did not have sex classes. I kept questioning her however, and she finally admitted they had an 'outline' to go by.

"She showed this to me and I made a copy of it to study.

53

It dealt more with humans than with animals. I asked if they were going to have any slides or films, and she said only if their level of 'maturity' required it.

"I then asked about the other grades, and she said the program would be at their level of sophistication. She believed very strongly in the 'teachable moment.'

"When I first entered the classroom, the students were at recess. The first thing I noticed was a large colored drawing in chalk of a chicken in embryo on the blackboard, and on the browsing table were two books.

"One book was called the Egg, and it was all about fertilization and development of the egg. The other book had pictures of different kinds of eggs, from fish to animals, and at the bottom of one page was the picture of a human egg. Throughout the book it explained fertilization and development in full detail of these different eggs.

"I really don't think first graders need all that information, and besides, I didn't like them putting human beings on the same level with animals.

"In the classroom they had an incubator with chicken and duck eggs getting ready to hatch. That was — except for the other materials.

"Each child made two notebooks, one on frogs and chickens, copying from the blackboard. It explained the use of the reproductive organs and the differences between male and female.

"Then, at the end of the year, the children put on a program for their parents on chickens.

"During my talk with the teacher, she mentioned that my daughter did not draw a single picture of her daddy or any other male during the whole year. She wondered if we had a problem. This was a complete shock to me, since my daughter has always had a very close relationship with her father.

"Not long afterwards, I was talking with a friend whose daughter was in the same class with our daughter at the school where our problems began the year before. She asked me

54

what I thought about the sex films and slides our children had seen.

"I asked her what films she was talking about and she described a slide film called 'How Babies Are Made.' I was horrified and went straight home to talk to my daughter and husband.

"My daughter would not talk about what she had seen. She only cried. It took three weeks of continual talking to get her to say anything about it, and then only when her daddy and I were holding her close under sobbing of: 'Mommy, I've tried to forget and I can't.'

"She finally said she had seen the slides of 'How Babies Are Made,' and that the boys had laughed when they showed the mother nursing the baby.

"She said she had seen also a film of a baby (monkey) dying inside its mother before it was born. She said that she and another little girl went into the restroom and cried.

"My friend told me the children were given a test to see how much they learned from the films. The children were told not to tell their parents, because they wouldn't understand.

"When I was holding her, she said, 'Mommy, if you'd wear underpants to bed, daddy couldn't hurt you.' "

It is inconceivable that the American people have reached a place where this kind of indignity can be practiced with impunity by teachers in a public school classroom.

Humanists, who are promoting school sex instruction, always strive to make sex activity no more unusual than eating and breathing. It is, to them, just another function of the body and should be treated as casually as sneezing.

Under that philosophy, a person ought to sleep with anyone he or she finds physically attractive, with no other considerations.

For instance, in a book published by Laidlaw, called "Human Growth and Reproduction," we find the following words under page one of chapter three:

55

"Coitus takes place when the man's reproductive organ, the penis, enters into the woman's passage, the vagina. The activity that follows is a natural one, and it is partly guided by the natural inborn actions of man and woman. That is, it is *partly an automatic* action much as swallowing food and sneezing are automatic." [Emphasis ours.]

Well, since it is all that natural, why the need for sex instruction in the schools? Of course it IS natural, and that is precisely why all religions have made a point of wrapping the sex act in mystery and in a Sacramental state.

Pius the Tenth said it on Dec. 31, 1929 in his great encyclical on Christian Education for Youth.

"Far too common is the error of those who, with dangerous assurance and under an ugly term propagate a so-called sex education. They falsely imagine they can forearm youth against the dangers of sensuality by purely physical means, such as a foolhardy initiation and precautionary instruction for all indiscriminately . . . even in public. Such persons grievously err in refusing to recognize the inborn weakness of human nature . . . and also in ignoring the experience of facts, from which it is clear, particularly in young people, that evil practices are the effect not so much of ignorance of the intellect, as of weakness of a will exposed to dangerous occasions (to sin) and unsupported by the means (Sacraments) of grace."

Father Robert Burns, writing in the Wanderer, a national Catholic paper, put the spotlight on the sexologists.

"The Commandments are being soft pedaled, minimized and deemphasized because the strict and meticulous adherence to law can lead to legalism, and legalism is a bad word to advocates of the New Morality. This reasoning also applies to the precepts of the Church and its civil ordinances . . .

"The average common sense Catholic parent, with only a high school or grade school education can observe this corrupting of Catholic doctrine and the destroying of Christian virtue. Many of them have organized to defend the Faith in various parts of the country. Why then do so many of our

Catholic educators seem oblivious to the danger?"

The answer seems to be that they have themselves been corrupted, as the facts bear out that some priests and nuns have frequently led assaults not only against the social order (Render unto Caesar, etc.) and against the Church, but against the Faith and virtue of the children put in their care.

The origins and motives of people behind the sex instruction drive in Anaheim is, in the words of one newsman, "like unravelling a can of worms."

The following is a brief analysis of some of the forces involved. It will give the reader new insight to the vast interlocking network of these influences.

We begin with a psychological technique that has become a regular part of education in thousands of schools, in police and probation departments and in businesses. The technique, of course, is popularly known as Sensitivity Training, but it goes under many names.

When the nature of the dehumanizing technique was exposed, the promoters promptly adopted a vast number of names for the technique in order to disguise it. It is known, now, by such titles as: T Group; Group Dynamics; Auto-Criticism; Operant Conditioning; Human Relations; Synanon Games; Basic Encounter; Broad Sensitivity; Group Counseling (though properly used, group counseling is a proper psychiatric technique); Management Development; Leadership Class; Self-Honesty Class; Self Examination; Interpersonal Relationships; Interpersonal Competence; Self Evaluation and Human Potential Workshop.

Brock Chisholm, former head of the United Nation's World Health Organization (WHO) summed up the use of these mind bending techniques in a speech given in 1945.

"For a cause we must seek some consistent thread running through the weave of all civilizations we have known, and pre-

57

venting the development of all, or almost all, the people to a state of true maturity.

"What basic psychological distortion can be found in every civilization of which we know anything? It must be a force which discourages the ability to see and acknowledge patent facts, which prevents the rational use of intelligence, which teaches or encourages the ability to dissociate and to believe, contrary to and in spite of clear evidence, which produces inferiority, guilt and fear, which makes controlling people's personal behavior emotionally necessary, which encourages prejudice and the inability to see, understand and sympathize with other people's points of view.

"Is there any force so potent and so pervasive that it can do all these things in all civilizations? There is — just one. The only lowest common denominator of all civilizations, and the only psychological force capable of producing these perversions is MORALITY, the CONCEPT OF RIGHT AND WRONG."

In other words, "we must get rid of morality," he said. And how is this to be brought about? Through SENSITIVITY TRAINING, of course.

Nearly forty years later, an administrator in Pasco, Washington school district was to echo Chisholm in a much more explicit way.

Harold J. Prairie, the superintendent of the Pasco schools, gave a speech before school administrators at the Eisenhower High School in Yakima, Washington.

Prairie called upon his fellow administrators to lead the revolution now going on in the schools in the following words.

"It seems imperative that educators adopt some of the new techniques for behavior modification which the social sciences have found efficacious to the classroom situation, so that education may lead a revolution to a better way of life for all America's people, instead of maintaining a posture of dedication to the status quo.

"Education has the basic potential mechanisms to give direction to and help control the tempo of the revolution that

58

is the main, continuing and disruptive influence in our society.

"As the effective (emotional) behavior of the mass movement meets the purely cognitive (rational) resistance of the reaction, the potential for the destruction of the very lifeblood of the nation is generated. It is for education to recognize and respond to the societal demands of the here and now, rather than to the desires of what DuBois (Communist) termed the elitist ruling class.

"It is this writer's opinion that the commingling of the effective and cognitive domains, and the utilization of teaching techniques which recognize the usefulness of such a commingling, can lead to peace, brotherhood and full equality in our country.

"Social scientists and writers have done, and are doing, their work well. The experimental support for programs in education which are being explicated today, point to the outstanding fact that if one wishes another to learn something, one must first effect the learner affectively before one can effect the learner cognitively."

In all that educational mumbo jumbo, the superintendent is simply stating that the schools have to be turned into social science laboratories in order to help promote the "revolution." The reader can imagine what kind of revolution he is talking about.

But what is the practical use of Sensitivity Training? John Dewey, the Marxist father of American education, summed it up very well in 1916.

"From a social standpoint, dependence denotes a power rather than a weakness, involving interdependence. There is always a danger that increased personal independence will decrease the social capacity of an individual. In making him more self reliant, it may make him more self-sufficient; it may lead to aloofness and indifference. It often makes an individual so insensitive in his relations to others, as to develop an illusion of being really able to stand and act alone — an unnamed form of *insanity* which is responsible for a large part of the remediable suffering of the world."*

So it was that John Dewey was looking into the future and envisioning the modern American classroom under the control of behavioral scientists.

Sensitivity Training has been described irreverently as Group Grope, and that is as good a description as any.

In the SIECUS Newsletter, Fall, 1965, there appears an article that begins: "Early in December, SIECUS Newsletters 1 and 2 will be sent to all Human Relations Aid Packet Subscribers, as one of the enclosures in their pack number 68."

Human Relations, in this context, refers to the kind of mental manipulation now coming out of behavioral science labs.

The SIECUS Newsletter continues, "A one page descriptive notice about these materials, and about SIECUS, will be included. The packet will present a topical emphasis on sex education and will include "Sex and the College Student," a new study by the Group for the Advancement of Psychiatry, material from the YWCA Sex Morality Teaching Record Kit, and the American Academy of Pediatrics selected references on sex education. Human Relations kit is a bimonthly subscription service of programs and resource materials in the field of family life-sex education, Mental Health and mental health problems and human relationships, and is produced by Mental Health Materials Center, 104 E. 25th St., New York City."

In other words, the Pavlovian technique for launching a frontal assault upon America's young people was being promoted by SIECUS.

So there you have it. SIECUS, the number one agency promoting sex education was up to its navel in Sensitivity Training and so-called Mental Health work.

Sensitivity Training had its origin at the time of the Communist revolution in Russia. Thomas Woody, a John Dewey

---

*Dewey, John; *Democracy and Education;* 1916, MacMillan, page 44.

disciple, writing in a book entitled "New Minds and New Men," tells how mind conditioning was practiced on the children of that beleagured land.

Those early forms of the technique involved self and group criticism and attacks upon those who would not conform to group thinking.

However, it was left to social scientist Kurt Lewin to introduce it with a vengeance into America. Lewin did his work in the field under the sponsorship of the National Education Association (National Training Labs) and that work, early in the 1950's, has led to the crisis in the area of mind bending today.

When the UN brought WHO (World Health Organization) into existence in February, 1948, it was ALGER HISS who gave Sensitivity Training its impetus.

Hiss stated, "Health is a state of complete physical, mental and social well being, and not merely the absence of disease or infirmity."

Interestingly, Woody, in his pro-Communist Russia book, used the exact same words in 1932.

The head of WHO, Brock Chisholm, also used the same words, and went on to state that those who do not believe in a one world government are mentally ill.

Frank Calderone, the husband of leading sexologist Dr. Mary Calderone, was the administrative head of WHO under Chisholm.

Dr. Mary Calderone is particularly unhappy about the demise of the Anaheim sex program.

Chisholm, in a book, the foreword of which was written by Hiss, said, "Universal Mental Health means One World."

To cure what he called a "sick" world, Chisholm suggested the use of Group Therapy — nothing more or less than Pavlovian brain washing.

Now, as a result of ground work laid by DR. SAMUEL BLAIR, director of the California State Department of Mental Hygiene, and Alger Hiss, the techniques practiced on American prisoners by the North Koreans are the latest 'in' thing on campuses, in churches and even kindergarten.

However, there is one slight difference. This time the older victims have been conditioned in advance to eagerly cooperate in their own brain scrambling.

How did it get into local schools? Don't we have school boards to prevent just such a thing from happening?

Yes — and we also have the world's most powerful political and ideological lobby, the National Education Association (NEA) which has been pushing Sensitivity Training for years through the National Training Labs of Kurt Lewin.

And how does SIECUS come into the picture?

Remember, the labs promoting the first techniques were first organized by state agencies in Connecticut. Mary Calderone is the head of SIECUS. She was also, according to the SIECUS Newsletter of Fall, 1965, in residence as a *"consultant to the public schools of the Hartford area, under the auspices of the State of Connecticut, Department of Education."*

Yes — and the Gordian Knot gets even more entwined and entangled.

The National Institute for Mental Health, whose first director was the infamous Red fronter and fifth amendment taker JULIUS SCHREIBER and the U.S. Office of Education (HEW) has, and still have, a lot in common.

Both agencies proposed the supplying of federal funds for sex education, and for its twin, Sensitivity Training. HEW, at the same time, pours money into the far flung activities of the National Institute for Mental Health.

There are those who have stated the SIECUS program is not only anti-Christian, but that it is actively promoting a religion called Humanism.

SIECUS lends credence to this charge in their choice of a symbol, the ancient YIN and YANG symbol of male and female.

Gudrun Maddox, a member of SIECUS, recently described the origin in a newsletter.

"Originally this symbol was at the center of a larger, circular symbol which, in Buddhism and Taoism, established the mystic relationship between man and the universe. In the central symbol, the dark half is YIN, the female principle, representing the moon which was considered negative and evil. It is balanced by YANG, the male – the positive, bright beneficient principle representing the sun."

"The two symbols together," she adds, "form the perfect circle representing man in his conscious existence."

Tax supported schools are the number one vehicle for the social engineers. Without that crutch, the entire attack upon this generation of young people would come to a screeching halt.

One social engineer who summed it up was former President Conant of Harvard University.

"I do believe there is some reason to fear, lest a dual system (public and private) of secondary education may, in some states, come to threaten the democratic unity provided by our public schools. I refer to the desire of some people to increase the scope and number of private schools. Our schools should serve all creeds. The greater the proportion of our youth who attend independent schools, the greater threat to our democratic unity."

Another social planner, Dr. Worth McClure, told the American Association of School Administrators in 1952, "Denominational schools build prejudices (and) . . . destroy the unity now found in our democracy."

The case for the independent, non-governmental school was given by HAROLD DODDS, president emeritus, Princeton University. He wrote, "The independent school in America is one of several voluntary non-governmental and non-political islands of independent thought and opinion indispensible in a society which is rapidly politicizing wide areas of life which not long ago were the responsibility of individuals and volun-

63

tary associations."

But of course, the professional change agents and social engineers want only state owned schools so that children can be mandated into their laboratories.

Recently a test was given to students in a California junior high school. Consisting of various matching questions, the test included such queries as, (1) The enlarged and firm condition of the penis is called ———; (2) The highest point of excitement sexually in a man or woman is ———; (3) A man's or woman's external sex parts are ———; (4) A woman who has intercourse for pay is called a ———.

If that seems somewhat amazing, remember that in November, 1967, the president of San Jose State College promoted to a post of full professor a man who had been convicted of performing a sex act with another man in the men's room of a department store just three months before.*

And if that is surprising, remember that DAVID LUCAS, professor of psychology at Sacramento State College, vigorously defended the San Jose professor.** (San Jose is the campus where the students recently demanded an official campus club for sex deviates.)

*Testimony of Professor John Gilbaugh before California Senate, April, 1968.
**The Voice of the Faculties, October, 1968.

V

CREATING ROBOTS

Where did the sexologists make their mistake in regard to the Anaheim program?

First, they underestimated the volatile nature of the material they were dispensing in their classrooms. It was inevitable that sooner or later some of those students would start to talk – and talk they did.

Second, they underestimated the incredible way in which Townsend and his sex education battlers could ferret out what what was really going on behind those classroom walls.

This is not to say that the classes were dens of vice – however, just enough was going on to give the opponents material to stoke the ever-growing fires of controversy in the community. School officials soon found themselves caught up in a raging inferno that no amount of verbal drooling would quench.

The sexologists tried desperately to paint their opponents as sexless beings with all kinds of hangups. Nothing could be farther from the truth.

Most of those who figured most prominently in the sex education battle were not trying to foist their own moral standards off on the whole community. As a matter of fact, the biggest complaint they had was that the school district was trying to foist its own standard onto the young people.

That standard, they decided, was not their standard and therefore they figured the school district was getting dangerously close to teaching a form of religion – Humanism – in the public schools of the city.

Townsend, Howe, Kelly, and all the others really didn't care what their neighbor's sex life was like. In fact, they figured sex was pretty much a private thing and that was one reason they opposed public exposure in classrooms.

If you were to take any six sex education opponents in Anaheim and ask them about their moral code, you would doubtless get six different answers. Some would allude to the 10 Commandments as a basic guideline, admitting at the same time that they didn't always match all the requirements.

Others would recite a few chapters or verses from the New Testament, stating they believed what St. Paul or Jesus Christ had to say about it, while disagreeing with each other over the details.

Still others would tell you they really didn't have any formal moral code at all, but that it was tied in with Jewish-Christian standards. Those same people would insist that it really was nobody's business but their own.

The death of the SIECUS type Anaheim sex program would not have taken place, however, without the usually secret help of countless numbers of teachers, including some administrators in astonishingly high places.

And Sam Campbell brilliantly summed it up in an editorial on the subject; "They could not meet in secret without the very words from their mouths being shouted from the rooftops for all the world to hear."

Of course, there were some who attributed much of the controversy to your author, insisting he did this or that to aid and abet the sex education opponents.

To that I can only say that I was highly flattered by the attention, but I do not *make* news, *I only report the news.*

The Anaheim sex program was news — BIG — news — and I am proud of one thing. My newsman's nose smelled the story and Campbell gave me every opportunity to develop it. A reporter could ask for nothing more.

In the fall of 1968 I sent a letter to Walter Winchell, with whom I had been associated when he was investigating the Sirhan Sirhan case. "Without the aid of a crystal ball," I said, "it seems apparent to me that the sex education controversy is going to prove to be one of the biggest stories of the year, if not the decade."

Winchell wrote back and thanked me for the information I had sent, and added he had sent the information on to his good friend, J. Edgar Hoover.

By winter of 1968 it appeared evident my rather hasty prediction was beginning to come true.

It didn't take long to discover that the Anaheim curriculum planners had made serious errors in strategy.

First, they had aligned themselves with SIECUS, which had such a suspect beginning that it could not stand much public scrutiny for a variety of reasons. Second, the philosophy embraced four ancient Christian heresies that made the program, in effect, just another religious form of cultist indoctrination.

The first heresy was that of Manicheanism, which was anti-life and anti-social. A second heretical aspect came close to the teachings of Rousseau, embodying within it a false and immoral optimism about human nature.

The program, by its very nature, sought to glorify the human body, matter and all physical pleasures and processes except that of procreation. Love was robbed of its spiritual nature, making it serve materialistic ends, denying any supernatural life.

Nothing was essentially evil, since all was to be considered in the light of the circumstances. The actions of man, they implied, never fell to the level of intrinsic evil, nor did they rise to the heights of intrinsic good. Hence, the program inevitably wound up denying the Christian concept of the all-good and all-holy God.

Sex became nothing more than a fetish and sex education the panacea for all human ills — a substitute for religion and morality and an almost Divine imperative.

In addition to this concept, the program possessed within its structure a streak of Gnostic elitism. Gnosticism, of course, was a philosophical and religious system of the sixth century, teaching that knowledge rather than faith was the key to salvation.

The sexologists are, to themselves, the light of the world but not the *salt* of the earth because they contradict nearly everything in the Christian tradition.

The scriptures simply say, "Thou shall not commit fornication," and goes on to describe the punishment.

The Anaheim sex program altered that dictum and made it a question of possibly abstaining from sexual relations only when it might be harmful to another person.

Try to tell that to two sixteen year old kids in the back seat of a car.

It was almost as if those promoting school sex instruction were totally devoid of sexual feelings, themselves.

The last heresy was that of Pelagianism. In their Humanism they sought to undercut the entire Christian dispensation of Divine faith and grace. They also held something of the view of the Anti-Nomians, undercutting the Divine and natural law.

In the words of St. Paul, "They spoke as if they were a law unto themselves, slaves of the body and innocent of the soul and its destiny."

Who and what were they?

The Catholic Wanderer newspaper has an answer to these two important questions.

"To the observer," the Wanderer editorialized, "they seem to be stool pigeons of Communistic atheism and stooges of Satan."

Pretty strong language, that.

Still, no matter how you try to understand the character of those most prominent in the sex education movement, and attempt to analyze their psychotic sex obsession, all true Christians would have to be aware and put up their guard against their machinations.

However, no matter how thin you slice the sex education loaf, the individual pieces are a real threat to Christian faith.

We don't expect the reader to buy that allegation unless it

comes right from the horse's mouth. The horse, in this case, is Dr. Mary Calderone, the SIECUS director and foremost spokesman for school sex instruction.

On October 3, 1969 she spoke before 400 teachers in a symposium at Kansas City, Kansas. The meeting was conducted jointly by the Kansas State Board of Health and the University Medical School.

She lashed out against the "evangelical and fundamental Christians" who stand four square against sex instruction and predicted there would soon be a change within the churches that would tend toward a more lenient and permissive attitude.

She proclaimed these changes must first take place before there could be any real advances on the sex education front.

Dr. Calderone's attack on the "fundamentalist Evangelicals" amused a great many Roman Catholics who were as dead set against her ideas as any Southern Baptist ever could be. They had never heard themselves called those names before.

Earlier in her speech she attacked the women who were picketing her lecture, calling them, "Hate mongers who call themselves Christians . . . they should be cognizant of the fact that the finest minds in the country support our views."

Those finest minds consisted of the most extreme, Leftist, fellow traveling odd balls in the nation, as witness a snake pit of them who signed a pro-SIECUS ad for the New York Times in the late fall of 1969. The nearly 100 names read like a reprint of government documents on subversion and suspect affiliations.

The Anaheim Bulletin devoted four days to chronicling the astounding backgrounds of the ad signers. It included among its list identified Communists, members of scores of Red fronts, members of everything from peace fronts to wild eyed leftist organizations and a small handful of what seemed to be simple dupes or professional joiners who didn't know what kind of company they were keeping.

Around the country, meanwhile, things were heating up.

In Grand Forks, North Dakota, a man named James Bradshaw was taking on the sexologists in the only way available to him. He was running huge ads in the daily paper, attacking the schemes of the mind benders right and left, simply because the paper refused to print his side of the story.

The true establishment in America is the public school system. When you dare to criticize their programs or their policies, you have not only invited the wrath of the professional educators and an assorted group of organizations such as the League of Women Voters and the PTA, but you have invited the wrath of businessmen who sell things to the schools and even architects who design school buildings.

Grand Forks was a hot bed for the behavioral scientists. In this small city is the state college, which has a behavioral science lab on campus. From that college went a group of students in the summer of 1969, to visit a small town called ZAP, and they proceeded to demolish the place.

Time after time Bradshaw's PAMS committee found itself losing, but they kept on persisting in their struggle.

Neighbor was divided against neighbor and friend against friend. Even husbands and wives stopped talking to one another by the summer of 1969, but young Jim was a persistent cuss. He didn't cave in easily. At last report the battle was still raging.

Around the same time, George Paules, a citizen of Parsippany, New Jersey, was singled out for persecution by the local school board and sued for libel, simply because he criticized the board's sex education program and the unprofessional conduct of some board members.

In addition to being sued, Paules and his family were threatened and harassed by school sex promoters.

He had to send his wife and daughter to another state for

70

several weeks and enroll his children in a private school, as well as obtain an unlisted phone number.

Not daunted, Paules says he welcomes the suit as a chance to expose the board's real sex program as "a doctrine of pornography, perversion and sexual permissiveness, and to expose the lies, deception, perversion and other illicit activities of school personnel."

At stake, according to Paules, is the basic question: Can a school board legally prevent a parent from making specific objections to a school curriculum which is contrary to morality and religion? The fact that the lawsuit was filed just prior to the school board election raises the interesting question of intimidating citizens during an election.

Paules has guts, pure and simple, and he is not about to be stopped by such a simple maneuver as a lawsuit — although word has it now that some people in the school administration would rather drop the matter.

After all, he believes, it's a matter of morality.

Teachers are not above reproach, unlike Pilate's wife.

They are subject to all the ills of the flesh, and just because they have the title of educator in front of their name doesn't make them any more or less moral than anyone else.

There are good, bad and indifferent teachers, just as there are good, bad and indifferent lawyers, doctors and mechanics.

Sometimes it appears there are more bad teachers than good ones, as witness one Deena Metzgar,* an English instructor in the Los Angeles Junior College District who regaled her fuzzy faced male students and her adolescent female students with the following poem.

It isn't a good poem, as poetry goes.

It isn't even good pornography.

However, it needs printing here, if only to prove to the reader that such things actually happen and that people

---

*Fired by the school board, she was reinstated in her job by a judge in Los Angeles.

71

charged with the education of young people can be involved in some mighty sordid interprises.

Some people will complain that this kind of obvious rot has no business in this or any other book.

Well, that may be true, of saner times — but you have to know the enemy in order to know what you are fighting.

Hence, we print this incredible bilge for the reader to ponder how much lower the American public school can sink!! If you can't stand filth, skip this poem.

JEHOVAH'S CHILD
or
In Christ's name, kindness is sucking the cock of a turned cheek — Jesus style — Jehovah would have bitten it off.
Straw legged Cindy
Now over the wall
dilates prismatic eyes
grinds unhabited wooden hips
mouse trap cunt
with vise and swivel just in case
leers and extends her pay-first
scanty chocolate and strawberry nipples
to be licked from crumbling sugar cones
a Thrifty treat — five cent Sunday special.
She extracts from a bloody napkin dispenser
a Volkswagen, folded mechanic and clubfooted daughter,
for entr'acts in her own private guerrilla charity show,
and a ball pointed German shepherd with retractable pecker.
Then she mounts her golden daughters on a
pay-as-you-go Zircon
and is off
through the American meatgrinder
seeking enlightenment by guru in gas stations across the
        country
teaching reading by billboard
and arithmetic by credit card.

72

$15,000 later she races, pussy first,
through Denver, Chicago, Florida
arrows through Seminole reservations
in a nylon cartwheel to the primitive soul,
then alligator lined, inside and out her quicksand womb
she rolls in the hospital bed out from under daddy
and wraps his heart in tin foil,
for possible transplant
when her own nickel and 17 jewel virgin is unsprung.
Then it's New York
and tea in a tenement
Blue point oysters in a three fantasy walkup climbed
on reefers filched in a $2 trick.
In October, when burning roaches provide little heat
she chirps a Robin's going S. for the winter — love you,
      love you —
for dough to roll into a moist and spicy
gingerbread, minklined, Morroccan cruise.
—No takers. Pre syphilitic, she
disconnects the nine month telephone silence
with husband, father, god, country and all creditors at sea
drops the mechanical spouse in the East River
with concrete daughter tied about his neck,
clamp's the dog's jaw on the postman's leg
and hailing Mary's on gold teeth
extracted in Catholic subway muggings,
she retreats to Convent Delores, Dolores, Dolores.
Repentant she reconciles testaments
fucks only Jehovah; sucks only Christ.

An unusual poem? Not really.

That kind of psycho-sexual-masochism is evident day after day on college campuses across the country. In fact, this entire book could be filled with illustrations even worse — so enough!

73

It was left to the sex education opponents in New Orleans to come up with a succinct analysis of those who are promoting sex classes in every school in the land.

"People who oppose sex classes," they wrote, "are frequently depicted as having sex hangups, and deliberate efforts are made to ridicule them. This is due to a psychological mechanism called 'projection,' which is the practice of persons having a problem, to project that problem unto other people. In other words, when sex educators say, 'You have a problem,' they really mean that 'They have a problem,' but they are projecting their problem onto others in order to relieve their own sexual anxieties."

It was left to the fledgling organization of doctors, SIECOP, to open a major salvo of opposition against the sexologists.

In the summer of 1969 they published a little booklet entitled, "The Medical Case Against Sex Education." Overnight it became a minor sensation, and a major irritant to the overworked libidos of the sexologists.

SIECOP was attacked right and left, meaning simply that they had scored a bull's eye.

About the same time your author was lambasted in the anti-Defamation League booklet published in the state of Michigan — meaning that I had probably scored one too.

The event that teed off the ADL was a meeting held in Grosse Pointe in the late spring of 1969.

Expecting a few hundred people, I was astounded when around 1200 showed up at the local high school for my talk.

It was later that I found out why.

Not only had the local committee done a good job in getting out an audience, but many in the audience were hostile to me from the outset.

Wayne State University in Detroit produced some of the audience. You name it, Wayne State has it.

In fact, some two months after I returned from Detroit, a newswire poll revealed that over half the pre-medical students at Wayne State were regular drug users of one kind or another. You name it, Wayne State has it!

Grosse Pointe, of course, is next door to Detroit, and nobody who can read needs to know anything more about Detroit.

More than 35 years ago Dr. Brock Chisholm, later to become the head of the UN World Health Organization, WHO, sounded like a forerunner to the Anaheim sex program when he cried, "The poisonous certainties fed to us by our parents, our Sunday and day school teachers is the root of the problem."

In a lecture entitled "The Reestablishment of Peacetime Society," Chisholm said that we are all citizens of the world, whether we like it or not, and in order to prevent future wars, human behavior must be permanently and irrevocably altered.

Of course, that is exactly what Christians believe, but Chisholm goes about it a little differently, since he doesn't accept the fact that man is a fallen creature.

In order to stop the world's ills, he said, there must be a cessation of all morality, self responsibility and individual integrity.

"If the race is to be freed from its crippling burden of good and evil," he said, "it must be the psychiatrist who takes the criminal responsibility . . . some help may well be found in possible developments of shorter, more effective techniques of treatment. Shock, chemotherapy, group therapy, hypno and narco-analysis, psycho drama and even surgery can all be used."

If that sounds a lot like a latter day Adolph Hitler it shouldn't be surprising. There is a great deal of the Fascist mentality in all those who promote these behavioristic schemes.

Chisholm gave that speech and just three years later George Orwell was to write his famous and horrifying book, "1984," developing in fiction the world that Brock Chisholm envisioned in reality.

And the instrument through which all this was to come about was through the so-called family life courses in Ameri-

75

ca's public schools.

In 1953 Bertrand Russell wrote a book entitled "The Impact of Science on Society," in which he pointed out the significance of changing all society through mass psychology. (UNESCO puts out a quarterly using the name of Russell's book.)

"The opinion that snow is white must be held to be a morbid eccentricity," he wrote. "It is for future scientists to make these maxims precise, and to discover exactly how much it costs per head to make children believe that snow is black and how much less it would cost to make them believe it is dark gray."

Russell continued, "Although this science will be diligently studied, it will be rightly confined to the governing class (Gnosticism, again) and the populace will not be allowed to know how its convictions were generated."

"When the technique has been perfected," he wrote, "every government that has been in charge of education for a generation will be able to control its subjects without the need of armies or policemen. Fichte laid it down that education would aim at destroying free will, so that, after pupils have left school, they shall be incapable throughout the rest of their lives of thinking or acting otherwise than as their schoolmasters would have wished."

He summed up his nightmare dream with, " . . . diet, injections and injunctions will combine from a very early age to produce the sort of character and the sort of beliefs that the authorities consider desirable, and any serious criticism of the powers that be will become psychologically impossible. Even if all are miserable, all will believe themselves to be happy, because the government will tell them that it is so."

In the State of Oregon, Mrs. Mary Kangas ran right into the spider's web of the mind manipulators.

76

A prominent resident of Portland, she was appointed by the State Board of Education to serve on a special committee set up to investigate family life, sex education and sensitivity training in the Oregon schools.

There were 12 people on the committee, and almost immediately they found themselves in a quandary.

At the very first meeting a chairman was appointed by a higher power, without any of the committee members having anything to say about it. Shortly thereafter, a vice chairman was similarly appointed.

Then the hanky-panky began.

Committee members were told they could not investigate sensitivity training and family life, since that was not a part of sex education and therefore did not come under the order issued to them by the state board.

Mrs. Kangas managed to reach a State Senator who was sympathetic to her views and he reversed the order.

Then the committee members were told they were not to set foot on any school campuses, since that would disturb the classes and upset the students. Any materials they needed would be picked up by the board and passed on to the committee.

Again Mrs. Kangas complained and again the manipulators at the state level backed away. The members were then told that there was to be no further publicity about the meetings of the committee and the members were not to ever speak in the name of the committee.

Mrs. Kangas simply ignored that request and went right ahead talking all over the state.

The head of curriculum for the Portland schools then informed the committee that the Portland sex program was entirely local in nature, that the guidelines were drawn up by local teachers and consultants independent of any outside forces.

Mrs. Kangas got out a copy of the 3M Company SHES concept number six and read it aloud.

77

It exactly matched, word for word, large portions of the Portland curriculum.

The school official still denied any outside counseling.

But the most incredible statement came from the head of the Ellis C. Brown Trust, located at the University of Oregon. Brown, now deceased, was a Portland bachelor physician who did his thing about sex. He devoted his life and his fortune to setting up one of the nation's first sexology factories.

In any case, in reply to a question, the head of the Brown Trust informed the gaping committee members, "I hate to step on any toes, but you (parents) have no rights at all."

Shades of Chisholm and Russell!

The two gentlemen have found themselves in complete agreement.

Remember, dear reader, this man, who is high up in the councils of the sex educators, tells you that, "YOU HAVE NO RIGHTS" when it comes to rearing your own children.

All that brings to mind the words of John G. Schmitz, a Congressman from Orange County. In reply to a question from your author, Schmitz stated he saw no hope of saving this country from the conspirators.

When asked why he was working so hard, Schmitz grinned and said, "Because I am not going to be judged by whether or not I won, but how hard I worked."

Townsend agrees with that.

"We kept our eye on the ball in Anaheim," he said, "and we know we haven't solved most of our problems. But we made a big dent. We brought a few people down to earth. Oh, we have people boring from within, all right, but we isolate them and plow right ahead. We will continue to operate that way."

Eleanor Howe agrees with Townsend.

"I know that if the schools can get away with this, the time will come when they will take the children at two or one or from the cradle. And they would finally end up rearing the kids in public nurseries. I was determined to do what I

78

could to reverse that drastic trend."

She turned from her busy telephone that rings night and day with calls from harried parents all over the nation.

"If that seems far-fetched," she said, the light glinting off her glasses and bouncing a yellow splash against the wall," remember that the Hawaii Master Plan for Education states the time has now come when the state must REAR the children."

And so it does!

On November 10 and 11, 1969, some 500 young people met at the Anaheim Convention Center. There were the so-called leading students from Southland high schools, meeting in Governor Reagan's Blue Ribbon Youth Conference.

With most of them staying at Anaheim motels, the beer flowed freely at parties where teachers and adult supervisors conveniently turned their heads while games went on in the motel rooms.

It was a swinging convention!

On the 11th, the young people passed a series of resolutions nearly unanimously.

First, they said, all laws governing sex activity must be abolished, since "old moral taboos" no longer exist in light of "new birth control information."

A sweet looking little girl, who could barely see over the top of the podium, piped in an adolescent falsetto, "Puritanism and the ethic of Calvinism must be abolished."

One adult onlooker said, "What she needs is a good crack across the mouth."

The sweet little thing called for sex laws that would be "relevant" for the young, and asked for the legalization of marijuana and the doing away with all abortion laws.

You would have sworn that you were listening to the toughest whore in town.

The young "leaders" called for other changes. Divorce,

they said, should be a matter between two people and should not be a matter for the courts to decide.

When your author asked one sweet thing who was talking about sex why she felt sex education was so necessary, since it sounded like sex was what they practiced night and day, I was advised that sex instruction was needed so that young people with Puritanical hangups could enjoy it more.

Further, she piped in her squeaky voice, "Many young people don't know how to guard against VD and against getting pregnant, so they need help from the schools in that area."

I had the distinctly creepy feeling that I was about to be propositioned by a 14-year old child.

On the way out of the building, it occurred to me that I had failed to ask her if she were, herself, a virgin.

Still, the question seemed rather out of place.

The building, by the way, was literally crawling with "relevant and responsible" teacher types, as they like to call themselves.

That new morality line laid down by the Convention Center kids was no morality at all. It was pure and simple hedonism. It was, in the words of one bystander, "the morality of a Billy goat."

Other demands made by the "relevant and responsible" students was that all California table grapes be instantly removed from their lunch tables or they wouldn't eat.

The Convention Center staff promptly acceded to their wishes, after a few noisy grumbles.

But those young people were more to be pitied than censored. They had been seduced, cuckolded by their own teachers, advisors and, in some cases, their own parents.

It becomes increasingly clear that no nation can survive this kind of psycho-sexual rape of its young.

Nor can it survive the young who are the product of that seduction.

****

Meanwhile, all hell was breaking loose in nearby Orange, California.

Villa Park High School, with a beautiful campus set amidst palm trees, is in one of the plushiest areas of plush Orange County. These are the lucky ones, the children who have everything.

Or do they?

The student body president refused to salute the flag on grounds that he owes no allegiance to his country. He also wanted to change the student government into a Presidium style administration. Funk and Wagnall's dictionery only gives one definition for that word. It is the "system of government found in Soviet Russia."

The school principal, Maurice Ross, caved in and surrendered to the student body president.

"Our students are responsible," he said, "and they will solve their own problems without interference (from parents)."

Well, why are you surprised? Remember, as parents you HAVE NO RIGHTS.

But all the brats have rights — *right?*

And so they did.

The students overwhelmingly voted to retain their non-loyal student body president, and a majority of the school faculty jumped to his defense. Most of the teachers were all for him. Relevant, you know, and RESPONSIBLE.

The same thing was happening in the nearby Garden Grove High School District. Again, the student body president would not salute the flag.

The superintendent, David Paynter, gave a speech about that time before the state board of education, defending the students and teachers of his district as "relevant and responsible" people.

Oh?

Not long before that the district held a mass meeting for teachers at which they were told by a behaviorist that they should all become change agents. How? Through Sensitivity

Training, of course.

A Garden Grove school would do nothing about its own Hippie looking, non flag saluting student body president, until, on January 26 something unpredictable occurred.

He was attending a luncheon for student body presidents of Orange County in the company of David Paynter, his school superintendent.

And — he was arrested by police for reportedly having a bag full of marijuana at school that very day — in his locker.

Poetic justice?

A lack of funds may kill the so-called public schools.

Lack of public confidence may kill them.

Internal dissension and subversion may kill them.

Meanwhile, they are killing the souls of millions of America's young people.

Cancer of the kidney cannot be cured by cutting off a toe nail.

The carcinoma now festering in the schools can't be cured by firing a few worthless or dangerous teachers and getting rid of a few students, even by arrests for dope possession.

Unfortunately, many adults are in the corner with the young radicals, egging them on at every chance and financing their activities. Without that support, the revolution would die.

Without the weakness and whining subservience of weak spined administrators, the revolution would die.

Without the tutoring of radical teachers, the revolution would die.

Without the support of tax free foundations, the revolution would die.

Without the support of lame brained clergymen, the revolution would die.

Without the support of spineless parents, the revolution would die.

Without the fawning and masochistic blandishments of jellyfish politicians, the revolution would die.

Without the deliberate plotting and conniving of conspiratorial agents and forces, the revolution would die.

But it will not die, because these forces are allied together into a vicious and no holds barred attack on America's children.

The schools are the battleground. The children are the prize.

And, in the words of the head of the Ellis Brown Trust, "We are all interlocked."

So they are.

It is time to unlock them!

The real battle is taking place in the behavioral science labs, where men look upon your children as guinea pigs for macabre experimentation. It takes place in classrooms, where children are taught faithfully to reject all the values of their parents, and it takes place in classes where children are taught that this nation's enemies are really our friends.

It takes place in churches, where children are told there is no such thing as right or wrong, that all is relative and there is no sin or salvation except through "social" service, and it takes place in sex instruction classes, where the young are psychologically raped by their own teachers.

It takes place in Sensitivity Training sessions, where repeated attacks upon the child result in total conforming to the group consensus, and it takes place in classrooms, where strangers called teachers are betraying daily the trust put in them by parents.

These strangers are creating the International Child of tomorrow, soulless beings with neither love nor hope nor joy.

VI

PARALLAX

Dr. and Mrs. Howard Scott (Margaret) of Belmont were dragged off to jail on December 30, 1969, mugged, finger-printed and treated like criminals — because they dared to stand up against the professional sexologists in the San Mateo County school system.

The Scotts, parents of 13 children, kept their children home, rather than to allow them to attend classes they felt were demoralizing and degrading.

Roman Catholics, the Scotts had previously enrolled their children in St. Matthews Parochial School, San Mateo, since their own parish school did not have room.

For this, they paid double the normal parochial school tuition.

When she militantly objected to her children being taught specific sex facts in their classes at St. Matthews, ALL the children were flunked. Thereafter, rather than enroll them in the tax supported schools, the Scotts simply kept the children home and taught them with the aid of friends.

The Scotts were jailed under a section of the California Education Code, number 12101, while several of their older children were serving their country on farflung military bases.

One was fighting on the front lines in Vietnam.

Vicious and demeaning forces within the school structure exerted exceptional pressure at the time of the arrest of the Scotts. Not only were they jailed and treated with brutal contempt and cynicism by the authorities, but they were not

84

allowed release under their own recognizance, which is done in practically every misdemeanor case and even in the case of felonies.

Within hours of their arrest, friends of the Scotts all over the nation had been alerted and funds began to arrive in Belmont to aid them in their plight. They were, after seven hours, restored to their family – but, as this is written, they await trial as common criminals for defying the all-powerful state.

But they are not the first.

The Scotts join the long list of martyrs who have dared to stand up against the mailed fist of the all-powerful educational force in the country.

If the reader thinks this is an exaggeration, we dare him to publicly stand and criticize his local public school system.

You can curse God and the church, and nothing will happen.

You can defile the flag, and few will complain.

You can defy the constitution, and practically none will object.

You can call the local police pigs and the armed forces murderers, and nothing will happen.

But when you raise your voice against the public schools, in any way whatsoever, you will find yourself tangling with a tiger. All the forces of the community will be brought to bear against you. Liberal preachers will rant at you from their pulpits. Businessmen, who make profits from selling supplies to schools, will give you the cold shoulder. The League of Women Voters and the PTA will castigate you in public. Even your local newspaper, generally a kept mistress of the school establishment, will rail against you in editorials.

Mrs. Emily Phillips found that out in 1963.

The beautiful mother of four children, Mrs. Phillips warned against the sex classes then creeping into the schools in the San Fernando Valley in Southern California. She made speeches about it, whenever she was invited to do so, and in particular, attacked the Socialist slant of the PTA.

That did it.

85

Herself a former PTA president, Mrs. Phillips knew what she was talking about. Her activities finally led to a phoney arrest, public disgrace and the breakup of her marriage.

Mrs. Phillips arrived at school one day to pick up her children. There, in the bright gold of the California sunshine, she saw a little boy, aged five, running from the school, crying as if his heart would break.

Taking the frightened little boy by the hand, Mrs. Phillips told him she would stay with him until his mother arrived.

However, the principal, who had a personal vendetta against her, I am told, ordered her to leave the school grounds. She refused, stating she had come to pick up her children and she would stay until the hysterical little boy's mother arrived, because she had promised him that she would do so.

Sometime later the mother arrived and Mrs. Phillips turned the boy over to her.

The principal signed a complaint against her — alleging she was disturbing the peace and loitering in a public place, the school.

At her subsequent trial, all charges were dropped when it was revealed that strange things had been transpiring in that particular school, including the use of obsenities in Spanish textbooks.

But they did not silence Mrs. Phillips, not then. She called a press conference and stated that if she had just been another parent, nothing would have happened to her. However, because she had once been an official in the PTA, and because she had dared to publicly challenge the immorality in the tax supported school system, she was arrested, charged with a ridiculous crime and had to post $100 bail.

Mrs. Phillips disappeared from the Southern California scene — and none of her former friends or enemies seem to know where she is today. The courageous lady was simply five years or so ahead of her time.

One of the early pioneers in the family life and sex education fraud was one Dr. Henry Meyer, who, in 1962, made a

86

small documentary film about the Danish Mother's Help program at the suggestion of a Danish colleague. He subsequently showed it to his colleagues in America and was in business.

Meyer is much more than a name.

The 12th report of the Senate Fact Finding Committee on UnAmerican Activities, Sacramento, puts the spotlight on him.

With his wife, Olive, he is listed as one of the leaders of the Palo Alto, California Fair Play for Cuba Committee and the Student's Ad Hoc Committee Against U.S. Intervention in Cuba. Both were branded Red fronts by the committee.

Henry Meyer's name pops up repeatedly in investigations of the people and organizations behind the sex education drive.

Then we get back to Dr. Mary Calderone, traveling ambassadress for sexuality, who is the director for SIECUS.

Revered by educators and fawned upon by teachers and school administrators throughout the nation, she is also the wife of a man who puts on girlie shows in his three theatres on Long Island.

Dr. Calderone, who has never practiced medicine a single day since getting her degree, is a graduate of the Women's Medical College of Philadelphia. Recently she received a distinguished service award from the Mental Health Association of Nassau County, New York, and she received the fourth annual award for distinguished service to humanity of the women's auxiliary of the Albert Einstein Medical Center, Philadelphia.

Usually dressed in funereal black, with just a touch of old lace at the throat, Dr. Calderone is the daughter of the famous Left tilting portrait photographer Edward Steichen. She is the niece of the late CARL SANDBURG, also identified with Leftist causes all his life.

Dr. Calderone spends a great deal of her time traveling, talking to groups of gaping, applauding teachers in a throaty semi-baritone voice, spicing up her conversation with an occasional four letter expletive for sexual intercourse.

87

For instance, on February 1, 1968, she showed up in Orange County, California for three meetings at St. Joseph's Hospital, at Garden Grove High School and at the Orange County Medical Association in Orange. The sponsor for the series of meetings was an ad hoc group calling itself the Orange County Council for Strengthening Family Life — a collection of weird characters if there ever was one.

Sally Williams, then the coordinator for the Anaheim sex program and Mrs. Bernard Paul, social gadfly who shows up at far out meetings with monotonous repetition, were on the committee that welcomed Mary to Orange County.

The startling ramifications of the SIECUS involvement can be seen in the list of sponsoring agencies for Dr. Calderone's Orange County appearances.

Taking part in the big show were the Academy of Religion and Mental Health; the Fourth District PTA; the Orange County Association for Mental Health; the Orange County Health Department; the Orange County Medical Association; the Orange County Psychological Association; the National Association of Social Workers of Orange County; Parent Effectiveness Training Organization of Santa Ana and the Psychological Guidance Center of Anaheim.

McCall's Magazine summed up the current all-out sex drive in an article entitled "Who Killed the Stork?"

"Sex, in case there's somebody who still hasn't noticed," they said, "has become such big business — like the arcane worlds of literature, art and politics — its own mystique and establishment have grown up — these sexual shock troops of the sixties are giving us all they've got — whatever that is — on all fronts."

And speaking of interlocking association, isn't it interesting that Vivian Cadden, an associate editor of McCall's Magazine, also just happens to be a SIECUS board member.

Further, Shana Alexander, who did the McCall's piece, just happens to be a member of the National Committee for Responsible Family Life and Sex Education, a SIECUS front

88

group that sports the strangest crowd of far out Leftists, pinkoes, radicals and free love advocates extant.

Still, the sexologists made some mistakes.

One of their worst mistakes was a film called "Time of Your Life," which was purchased for showing over New York TV by National Educational TV. When the film was shown in San Mateo, all hell broke loose.

The title of the film was a mistake, for one thing, because sex education opponents pointed out that it smacked of crass commercialism and frivolity in an area that sexologists constantly prate should be one of serious study.

Suffice to say, the sexologists found themselves on top of a hurricane when some of the parents in Northern California saw the film.

Disclaimers are voiced right and left, but the fact remains that most of the American sex programs are patterned after disastrous programs now in use in Sweden, the original home of the "skin flick."

The Swedish program for 14 through 17 year old children involves: contraception techniques; best contraceptive methods for teenagers; detailed description of orgasm; various methods of masturbation; discussion of venereal disease and techniques for abortion. In addition, intercourse between teenagers is encouraged, if both want it and if both partners agree to use contraception.

The results are seen in the following statistics.

A 1964 study showed that 83 per cent of all Swedish military draftees, mostly under 20, had engaged in sexual intercourse. The median age for relations was 16. In 1965, among college students, 87 per cent of the students had engaged in intercourse and the median age was listed as 17. The San Francisco Chronicle of May 17, 1968 reported that a new survey showed that 90 per cent of all Swedes reported sexual intercourse before the age of 20, and one in every three girls engaged in it before the age of 16.

Swedes attach no moral stigma to any kind of sex act, in

89

or out of marraige, and there is little sex crime for the simple reason that practically no sex acts are crimes any longer.

A plea to change all that was recently voiced by 200,000 Swedish mothers, but their words fell on deaf ears. Nobody can remove their children from the sex classes and nobody can stop the government's insane policies.

The moral implications of Sweden's sex classes were made clear by the Swedish State Board of Education when it said, "Those who want to postpone relations until marriage are free to do so and those who start earlier will, it is hoped, act more responsibly."

Now the tentacles of the sexologist octopus reach into every home and school in this nation, as can be seen from the following exchange between Shirley Bopf of Santa Ana, California and the Reader's Digest.

An article entitled "Sex Education" in their June, 1968 issue came under fire from Mrs. Bopf and she sent them a letter of protest.

A reply came back to Shirley from "The Editors," in which they praised SIECUS board member Dr. Lester Kirkendall as a "widely respected and recognized educator."

No one will argue that he is widely recognized.

The letter then stated the following:

"Sexology (magazine) has been published for a number of years primarily for newsstand circulation. Its authoritative articles provide access to accurate information for adult men and women who otherwise have no such access to knowledge they need.

"The titles are couched in language that will attract many people, while repelling others. Those who are attracted by the titles will then learn important facts from the articles, facts that may actually improve their personal lives in a more responsible and satisfying direction, very often in marriage."

Of course, the Digest did not say they were quoting Dr. Calderone. Rather, it was worded as if the language originated with the editors of that once prestigious little magazine.

90

However, in a letter to the Morro Bay [California] SUN, in answer to criticism of SIECUS, Dr. Mary Colderone uses exactly the same words that appeared in the letter from the Digest editors.

Sexology, of course, was published by ex-SIECUS board member and identified Communist, the late Isadore Rubin.

All this fantasically powerful interlock has alarmed many parents, and understandably so. They have been threatened, harassed and even driven into jail by the sexologists.

Is it any wonder that the following letter recently came to the Citizen's Committee in Anaheim from a panic stricken parent in a midwestern city.

"Don't write us about anything — don't send anything. They are trying to find out who the ones are who are against sex education here — and probably jail us, I suppose.

"We have no legal funds — so don't send any mail to me until I notify you. You know who I am — I'll not sign my name — disregard the name and address on the front."

Paranoid? Hardly!

The memory of Margaret Scott and Emily Phillips comes back to haunt us, and we know that the forces behind the family life program will stop at nothing.

In Spain, just before the Reds plunged that nation into one of the bloodiest civil wars in history, the nation was flooded with filth and pornography of every kind. Stands appeared on every street corner, selling pornography and giving it away to the young. The whole family structure was assailed and crumpled under the onslaught.

In concert, the high school and college students were whipped to a frenzy of rebellion and anarchy.

The whole world knows the result.

All that could not be happening in the United States if the American people had not been prepared over the years to accept it. In order to enslave this nation, one generation must first be demoralized.

In the words of Marxist college professor Herbert Marcuse, "The Marxian idea of Socialism is not radical enough . . . *we must develop the moral-sexual rebellion of the youth.*"

That is what is happening today, in your town, on your block, in your school, even in your home.

Weird gods and strange rites of occultism have permeated deep into the very bloodstream of American life. Witness the fact that the Florida Bar Journal for December, 1968 featured photographs of symbols of eight different religions – and made them all EXACTLY EQUAL. Significantly, the cross was pictured *last* in the lineup.

In Anaheim, a handful of astonishingly brave people dared to stand against the might and power of the educational establishment.

Joe Mullin, engineer and Anaheim chairman of the Citizen's Committee of California, was one of them.

Week after week he appeared before the board – slender, intense, and somewhat shy in his demeanor – asking questions.

And from his study came an interesting little paper he called Parallax, showing the relationship between the Anaheim family life program and the program of another all powerful establishment.

Widely circulated, and reprinted by many groups throughout the U.S., it even brought a disclaimer from the publisher's representative of William L. Shirer, author of "The Rise and Fall of the Third Reich." Mullin was highly amused at the controversy caused by the two page study he turned over to the Citizen's Committee and then forgot.

PARALLAX
(Read this side by side. We leave it to you to decide the similarity.)

1939 National Socialist (NAZI) Sex Education Experiment

1969 Anaheim High School District (AUHSD) Sex Education Experiment

The National Socialist (NAZI) sex education experiment, under the leadership of Adolph Hitler, was initiated in 1938. The Hitler Youth, the name of the tax supported National Socialist (NAZI) education system, was under the leadership of a minor bureaucrat, Dr. Robert Ley. One of the progressive courses introduced by the deception of gradualism was Strength Through Joy. The course, Strength Through Joy, was to enrich family life with an open minded examination, rationally questioning existing moral values, and to enlighten the sex education of the people in the new social order.

The Sex Information and Education Council of the United States (SIECUS) sex education experiment, under the leadership of a group of doctors, was initiated in 1964. The Anaheim High School System (AUHSD), the name of the local tax supported education system, is under the leadership of District Superintendent Paul Cook. One of the progressive courses being introduced by deception through gradualism in the Family Life Education is to enrich family life with an open minded examination, rationally questioning existing moral values and to enlighten the sex education of the people in the new changing society.

93

District Superintendent Paul Cook, to overcome opposition to the Family Life Education course, has the Sex Instruction Coordinator of SIECUS for the Anaheim High School system, Sally Williams, attack the self evident adult moral authority through the children. The education system promotes abandonment of personal, mature existing moral sex behavior. At the same time glorifying the freedom of thought in the new changing society as expressed in the collective and public discussions of sex and sexual emotions by youth.

The pre-marital sex resulting from this mass exposure to sex information in the new changing society is admitted and justified as the new youth relieved of materialistic values, communicating the knowledge of relative humanism to each other and honestly displaying their FAITH in themselves and the new changing society.

94

The cowardly Dr. Ley (he was to commit suicide by hanging while awaiting trial for war crimes at Nuremberg), to overcome opposition to the Strength Through Joy course, had the hirelings of the education system attack the self evident adult moral authority through the children. The education system promoted abandonment of personal, mature existing moral sex behavior. At the same time glorifying the freedom of thought in the new social order as expressed in the collective and public exhibitions of the naked body staged by youth.

The pre-marital sex resulting from exercise of the new social order morality was praised as the new youth, relieved of materialistic values, communication of the knowledge of relative humanism to each other and honestly displaying their FAITH in themselves and the new social order.

Originally, the devious Dr. Ley excused any child from the Strength Through Joy course upon the request of the parent. The law, however, was changed to make Strength Through Joy a required part of the curriculum in the education system when a minority of the children were deprived, by their adult guardians, of the State provided free opportunity to experience the full social joy of developing sexual behavior.

No adult was to deny the youth a relief from the stress of materialistic morality, a discovery of sexual freedom, a loss of self respect which would result in the youth begging at the altar of the State for grateful recognition of his self degradation that was required to be accepted as one of the FAITHFUL of the new social order.

Presently the District Superintendent, (formerly) Paul Cook excuses any child from the Family Life course on request of the parent. The law, however, may be changed to make it a required part of the curriculum in the education system, when a minority of the children are deprived, by their adult guardians, of the state provided free opportunity to experience the full social joy of developing sexual-emotional behavior.

Perhaps — under leadership of a National Education Association, no adult will deny any child a relief from the stress of materialistic morality, a discovery of sexual freedom, a loss of self respect which would result in the child begging at the altar of the State for grateful recognition of his self degradation that is required to be accepted as one of the FAITHFUL of the new changing society.

95

There is opposition to the Family Life course and Superintendent Paul Cook has admitted that the changes in society require changes in education which require an honest effort to understand; those persons who do not understand, do not honestly try. Individuals expressing opposition are insulted as having "hangups on sex," ridiculed as being against progress and complaining because of taxes.

There is a fringe group of dissidents (in Anaheim and around the nation) who think rationally about changing sexual attitudes. Society is rapidly changing and the basis for all authority has shifted from the mature adults and parents to the State. These resolute persons of the fringe opposition group have refused to abdicate their own adult authority to the powerful State, having refused to abandon

There was opposition to the Strength Through Joy course in the education system, and Dr. Ley's superintendents admitted that the new social order required an honest effort to understand it; those persons who did not understand it did not try honestly. Individuals expressing opposition were insulted as having "hangups on sex," ridiculed as being against progress and capitalistic exploiters complaining because of high taxes.

There was a fringe group of dissidents who did think rationally about changing sexual attitudes. Society was changing and the basis for authority had shifted from mature adults to the State. These resolute persons of the fringe opposition group, refused to abdicate adult authority to the State, refused to abandon their own reasoning to the State, refused to deny their own knowledge of right and wrong. These resolute persons opposing the new social order were therefore placed in camps to receive a concentrated course in education in the new social order. The administration of these camps tested mental and emotional "hang-ups" of these resolute persons opposed to the new social order. The result was 10 million persons executed because they were mentally and emotionally opposed to the society, the changing progress of the new social order.

their own reasoning to the State and have refused to deny their own knowledge of right and wrong. (Perhaps concentration camps wait for them, even as jails have already opened for them in 1968 and 1969 in isolated parts of the nation — concentration camps, followed by oblivion and they will be removed as a threat to the new social order.)

97

Ref: The Rise and Fall of the Third Reich by William L. Shirer. (NOTE: Mullin did not say Parallax came from The Rise and Fall of the Third Reich — he used the book as reference only.)

For the Family Life and Sex Education programs are nothing but an extension of the totalitarian mind that says, "Give me your child. You have no business rearing him, since the state can do it better."

In the words of the head of the Ellis Brown Trust, again the same replay, *"You (as parents) have no rights."*

That statement is coming true at an alarming rate — but here and there, isolated voices are crying out, "This far and no farther — we will not surrender our God given prerogatives."

Such a voice is that of Paul Victor, Twin Falls, Idaho, who nearly single handedly stood off the depredations of the Child Seducers.

Just an ordinary guy — a builder of homes where little chidlren can be reared in beauty and love — Paul Victor is also a fighter, a gut level battler who doesn't know when to give up.

Even when certain so-called conservatives in the town turned against him — he kept on fighting. Even when he was harassed and threatened — he kept on fighting.

And from his little farm in the valley a steady stream of materials flows — to teachers, principals, board members and district patrons. Miles are racked up on his speedometer as he drives the snowy lanes and highways of the state, working night and day to spread the word.

In Orange, California, Ruth Spencer, wife and mother (of six children), once was interested in social activities as well as being a prominent school booster. Suddenly, like a bolt from the blue, she awakened to what was happening in her school district.

The student body president refused to salute the flag and the principal of the school appeared to cave in.

Ruth, the Orange chairman of the Citizen's Committee of

California, Inc. went to work with a vengeance.

Her own beautiful daughter was the school mascot. It made no difference. Together they took a stand.

The daughter was subjected to unbelievable pressure from her school mates and especially from her teachers.

In classes she was reviled and her mother was publicly ridiculed.

Still supported by her loving husband, Dick, a highly successful businessman who treats his wife like a guy still on his first date, they stuck to their guns, determined to expose the cancer that was hidden in the Orange school system.

Standing there, one night, before the school board, with a hostile, jeering crowd of teachers at her back, Ruth spoke with moving and eloquent words about country, patriotism and her nation's flag.

It took guts, especially since they handed her a dead microphone, just to make sure the CCC supporters standing in the hallways could not hear what she said.

She had more courage than anyone knew as she declared above the voice of calumny and evil spite:

"My being here tonight is a direct consequence of the flagrant contempt shown by the Villa Park High School student body president, when he announced in his arrogance of ignorance that he owed no allegiance to his country and would extend none, and refused to lead the student body of that school in the pledge to our nation's flag.

"We who have assembled here view his statements and his position as a carefully contrived and calculated insult to every man who has served or sacrificed for his country, and to every woman and child who loves it; not only for what it was and is, but for what it can be."

There were stirrings and loud murmurs in the room. How dare this woman stand before her school board and defend the flag of her country?

And in the shadows of that room, it was as if a thousand patriots from the past were slowly gathering, murmuring and muttering in the recesses of the halls of that building . . . voices that rang down all the corridors of time, to the corridors of that board of education building.

"We find this student body president and principal unfit for their respective positions in our Orange public school system," she cried, "and we respectfully request that they be removed from those positions so this community can hopefully have a share of its confidence in the system restored. We will not be placated with an apology or a retraction. We have no intention of being tolerant nor compassionate of this incident or of the people involved. Respect for that flag, and what it stands for to loyal Americans everywhere, is absolutely non-negotiable. Ladies and gentlemen, make no mistake about this issue. The people, the industrious, loyal, God fearing, taxpaying people of this community do not understand, do not condone and will not tolerate callous and cynical disrespect for their flag."

Courage? Yes, indeed.

The murmurs from the 410+ teachers and parents of the largely hostile crowd who had jammed into the board room two hours earlier in order to prevent Mrs. Spencer's supporters from gaining entrance, were subdued now.

It was the calm before the storm.

Teachers and their liberal followers went on the offensive shortly thereafter. Threats were made against Mrs. Spencer's family. Two women came to the door — and threatened her life, disappearing as rapidly as they had come.

All the evil, demeaning forces were loosed against her. She stood her ground and waited.

Two weeks after that explosive speech before the school board, Mrs. Spencer and her committee put on a rally at one of the school auditoriums in Orange.

By seven o'clock the hall was jammed — with over 350 people standing out on the sidewalk and walking away in frustration because they couldn't get in.

Again, the enemy was there in force — trying to disrupt the

meeting – shouting threats from the floor – accusing Mrs. Spencer of demagoguery.

She was not importuned by their angry outcries.

One month later she was to see her courageous position vindicated. The school board voted to require all student body officers to sign an oath to uphold the constitutions of California and the United States and to pledge allegiance to the flag. Later, Ross resigned his post.

Just one woman – who cared enough to fight, and her husband, with enough courage to back her to hell and back.

There was another woman – far to the east – in the state of Massachusetts.

In August, 1969, your author was in Massachusetts to cover the Edward Kennedy story.

One night, near the city of Springfield, on a porch overlooking a magnificent lake, I talked to Eva Orsini.

Lightning flashed across the sky, cutting jagged streaks across the black water, clouds scudding overhead while thunder rolled and crashed against the woods across the way.

It was a setting from a Hollywood film.

But another storm was brewing in Massachusetts, one that would soon break over the schoolhouses of that wooded state, a storm that centered around sex education in the schools but that would soon widen into a larger fury.

Mrs. Orsini felt she was nearly alone, battling against insuperable odds. She knew the problems for she had done her homework well.

Unfortunately, she could not persuade anyone else.

Only one lone minister in Springfield understood what she was trying to say, and his support was, of necessity, slight.

Six months later, all that changed.

A letter reached my desk at the Anaheim Bulletin dated

101

January 26, 1970.

"Massachusetts is, through the Willis Harrison act," she wrote, "going to try and make sex instruction mandatory in all our schools. I called all the ones here I knew were opposing it and we found a Representative Langone from the Boston area. He has a bill up that would ban the compulsory requirement.

"Then I got a few names from the Boston area, called my Worcester contact and we plan to form a statewide organization. Mothers from Burlington begged me to come over, and I was there for two whole days.

"I was heartened to see that at least 30 cities are now opposing sex instruction, in the eastern part of the state.

"We are having a meeting with members of the clergy and a public rally on February 2 here in Springfield.

"The four clergymen I have been working with here asked me to find a speaker, and through my contacts in the Boston area I found a doctor William Lynch, a well known gynecologist who has joined our fight.

"I heard him speak in Burlington and he is very good.

"As a result, my telephone bill is terrible.

"Springfield is about to explode, I have four speaking engagements and the mothers in Lexington, Burlington and Concord are asking me to officiate at the state meeting. I'm actually getting dizzy.

"My phone rings all the time and I have helped eight cities in the immediate area. I also have to supervise printing of materials.

"While I was in one town, I received a terrible shock. The parents kicked out the superintendent of schools and the one who replaced him gave this one mother a large number of school textbooks with the most pertinent pages marked off.

"In the English book — hatred, murder and violence; in Social Studies — revolution and hatred of country. One story tells how the children destroyed the eagle symbol of America and a cartoon encourages rioting. The children's second grade reading assignment – Charlie in the Chocolate Factory – refers to the boy's mother as a 'silly ass' and a 'fish face.' In all the surrounding cities the parents are upset over the books. The children are not allowed to bring their books home from school and a third grade social studies book tells them not to tell their parents a thing.

"Believe me, tell your editor to send you out here and he'll have a story that will blow the lid off education.

"We are going to print excerpts and mail them to every organization opposing sex instruction. Most of these books are published by Laidlaw Co.*

"Oh yes, one magazine assignment for English has dope addicts featured all over it. Believe me, this is as bad, or worse, than sex instruction, and I am SCARED."

Eva had reason to be frightened.

She remembers the night when she first learned what was happening in her state – when all the pieces fell together and overwhelmed her.

It was raining. Chain lightning flashed across the New England skies as she opened the car door, slid under the wheel and started the motor.

The car purred, but she did not notice the comforting sound. Backing out of the garage, the wheels slithered across mud that had poured down over the driveway, then gripped as the tires caught the asphalt of the street.

She kicked the headlights into high beam – a slash of brilliance cutting through the rain splattered night – and started down the winding road toward town.

Over and over, like a churning wheel, went the same old refrain, the nightmare that had been steadily growing for the past several weeks as more and more information and evidence came to her, plaguing her waking hours and coming to spectral reality in fitful dreams.

_____

*Mrs. John Laidlaw was a sponsor of the second annual SIECUS dinner; Winn Laidlaw is on the SIECUS board.

Something dark and horrible was settling over the classrooms of America — far-reaching in its implications. In fact, she still found it almost impossible to believe.

Lights of passing cars intermittently flashed against her rain-smeared windshield — yellow beacons in the night, going somewhere too, she thought.

She too was going somewhere — to the one place where she thought she would find help.

Neon lights of the town were ahead of her, now — and then they were beside her car, splashing red and yellow, and the glowing windows of light where families were sitting around dinner tables.

She glanced at her watch. It was seven o'clock and she wasn't hungry — not for food. She was hungry for some answers.

At last she reached the small Catholic church, a flash of light illuminating the cross on its steeple as it loomed up out of the mist.

It was then she remembered that she had forgotten her raincoat and umbrella.

Still, it mattered not that she was wet and cold. The church would be warm.

Eva reached out blindly for the knob, grasped it and tugged as the door opened with the faint creaking of unoiled hinges, the threads of water beading down the door jam and trickling away in tiny rivulets.

Seconds later she was inside, candles winking red in the distant gloom, the rich perfume of incense folded around her — she fell to her knees, oblivious of the drops of water forming a ring around her feet.

"Oh God our refuge and our strength," she gasped, "look down upon thy people who cry to Thee . . . "

Unconsciously, without knowing what she was saying, she found herself murmuring the ageless prayer to the Archangel, St. Michael.

"Oh God," she said . . . and she was praying out loud . . .

104

but there was no one else in the sanctuary. She didn't know she was praying out loud. She only knew that an answer would come to her in this place.

"Holy Michael the Archangel," she said, "defend us in battle. Be our protection against the wickedness and snares of the devil. May God rebuke him, we humbly pray – and do thou, Prince of the heavenly host, through the power of God, cast into hell Satan and all the evil spirits who wander through the world seeking the ruin of souls ."

That was all. It was the end of the prayer. Now she was silent, shaken, her head bowed, tears on her face – or was it the rain?

"Oh God," she said, and it seemed to her she was talking to a friend who was very near, "preserve the souls of the little children."

Slowly, with effort, she pushed herself to her feet. No answer had come to her – no voices out of dim corners – no flash of metaphysical insight. Nothing. She had never felt so cold and alone.

She didn't know how she got there, but suddenly she was standing in front of the rectory, her hand on the doorbell.

With a rush of warm air swirling out into the dampness, the door was opened, and a lined face peered into the darkness.

"Yes?" The housekeeper looked suspiciously at the dripping woman standing before her.

The housekeeper's mouth drew down and she frowned. "Not now lady. He's having his dinner. Surely, not now. No, it's quite impossible. He can't see you now."

The door closed with a bang.

Maybe it was just as well, she thought, because what she had to say might spoil his appetite.

She was alone again, the wind whistling around her as she walked to the car, drops of rain beating a steady tattoo on top of her head.

She slammed the door shut and sat there, soaked, shivering

and chattering, letting the motor idle while she soaked up the warmth from the heater.

What now, St. Michael?

Later she was to say that she didn't really remember making up her mind, but suddenly she found herself driving up a steep hill in a neighboring town, the ancient facade of the Catholic rectory looming up out of the darkness on the crest of a hill.

Again there was another long, rain-soaked walk to a door, and again her finger was on the doorbell. She heard the distant clang of the bell, and the sound of heavy footsteps approaching.

"Yes, my child?" A priest stood there against the warm glow of yellow light, grey eyes looking intently at her, his silver hair framed by the light from a bulb burning behind him.

"Father," she said, "I must talk to you."

There was a slight hesitation as he looked at her soaked and unprepossessing appearance. But it was only for an instant, and then he smiled.

"Come in," he said, calling his housekeeper at the same time. "Come in, my daughter."

And then, to his housekeeper, "Take her to my study — and bring us a nice pot of hot tea — yes, a pot of tea."

Gratefully, she stood dripping near a blazing fireplace and waited.

The priest entered, standing there for a second, looking at her.

It was then that she saw it, over his right shoulder, a painting on the wall.

"Suffer the little children to come unto me," she thought in a flash, "for of such is the kingdom of heaven."

It was an oil painting of Christ — and around him, with one sitting on his lap, were three children, dressed in modern garb.

For the first time Eva smiled and relaxed.

"Suffer the little children," she repeated, as she nodded toward the painting.

"What?"

106

He turned and glanced at it.

"Ah yes, lovely, isn't it? Perhaps it should be, "Woe unto those who would harm one of these, my little ones . . . "

Her head snapped back and she riveted her eyes on his face.

"Father, why did you say that just now?"

He shrugged, dropping his long frame into a chair that seemed much too small.

"It seemed appropriate — although I'll admit, I hadn't thought of that passage in years."

"It's far more appropriate than you know," she said, beginning her story.

One woman, Eva Orsini, dared to stand alone — for awhile — until her faith and courage gathered others around her.

Winston Churchill, at the height of England's World War II cheered his fellow Britons with these hopeful words:

"See while the tired waves vainly breaking,
Seem here no painful inch to gain.
Far back through creeks and inlets making,
Comes flooding in the main."

And all over America, little drops of water are falling into rivulets and inlets — forming the mighty cataract, the mighty rushing flood that will sweep away all the impurity and the dross and cleanse this land once more.

VII

BATS IN THE BELFRY

The phone rang on my desk at the Anaheim Bulletin. It seemed to be nothing unusual — just another of the interminable long distance phone calls I had been receiving from all over the United States since the family life and sex instruction mess had become front page copy.

It was a young lady named Clarice Sass, a lovely little dynamo who had been leading the assault against the sexologists in Grosse Point, a suburb of Detroit.

She was interested in a particular man — a Reverend Harry Meserve who had come to Detroit some time before and had taken over the Grosse Pointe Unitarian Church.

His church had become a center for youthful revolutionary types, and Mrs. Sass wanted to know something more about him so she could spread the word.

After promising her I would try to find out something, I made a few phone calls to some high places in Sacramento and received some astounding information.

It begins in San Francisco, where Louise Meserve, his first wife became president of the Madison School PTA on March 16, 1953. She prospered in her job because on October 10, 1954 she was appointed to the chairmanship of the parent education committee of the San Francisco Second District PTA, quite a boost up the ladder of that strange organization.

The San Francisco Chronicle of April 25, 1957 reports, "Dr. Harry Meserve has resigned as minister of the First Unitarian Church of San Francisco, and has married the former Margaret Swann Reydel of New York."

The article continued, "He resigned his pastorate last winter (December) and was divorced in Reno early this year. His second marriage took place in Nevada. His former wife, Louise, and their three children, Emily, Harry and Peter live in San Francisco.

"Mrs. Louise Meserve confirmed news of the marriage last night. She plans to remain in San Francisco with her children."

That neatly worded item was preceded by a not-so-nice article in Herb Caen's column of January 24, 1957, "Talk of the know-it-all-set — the prominent man of the cloth who renounced his pulpit, left his wife and children and moved east to join his lady friend; the flock he left behind is still aghast and agog."

They should not have been surprised or aghast!

Meserve's Left Wing radical views on everything were known to me as far back as 1951 when I was living in San Francisco. At that time, Harry Meserve was the pastor of the San Francisco Church and involved in every extremist Left movement extant.

Ex-wife Louise continued, after the divorce, to attend the San Francisco church because there was a society item in the church bulletin on November 29, 1957 to the effect that the Unitarian youth met at the home of Louise Meserve on November 10.

But now I really began to discover Meserve on the pages of the old Dies Committee Appendix IX reports on page 1252. At that time he was the pastor of the Unitarian Church in Buffalo, New York and signed the statement of the National Federation for Constitutional Liberties in opposition to that same Dies Committee.

Nothing like accusing your own accuser.

On February 28, 1950, Harry Meserve became pastor of the church in San Francisco, located at the corner of Geary and Franklin Streets.

Readers should remember that although basically deistic in philosophy in the early days, the Unitarian Church is now nothing more nor less than a front for the atheistic beliefs of Humanism, the same philosophy now embraced by our public school system.

October, 1950 rolled around, and Harry Meserve was elected to the executive committee of the American Civil Liberties

109

Union (ACLU) an outfit founded by Socialists and Communists, mostly. On April 17, 1951 he was publicly deploring the fact that the regents of the University of California were "falling for the ideology of anti-Communism."

Heavens!

On March 16, 1951 he led a panel discussion at the San Francisco Forum on the subject of parents, youth and war. The meeting, as could be expected, was sponsored by the Humanist organization known as the American Friends Service Committee (AFSC).

On January 26, 1952, Meserve sponsored an appeal for the abolition of the Levering Act, a law covering the registration of Communists.

It just wouldn't be fair to have the poor Communists registering as agents of a foreign power, you know.

On April 4, 1952 he spoke over KNBC on the theme, "Communism: A Clinical Analysis."

To which I can only add that he was not very hard on the Comrades.

That same month he drove to Oakland to attend a meeting at the home of UC professor Harold Winkler, a meeting under the auspices of the Repeal of the Levering Act crowd.

April was a busy month for the gad-about Mr. Meserve, for on the 30th he signed a statement urging, nay, *imploring*, the Supreme Court to rehear the case of the top Reds in the nation who were locked up in durance vile in the federal pokey. He also called on Congress to repeal the Smith Act for good measure. That was the law that had helped to lock up the Comrades.

On May 21, 1952 Meserve spoke to a small crowd at Grattan Grammar School in San Francisco on the subject, "The World United for Peace and Progress."

And, on June 12th he sent a letter as a member of a Leftist outfit called the San Francisco Council for Civic Unity.

The 30th of that month saw Meserve as the featured speaker at the Japanese-American Citizens League 12th biennial convention.

On September 8 he was the speaker at a meeting of a Leftist pacifist group called the Fellowship of Reconciliation.

Harry penned an article for the Churchman magazine which appeared on August 1, 1953 entitled "Investigating the Investigators," and squawked loudly on January 1, 1954 when he spoke to the Friend's Committee on Legislation at his church on the theme, "Is the Fifth Amendment a Proper Refuge for an Honest Man?"

His answer to that question was YES.

On February 1, 1954 Meserve signed an appeal on behalf of Wesley Robert Wills that appeared in the Communist People's World newspaper.

Meserve, despite all this flitting around, was getting itchy feet.

He announced on March 20, 1954 that he would resign his San Francisco pastorate on September 30 to assume the post as minister of King's Chapel, Boston. At that time he was described as a member of the ALCU, the Mental Health Society, Council for Civic Unity and was described as a graduate of Haverford College and Harvard Divinity School.

Maybe the fact that King's Chapel is sitting in the midst of a graveyard that is filled with the mouldering bones of American patriots of 1776 or so helped to change his mind. Their ghosts might have haunted the pulpit of King's Chapel.

In any case, Meserve announced on June 1, 1954 that he had changed his mind and had decided not to become the minister of the nation's oldest Unitarian Church.

Meserve was re-elected to the executive committee of the ACLU in February, 1955.

On October 4, 1956, it was reported that he was slated to become the chairman of the Northern California ACLU,* and

---

*SIECOP has established a definite link between SIECUS, the ACLU and the President's Commission on Pornography that wants more freedom for pornography.

111

on December 24, 1956 he said he was going to resign his pastorate in San Francisco to take a position – and a new wife, no doubt – in the east.

He would not publicly comment on his reasons for leaving.

On January 3, 1957 Meserve said he was joining the Rockefeller Foundation on April 1 in order to work in the field of "humanities and social science."

He did journey east, and on April 25 his new marriage was announced and it was simultaneously announced that he was employed by the "Rockefeller Brothers Fund."

Meserve rose rapidly – as could be expected – in the ranks of the Rockefeller Foundation and on January 9, 1959 he left the executive staff and was named director of the Fund's Academy of Religion and Mental Health. He was also the minister of the Unitarian Fellowship Northern Westchester, New York, and was a member of the national board of the ACLU and vice president of the Unitarian Service Committee.

Meserve surfaced in the Communist People's World newspaper a total of 23 times between April 24, 1952 and May 8, 1956.

And most interesting of all, he was listed as the president of the board of the occultist Temple of Understanding.*

He now pastors the beautiful grey stone church in Grosse Pointe, where it is reported that young people flock from all over Detroit to hear his words of wisdom.

His is a typical story in the tight little world of the secularists.

Once again my phone rang – in the middle of the night. I awoke, groping in the dark for the receiver, knocking the

---

*See my book, "RFK: The Man, The Mysticism and The Murder," in which the Temple of Understanding is dissected. Impact Publications, Box 64500, Los Angeles, California.

telephone off the nightstand in the process.

The clock showed 2 a.m. It was cold in the room. Somewhere in the distance a siren wailed, with two dogs joining in high pitched protest.

I was wide awake by now.

Who could be calling at this hour? The phone was unlisted and only a handful of people knew the number.

"Mr. Steinbacher?"

The voice crackled across what seemed to be a thousand miles of space.

"Which one?"

"Do you work at the Anaheim Bulletin?"

"That's right."

"You don't know me," said the voice, "but I live in New York. I won't take any more of your time, but if you want an interesting story I suggest you call William Cahn, the District Attorney of Nassau County in New York. Ask him about the Calderone girlie shows."

The line went dead.

Back at the Bulletin office, I was too busy with deadlines to think about the nocturnal caller until about 2 o'clock in the afternoon.

I approached Sam Campbell, wondering if he thought it was worth wasting a long distance call on such an anonymous tip.

He grinned, and took only a half second to give me the green light.

From that interview with Cahn's aide came a story that not only put the whole sex instruction issue into a different perspective, but also indicted Dr. Mary Calderone for, at least, some astonishing hypocrisy.

It was the astounding story of the Calderone theatres – all three of them.

Two days later I was handed a letter from Rose Marino in New York, verifying what I had learned in the late night phone call.

113

In 1967 and 1968, according to Cahn's aide, Dr. Frank Calderone, Mary's husband, imported Minsky's Burlesque Follies to his Mineola Theatre on Long Island, a theatre specializing in try-out stage productions and other stage shows.

According to the official, the show was so raw that the district attorney, after previewing it, told the male half of the Calderone team that he would have to clean it up or it would not be allowed to open.

One act featured a male and female dancer, in which the male's tights were so small "the pubic hairs showed down front."

Of course, that seems rather dull in the days of "Hair" and other assorted shows staged in the total buff, but remember, that was clear back in the neanderthal days of 1967, when people were still shocked by such things, even police officials.

What a difference three years can make in the life of a revolution. Now the entire staff of St. Patrick's cathedral could do a review in the nude on the high altar and most people would accept it.

Another act in the Minsky Revue featured a flamboyant, well-endowed redhead who danced with a life sized male dummy.

"The act was just like fornicating on the stage," said the official, using saltier slang in his description.

After some discussion – and considerable protest – Calderone agreed to change these acts.

Placing a call to Frank Calderone, we found he had a controlling interest in three theatres, the Mineola, Hempstead and Calderone. The latter two are movie houses that screen every film to come out of Hollywood, including such gamey productions as "Three in the Attic" and "The Killing of Sister George," however, Calderone said the Calderone Theatre was leased to United Artists Corporation.

Searching further, I discovered the three theatres were purchased by the Calderone Corporation, the Erone Corporation and the Fracal Corporation, all derivations of Calderone's name.

114

Denying that he was responsible for the Minsky's presentation, Calderone said it was staged by the Long Island Theatre Association; however, a careful search of the records by a Title Company and other sources revealed no such organization existing in 1969.

The "Three in the Attic" film is all about a handsome young man who is locked into an attic by three girls, a Negro, a white girl and an oriental; they then force him to have sexual intercourse to the point of exhaustion.

Nice, clean family fare, as well as a defilement of the scriptural admonition found in both the 10 Commandments and in the New Testament.

I had been claiming right along that there was an incontrovertible link between the smut and pornography peddlers and the sex instruction promoters. This tie becomes clearer every day.

For instance, I discovered that the very first nudity group in the nation was an outfit called Nature Friends. They established the first "skin camps" in America through the auspices of the Communist Party in the early Thirties. The name of the camp was Midvale and it was located just off the Snake Dew Road, Wanaque, New Jersey.

Midvale is still in existence, with FBI director J. Edgar Hoover announcing that the camp is a "Communist training area."

The club they referred to was the W.E.B. DuBois Club, a Communist youth group named after a Negro traitor who fled to Africa and died there some years ago.

The camp was a permanent facility maintained by the Communist Party and top Party officials who acted as teachers for youth in attendance there.

In 1967 a group of campers was raided by South Carolina mountaineers who had heard all about their nudity, free love

115

and integration in a summer camp in the Blue Ridge Mountains.

A number of those campers fled north to Midvale, where they could be safer.

Nature Friends was, and still is, an international arm of the Communist conspiracy, formed in most countries of the western world, with chapters and camps in scores of cities and states in America.

The purpose of the camps was described in the hearing of the Special Committee on UnAmerican Activities, 75th Congress, Volume One, page 556.

"Nature Friends seem to receive more attention than any other unit. This organization is widely organized throughout the country. It not only maintains outdoor activities, but it also operates an agit-prop (agitation and propaganda) section, music groups, film and photo sections (lewd, nudie films), chess groups, gymnastics, dance groups, scouts, lecture groups and summer camps."

In the Guide to Subversive Organizations of the United States Congress, "Nature Friends" is called "an international Communist affiliated movement which swept over our nation through its appeal to lovers of outdoors."

At one time the camps had 170,000 American members who took part in 400 physical activities.

The UnAmerican Activities report ends with, "Whether or not Nature Friends are in any way connected with the nudist fashion is not yet known, but it is common knowledge that nude bathing among mixed sexes is practiced at Communist summer camps."

Of course, skinny-dipping and what not, is *de rigeur* these days on college campuses, at hippie festivals and at Sensitivity Training sessions.

Since the Congressional report was issued it has been proven that nudity did prevail at Midvale and the other related camps.

Herman Thomas, an FBI undercover agent, reported to the 84th Congress, "I attended several closed meetings of the Communist Party with Frances (Grabow), but on one of the

116

latest occasions, after the party went underground in 1950 (when Joe McCarthy was hot on their tails before the U.S. government shut him up permanently), I met her and another member friend of the Communist Party at an affair at the Nature Friends Camp near Valley, Pennsylvania. I made arrangements there with the other person to pick up Communist Party literature in Philadelphia, inasmuch as they weren't using the mails . . . "

So, what does all this have to do with the public schools and sex instruction?

Well, read on and you'll find out.

The Los Angeles based Elysium Institute exists for a variety of reasons, not the least of which is to promote free love and nudity.

Ed Lange,* head of the group, publishes a number of magazines such as "Ankh," "Nude Living," "Sun Disc," "Nude Lark" and "Nudist Idea."

He also publishes the official magazine of the American Sunbathing Association called Nudism Today.

Lange is vociferously in favor of school sex instruction and in his magazine was listed a chart of affiliated organizations. Among that assorted group of not-so-odd outfits (if you really know what they are up to) is dear old SIECUS, along with assorted nudie and psycho-political organizations.

For instance, Elysium describes itself as "a non-profit organization whose real purpose is research and dissemination of information in the behavioral sciences relating to nudity and the body taboo neuroses so prevalent in our nation. The Institute promotes self acceptance of others through a wholesome attitude toward the human body and its functions, both physical and emotional, including sexuality."

Now, if you substitute the word "sexuality" for the word "nudity" you have pretty well found the self description used by SIECUS.

---

*Lange was arrested in July, 1970 on a variety of charges.

When Dr. Mary Calderone spoke in Santa Monica in 1969, she was approached by Mrs. Lillian Drake, co-producer of an anti-sex instruction film called "Pavlov's Children." Mrs. Calderone first attempted to deny that her group's name appeared in nudie magazines, according to Mrs. Drake, and then, when faced with the magazine as evidence, "flew into a huff and brushed me off."

That was the meeting where Mrs. Calderone was taped using the four letter expletive for sexual intercourse during her speech.

Dr. Calderone apparently learned her lesson in Santa Monica because, when she was slated to speak in Kansas City, Kansas to a meeting of the University of Kansas Medical School, the printed program stated *no taping* would be allowed.

Carl Rowan, leftist and former head of the United States Information Agency and a senior editor of the Reader's Digest, suddenly appeared in the Bulletin offices.

He was writing an article for the Reader's Digest, he said, and had a task force of people working for him.

When the great task force got around to regurgitating its masterpiece in the October, 1969 issue it turned out to be a shoddy piece of old wives tales, half truths, innuendoes and sometimes clever way of making the sexologists look like the greatest thing that ever happened to American education.

But even the Reader's Digest couldn't make a skunk cabbage smell like a rose.

The sex education war and the Sensitivity Training war and all assorted, related battles are being fought by a woman's army, an army of damned angry women.

Sensing that their children are in deadly peril from those who not only covet their bodies but their souls, in city after city it is the women who take up the cudgels.

These are not professional Communist fighters. By and large, wherever I have been, I have discovered that the women are from the PTA, tea party and canasta (or bridge) set.

Suddenly they have sensed danger to their children and

118

they have gone into action – just as the women of Brazil, two million strong, went on the rampage that nearly wiped out the Communist influence in that country.

There they were, by the hundreds of thousands, marching down the streets, praying their rosary beads, while their husbands and sweethearts in the armed forces had no choice but to turn the other way. After all, they couldn't shoot their own sisters, wives and sweethearts.

In Anaheim, Jim Townsend laughingly refers to his workers as "Townsend's female army," and that is exactly what it is. There are men involved, but by and large it is the women who have carried the big stick from the first day of the conflict. It was the women who went door to door with the flyers, informing the public. It was the women who stood and looked the school board members in the eye while they read the riot act to those august gentlemen. It was the women who got out the vote that turned the tide in the spring of 1969. It was the women who used their allowances to print materials, who traveled around the state giving speeches and alerting hundreds of thousands of their fellow females. It was the women who talked and walked and worked – and prayed.

Santa Monica was a good example.

Led by Marilyn Angle (CCC chairman, Santa Monica) and a marvelous man named Yolk Lew, the women of that city went to work, alerting and warning in the spring of 1969.

Finally, in the late fall of 1969, the program of sex instruction they had been concerned about died a death by administration fiat – quietly and in an unheralded fashion.

Superintendent of Schools Alfred Artuso disclosed in February, 1970, that a decision had been made in his office that no sex education courses would be offered in the district.

"So many hurdles were put in front of us," Artuso moaned, "such as restrictions from the State Board of Education, restrictions from the state legislature – you can do this and you can't do that. By the time you set things up, you don't have a program it's so watered down.

119

"The main reason we decided not to go ahead with the program here is because every place it's been tried it has failed."

Amusingly, Anaheim's Sally Williams was the person who ran the pilot program for teachers of sex instruction in Santa Monica.

So, once again Mrs. Williams was defeated.

It has become increasingly clear, after nearly two years of raging controversy, that school sex instruction has a rocky road to travel before the mind benders complete their sinister task.

VIII

AMERICA

The plane cut down through clouds that seemed to stick to the fusilage, banked left over a clump of houses and straightened up for its descent into the Waco airport.

It was a prop plane — part of the "tree top" airline that services dozens of smaller cities out of Dallas and Houston.

My first impression was of flatness — the same checkerboard table I had glimpsed through the clouds all the way down from Dallas.

"Fasten your seat belts please," the lone stewardess drawled over the intercom. "Texas International Airlines welcomes you to Waco. We hope you have a nice pleasant stay hereabouts, and do fly with us again."

Sound advice I thought, since there didn't seem to be any other plane service out of town.

I was the last one off the plane — the small clump of people waiting at the entrance to the airport terminal were beginning to stir restlessly, looking at each other and then peering toward the plane with hands shielding eyes against the glaring sun.

They spotted me then, and broad grins broke out under large Texas style hats as the men walked hurriedly toward me.

"Welcome to Waco," said the younger one, sticking out his hand and gesturing toward the other two.

The usual amenities and we were off and running — toward the radio station for an interview, then to the newspaper office and finally a conversation on the local TV station.*

It was like playing an old record, I thought, listening to the men talk about their problems in the local tax supported

---

*In all fairness, I must commend most of the news media people all over America for the cordial and respectful way they received me.

121

school system — nothing had changed except the setting.

I was reminded of my grand entrance into Grand Forks, North Dakota a few weeks earlier — when the hostility from the state college crowd had spilled over into the Armory.

That was the first time I had been called a demagogue — but it wasn't to be the last.

Then there was Casper, Wyoming, and a snowstorm in late June — but an even colder blizzard kicked up by the local newspaper which, in effect, practically ordered me out of town.

Casper — that was one town I wouldn't forget for awhile. That was the city where a woman called me at the radio station, identifying herself as the wife of a local teacher, and promptly began to shriek, "I'm sick and tired of hearing the name Steinbacher — that's all I've heard around here for the past month. I'm sick of it — Sick! Sick! Sick!"

However, the same woman showed up at my talk that night — and promptly began a haranguing monologue of her own.

So many towns and so many strange faces — that weren't very strange after all, because they were all saying the same things I had heard over and over again in Anaheim. The change agents were, it seemed, romping all over the American landscape.

Waco was just another stop on a whirlwind tour of America that had begun with a talk I delivered at the Public Affairs Luncheon Club in Dallas.

The phone rang one day, at the Anaheim Bulletin, and a sweet Southern drawl identified the owner as Mrs. Milam Pharo, president of the club.

It seemed they had sex instruction problems in Dallas — or at least they thought they did. Dr. Mary Calderone had been in and out of town — and a member of the SIECUS board was a big shot in the local education establishment.

Gwen Pharo, lovely wife of one of the city's most important physicians, wanted to know if I could come to Dallas and talk to their group.

And so it began – a merry-go-round that went on for over a year and that was to take me to nearly every state in the union.

With a capacity crowd jamming the Hilton Hotel in downtown Dallas – we were able to kick off a minor revolution that continues to this day, a revolution led by the men and women who were determined to regain their school system from those who had ulterior plans for their children.

Then there was Grosse Pointe, Michigan, and a committee led by Clarice Sass, a little lady whose love for children led her to adopt three babies – all of whom looked astonishingly like they were flesh and blood relatives.

Grosse Pointe – and again the same problems, the same stories, the same complaints, the same feverish worries about what was happening to their children – and the search for miraculous instant answers from a stranger from California.

Any one of those towns, it seems, would make a book in itself – the story of men and women, and some of importance in their communities, determined to regain control of their school, first, and control of their children's destinies, second.

Then there was Ginny Cracraft and her committee in Charleston, West Virginia. Charleston is a beautiful city sitting between its two rivers like a contented, elongated, lively animal.

Again, the same disappointments – as for instance when we went to see a couple of attorneys who had volunteered to work with the committee in bringing suit against the school district over the sex instruction issue.

I wasn't quite prepared for their Southern kindness and their manners that should have gone out with the Civil War. Also I wasn't quite prepared for the genteel way in which the two attorneys informed Mrs. Cracraft and her committee ladies that they just didn't have time to take the case, after all.

What happened? Ginny was stunned – and surprised and disappointed – and she kept shaking her head, wondering if perhaps someone hadn't gotten to the attorneys, but that,

123

she kept saying, was hard to believe because the two men were such fine, upstanding and conscientious citizens.

I wasn't prepared, either, for the enormous crowd that jammed the city's biggest auditorium on that hot summer evening — an enthusiastic — though worried and frightened — crowd of people who again were determined to take on the education establishment.

Newark, Ohio and a young and energetic principal of a local school — who knows what is going on and who doesn't like it. It was a refreshing change to find one school man who had the courage to take a public stand.

The roll call of those who contacted me at the Anaheim Bulletin during those feverish and hectic days of 1968 and 1969 is a roll call of some of the most important people in America — people who care and who are determined to stand against the floodtide of educational disintegration.

The Concerned Citizens of Greater New Orleans; Concerned Citizens of Hawaii, and Smokey Bird and Dottie Morrison; John Norris, Denver; Mrs. E.L. Parrish, Rocky Mount, North Carolina; Dr. James Parsons, Florida; Don Riddle, Casper; Mrs. F.E. Ruedebusch, Lee's Summit; Mrs. Herman Swigert, Butler, Pennsylvania; George Wagner, Fort Thomas; Marshall Covington, Eight Mile, Alabama; Paul Sikes, Greensboro, North Carolina; Chris Smith, Raleigh; Dr. Thomas Suiter, Rocky Mount; Minnie Berg, Dahlen, North Dakota; LaVerne Gaarder, Edmore, North Dakota — who was inspired to run for the school board after my appearance in Grand Forks, and who, to everyone's surprise, won; Ragnhild Lima, Copperstown, North Dakota; Leo Gauthier, Grand Fords; Dr. K.G. Mauerer, Fargo; Mrs. Jacob Passa, Grand Forks; Marcus Bailey, Norcrosse, Georgia; Shirley Bratten, Forest Park, Georgia; Nelda Cain, Columbus, Georgia; M.C. Pawley, Atlanta, Georgia; Mrs. B.E. Worrell, Marietta, Georgia; Dr. Ed Brown, Pocatello, Idaho; Teresa Hendry, Jerome, Idaho; Mrs. John Howell, Boise; Mrs. Steve MacKay, Weiser, Idaho; Ann Stalder, Pocatello; Paul Victor, Twin Falls, an incredible man who spends

124

most of his waking hours striving to improve his country and his city; Reba Young, Idaho Falls; Paula Derbak, Chicago; Mrs. J.A. Dowthitt, Edwardsville, Illinois; Emily Winter, Clarendon Hills, Illinois; Chriss Bender, Kalona, Iowa.

Ah yes, Chriss Bender and that amazing group of people known as the Amish who peacefully farm their lush and fertile acres in America's heartland — and who want only to be left alone to rear their children in their own way.

But the government won't let them alone, and so they have fought and they have fought again and again in a day when the rest of America thought of them as only quaint relics of the past.

And there was that never to be forgotten meeting, in Kalona, in the patriarchal world of the Amish, when time fled backwards for me to a glorious time when things were much less complicated and when everything was slower and made more sense.

There was that meeting in the Amish church, when the women sat by themselves in their quaint hats and long dresses, and the men ran the whole show.

And there were the two schoolteacher types who, in a burst of arrogant superiority, hissed loudly, "Just look at those ignorant women in the front row."

Ignorant? Those women were far from ignorant. They were fighting for one thing — they were fighting for the right to be free — just as they had fought for the right of their children to stay out of the government run schools for a hundred and more years.

They would continue to fight — despite the arrogant superiority of the educators who looked down patrician noses and scoffed at their simplicity.

And there were others, all across America, Barbara Richards in Santa Ana and Virginia Beebout in Downey, California.

There are Mrs. Dexter Woods, Dodge City, Kansas; Mary Campbell, Wichita, Kansas; the Catholic Action Committee of Overland Park, Kansas; Mrs. Forrest Fenn, Prairie Village, Kansas; Mary Jo Heiland, Wichita, Kansas; Kathleen Taylor,

125

Pittsburg, Kansas; the Reverend Richard Wilson, Winchester, Kansas; Marcia Kemp, Ann Arbor; Dorothy Sherrit, Madison Heights, Michigan; Gerald Smith, Detroit; David Sponseller, Ann Arbor; James Erickson, Larimore, North Dakota; Dr. M. Glover, Livonia, Michigan; R.L. Gordon, Mount Clemens, Michigan; Raymond Jones, Birmingham, Michigan; C.W. Mallory, Flint, Michigan; Robert Ewing, Minneapolis, Minnesota; John Schroder, Moorhead, Minnesota; A.G. Thiessen, Minneapolis; Elsie Zimmerman, Minneapolis; James Chu, North Haven, Connecticut; Mrs. Attilio Gambardella, North Haven; Mrs. Norman Murray, Freedom, Maine; Eva Orsini, East Longmeadow, Massachusetts; Mrs. Willard Grothe, Omaha; Merritt Newby, Lincoln, Nebraska; Neva Schram, York, Nebraska; the Reverend Jack Keep, Parsippany, New Jersey; George Paules, Parsippany; Audrey Piel, Neptune City, New Jersey; Gordon Whitney, Trenton, New Jersey; James Allen, North Tonawanda, New York; Catholics United, New Rochelle; Mrs. J. Dowling, Pelham, New York; Joseph Dwyer, New Rochelle, New York; Howard Hurley, Utica, New York; Rosemarie Marino, Dix Hills, New York, who was one of the first to discover the theater ownership of the Calderones; Ruth Spirito, Bronx; Mrs. Daniel Suida, Cheektowaga, New York; Mrs. Paul Marmet, Glenmont, Ohio; Mrs. Fred Saceau, Parma, Ohio; Ira Brandon, Columbus, Ohio; Stanley Ingram, Lewisburg, Tennessee; James Johnson, Nashville, Tennessee; Fred McPeake, Knoxville; David New, Nashville; Dr. and Mrs. C.H. Cowart, Waco; Dan Smoot, Dallas; Edward Hunter, Virginia; Evangelist A.G. Hobbs, Fort Worth; Dr. W.I. Fox, Abeline, Texas; Ruth Godbey, Houston; Mr. and Mrs. George Goody, Waco; H.A. Jessup, Waco; Mrs. Carl Lindhoff, Waco; Mrs. Phillip Collins, Dallas; W.T. Rea, Dallas; Mrs. Andrew Small, Dallas; H.C. Willis, Garland, Texas; Mrs. H.N. Wharton, Waco; Marie Bell, Wichita Falls; Mrs. Paul Bottorf, Portland, Oregon; Mrs. A.C. Bufka, Dallas, Oregon; Citizens for Constructive Education, Seattle; Don Tait, Yakima; Mrs. Ray Evanson, Tigard, Oregon; Mrs. Edward Elkins, Portland, Oregon; L.A. Garland, Roseburg;

Jean Hess, Veneta, Oregon; Mrs. J.H. Jeppeson, Eugene; Alan Knudtson, Roseburg; June Larson, Lynwood, Washington; Mrs. Robert Lund, Tacoma; William Scheele, Moses Lake, Washington; Kitty Thomas, Walla Walla, Washington; James Weitzel, Enumclaw, Washington; Doris Wood, Portland; Mr. and Mrs. Richard Wright, Wenatchee; Mrs. Fred Dehne, Milwaukee, Wisconsin; Lenore Rock, Milwaukee; Valerie Setter, Oshkosh.

And in California, so many names and committees they cannot all be named. Yet, some of them stand out in my memory.

Gloria Beihl, Anaheim; Mr. and Mrs. Bill Jollissant, Anaheim; the Reverend and Mrs. Willard Conradson, Anaheim; Bernice Monson, Anaheim; Joe Mullin, Anaheim; Lee Regis, Anaheim; Mr. and Mrs. Richard Spencer, Anaheim; Ethel Weimer, Anaheim; Earl Woodhull, Anaheim; D.C. Parks, Bakersfield, who though blind, works tirelessly on behalf of those afflicted with drug addiction; Alice Weiner, Belmont; Coleen Brown, Buena Park; Frank and Barbara Dooher, Culver City; Mrs. Raymond Ball, Camarillo, Lee Olsen, Claremont; Robert Easter, Chico; Willard Bullock, China Lake; Fern Herbst, Chula Vista; Irma Liberator, Culver City; Don Marcoe, Los Angeles; Marge and Raymond Isitt, El Segundo; Mrs. R.A. McMahon, El Segundo; Shirley Morgan, Escondido; Joe Shimes, Escondido; R.E. Combs, Fresno; Mary Whealen, Fresno; Barbara Toth, Garden Grove; Ronald Hewitson, Garden Grove; Frank Jaacke, Glendora; Letitia Bastiani, Hanford; Joseph Bean, a courageous, fighting school board member from Glendale; Mrs. Clinton Hill, La Jolla; Mrs. Edward Stahl, La Jolla; Doris Juan, La Mesa; South Bay Citizens for Constitutional Government, Lawndale; the Reverend David Bryant, Lemon Grove; Wanda Bybee, Long Beach; Mrs. Harry Traffert, Long Beach; Dr. and Mrs. Phillip Voight, Long Beach; Mr. and Mrs. Gerald Knudson, Los Angeles; Yolk Lew, West Los Angeles; Mildred Thrasher, Monterey Park; Faye Brice, National City; Doris Wise, Petaluma; Pat McClendon, Ridgecrest; Lorrie Wicker,

San Mateo.

On and on the names go — thousands of just plain Americans who contacted us at the Anaheim Bulletin over the two year crisis period when sex instruction in the public schools was a major issue throughout the land.

Their names appearing in this book will surprise some of them — and it might even annoy some of them, for none of them are looking for publicity. They are just like you, Mr. and Mrs. America — and they care about their children or their grandchildren or someone else's children. And of course, thousands of deserving names are missing.

They care — like Dorothy Steiner of St. Louis, Missouri, who dared to stand up against her own school district, as a teacher, and demand that the administration stop its wildly innovative programming and get back to fundamentals.

Finally, then, she was given an ultimatum — shut up or get fired.

Since she had tenure and had a record as an outstanding teacher, she wasn't about to surrender that easily.

She stood up to them — one woman alone — and she won her battle.

Stories — one after another — all over America, from Eight Mile, Alabama to the Bronx and from Escondido, California to the far reaches of Alaska.

In some cases the parents and their committees can rack up a solid victory for constructive education. In other cases it was a standoff, and in others a defeat — for the time being.

The battles continue, and they will keep on, until once again the parents of America control their children's destiny.

It was election eve, 1969. Darkness had settled over the city of Anaheim. At the board room for the high school district, a crowd jammed the few available seats, waiting expectantly for the vote count.

128

And, in the Anaheim Bulletin office, Sam Campbell, Richard Doyle, the paper's Managing Editor and an assorted group of reporters also waited — with something akin to trepidation.

The die was cast. For weeks and months the battle over the sex instruction program had raged. Now the public would speak, clearly and loudly.

Indeed, the die was cast.

William Almand, Irving Pickler and John Barton — who had played a major role in installing the controversial sex program — were up for re-election to the school board.

Almand and Pickler had particularly taken a strong stand in the closing days of the hard fought campaign, with both men publicly stating their school board seats would rely on public acceptance of their sex instruction stance.

Two men opposed them — James Bonnell, who had publicly opposed the sex program from the outset and a former narcotics officer, Robert Bark, whose opinions of the sex program were not quite as clear as those of Bonnell. Still, both men were publicly known as being far more conservative than their two opponents, Almand and Pickler.

The Citizen's Committee of California, led by the state chairman, Jim Townsend, and the Anaheim chairman, Joe Mullin, had fought a tremendous campaign agains the program, and had worked to elect both Bark and Bonnell.

All that didn't matter, to the men who gathered that night in the Anaheim Bulletin editorial offices to watch the returns.

As a public service, the Bulletin regularly maintains a vote count center at their offices, and the citizens phone the Bulletin for the returns into the late hours of the night.

This time there was a difference. Sam Campbell, who opposed the sex program from the outset, who had waged a titanic struggle against it in the pages of his paper, was understandably nervous.

After all, a newspaper is in business to make money, because without a profit it won't be in business at all. Even though many citizens of the town had shown their displeasure

129

over the sex instruction controversy, it was hard to gauge exactly where their sentiments lay.

If there had been a great loss of readership, Sam would have known that he had alienated a good part of the town. On the other hand, since there was no great surge in subscriptions, he was understandably apprehensive as to how many people were on the side the paper had chosen to take.

I was at the board room, passing on the results to the Bulletin as the vote came in.

In addition, various campaign committees for Bark and Bonnell had already run counts of their own — and the word was out that Bark and Bonnell had won.

A third candidate, the one opposing John Barton, didn't look very good they said, since Barton had taken a sort of middle stance on the sex issue.

Still, as the votes came in, it looked as though the sex instruction forces were going to win an easy victory. By 10 p.m., with over half the vote counted, both Almand and Pickler were far ahead of their opponents, and Barton was already a sure winner.

There was quiet despair in a number of circles that night — and Sam Campbell must have been breathing a prayer or two, though outwardly he remained his usual jovial self.

Still, the campaign committees for Bark and Bonnell kept saying, "Don't worry." Their men would surge ahead when the Anaheim city vote came in, they said.

Something had happened just days before the election that should easily have thrown the election to Bark and Bonnell. In the early days of the sex instruction battle, the real leadership seemed to come largely from certain Catholics such as Lucille Townsend, Eleanor Howe, Blanche Kelly and others. There were, of course, such protestant stalwarts as James Garner, pastor of a local Church of Christ, who had also joined in. But by and large it seemed to be spearheaded by Catholics.

As we say, something happened. The Mormon church met in convention in Salt Lake City and a number of their leaders took strong and unequivocal stands against the very program

130

we were fighting in Anaheim.

Overnight the local Mormons – and there are thousands of them in Anaheim – joined in the fray.

Later I was to describe it in an article as a time when the Catholics were in their churches praying and the Mormons were sitting home saying, "Don't worry, God is still on his throne."

Maybe there was a lesson there for someone, because the Mormons turned out to be quite correct.

Around 10 p.m. that election night the results began to change – almost imperceptibly at first. Bonnell and Bark began to creep up, vote by vote, upon their front running opponents.

District personnel, such as Hank Davis, who had been jubilantly predicting a victory as early as 8 p.m. were suddenly very quiet. The victory was slipping away from them, vote by vote – and by midnight it was all over.

The parents of Anaheim had dealt a mighty blow to the education establishment that had taken them for granted.

And in the Anaheim Bulletin office there was a united sigh of relief, as the letters and telegrams and phone calls flooded into Sam Campbell, congratulating him on his personal victory.

But Sam, as could be expected, refused to take any personal credit for the smashing defeat of the sexologist forces.

"Just give the public the truth," he smiled, "and they will react accordingly."

And so they did.

Six months later the sex program was demolished, Royal C. Marten had resigned, Paul Cook was gone, Sally Williams was demoted and a third anti-sex instruction board member had been appointed.

The will of the people had been expressed – but Hank Davis promptly released the information that nobody was to take the election results as any kind of mandate. After all, he said, the turnout of voters was much too small for that.

He forgot that an even smaller turnout of voters had elected the pro-sex instruction board members four years before.

XI

COUNTERATTACK

The kooks, radicals and revolutionaries in the Anaheim Union High School District went on the counterattack in the fall of 1969.

They had suffered a series of serious ego-deflating defeats, including the ouster of most of the old school board.

Their prize sex program had been demolished, at least temporarily. Sally Williams and Paul Cook had lost their jobs. Three apparent conservatives now sat on the school board. The controversy over the sex education program had shaken them to their eye teeth.

Like homogenized peanut butter, they began to ooze their way out of the cracks and crevices in which they had been hiding.

Men and women with no private lives—having been stripped psychologically naked in sensitivity training sessions — the thing they feared most of all was the individual man.

With a value system built on total evil, they could only accept lesser degrees of evil.

Now they were someone, a mob, looking for a leader. They were determined to destroy the system, and in doing so, they had destroyed themselves and their own sense of pride. They were looking for another person who could give them a new value system.

They found it in Harold Rice.*

Harold Rice is a tall, cavernous looking man, balding, with glasses much too large for his peaked face.

He was a former family life and sex education teacher in

---

*In the fall of 1970, he put a photo of Angela Davis on the board in his room, intoned "God Bless, Angela Davis" to his students and then printed the four-letter word for sexual relations.

132

the district. Now he was elevated to the position of the head of the American Federation of Teachers, a rump group of 17 teachers or so who had broken away from the more conservative Anaheim Secondary Teacher's Association with a membership of nearly 1500.

Rice had made one public mistake.

In the spring of 1969 he had stood before the school board and confessed that he had been brainwashed in sensitivity training sessions.

In that confessional to the board — kicked off no doubt by the same kind of subconscious masochism that had led him into the family life program — Rice admitted that he had been unable to say the four letter obscenity for sexual intercourse out loud in his inservice training class while sitting in a circle on the floor with other teachers.

Finally, after great effort, he was to blurt out the word — to the applause and cheers of his fellow educators. Rice had crossed the threshold. There was to be no turning back for him now.

Somehow, the momentum built up by the Citizen's Committee had to be crushed, and the opportunity presented itself when a $23 million bond and tax override issue came up for a vote within the district on December 13.

Teacher power went to work — aided and abetted by all the way-out extremist individuals and groups in the community. It was a veritable juggernaut.

An organization was formed called COPE, for Council On Public Education. Was it an accident that this was the same acronym for Walter Reuther's political action group in the AFL, Reuther, who had signed a letter to his brother, Victor, "Yours for a Soviet America"?

Teachers in the district were assessed a set fee. Some say it was five dollars each. A war chest of large proportions was prepared.

The ubiquitous Henry Davis, public relations man for the district, went to work with a vengeance. This was his day, his chance at last, to get even with the Anaheim Bulletin, the Citizen's Committee and all those real and imagined foes out there.

For nearly a month he operated the COPE election machine in school hours, paid by the taxpayers for doing his job as a public relations man. The district superintendent was to admit later that Davis had broken the law in doing so. It made no difference.

Numerous "irregularities" and illegal activities were reported within the district.

Children in school rooms were harangued over the loudspeakers. They were given special awards to deliver COPE material door to door. They were told to encourage their parents to vote yes.

And all that scandalous behavior was done in the name of education. Lies were told, about what courses would or would not be dropped if the tax override failed.

So, with all the fabrications and the duplicity, the bond and tax override passed on January 13, 1970.

The sex education proponents were jubilant.

Their impassioned cheers were voiced at every opportunity. The people of the school district had played right into the hands of the revolutionaries and the radicals. They had given them the money they needed — $23 million — to continue a program of systematic change agentry and experimentation upon the helpless youngsters of Anaheim.

At the very first meeting of the board, following passage of the bonds, a parade of extremists marched to the front to thank the board for its support in passing the bonds and to pledge their loyalty to the cause of institutionalized crackpotism.

But James Bonnell, who had been elected in the spring of 1969 on an anti-sex education plank, found out that it doesn't pay to compromise with evil.

He had supported the bond and tax override measure, buying the line of the liberals that the district could not function without all that extra cash. But his glory was shortlived.

One partisan bond supporter charged to the front of the board meeting and denounced him as "some kind of sex nut" who wanted to do away with the sex instruction classes.

"The election results," cried the patron, a long time supporter of extreme causes in the district, "prove that the people of Anaheim have no confidence in the present board and they want their sex classes back."

Which reminds us of what a Dr. David Rubin said on the Tonight Show about that same time.

"Most parents who want sex education classes do so because they have a guilty conscience about not teaching their own children."

What kind of sex education were these League of Women Voters and PTA types demanding? It seems evident they demand the sex instruction now being promoted by the professional self-styled sexologists of SIECUS.

And one of those sexologists — and a leading SIECUS defender — Albert Ellis, recently declared before a mostly student audience of 600 at the University of Bridgeport, "Have as much sex as you possibly can before you get married — as intensely as possible."

He also said, "Petting is not harmful — heavy petting to the point of climax can be especially beneficial. Swinging group sex for married couples in a room, at the same time, is not objectionable — I encourage trying these things."

Ellis, who looks like a wizened Woody Allen with fuzzy, wool like gray-black hair, recently wrote a film script on sex with ANN LANDERS. The film is called "The Merry-go-round."

Readers are invited to write to Miss Landers and ask if she agrees with the Ellis philosophy, and if not, why she writes film scripts with him.

In Anaheim, the battle continues to rage, led in part by the extremist, far-out fringe group of teachers who belong to the AFT.

135

They monopolize board meetings, shout and scream and applaud wildly whenever anyone says something with which they agree, and in general act like characters in Orwell's "Animal Farm."

The people promoting school sex education are not interested in reducing venereal disease and pre-marital pregnancies. They are interested in establishing a new code of ethics that is void of all morality. In other words, they seek to make immorality the moral of the schools.

They have succeeded admirably.

Their aim is to promote promiscuity as a healthy attitude that one should have toward fornication of all kinds.

The study of reproduction can be scientifically presented, but the study of sex cannot; e.g. there is no way to determine the degree of sensuality that different people might experience when sex and more specifically, the sex act, is presented in a classroom.

They seek to totally destroy the established standards that history has proven must exist if civilization is to survive.

Val Davajan, distinguished assistant professor of obstetrics and gynecology, section of reproductive biology, Los Angeles County and USC Medical Center, agrees that sex education is bad.

"I realize that sex outside of marriage always has been and always will be practiced," he writes, "but when extramarital sex is established as the 'normal code of behavior' and is uniformly practiced by society, the society disintegrates."

Davajan adds, "When marriage goes, so does the family unit, and when the family goes, so does the nation. Anyone denying this series of sequences is totally ignorant of history and human nature. Therefore, I am not against sex education, but I am totally opposed to it as it is being promoted today."

The physician has some other complaints about the sexologists' methods.

"I have repeatedly asked them [the sex promoters] what effect such education is having on primary school children, and not one has been able to give me a proper answer. The reason is that up to the present there has never been a well designed control study whereby the effects of the psyche of the child can be scientifically evaluated. Since I am in medical research, these so-called educators cannot get away with a quote from some sociological study done by a doctor so-and-so, because they know I can look up the reference and tear it apart as to its experimental design and interpretation of results. So I suggest the layman demand the exact title of the paper, the author's full name and the name of the journal (including exact volume and date), if one of these 'experts' quotes statistics from a study. I assure you, no such study has ever been done — by that I mean a study that is scientifically valid. And you can quote me."

Reproductive biology, says Davajan, can be taught without promoting promiscuity to young people who have reached the maturity level of the 10th or 11th grade. Prior to this age (15-16), reproduction CAN NOT be taught without stirring up the child's sensuality.

Davajan states, "The most dangerous time to teach reproduction would be in the nine to 14 year bracket, when most children undergo puberty. It is during this period of time that moral ethics limiting sexuality must be taught. It takes time and it must be taught by qualified people. Unfortunately, those 'experts' uniformly teach that sex education must be void of morals — the very thing that should be stressed."

Davajan also states he would "absolutely, unequivocally" not allow his children to take a sex education course in grade school.

"It is not and never will be the teacher's job to teach my child anything about sex," he states. "I assume that responsibility absolutely and totally and I will bring a law suit against any teacher who violates that code against my wishes and I encourage all parents to do the same. No person in his right mind would allow any teacher to impose his or her moral standards upon his own children. To think that sex can be

137

taught without some kind of moral code is absolutely absurd. Just the fact of teaching sex without a moral standard is in fact establishing a code of immorality. I know some of the leading sex education proponents personally. All of them promote their own brand of immorality under the disguise of staying away from moral issues. All of these people I consider sexually unstable."

Davajan winds up his blast with, "Sex education is designed for promoting promiscuity and destroying the moral standards of this nation . . . I realize there are dupes who do most of the active sex education promotion, but there are also people in this country who, because of personal bitterness and hate for this nation and for all America stands for, are bent on destroying it from within, and I mean destroying the very souls of a whole generation of young Americans. Any parent who remains ignorant or apathetic about this attack on youth is helping and abetting that destructive process. MAY GOD HELP US."

Back in Anaheim the deadly forces continue to operate around the clock — leveling all they have against the Citizen's Committee.

School board meetings have turned into shouting, abrasive travesties, while behind the scenes scheming and plotting proceed apace.

It began to look like a showdown between the two teacher's organizations, ASTA, with 98 per cent of the teachers of the district enrolled and the American Federation of Teachers (AFT) by the end of the 1969-70 school year.

The way in which AFT came into existence is in itself an insight into the kind of organization it is and the kind of people, parents and teachers it represents.

A check into the background of the newly formed AFT

revealed that the hardest push for union organization (AFT) was made behind the scenes by a former president of the Anaheim Secondary Teacher's Association (ASTA), who applied for, but did not get, the job as ASTA executive director.

This director position currently pays between $18,000 and $20,000 per year plus fringe benefits and allowances. The position was first established while this individual was president of ASTA.

After being turned down for the job, because the board felt it would lead to inbreeding, he resigned his teaching job in Anaheim, in a tiff, and tried his luck as a teacher in another district.

Being no more successful there in his efforts to receive higher pay outside of the classroom, he returned to the Anaheim district and immediately began agitating full time for the formation of a union under AFT auspices.

Since then, as a member of the union's editorial board, he has launched several attacks upon ASTA, the organization which refused to employ him as executive director at the end of his year's term as president.

At present the AFT is too small to employ an executive director. However, if the local within Anaheim, through creating dissent and unrest, is able to increase its now puny membership, it will then be able to establish a director's position. That same individual would then, of course, be eligible to apply for the job.

Meanwhile, ASTA finds itself in the strange position of being forced into a corner by the AFT over the sex education issue, since the AFT has sought to link ASTA with the new school board and the ouster of Cook, Williams and the sex education program.

On January 9, 1969 a pro-sex instruction meeting was held at Anaheim High School, attended by around 1200 people on both sides of the issue. In the audience were a great many young people — many of them sporting the now familiar long hair and unkempt look of the student radical.

Leading the assault on the Citizen's Committee was one ex-reverend Robert Kevorkian, formerly the pastor for nine years of the First Baptist Church in the city. He had been allegedly forced out of that position by the church board — with some strange charges against him — and is currently a marriage counselor in Santa Ana.

Also present that night were three other so-called ministers, all noisily advocating sex instruction in the classroom — and all mouthing the now familiar humanist notions.

The meeting had been arranged so the proponents could air their views publicly, although the school board, which arranged the meeting, claimed it was for their benefit.

Board members claimed they had given the other side equal treatment a month or so before when they had been present as a presentation by the opponents of the program. However, all the board members, except Royal C. Marten, had promptly disappeared as soon as the meeting began.

But on this night they were, as we recall, all present, and all fascinated by the presentation made by the sexperts.

This was the *old* board — the one that had put the sex program into the district. They were allegedly getting the facts so they could make up their minds as to the merits of the program. It was later to be shown that they had already made up their minds to continue it.

Only the election of the two new board members — and later the appointment of a third — was to change that situation.

Letters had been sent home with children in the district, urging parents to attend the meeting, and there is evidence to show that certain teachers were literally pressed into service for the night.

Nearly three hundred students showed up to side with the

140

sexologists, plus about 400 curious supporters of the Citizen's Committee of California.

It was the last big gasp of the sexologists. Just a few short weeks later the election was to be held that dashed all their hopes and dreams.

Some months later the executive vice president of the Chamber of Commerce, Larry Sierk, was to complain that the controversy had hurt not only the image of the city but business as well.

One of Paul Cook's complaints, later to appear in print in the October, 1969 edition of the SIECUS newsletter, was that some scurrilous person had reported that sailors and marines hung around Anaheim's high schools, picking up the girls because they were so "available."

This was a typical strawman trick, designed to con the gullible.

The original charge was leveled by this reporter – and it concerned the fact that numerous interviews with Marines (who flood into Disneyland) revealed that the main reason they came to Anaheim was because there were a lot of "available" girls in town.

That is not to say that all the girls are immoral. It is simply to state a fact of life.

Some months later, in Wenatchee, Washington, a young ex-Marine was to echo the charge and agree with it.

"That's absolutely right," he told his mother, getting the reply, "I'll have to tell your father about you."

In any case, no charge of Marines and sailors hanging around high schools was ever made.

It was a pure fabrication, so far as we have been able to discover.

Cook also used another favorite gambit.

Someone, he kept repeating, has issued the base canard

141

that 50 per cent of the girls in Anaheim were pregnant and that the homes for unwed mothers in the area were overflowing with patients.

Triumphantly, he would then declare that no homes for unwed mothers existed in the county and the pregnancy rate was actually quite low.

Again it was a case of building a strawman, for implicit in his declaration was the charge that the two remarks had stemmed from someone in Anaheim.

Neither of those charges was ever made in Anaheim, by anyone, since everyone opposing the sex program knew they were not true. Everyone in Anaheim knows there is no home for unwed mothers.

The sex program in Anaheim — and those now being promoted around the nation — is purely naturalistic. That is, the program ignored the doctrine of original sin and was simply unChristian.

Second, the programs are purely intellectual and scientific (or pseudo-scientific). Mere instruction can be illuminative but it is not operative. Increased knowledge implies no increase in virtue. Some of the most wicked and evil men on earth are the most highly educated men. Morality has nothing whatsoever to do with knowledge.

As St. Paul said, "I do not that good which I will, but the evil which I hate, that I do."

St. Paul certainly had more defenses against sin and concupiscence than the children of Anaheim or anyplace else.

As G. Stanley Hall of Clark University puts it, "Sex education is a psychic rape of the young."

Mere teaching about evil does not cure that evil. If that were so, the Marquis de Sade should have been the most moral person on earth. HUGH HEFNER should be a paragon of Christian virtue. Playboy Magazine should be a manual for chastity and clean living.

Further, sex instruction is public, and does not consider the individuality of children.

142

Liberal Catholics who speak out in defense of these programs should remember the words of Pope Paul VI, in his Humanae Vitae. "On this occasion we wish to draw the attention of educators and of all who perform duties of responsibility in regard to the common good of human society, to the need of creating an atmosphere favorable to education in chastity, that is, to the triumph of healthy liberty or license.

"Everything in the modern media of social communications which leads to sensual excitation and unbridled customs must arouse the frank and unanimous reaction of all who are solicitous for the good of the human spirit. Vainly would one seek to justify such depravations with the pretext of artistic or scientific exigencies, or to deduce an argument from the freedom allowed in this sector by public authorities.

"To rulers, who are those principally responsible for the common good, and who can do so much to safeguard moral customs, we say: Do not allow the morality of your peoples to be degraded; do not permit that by legal means practices contrary to the natural and divine law to be introduced into that fundamental cell, the family . . . "

Nearly two thousand miles from Anaheim, the bishop of Nashville, Tennessee, the Most Reverend William Adrian, was speaking out against sex instruction and other strange innovations in the schools.

"In the last few years," he said, "the enemies within the church — some priests, religious and lay persons — have been teaching false doctrines and morals to the children in our Catholic schools — principally in the religion classes. But these false doctrines spill over into almost every subject taught, like history, biology and social science. I dare say that one half of the teachers in our high schools — probably less in the grades — are imbued with the errors of Teilhardism, which denies the existence of original sin and so makes Christ's redemption useless — and the errors of Situation Ethics, which practically destroys all norms of morality, including the 10 Commandments — and now these enemies of religion, agents of the

143

devil, having to their satisfaction destroyed the faith of our children in the supernatural, are playing their last trump card designed to destroy that last bastion that can protect the morality of our children, in the public, private and Catholic schools. It is part of the Sensitivity Training program, which has been so devastating to faith and morals . . . a program capable of destroying the moral fiber of our children in a widely established program of sex education. It purports to dignify man's sexuality, but has, in fact, exploited it."

Pretty harsh words from a leading Roman Catholic shepherd.

The speed with which the two twins, sex education and Sensitivity Training, are being implemented is evident in the fact that it can now be found within such organizations as the YMCA, Girl Scouts, Boy Scouts, churches, schools, hospitals, industry and even in service clubs.

A psychologist, who was very angry because a Long Beach [California] YMCA had recently dropped Sensitivity Training after some unfortunate results, remarked, "After all, you can't expect to make an omelet without breaking a few eggs."

It is obvious that the people promoting these programs are either knaves or fools. The evidence shows they are not fools.

Sex education fighters were to discover that the whole process had a great many more tentacles than they had at first imagined.

The people promoting these programs are few in number, but they have known each other for years. By and large, they have been associated over and over again in a variety of projects dating back several decades.

They have known and worked with each other, have promoted each other, have bestowed public honors upon each other and have prepared for this day with great care.

It was clear back in the 1940's, when UNESCO, an education arm of the UN, was first formed by a heterogeneous

144

group of radicals, revolutionaries, fellow travelers and Communists.

The beginning was in 1946 when the UN Charter was ratified by the United States.

Sex education and other aberrations stem from the UNESCO Declaration of the *Rights of the Child,* a shocking document that has received little if any publicity.

A copy of the declaration can be obtained from the United States Commission for UNESCO, Department of State, Washinton, D.C.

The UN has had total control of your children and all education in this country since October 24, 1946, but most Americans don't know it.

A deadly and vicious attack upon the rights of parents, the Children's Declaration is a diabolical instrument if there ever was one.

The day is not far off when parents will be prosecuted for violations of precepts of that declaration – parents will be subject to imprisonment and their children will be reared by the state.

The Honorable John Woods, Idaho, told his fellow Congressmen on October 18, 1951, "Just how careless and unthinking can we be that we permit this band of spies and traitors to exist another day in this land we love? Are there no limits to our callousness and neglect of palpable and evident treason stalking rampant through our land, warping the minds and imaginations of even our little children, to the lying propaganda and palpable untruths we allow to be fed to them through this monstrous poison? It is my sincere hope that every parent of every child in America may be able to read the inroads that this infamous plot has already made in the educational system of America, and, reading, may feel impelled to do something about it, both locally and nationally; and particularly at the voting booth."

Unfortunately, a majority of people never heard his words, and those who did, paid him no heed.

145

The children's charter is simply unbelievable. In its utopian language lies the veiled threat of state rearing of all the children in this nation.

"The child shall enjoy special protection," it reads, "and shall be given opportunities and facilities, by law and other means, to enable him to develop physically, mentally, socially and spiritually in a healthy and normal manner and in conditions of freedom and dignity."

Doesn't that sound fine? Of course it does, and that is precisely what the plotters had in mind.

The reader must ask several questions. Whose law and what means are they talking about? When Communists talk about freedom and dignity, they are talking about a collectivist society. Communists helped write the declaration.

"The child shall be protected from practices which may foster racial, religious and any other form of discrimination. He shall be brought up in a spirit of understanding, tolerance, friendship among peoples, peace and universal brotherhood, and in full consciousness that his energy and talents should be devoted to the service of his fellow men."

That is the final quote from the lengthy children's charter.

They are saying that if you are a Mormon, for instance, the state could demand that you stop teaching your church doctrine to your children.

The so-called racial balancing of schools in this country is part and parcel of this treaty.

And now a Congressman from Washington State has introduced a bill to set up federally run nurseries based on the communal Israel Kibbutzim. "It's pure Communism," he exults, "the essence of Karl Marx."

In the middle of the Anaheim sex instruction controversy, an ad hoc committee was set up by the sex instruction opponents that turned out to be a perfect pipeline for finding out what was going on in the minds of such people as Paul Cook and Sally Williams.

Called RESCUE, the committee purported to be one hundred per cent on the side of the sexologists, and in an opening newsletter the author attacked the Citizen's Committee unmercifully and offered its help to Cook, Williams et al.

RESCUE workers were under only one order — they were to be entirely independent as to financing and as to activities — and their findings were to be promptly turned over to the Citizen's Committee to help fill their fattening files.

Sally Williams did her best to help RESCUE.

She promptly sent 10 dollars to the "committee" along with a glowing letter. They never cashed her check and sent it back when RESCUE went out of business.

Paul Cook also wrote a letter, excoriating the opposition in the following words:

"I have read with interest and appreciation your RESCUE newsletter and agree with you that there is far more behind this than a simple attack on sex education. The extremists suddenly realized about a year ago that most of us are raised to be tense and sensitive in the area of sex, and that through distortions and outright fabrications it is possible to fashion a very dangerous club.

"A list of people was sent to you who I feel should know about your plans and your newsletter. The address of Mrs. Sally Williams is 13251 Safford St., Garden Grove.

"We have received information on some of the key 'nuts' from Paul Putnam (National Education Association; ed.) in Washington, a copy of which is enclosed, and this might be a reasonable source for you to obtain objective information. I have contacted the Anti-defamation League in Los Angeles, because we have seen in our last election some tendencies toward anti-Semitism, since at least one or two of our candidates were Jews, and of course the right wing has always had a weakness in that direction.

"I would be very glad to sit down and talk with you, in-

147

dividually or together at some time that would be convenient in time and place to you both."

Of course, Cook was ready to talk with anyone, at that point — since he must have felt like the loneliest man in the city of Anaheim.

In regard to his reference to anti-Semitism, the Citizen's Committee had a choice of various candidates on the school board ballot. Among those candidates, favored by a great many of the "right wing," was an outstanding, fine Anaheim businessman named William Silverman.

Mr. Silverman is a Jew.

Sally Williams was writing letters, too.

"All I can say for the moment," she said, "is God bless you. If there is anyway I can help, please ask me. Sincerely, Sally R. Williams."

After speculating as to the identity of the RESCUE committee, and stating some fearful thought that RESCUE might be a "cover" for the anti-sex education forces, Mrs. Williams said, "I do think that if you will meet with us we can unify our efforts for the benefit of the students in the Anaheim Union High School District."

RESCUE's planned propaganda was shortly picked up by leftist Cal State, Long Beach, journalism professor Dixon Gayer. In his monthly "Dixon Line" he dutifully repeated the canned falsehoods about your reporter and other planted stories the CCC wanted the pro-sex cult to fall for. It may come as a surprise to Mr. Gayer, but he was printing the Citizen's Committee press releases all the time.

Sam Campbell's prediction was coming true. The other side had no secrets, and whatever they said was shouted from the rooftops for all the world to hear.

Phone calls flooded into the Citizen's Committee from teachers in the district, reporting every move of the sexologists.

If the sexologists thought that the anti-sex education forces were omniscient it was an understandable error.

148

The sexologists talk about four kinds of standards existing in our society.

Those standards are, (1) affection-centered; (2) total abstinence; (3) double standard and (4) permissiveness without affection.

Of course, many of them embrace standard number four with exuberance and gusto.

American Baby Magazine opined, "To the small child, mother and father are synonymous with husband and wife. Stay away from the husband and wife concepts in your (sex) answers, because it will be a great shock to the children when they learn that people don't have to be married to have intercourse."

Leading SIECUS board member Ashley Montague (alias Israel Ehrenburg) writes, "Unmarried persons who are sufficiently responsible will be able to enter into a responsible sexual relationship in a perfectly healthy, normal and reciprocally beneficial manner."

Former SIECUS board member Isadore Rubin insists we must, "Cleanse every trace of dirt from the use of contraceptives so as to make premarital sexual relations more convenient."

The real sin, he adds, is to bring an unwanted child into the world.

Rubin's writings were an integral part of the Anaheim program.

The people of Anaheim discovered that the Socialist school system could not teach sex instruction in a moral setting.

The die is cast and the public will make the final choice whether parents or the state will have the say in regard to the rearing of their children.

Parents in Anaheim taught the sexologists that an aroused public can make an impact heard around the nation.

That impact is still causing shock waves throughout the halls of academe wherever the sexologists gather to plot their little schemes.

X

THE MIND BENDERS

James Bonnell, newly elected Anaheim school board member, has been a tower of calm strength in the midst of the hurricane that swirled around him.

A handsome man, with a frequently brooding look on his face, he appeared suddenly one night in the middle of 1968 at a district board meeting.

Nobody knew him – but it didn't take long for the Citizen's Committee to know they had found a man of principle.

Bonnell, frequently standing alone since his 1969 election, has obeyed the injunction of the Methodist leader, John Wesley – "Turn your face toward the mob."

In turning his face toward the mob, Bonnell frequently found himself struggling against the tide, as well.

No one will ever know the psychic agony that Bonnell endured his first few months in office.

A clever man, he has a calm assurance and a soft spoken manner that disarms his attackers and frequently makes them look rather foolish.

Robert Bark, elected by conservative votes, was frequently on Bonnell's side – but he as frequently hedged his bets and kept his cards close to his chest. Bark could not always be counted on to side with Bonnell, even though the principle seemed clearcut enough to the onlookers.

So it was that Bonnell engaged in a mighty game of musical chairs – stalling for time when it was necessary and frequently throwing everything in the parliamentarian's book at his fellow board members in order to stop what he thought would be deleterious decision making.

That was especially the case when it came to sex education and Sensitivity Training. Elected on a strong anti-sex education stand, Bonnell realized he would have little chance to close down the program – because he was outnumbered on

150

the board.

Still, something happened behind the scenes that will never be made public. Time and again Bonnell was able to enlist the support of three other board members, leaving only Edward Hartnell to fume and fret and complain bitterly that he was being ignored.

It was a game of wits, with Bonnell ever the master of the situation – though to the public it frequently looked as if he were losing badly. Still when the final chips were down, he had nearly everything he wanted.

That is, he had them for awhile.

The opposition promptly launched their counterattack that is still raging to this day.

Bonnell understands the nature of the enemy. He has done his homework and he is not importuned by the raging fury of the mob.

"Be my guest," he frequently smiles to a fuming, foaming and enraged opponent who is taking him over the hoops during a board meeting.

This kind of understated reaction generally disarms the opposition. Frequently they sputter to a halt and end up apologizing. Other times they moderate their language.

Bonnell has that elusive thing known as charisma, though he would be the last one to admit it.

As a matter of fact, he has so much charisma that he was promptly threatened with a recall election only weeks after getting into office. The same rabid, wild eyed and frenetic revolutionaries who have opposed every sane move in the district for years are today plotting and scheming to throw Bonnell out of office.

They have no chance of succeeding.

One of the things that concerns Bonnell is the sneaky way that Sensitivity Training has been introduced into the district.

Disguised in countless ways, Sensitivity Training plays a major part in most school sex education classes.

For instance, Sally Williams and Paul Cook were slated to

151

appear as faculty members at the Paul Popenoe Institute in Los Angeles from June 23 through July 3, 1969. However, they cancelled out after the sex education furor erupted in Anaheim.

On page six of Popenoe's catalog, in which the names of Williams and Cook are listed, it states, "All participants in the seminar must undergo daily Sensitivity Training."

Kurt Lewin of the National Training Labs in Group Development died in 1947, but his work lives on.

An earlier day experimenter in sensitivity techniques, Lewin left behind a body of research and work that was incorporated, in 1954, into an organization called simply the National Training Labs, NTL, in order to embrace the growing involvement of sensitivity in the many areas of American industry, education, religion and science.

The National Education Association, NEA, was a prime mover behind the NTL experiments.*

The purpose of the NTL was to experiment in human change agentry and figure out ways to bring it about.

The first laboratory sponsored workshop for industrial administrators and church executives was held in 1955, years before the public even knew that sensitivity training existed. In 1958 the NTL sponsored a laboratory for educational adminstrators and key executives in volunteer organizations. The NTL was well on its way.

Young social scientists underwent training in 1960 and the NTL program has been in continuous operation ever since.

From its NTL labs in Bethel, Maine, the NEA coordinates the work of several hundred trainers or change agents in training centers and universities throughout the nation. People from every social strata and profession in the United States are involved in the programs, all the way from teachers to judges and from housewives to ministers.

---

*Mrs. Elizabeth Koontz, President Nixon's head of the women's division of the Labor Dept., is a past president of NEA and a SIECUS board member.

152

For instance, at UCLA, more than 75 people work full time in setting up seminars in sensitivity for everyone from businessmen, teachers and clergy to students and housewives.

In turn, the NEA cooperates with and obtains the aid of change agents from the National Institute of Mental Health.

Further, regional centers stressing Sensitivity Training have been established at such places as Boston University, Temple University, George Washington University, the University of Texas, the University of Chicago and at the Rocky Mountain Laboratory and the Intermountain Laboratory sponsored by the University of Utah. Practically every university in the nation has Sensitivity Training courses, clinics and seminars as a regular part of their routine.

Other places are the above named UCLA and all the campuses of the University of California, as well as the Northwest Laboratory, which was initiated by the Seattle Public Schools, aided by the University of Washington.

Change agent centers are also located at such far flung places as Esalen (California), and Ontos (Illinois), as well as Western Behavioral Sciences Laboratory in La Jolla (Calif.).

Extensive training sessions are carried on in such places as Puerto Rico; Nigeria; India; England; France; Belgium; Denmark; Norway; Sweden; Australia; Germany and the Netherlands.

Those promoting the programs use an almost incomprehensible jargon all their own that is supposed to make the whole process sound legitimately scientific.

For instance, they claim that "cross-national-T-groups are an excellent milieu in which to examine culture shock, internation conflict and the idea of a common human nature."

Actually, what they are saying is that Sensitivity Training is precisely designed to merge science and "democracy" into a total personality system and a total world social system. In other words, a new secular religion of the world is their goal.

Though going under a variety of names, from group confessional to interpersonal competence and from T grouping to Interpersonal Relations, the programs are all in a constant state of flux and transition in relation to objectives, designs and methods.

Originally the trainers concentrated upon the external or objective factors, but in recent years the emphasis has shifted to subjective matters involving "gut level," here and now events, with attention riveted upon "central life values" and personal attitudes toward the home.

James Bonnell was clever enough to see that the Anaheim program was nothing less than an extension of the Pavlovian change agentry found in the NTL programs. Once he saw that, nothing could shake him from his determination to change things himself. He became a change agent – but a different kind.

The NTL seeks to recruit those within the community who are already leaders or people of prominence. They enlist teachers, ministers, businessmen and even policemen and military leaders. In Anaheim, these were exactly the kinds of people who were put on a citizen's advisory committee for the purpose of instituting the sex education program five years ago. It was an entirely one-sided kind of group with a few sincere people thrown in for good measure.

There are two basic things that the labs hope to accomplish – changed behavior and increased knowledge.

Since there is natural innate resistance to change in all of us, the labs seek to involve the person in a deeper and ever deeper relationship with the "group" so that this reluctance can be overcome.

Lab trainers constantly stress the importance of the participants becoming more deeply involved than would be the case if only the gaining of knowledge was their goal.

Permanent change in the attitude of the participants is the end goal of Sensitivity Training – hence, it is important that the attitudes of those back home, with whom the 'changed' individual relates, are also changed. That is why the labs stress attendance by groups rather than by individuals, and that is why the participants become 'change agents' in their own

154

communities.

Some change agents are used for the supposedly constructive purpose of increasing production or industrial efficiency. However, the duty of other change agents is to bring about radical changes in political, moral and religious values when working in schools, churches, universities, clubs and so forth.

Family Life teachers in America's schools are frequently those very change agents. They may not have learned the techniques at the NTL, but they have learned them from someone who has.

Exactly what goes on in these training sessions?

First of all, the learner is involved in the training situation to a point where he feels it is vital to become a member of the group in which he practices 'new, improved and appropriate' behavior.

During the training process, the trainee can easily become threatened through such things as criticism by others, rejection by the group or trainer, loss of status, fear of ridicule or the failure to measure up to the standards and expectations of the others.

It then becomes the trainer's duty to dispel these anxieties without making it possible for the trainee to escape from the change process.

This is the crucial point in the whole brainwashing procedure.

The trainer is a combination agenda planner, initiator, mediator, behavior model, source of new values and a facilitator of the learning process. His job is to manipulate, plan and create situations that will cause total change in other people.

Unfortunately, the victim of this mind manipulating does not know that he is a victim. He cooperates with the trainer even while his very soul is being stripped from him and he becomes a walking and talking example of whatever the trainer wants him to be.

All the while, the one being manipulated thinks he is doing something worthwhile and at no time does he realize he is nothing but a puppet.

As the training sessions begin, ground rules are agreed upon by the trainer and the trainee, so the trainee feels duty bound to abide by them since he has had a part — though superficial — in the planning.

Some of the rules are: agreeing to stay in the entire time; being completely open and honest with the group; keeping nothing back; not talking during non-verbal exercises; not engaging in side conversations, because all thoughts, feelings and ideas are now group property.

The use of language normally thought objectionable is encouraged for free expression.

During the sessions, self and group criticism techniques are used to discover personality changes the trainer believes need to be made within the trainee.

Written tests are often administered at the beginning and at the end of training as an instrument for measuring the degree of change that will be accomplished before the sessions have ended.

Periods of silence are often coupled with the call to close one's eyes and is used whenever a person's defense mechanisms have stifled the group from reaching the pre-established goals.

Trainees record in writing their most potent feelings. This gives the trainer further insights as to trainee reactions at different stages of the session.

During a specified period of time, participants are to convey their feelings by means other than the spoken word. They may use their eyes, facial expressions, body movements and so forth. At times these exercises are accompanied by music.

Along with the non-verbal exercises come so-called body awareness exercises, in order to more readily achieve a 'feeling level' in the trainees. In one example, all lie on the floor and push in toward one another to achieve a psychological unity. Another is to forcefully push another person to the ground so he can feel hostility. Then the group hastens to help him up, offering 'love' and solace to assure the person that he is 'loved' and cared about. This gives the support needed for the individual to feel he can trust the group and be able to accept the group's standards, values, morals and ideas.

Participants meet for a marathon of several days to a week or more, during which they do not sleep except for catnaps, and never leave the group except to freshen up or get something to eat. This uninterrupted pressure is intended to lower the natural defenses and drive participants to interact truthfully, authentically and transparently. They are urged to talk on the 'gut level' and to be intimate and authentic.

Nude marathons, used widely, are rationalized as an attempt to strip away the emotional inhibitions that man has hidden behind his clothes. Clothing, they say, is a mask which we traditionally remove only in the presence of persons with whom we are intimate. In the case of the nude marathon, the clothes are removed as a facilitator of emotional transparency and interpersonal honesty.

The wrapup is a device used by trainers to summarize what the trainees were supposed to have learned. One wrapup message, frequently used, is: "In the outside world they are no longer on the same wave lengths as you are. You have reached a wave length not many others have ever achieved. They can't possibly understand unless they also have been in a group."

This was echoed recently by Angus McCloud, head of a Sensitivity Training lab at UCLA which puts on sessions for teachers, students, industry and so forth.

Reminded that many psychiatrists are opposed to the very techniques his organization uses, McCloud angrily asserted, "How can they know unless they have been through one of our sessions? I suggest they take one of our sessions and then they will understand."

In other words, the critics will then be locked in psychologically.

Since, in these sessions, some people 'blow their minds,' as if they had taken LSD, they become 'hooked' on it. Sensi-

157

tivity Training becomes an obsession with them and nothing else in life has any meaning for them.

The NTL said it succintly in their booklet, "Issues in Training," on page 47: "(It) includes coercive persuasion in the form of thought reform or brainwashing as well as a multitude of less coercive, informal patterns."

There you have it. They admit to brainwashing procedures.

The NTL then describes three steps to bring about what they call "integration of attitudes."

First, they refer to UNFREEZING, which is force acting as resistance to change.

Second, CHANGING is a process of actually learning the new attitudes.

Third, REFREEZING is the integration of the changed attitudes into the rest of the personality.

The essential elements in the original unfreezing are: (1) Removal of the supports for the old attitudes; (2) Saturation of the environment with the new attitudes to be acquired; (3) Minimizing threats from the new attitudes; (4) Maximizing support for the desired change.

Proponents of these programs all agree that major similarities exist between Sensitivity Training programs and some forms of group psychotherapy. The rather distinct differences that existed a few years ago appear to be more and more blurred. These proponents feel that it is unnecessary to draw clearcut distinctions between them, and seem to agree that what is needed now is a general theory which would bring under one conceptual scheme the various psychotherapies, Sensitivity Training, psychiatric case work, counseling, guidance and existential psychology. This would then become the preventive mental health field of the future.

These programs are designed to make well persons sick.

For instance, the NTL, in its 1962 publication, "Issues In Human Relations Training" writes: "Ill persons reach out for

158

help, while relatively well persons find themselves in a dilemma. Although they *appear* to behave appropriately and *seem* normal by most cultural standards, they may actually be in need of mental health care in order to help them change, adapt and conform to the *planned society* in which there will be no conflict of attitudes or beliefs."

The Department of Health, Education and Welfare has been promoting these programs for years, together with the National Education Association, the NTL and other related groups.

In "Concepts of Community Psychiatry," the HEW states, "(Psychiatrists) must not wait for patients to come to them, because the psychiatrist carries equal responsibility for all those who do not come." Thus he will be "dealing with those who are not yet sick," but those who have "been defined as maladjusted in the educational, social, occupational or religious fields and may be struggling on their own . . . "

(A new TV series has the star playing a psychiatrist who goes into the community looking for sick people.)

Can you believe that?

Well, you better believe it.

In the city of Wichita, Kansas, for instance, the entire community has become a therapeutic clinic.

There, as in other cities across the nation, the behaviorists are treating the whole community instead of sick individuals.

In the second grade, the children of the city are subjected to unbelievable invasions of privacy — carrying out the role playing first suggested by Dr. J.L. Moreno, the inventor of psycho-drama.

The children are forced to discuss each of their family members. Then they put on masks made out of paper bags, drawn to resemble members of their family and are urged to "role play" the different duties performed within the home.

By encouraging subjective emotional dramas, the children are encouraged to act out everything they see and hear within the home; nothing is sacred.

159

Next, the children are forced to make "socio-grams," which were designed by Moreno.

The class members are then asked to decide how a child should respond after he has done something wrong.

Is the class also to decide what is wrong and what is right?

The second graders are then divided up into pairs and given three minutes to tell each other something about themselves. Each child is then to tell the class what he has learned about the other.

After that, the children are asked to write a paragraph, using the topic, "Why I chose Johnny Smith as my best friend."

What happens to those in class who are not chosen as a best friend? Moreno's cruel sociograms would suggest the unchosen ones be clumped together as a bunch of sorry losers.

The children are asked to "discuss the need and importance of proper elimination, and learn the parts of the body that are responsible for elimination."

These children are around eight years old. Can you visualize them sitting around in class discussing such a private function? Furthermore, it is doubtful if the teacher knows any more about it than the child's parents. The parts of the body used in elimination are also sex related — so here we go again.

Those same little tots are asked to "discuss the differences and likenesses in the physical makeup of boys and girls."

They are also to be involved in a discussion of how all living things reproduce, and they are to check their family newspapers for articles dealing with conflicts in the home.

Needless to say, the only conflicts that would be reported in a daily newspaper are "adult" conflicts. Since when do eight year old children have to concern themselves with adult conflicts?

Well, since Moreno came into the picture; perhaps it is time to discuss him more fully.

Readers are referred to the 1957 report of the California Senate Investigating Committee on Education for a comprehensive report on Moreno and his psycho-drama and socio-

160

drama. We will have to stick to a bare outline of the man and the subject for reasons of space, and this material is based on the same state report.

The term 'psycho-drama' is broadly used in much the same way as cognition was used some 50 years ago. It includes, simply, the whole range of skills, techniques and processes which are involved in the unrehearsed but not unplanned *dramatization of human problems*, for the purpose of dealing with them more effectively.

It offers a method whereby individuals and groups may be analyzed with respect to their potentialities for some kind of future action.

Educational psycho-drama is concerned with the control and direction of normal behavior toward desired goals. It is a group process that seeks to modify existing behavior.

In a book entitled "Psycho-drama and Socio-drama in American Education," the author Robert Haas of UCLA, talks about the use of the techniques in junior high school.

"As a new school year begins," he writes, "it is gratifying to see how well a number of teachers have integrated sociometry into their teaching and how often they refer to their charts in analyzing and treating behavior of children. *They seem to give more concern than formerly about the values a group places upon a given classmate* (emphasis ours), his attitudes toward the group, the interaction between the individual and his group and between individuals within the group. Strangely enough, while teachers seem to place less value upon the infallibility of their own judgments of child status with his fellows, they seem to find more security in the new broader and more objective procedure. They take keen delight in discovering new relating techniques for bringing the outcast into better relationship with his group and in observing the changed position in successive sociometric charts."

Can you believe that your children are being used as guinea pigs in this kind of head shrinking clinical study?

Haas writes, "As a further attempt to help the children

build security in their groups, teachers kept anecdotal record cards for each highly rejected or underchosen child."

Of course, the usual subterfuge is employed.

On page 266, Haas writes, "The superintendent can direct that one of his staff members, *in a rather secretive way*, have tests given and corrected in order to know the status of pupil achievement in the several schools under his jurisdiction."

The ideological bent of Haas can be easily discovered in the following quote from his book: "If the nationwide propaganda campaign against Russia would be stopped, it would be a long way forward . . . Well, I believe I'll try, anyway, to get something started."

Moreno is promoting Sensitivity Training under new names, although he was one of the real pioneers in the field. He says, "The degree of participation is at a possible minimum when the individuals composing the group are willing to answer questions about one another. Any study which tries to disclose with less than maximum possible participation of the individuals in the group, the feelings which they have in regard to one another, is near Sociometry."

Who is Moreno?

His real name is Ivan Vladimir Morenovsky, and he was born in Siberia or possibly Rumania. His Sociometric methods were used to overthrow the Russian government in 1917 and in Communist lands these group confessionals — depending upon the group for survival — result in individuals conforming for fear of betrayal by other members of the group.

In his book, "First Psychodramatic Family," Moreno describes his first meeting with Sigmund Freud, at which time he told Freud, "You analyze their dreams, I try to give them the courage to dream again. I teach people to play God."

Moreno developed the concept of group evolution, in which everyone has his own group and what you do and believe is decided by the group — admittedly conforming to the lowest denominator. (The Manson family?)

And then comes the clincher. Moreno admits that his techniques were picked up by the NTL through the National Education Association, spreading his message faster than he could have done it himself.

The Marxist Russophile, John Dewey, father of modern American education, said of Moreno's techniques, "Sociometry appears like the next stage and its techniques are already far developed."

Moreno hates religion, particularly Christianity. He says, regretfully, that attacks made upon Christianity by Marx and Nietzche failed because their methods were repressive and Christianity is repressive, so they end up paralleling themselves.

He has devised a better plan of attack — now being used in thousands of American schools and colleges — which he believes will succeed. That is, people are simply to be permitted to destroy themselves in pursuit of pleasure.

"In considering this," he states, "we began to speculate over the possibility of a therapeutic procedure which does not center primarily in the idea of sublimation, but leaves man in the state in which he is spontaneously inclined to be and to join the groups he is spontaneously inclined to join (Sociogram); which does not appeal to man either through suggestion or through confessional analysis, but which encourages him to stay on the level toward which he naturally tends; which does not forcibly transgress the development of individuals and groups beyond their spontaneous striving as has often been attempted by sublimating agencies."

In that Moreno concept is found the rejection of Original Sin, and he is promoting Hedonism. Translated from the Greek, it means self indulgence or pleasure for the sake of pleasure. That is the Playboy mentality and it is the SIECUS mentality.

It is interesting that the head of the State Department of Health in Kansas, where Moreno's concepts are now full blown in the tax supported schools, is Dr. Evelyn Gendel, a board member of SIECUS.

Moreno is simply preaching the ancient heresy of Manicheanism in a new form. The Manicheans denied the objective nature of reality, and believed that everything is possible as an operative principle. They propose to free man from social disorder by *revolutionary political action*, thus realizing the transfiguration of man and the final realm of freedom within history. There can be no clearer expression of this revolutionary gnosticism than a movement that seeks to transform man and create a contraceptive society by means of an aphrodisiac education, control over the origins of life and genetic experimentation with the very nature of man, himself.

The philosophy expounded by Moreno — and his myriad of followers in the NEA — strikes at the very heart of civilization. It first attacks what the theologian, Martin Buber, has called the "exemplary bond" of the social and political order which is the family. Finally, it undermines the fine balance of freedom and order which marks viable society. It dissolves the rationale for interior moral restraint in the individual and encourages the state to assume a totalist interference in the most basic personal realms of social existence.

The Moreno philosophy is not confined to the state of Kansas. In my travels, I found traces of it in such far flung places as Waco, Texas; Casper, Wyoming; Roseburg, Eugene, Astoria and Portland, Oregon; Dallas, Texas; Minneapolis, Minnesota; Detroit, Michigan; Boise, Idaho; Seattle and Tacoma, Washington and in every city, town and hamlet.

In most cases, the center for the propagation of the concepts is a local university.

In Waco, we believe, it is Baylor University. In Grand Forks, North Dakota it is the state college, which has one of the largest behavioral science labs in the nation. In Dallas it is at the Methodist University and in Detroit it is at Wayne State University.

In California it is coming out of the state colleges and the massive statewide campuses of the state university system, as well as many of the smaller private colleges.

Here and there, small bands of valiant parents are fighting this and similar programs — like little Davids swinging against the full scope of the problem with which they are contending. They only sense that there is something very wrong.

The full scope of the interlocking agencies that sponsor programs stemming from Moreno and the perfected techniques of the NTL-NEA can be seen by the following partial list of Sensitivity Training centers.

Berkeley Center for Human InterAction; Caselya; Center for Human Communication; Esalen Institute - Stanford; Institute for Creative and Artistic Development; Kairos; the State Colleges; the State Universities; San Francisco Gestalt Therapy Institute (all in California).

In other states we have, in addition to the state colleges and universities, such places as Shalal, (Canada); Amare, Institute for Human Relatedness (Bowling Green, Ohio); Cambridge House, (Milwaukee, Wisconsin); Evergreen Institute, (Littleton, Colorado); Gestalt Therapy Institute of Cleveland, (Cleveland Heights, Ohio); Kopavi Inc., (St. Paul, Minnesota); Laos House, (Austin, Texas); Oasis, Midwest Center for Human Potential, (Chicago, Illinois); Ontos, (Clarendon Hills, Illinois); Shadybrook House (Mentor, Ohio); Adanta, Inc., (Atlanta, Georgia); Aureon Institute, (New York City); Bucks County Seminar House, (Erwinna, Pennsylvania); Boston Tea Party, (Boston, Massachusetts); Human Resources Development, (Hidden Springs, New Hampshire); Orizon, (Washington, D.C.); Plainfield, (Plainfield, New Jersey); Sky Farm Institute, (Calais, Vermont); Synergia, (Montreal, Canada); Tarry Town House, (Tarrytown, New York); Wainwright House, (Rye, New York); Western Behavioral Institute, (La Jolla, California).

Thus the entire nation is blanketed with change agentry factories, ready to perform their function in shaping and molding the next generation and preparing them as ready and willing models of the International Child.

Where does the money come from?

Perhaps a Western Behavioral Laboratory brochure will give you a small idea.

"Our work is supported by grants and contracts from government agencies," they write, "(e.g. Office of Education; Vocational Rehabilitation Administration; Office of Naval Research; Office of Economic Opportunity) and from philanthropic groups (e.g. the Charles Kettering, Babcock, Eli Lily and Ford Foundations). In addition, some of our research is underwritten by private donors . . . our budget for 1967-68 is $750,000 . . . among our current projects (13) are studies on attitudes and values of youth elite groups in more than a dozen countries; new uses of the mass media; development of programmed instructions (audio-taped) for small basic encounter groups; designing and testing 'simulation games' as classroom technique; use of intensified group experience as an aid to educational innovation in an entire school system; a large scale evaluation of San Diego's Community Action Program, and the development of a policy research program to aid educational planning for the future."

Carl Rogers, who worked with the Western Behavioral outfit for some years, said recently in the Oracle, an underground newspaper, "In the future there will be greater freedom in sexual relationships in adolescents and adults; prurience is dying out; obsessiveness of another individual will be diminished; by the year 2000 each individual will be assured of infertility in adolescence; it will take positive action to re-establish fertility; most unions will be childless; temporary unions may be legalized as a type of marriage with no permanent commitments, no children and no alimony."

Is that why more than one out of ten teenagers in California will contract venereal disease in 1970?

Richard Farson, who is an advisor to Esalen and was formerly with the Western Behavioral outfit as the director, has publicly proposed establishing networks of families around the nation who would monitor each other's marriages.

The United States Congress funded a project for Richard Farson at the Education Policy Research Center, a branch of the Western Behavioral Sciences Institute. The starting date of the project was June 1, 1967 and the ending date was December 31, 1968.

Consisting of a "group of pilot studies on a variety of problems in educational policy," the project was to find a "basis for the design of an operational policy research center."

Included in the operation of the center would be courses for teachers, providing educators at all levels with information that has implications for education. Among the studies carried out would be, (1) economic consequences of changes in educational policy, (2) simulations (socio-drama) as a tool for educational planning for the future, (3) future role of the school board, (4) predictive study-attitudes and values of future decision makers and (5) future-focus, the human condition format, a T Group conference technique.

Robert Grist, who works with Esalen and Stanford University, is the director of the Mid-Peninsula Free University. He is also a rutting sex machine, according to his own boast.

"I'm a living experiment in community sexuality," he said in the San Francisco Chronicle on March 10, 1968. "We believe that in today's climate of sexual permissiveness, traditional moral questions are no longer even questions."*

Michael Murphy, brother of Denis Murphy who wrote the best selling novel about a homosexual Army sergeant, is a cofounder of Esalen.

In a recent article in the official publication of the American Association of Humanist Psychology he wrote, "50,000 people, from all walks of life, have participated in our program at Big Sur (laughingly called Big Sewer among those in California who know what goes on there). We have also worked with groups from the Peace Corps, the California Teacher's Association, CTA, various schools, colleges, clinics and major American corporations . . . educators are increasingly aware

---

*On Nov. 16, 1970 the National Public Health Service declared venereal disease to be "pandemic" in the United States. "V.D." they said, was a "raging conflagration totally out of control."

that life's important lessons are learned early in a child's development, and many teachers are trying to reach children with Sensitivity Training before their creativity and spontaneity are stifled in the classroom."

Esalen received a $21,000 grant for experimentation in all phases of Sensitivity Training at the University of Santa Barbara, on all levels of elementary and secondary schools.

Title III of the Elementary-Secondary Education Act of the United States Government provides the clue to the powerful mechanism operating within the various change centers.

Funded by the Office of Education, the program is "for the exploratory development of models of planned change in education."

That is the link between the behaviorists and the public schools.

Programs for interdependence among universities and school systems, both public and private, were created through grants from the Office of Education and the Fund for the Advancement of Education of the Ford Foundation.

Those programs permit the federal government to serve as a catalyst for bringing about "desirable" educational changes. Two of the programs are the "Co-operative Project for Educational Development," COPED, and the "Project to Accelerate Creativity in Education," PACE.

Since Sensitivity techniques can be incorporated into any class and into any subject, parents seldom know when their child is being experimented upon.

Even principals and other school officials are frequently unaware that change agent teachers are at work in their schools day after day.

A permissive attitude is created in the class, during which students are encouraged to freely express themselves.

Psychodrama and role playing require students to divulge home-family situations, and family authority is undermined by student acceptance of peer group opinion. Assignments may include diaries of innermost thoughts, or essays are written

168

incorporating self criticism and confession.

Students may volunteer for peer analysis (criticism by classmates) and are encouraged to make personality changes deemed by the class to be necessary. Debates involve such topics as legalizing narcotics, prostitution, abortion, the sexual revolution, the generation gap, hippies and so on. These debates are frequently steered so the student adopts the "objective" view.

Gym and drama classes frequently include body awareness exercises.

Despite after-the-fact disclaimers, students have been urged to embrace in darkened rooms, feeling each other, and are asked to write essays on the sensations they experience.

One such course at the Davis campus of the University of California ended up with everyone stark naked. The same thing happened at the State College, Long Beach, California, with the participants before the class as naked as jay birds.

The educators generally make the following pitch to the gullible students.

"We are building a new social architecture and education is no longer relevant. Students should be educated in the area of the senses rather than the intellect. Youth has more to teach than does the older generation. Students have the right to their own influences and their 'life style.' Students can teach other students best, just as convicts can work with convicts better and mental patients can best help their fellow mental patients. There should be no examinations, grades, terms or credits (Schools Without Failure). The only meaningful changes in education will come through student rebellion, when the students take over the design of their own education as they are now in the process of doing."

Dr. T.M. Stinnett, a former NEA official, agrees.

"Tomorrow's teacher," he writes, "is going to be a director of learning instead of a ladler of facts or alleged facts . . . education for the future must be *humanistic* (emphasis ours) and humanizing."

169

Frank Bowles of the Ford Foundation agrees in the NEA Journal, December, 1966.

"The goals in short are behavioral," he writes. "If we claim they are intellectual, we fool ourselves. Our colleges and universities are the board of strategy for the intellectual and social revolution . . . "

Dr. Stinnett adds, "Education has gained the power to change society against the wills of the politicians. It is the key to economic progress and to the constant renewal of society. It is now master as well as servant for the first time in history."

John Goodlad writes in the February, 1968 NEA Journal as follows:

"The most controversial issues of the 21st Century will pertain to the ends and means of modifying human behavior and who shall determine them. The first educational question will not be, 'What knowledge is of most worth?' but rather 'What kind of human beings do we wish to produce?' The possibilities defy our imaginations . . . sedatives, barbiturates, tranquilizers and various psychedelic drugs provide powerful ways of controlling behavior by direct action on the brain. Similarly, we can manipulate behavior by applying electrical currents to regions of the brain. Experiments are now underway with drugs and brain extracts designed to enhance learning or memory. Aldous Huxley long ago introduced us to the possibilities of genetic selectivity through the availability of sperm and ovum banks. The means of drastically altering the course of human development through artificial insemination, chemical treatment and electrical manipulation are with us. We are already tampering with evolution."

Robert Maynard Hutchins, writing in the California Teacher's Association, CTA, Magazine, the Valuator, said, in the Fall, 1969, " . . . the teachers must control the educational programs. They must have organizations which will attempt to resist the impositions placed on the teaching vocation by superintendents, by school boards, the legislature and governors."

"Our real war is not a battle of bullets," warned educator E. Merrill Root recently, "but of brains; not of space, but of spirit; not of missiles, but of minds; not of weapons, but of wills . . . Thus, our greatest danger today is not atomic fission, but academic fission; our greatest peril is not nuclear fallout, but scholastic falldown. Teachers and texts that accentuate the negative can be of far greater danger to America than the loosing of one hundred Panzer divisions or the launching of a thousand missiles . . . "

Around 1957, in California, the State Department put out Guides for the schools that were designed to bring about the changes the NTL-NEA wanted.

Those guides quote extensively from the Marxist, John Dewey and his disciples, William Heard Kilpatrick, Boyd Bode and George Counts. Other radicals such as Fritz Redl, Kenneth Benne, Theodore Brameld, Ronald Lippit, and Ernest Melby also appeared.

Though a section of the education code specifically charged teachers with the duty of inculcating patriotism, a check of the Guides showed nothing that would stir a child's love of country. In fact, the child was to be specifically educated in world mindedness, and religion was to be treated as a factor contributing to bias or undesirable prejudices.

The group philosophy of the Guides was a collective one, in which the welfare of the group was uppermost above all personal ambitions, desires and incentives. The children were to submerge their identity in the group. Such personal ambitions as improving of status and striving for success would interfere with the functioning of the group. The child was not to work for personal improvement or for personal gain but for group acceptance and group welfare. Independence, in the guides, is described as "poor mental health."

In solving the mental health problem, teachers were told to keep track of every act, every word, every deed, every attitude and every incident. and record it all in the child's permanent record.

"Learning," the Teacher's Guide to Education in Early Childhood reads, "is changed behavior. The test of learning is in the changed behavior of the learner. Little meaningful learning takes place on a purely verbal level; meaningful learning results in changed feelings, understanding and behavior."

Sociometry is recommended in the guides as a means for identifying a child's status, the very technique perfected by Moreno.

Moreno, said the Los Angeles Times of May 4, 1957, is a "New York mental expert famed as the discoverer of psychodrama, group therapy and sociometric technique in psychotherapy."

In describing his sociometric techniques, the Times quoted Moreno, "This is designed to measure human relations. It gives an idea of the emotional picture of the group."

In 1927 he came to New York and was naturalized in 1935. He did his first psychodrama work at Hunter College in 1929 and was responsible for the first psychometric conference at Philadelphia in 1932. He was a special lecturer at the radical New York School for Social Research from 1937 to 1938. He was a special lecturer at Teacher's College, Columbia, from 1939 to 1940.

"Highly directive sociodrama," he writes in his book, *Who Shall Survive*, "can be used for indoctrination of any set of values — religious, Communistic or Fascistic."

The report put out by the California State Legislature Joint Interim Committee on the Public Education System, 1961, sums up the entire sordid situation.

In speaking of certain tests being administered to the children of the state, the committee said, "These tests compel a child to expose his secret thoughts, snoop into a student's beliefs on spiritual values and religion, and will lead him to question his beliefs; (They would) direct the child's mind toward criticism of his home, parents and teachers and undermine America; (They would) encourage students to spy and report on those for whom they should have the highest re-

172

spect; (They would) dirty the children's minds in the garbage pit of human thought and force the child to testify against himself."

What more need be said?

The child seducers have even reached down into the nursery, into that golden time when mother and child should be learning to know one another, growing and sharing together.

But the predators are not content with twisting and perverting the minds of half grown children – the pre-school child is a much more susceptible target.

Evelyn Barnes, mother of four children and a resident of the rolling hill country of Southern Idaho, is an example of what can happen to someone who stands against the spoilers.

On January 4, 1970 she took a plane to Lawrence, Kansas to take a leadership course in the Headstart Program.

But let her tell it in her own words . . .

"I was to receive $135.00 a week for this training, plus all my expenses for travel as well as board, lodging, tuition and books at the University of Kansas. I was told I would receive six hours of college credit for my studies in Leadership Development. Since I am working toward a degree in hope of becoming a teacher this was very interesting to me.

"I arrived at the University of Kansas on January 5 and was assigned to Lewis Hall. The courses I was to take were called Child Development and Human Relations.

"In the Child Development course the instructor (called a trainer) was Jesse Esqivil, and the Child Development specialist was Mrs. Phyllis Connelly.

"In the Human Relations course the instructor was Ed Skaggs.

"Each of these classes was to meet every day, except when there were other activities. Goals for these classes were to be that we would be (1) Better Organizers, (2) More Deft in the

173

Training Areas, and (3) More Aware of Group Processes.

"Classes January 6 started at 1 p.m. with Ed Skaggs, Jack Connelly, Phyllis Connelly and Jesse Esqivil present; also Jean Shields.

"We were told about the Parent Involvement Program (PIP) which meant that Head Start pupils' parents were to hire and fire the teachers and teachers' aides with no school system involved. There was to be a grant of $250,000 to get PIP organized. We were told that the school system must be thrown out of Head Start. (At home at Malta, Idaho I work under the school system and have found it very desirable and pleasant.)

"Later in the class session we had a talk by Dr. Arthur Katz of the School of Social Welfare. He told us that Head Start was not just for children, but for all members of the family. Dr. Katz said the gross national product was around $400 billion dollars, and that we, the poor and the underprivileged were not getting our share because of The Establishment. 'The Establishment' he said, 'will not let us out of our poverty. The Establishment is the enemy of poor people, and we must do something about it.'

"All professional people, Dr. Katz told us, were part of The Establishment. Some people, he told us, would say that socialism was close to communism, but for us not to buy that. Socialism would give us our fair share of the gross national product, and it was up to the poor people to demand a change in the system. Dr. Katz said nothing about our working to earn our fair share of the gross national product.

"In getting to know the other students I learned that 85 to 90 per cent of them were welfare recipients.

"January 7, I had no classes until 1 p.m. when Child Development in Today's World was in session. Phyllis Connelly was the lecturer. She told us The Establishment was not letting poor children have a better life, and that we must teach children to be more aware of today's world.

"We were asked to write every few days on the following questions:

174

1. How today's world affects me as a person?
2. What is my reaction?
3. Is there any problem?
4. Do you need to deal with it, and if so, how?
5. What do you feel you need to do?
6. What are you going to do?

"On Thursday, January 8, we had Human Relations class in the morning. Mr. Skaggs told us the PAC (Parent Action Committee) was for parent involvement. The Board of Education, he said, was part of The Establishment and poor people are not usually represented on the Board of Education. Head Start needed to get the Board of Education out of the program, he said.

"Friday, January 9, we all went to the Student Union Building for a film and lecture about the grape strikers in Delano County, California. We were told we had to see this. The grape growers were shown as the villains, the strikers as heroes. The speaker was from the California strikers group and a personal friend of Cesar Chavez. He was in Lawrence, he said, to get supporters and ask people to help in the boycott.*

"Next we heard Tex Samples, a liberal theologian, who referred to himself as being in the tinker's trade. His talk was Conflict and Consensus.

"A man asked if our group would come hear a lady speaker on Welfare Rights. Jack Connelly said that we would go. We were not asked to vote on whether or not we would go.

"Monday, January 12, we had Human Relations in the morning, and Child Development in the afternoon.

"Miss Esqivil did say a few words about child environment, but Mrs. Connelly soon took over, telling us how wonderful the Hippie Movement was for our country. She wore a peace sign pendant on a long chain.

"Tuesday, January 13, we had Human Relations in the morning, starting T-Group Therapy, which I felt was sensitivity

*See BITTER HARVEST by John Steinbacher, available from Educator Publications at $2.00 pp.

175

training under another name. We were given a manual for this course — mimeographed. It read exactly like sensitivity training and I have a copy which I can show anyone interested.

"We divided into little groups and discussed each other as part of the T-Group Therapy.

"Later, in a class under Dr. Katz, he continued his talk about the war on the causes of poverty. He said The System had to give way to include the poor people.

"Wednesday, January 14. We were told in Human Relations class about Johari's Window, a sensitivity device.

"Mr. Skaggs told us that in the class we were in our own little world and no one would know what we were doing. 'The folk back home won't understand you when you get home,' he said. I felt this was probably true when I read in our T-Group Therapy manual that 'in the most close (maximum contact) phase, the muscles communicate. Pelvis, thighs and head can be brought into play, arms can encircle.'

"In the afternoon we had a film for Child Development class . . . Jenny Is A Good Thing. This is a Head Start film.

"Thursday, January 15 — There were no classes on this day in honor of Dr. Martin Luther King.

"Friday, January 16 — We were told that Human Relations goals were: What Is A Leader? Leadership Roles. Problem Solving. How to Deal with Conflict in Ourselves. Our Frustrations. Finding out About Ourselves.

"In Child Development class we had a speech by Phyllis Connelly about The Establishment, race, etc. One day she spent a whole class period telling us not to say "blackboard" because it was injurious to the black people, etc.

"Monday, January 19, in Human Relations we were asked to look at each other eyeball to eyeball, then tell what we were thinking about at this time.

"Tuesday, January 20, in Child Development we had another lecture by Mrs. Connelly on how to get rid of the school district in Head Start.

"Wednesday, January 21 — in Human Relations class we

stood in a circle (all but me) and everyone was to shut their eyes and feel the person next to him with their hands.

"On this day we were taken in a bus hired by Head Start Leadership Development, to Kansas City to hear the lady speak on Welfare Rights, as outlined in our class on Friday, January 9.

"We were almost to Kansas City when Jack Connelly got up in the bus and announced that the woman who was to speak was ill, so we would be part of a demonstration to protest about a song being played over a radio station. We were not asked if we wanted to go.

"The radio station was housed in a tall building. Some one locked the elevators and closed off the stair wells so we could not get up to the station. In the lobby on the main floor were many people trying to get upstairs. One of their leaders rode with us in the bus to the Kansas City Star. We went in the Star office and demanded to see the editor for an interview. Everyone was singing "We Shall Overcome." I stood off to one side like I didn't belong to the group. The man who had originally invited us to hear the lady speak was there. Someone said, 'What are we going to do if we don't get what we want?'

"The crowd yelled, 'We will tear the place apart.'*

"Then a reporter came up and heard the complaint about the radio station.

"After leaving the newspaper office we went to the National Welfare Rights building. We were told how badly the Establishment treated the people on welfare, and how the National Welfare Rights Organization is becoming a power to fight the system.

"At this place there were many people who were using filthy language, and there was talk of a demonstration of some kind at the Kansas State capitol at Topeka. Jean Shields from our group said if they needed any help, our group would come to help.

---

*The crowd used the foulest profanity.

177

"January 22. On this day we went to the Creative Playthings warehouse. Here we saw some interesting toys for children, but I was somewhat alarmed when we were shown some boy and girl dolls with complete sexual parts, so that children could see the different sexual parts of their dolls. I understand there is an effort being made to secure these dolls for Head Start children. It seems to be a bit too much.

"We spent the entire morning at this warehouse. There were no classes in the afternoon.

"Friday, January 23. Human Relations in the morning. T-Group Therapy. This time we were to name names and tell the group what we didn't like about each other. I did not take part. However, I did observe. There was a great emotional binge, and then the class was dismissed.

"We had no more classes that day.

"Monday, January 26. Ed Skaggs told us that people from Kansas City would come on Wednesday to evaluate the sessions. We were given an outline in order to make a good impression.

"January 27, Tuesday. On this day we visited the Special Education Center at Kansas University. This visit was the most educational thing of the whole training course as far as I was concerned.

"There were no classes in the afternoon.

"January 28. We arrived at 9 a.m. for Human Relations class. No one showed up to teach us until 10:30 or later. The trainers were with the Kansas City people and the students were being ignored. After 10:30 we were taken up stairs to the staged program for the people from Kansas City.

"Then at 2 p.m. we all left for a long weekend.

"My transportation was paid by plane back to Idaho.

"As I got on the plane and thought about the whole training session, it seemed to me we were always being reminded how badly we were being treated by the system, and how we had to get rid of the system before we could get our fair share of the gross national product. This was the theme of the entire program.

"Monday, February 2. I returned from Idaho to Lawrence. Only four of us were there for classes out of the 24 students.

"My roommate and I worked in the Head Start center in the basement of Jolliffee Hall.

"The classroom was dirty, and smelly, a ghastly place for little children to be.

"This was the first time I had done any work there with the children.

"In the afternoon we had Human Relations class. Ed Skaggs told us how impressed the career people were with the training session they had seen the Wednesday before.

"We were given a problem to solve in class.

A PAC (Parent Action Committee) is dominated by a community representative, who is superintendent of schools, age 60. He has a theory regarding people-seen but not heard. A powerful person in the community, and parents are dropping out of meetings. The Head Start is in the school system. How to get Head Start out of the school system?

"Tuesday, February 3, My roommate and I worked in the Head Start center in the morning.

"I had an opportunity to observe what happens when Head Start centers are not operated under the public school system, but run by the parents as advocated by my instructors at the Head Start teacher training session.

"Besides being very dirty and in disorder, the room smelled of urine. It was also extremely noisy. In fact, it was bedlam. The children were allowed to run everywhere, yell and scream and do as they pleased. They were even allowed to hit the teacher without protest. There was very little effort that I could see to teach the children listening skills, hand-and-eye coordination, or anything else. Once the teacher did tell a story, but only those who wanted, listened. The others ran about the room, talking and yelling, and doing whatever they desired.

179

"There was a desperate shortage of materials. There were a few old stubs of crayons, and two old tin cans of dirty, dried up finger paint, just two colors. There were a few disreputable looking books in the room, and a few more in another room, some of which did not seem to me to be suitable. There was a record player but no piano.

"The children were mostly ages four to five years. The teacher told me it was impossible to hold the children's attention for a very long period, although I found the little group I had was desperately eager to learn and participate in supervised play or any of the other activities I suggested. Of the four little girls I worked with twice, I found not one could coordinate her body well enough to walk around the rim of the little sand pile without falling off, an easy feat for the average child.

"The toilets for the children were unfit for human use. One colored lady complained while I was there. She was told to go to the parents. No effort was made that I saw on the part of the staff to clean either the toilets or the room.

"I noticed the teacher was wearing the same outfit I had seen him in for a week, a dirty sweat shirt, etc. When we inquired why he didn't dress as a regular teacher should so the children could see how one should be well groomed and clean, he told us that it was more comfortable to dress the way he did, and anyway the children were in poverty and would never get out, and what difference did it make anyway, they didn't expect anything else.

"In the afternoon of February 4 we were ordered to go hear a speech by Saul Alinsky on the subject, The American Revolution, Act II.

"This was an assignment. One student asked, 'Are we required to go?' Jesse Esqivil said, 'Yes, this is an assignment. You are required to go.' At no time did we vote on whether or not we wanted to go.

"At 8 p.m. we heard Mr. Alinsky.

"He said, 'What we need is a new society . . . the Establish-
180

ment is the enemy. Once you leave the radical movement you are gone. You might get a job. Conflict is a way of life. Approaching people on a nice basis gets you nowhere. The middle class have the power . . . The Establishment doesn't listen with ears . . . only with its rears . . . You have to organize to break down the middle class. You have to go home and start to organize. Then you become the delegates to the conventions and conferences. You have to organize and get in the system. Do your stuff where you come from. Organize and get stock proxies in your middle class society. This is the only way to break it down.'

"February 4, Wednesday. We were told we would go to Kansas City to hear lectures all day. We were not told what kind of lectures we were going to hear. Sack lunches were prepared for us and we left by bus at 8 a.m. There was never at any time a vote on whether we wanted to go or not.

"All 24 of us were bussed to Kansas City to a medical building. Here a Dr. George Wiley,* executive director of the National Welfare Rights Organization spoke to us. He said the goal of the National Welfare Rights Organization was political power. We, as the poor, were only a step away from welfare. If we separate ourselves from welfare and don't identify we not only hurt them, but we hurt ourselves and cut ourselves off from the power. We need political power. Welfare needs more people, and people working for welfare is a good sign. Professional people like us should get out and organize and get groups to apply pressure on The System. The more you learn about the system and how it works, the better you can organize to fight the system.

" 'If you don't want to riot right in your own community,' Mr. Wiley said, 'fine, but you still have the power because you are part of a powerful organization. You can use the threat of a riot right in your own community, because there are riots going on elsewhere.'

---

*"Being a subversive is the best way to get power," Wiley said.

"Dr. Wiley also said, 'Benefits from the Welfare Rights Organization should only go to the active members. If you don't join with the Welfare Rights Organization, you don't get the benefits. You have to be active to receive.'

" 'Being a subversive is the best way to help get power,' he said.

"Our instructors nodded their heads and applauded Dr. Wiley. At noon time we were bussed to the University of Missouri to hear Dick Gregory.

"We were told we would have to pay 75¢ admission fee, but we never could find Ed Skaggs to get our tickets, so we all sat on the floor in the library as part of an overflow group and listened over a loud speaker. This was part of the program for Afro-American week. The program was entitled 'The Black Revolution.'

"Mr. Gregory's language was dirty in the extreme. Among the many things against American people he said was, 'Baby, we are going to burn America down.' He spoke against our flag and our country. It was so terrible I got sick to my stomach.

"We had three hours of his ugly, hate filled, nasty talk. In all my life I have never heard such profanity. He spoke against the American Legion, anything and everything patriotic. He said white people had better tell their children they had written them a bad check and it would bounce.

"Gregory's whole talk was hatred for America, but Ed Skaggs and Jack Connelly taped the speech because they thought it was so great.

"In the audience were both black and white children, who had been brought to hear the talk. As a teacher this was disturbing to me. I had to leave because I was sick and felt I would like to vomit.

"After the Gregory talk, we went to hear James Jackson. His jokes were dirty.

"Then at 8 p.m. we were shepherded by Jesse Esqivil to hear Father Groppi, the priest from Milwaukee. He said, 'No

182

government that does not provide for widows and children has a right to exist.' He also said, 'You folks should go home and and vote out the pigs.'

"Father Groppi also said, 'I believe strongly in civil disobedience . . . the church burns draft cards at mass with candles . . . the kids who loot and burn are heroes.' He told of the Milwaukee riots, and how the police were the villains. 'Bobby Seale,' he said, 'is a political prisoner. What they did to him was like Nazi Germany . . . we have to throw out racism and the Churches.' About this time the entire audience (except possibly my roommate and I and one or two others) stood up and applauded and cheered.

"February 5. We were told on this day to be ready the next day to go to Kansas City and hear more lectures.

"I said, 'Do I have to go?'

"I was told that I did.

"I said, 'I am not going. I will work in the Head Start class.'

"Mrs. Connelly said, 'I'll go tell Ed Skaggs.'

"I said, 'Go right ahead. I am not going to Kansas City to hear more lectures. I have heard all the anti-Americanism I can stand. I have had it. None of you have a plan of government as good or better than our Consitution.'

"Jesse Esqivil said, 'The Americans were worse than the Nazis at the Nurenburg trial.'

"Mrs. Connelly said, 'I will go tell Ed.'

"When she came back she said I was to see Mr. Skaggs. Before I went in to see Mr. Skaggs, Jesse Esqivil said if I didn't go to Kansas City to hear the lectures, I would have to read three chapters in our text book. We had scarcely opened this book in class or discussed any of the things that we did read because of going off on a tangent about other things. She also said I would have to turn in an essay on Monday on the three chapters. And go see Ed Skaggs.

"At 1 p.m. I saw Mr. Skaggs. I told him that all the time I had been at the training session, I had never heard a better plan of government than the one we already had, and our

183

Constitution.

"Mr. Skaggs said, 'Oh, you are just a classic example of being brainwashed by the Establishment. In the next two weeks you will change your mind . . . or else . . .' *

"I said, 'I love America. Even with all its faults, I still love America. I came here to learn about children. Children are my love.'

"Mr. Skaggs told me that Dick Gregory was a close friend of his, and that he and Dick Gregory had both grown up together in the slums of Chicago.

" *'There is revolution coming,'* he said, *'You are in power now. But we are going to be in power, and then you will do what we tell you.'* " †

Mrs. Barnes was fed up. She fled from Lawrence and came back home to her farm in Idaho.

Troubled and alarmed by what she had experienced, she sent an affidavit to Elliot Richardson, Secretary, the Department of Health, Education and Welfare, outlining the revolutionary designs of the program and demanding that HEW do something about it.

Richardson, instead of investigating the outrageous situation in the Headstart Program, turned upon Mrs. Barnes for alerting him to a fact he no doubt already knew, since it is apparent that HEW is participating in the subversion being taught in the leadership school.

One day, Mrs. Barnes was out in the hay field when she saw a big new white car approaching in a cloud of dust. The instinct that had been honed to a fine edge during the terror-filled days in Kansas told her that these were men from the government.

And so they were, two of them, from the Office of Eco-

---

*He added, "We are going to put you into intensive sensitivity training."

†Skaggs, with a big gold ring flashing in the light, struck the desk repeatedly to emphasize his words and his towering rage.

184

nomic Opportunity.

They upbraided her, harassed her and told her that she should "shut her mouth."

After a series of other threats, they left.

Sometime later she was contacted at her school by officials from HEW who asked to see her at her home.

Her principal told the callers that she could not see them alone, that she would have to have a witness on hand or the meeting would not take place.

They agreed, after much grumbling, and so her husband and a neighbor woman sat in on the incredible scene that followed.

She was abused, ridiculed and subjected to threats and intimidation.

They began to question her — How much money did she make? What was the net worth of the family? Who was responsible for the affidavit she sent to Washington?

Accused of being a racist, she was again told to "shut your mouth" and stop making trouble for the department, and was advised that she had not heard the end of the matter.

XI

CITIZENS OF THE WORLD

"We are all now, perforce, citizens of the world," Brock Chisholm once pontificated, "whether we are sufficiently mature to adequately carry that responsibility or not. In the face of this new status as world citizens, we must accept the uncomfortable fact that we are the kind of people who fight wars every 15 or 20 years. We always have, for as far back as we know anything about the race, and if we go on being the same kind of people, it is to be supposed that we will continue to fight each other."

Chisholm, the first head of the UN's World Health Organization, knew exactly how to solve the dilemma.

"The responsibility for charting the necessary changes in human behavior," he said, "rests clearly on the sciences working in that field — psychologists, psychiatrists, sociologists, economists and politicians must face this responsibility. It cannot be avoided."

And why are we in this fix? He has the answer for that, also.

"We have swallowed all manner of poisonous certainties fed us by our parents, our Sunday and day school teachers, our politicians, our priests, our newspapers, and others with a vested interest in controlling us. The reinterpretation and eventual eradication of the concept of right and wrong which has been the basis of child training, the substitution of intelligent and rational thinking for faith in the certainties of the old people, these are the belated objectives of practically all effective psychotherapy.

"The suggestion that we stop teaching children moralities and right and wrong and instead protect their original intellectual integrity has, of course, to be met with an outcry of heretic or iconoclast. We all recognize these reactions as those of the immature, the inferior and the guilty, which are not found in the mature, integrated personality. Freedom from

186

morality means freedom to observe, to think and behave sensibly, to the advantage of the person and the group, free from outmoded types of loyalties and the magic fears of our ancestors."

He then has a plan.

"If the race is to be freed from its crippling burden of good and evil, it must be psychiatrists who take the original responsibility. Should discounts be offered for treatments of whole families? Should attempts be made by professionals to induce governments to institute compulsory treatment for the neuroses as for other infectious diseases?"

By now you are saying, "This guy has got to be kidding."

Unfortunately, he was serious.

"Some help may be found in possible developments of shorter, more effective techniques of treatment," he continues, "such as shock, chemotherapy, hypno and narco analysis, psycho-drama and even surgery can all be used, and some of these methods may be employed by other than trained psychiatrists."

Such as your child's third grade teacher?

With Chisholm's words as a background, it is easy to understand why Dr. Mary Calderone hedges whenever the question of morality is raised in one of her frequent lecture appearances, especially since her husband, Frank, was Chisholm's administrative assistant.

Sexologists are very elusive people. They remind us of the little grunion fish who invade California beaches every summer. Thousands of people try to grab them by the gills, but just when they think they have them securely in their grasp, the squirmers are free and heading for the water.

SIECUS, for instance, claims it has no program. They say they write no materials and publish no books. The American Medical Association insists it is no propaganda organ for

187

SIECUS, yet, on the SIECUS letterhead, the AMA is prominently listed and the AMA promotes such books as "Love and the Facts of Life" by Evelyn Duvall, a SIECUS board member.

With Chisholm's immorality position clearly in mind, it should come as no surprise to learn that the parents who attended a PTA meeting on sex education at Stevens Elementary School, Fountain Hill, Pennsylvania, were slightly more than nonplussed to discover the following signs displayed on the blackboard.

"Legalize Abortion" — "More Deviation - Less Population" — "Fornication is Fun" — "Make Love and Not War" — "Plan Ahead - Use Contraceptives" — "Pray for the Success of Atheism" — "I'm for Sexual Freedom" and "Support Your Local Pornographer."

Of course, that "More Deviation - Less Population" should interest Dr. Mary Calderone. She is past president of Planned Parenthood and her number two interest, next to sex, is contolling the population.

In 1963, Elizabeth Force, director of Family Life Education for the American Social Health Association, ASHA, gave a talk in Rio de Janeiro. SIECUS lists ASHA under their name on their letterhead.

She deliberately linked sex education in the United States with a movement she said was "world wide in scope."

She then quoted UNESCO to prove her point.

Marilyn Angle is a little lady from Santa Monica, California, who was scared to death the first time she got up in public to oppose school sex instruction.

At the request of the California State Board of Education, Mrs. Angle served on a family life and sex instruction abstracting committee.

The project was paid for under Title III funds and the purpose was to find out exactly what was being taught in that area in the state's schools in 1968.

They were to report back to the Education Research Center of HEW.

The majority report from her five member committee must have startled the people in Washington, D.C.

The report reads as follows:

"Inasmuch as the state is assuming it is protecting the child from harm from a lack of sex knowledge, is the state willing to assume the liability if this instruction proves harmful? There is a distinct lack of spiritual and moral instruction in all the (15) guides studied. There is no recognition of Biblical prohibitions or moral or civil law.

"The guides do not define responsibility in relation to biological information. They list no definite qualifications for teachers, yet the course is designed to change or set attitudes and behavior.

"The guides are based on an evolutionary point of view. What qualifies a teacher to do an analysis of character and personality traits? What authority gives him that prerogative?

"What training has the teacher had to guide children in self analysis?

"The child should be considered as an individual, not as something to be standardized, plied with information as in computer programming and wound up like a spring with pre-set attitudes and behavior patterns."

They went on to say that if the public school system did not set its own house in order and stop subverting the nation's children, then the public school system should be *abolished.*

What Mrs. Angle and her fellow committee members had stumbled onto were the workings of the change agents.

The California State Department of Education, in mealymouthed fashion, recognized dangers inherent in sex instruction in 1969 when they passed a series of guidelines that condemned the philosophy held by SIECUS board members and, in effect, requested school districts not to use anything identifiable as coming from SIECUS.

However, since the guidelines were not binding on local districts, most administrators promptly ignored the state.

189

That made Senator John Schmitz, then a State Senator from Orange County, California, rather angry. An ex-Marine pilot, he has a very short fuse when it comes to the nonsense now parading under the disguise of education.

He promptly rammed a law through the state legislature that, among other things, did away with any mandatory requirement in regard to sex instruction. Parents had to be informed of the course and they had to request that their child be put into a class.

However, he submitted an additional bill, one year later, since he discovered that hundreds of districts were getting around his law by sneaking sex into everything from English to arithmetic.

One and one make three, perhaps?

Schmitz* is a very astute young man. He realizes that when the tax supported school system recognizes no higher authority than the state, then its potential powers are simply unlimited.

When such a system is part of a social order that has lost recognition of man as a spiritual being, then literally anything can, and does, happen.

There is no manipulation of children that is outside the power of the schools.

In the middle of the 19th Century, when states were just proceeding to operate their learning factories, proponents of the "public" schools claimed universal education would cure every social ill in one generation.

The schools, in the long run, would cost the public nothing, they said, since the educated children would become civilized, honest men. The cost for jails, poor farms and homes for the aged and indigent would disappear.

We need not comment on how successful they were in their

---

*Now a United States Congressman from Orange County, California.

crystal ball gazing, as a stroll down any city street will suffice to convince anyone that they were totally in error.

They have been wrong ever since, on most things.

If, in fact, the public schools now claim they can educate all children to be well balanced, adjusted adults — are they willing to take the blame for the rise of the current squalid Hippie generation? After all, the public schools have had most of the children in this country under their care during most of the children's waking hours.

The state of Washington recently adopted a sex education program that includes most of the names frowned upon by the California State Department of Education.

Such SIECUS stalwarts as Isadore Rubin, Lester Kirkendall, Mary Calderone, Evelyn Duvall and Johnson and Masters appear in their materials.

In other words, the state of Washington is pushing the very program deemed unsuitable for children by the state of California.

And, despite the condemnation by California's highest educational body, the state organization of teachers, CTA, was still pushing SIECUS in its official Journal six months later.

But SIECUS was really feeling the sting of the attack by the fall of 1969. They organized a front group called the National Committee for Responsible Family Life and Sex Education and took out a full page ad in the New York Times on October 15th.

"Where will our children learn about sex?" they thundered. "From the movies? TV? From the boy next door?"

Of course not, silly. From the professional sexologists.

"Let us join together to educate these children in what it means to be a man and woman in today's world," they pleaded.

They then gave an impassioned speech in defense of SIECUS and sex instruction without once talking about morality.

Well, what does it mean to be a man and woman? Maybe it means to be the kind of man and woman who signed the pro-SIECUS advertisement?

191

Let's see now, just what kind of men and women are they?

First there is Stringfellow Barr, former president of St. John's College, Maryland and the man who introduced the non-elective four year system wherein degree candidates were required to read the Great Books of the Western World. And no wonder – he helped to prepare them, since he was on the advisory board of the Great Books division of the Encyclopedia Britannica from 1944 to 1946.

From 1948 to 1959 he was president of the Foundation for World Government, which was funded for $1 million by Leftist, one-time vice chairman of Henry Wallace's presidential campaign, Mrs. Emmons McCormick Blaine.

She also contributed $2 million to the pro-Communist Compass, successor to Marshall Field's defunct PM newspaper, which a committee of Congress once called a Communist mouthpiece.

Barr has been a member of at least 28 Communist fronts, including the National Committee to defeat the Mundt Bill; the Emergency Civil Liberties Committee and the National Federation for Constitutional Liberties.

He has frequently whined about the House Committee on UnAmerican Activities and was a sponsor of SANE.

Dana Greeley also signed the ad. He has belonged to 14 Communist fronts at one time or another.

Harold Bosley, pastor of Christ Church, New York, signed the ad. He has belonged to the Leftist Fellowship of Reconciliation, and argued for amnesty for 11 convicted Reds in 1953. In 1961 he signed a petition to John Kennedy, asking for clemency for identified and jailed Communist Carl Braden.

Bosley, at last count, had either 17 or 18 Red front affiliations to his name – take your pick.

Rabbi Balfour Brickner signed the ad, but he must be a small fish. We could only find two Red front affiliations attached to his name.

But then there is the so-called Rev. Donald Harrington. He is pastor of New York City's Community Church where some

192

pretty far out and strangely swinging things went on for the past few years.

He has been an officer in the Socialist League for Industrial Democracy, of SANE and of the United World Federalists (UWF).

Harrington also supported appeals on behalf of convicted atomic spies Ethel and Julius Rosenberg, wanted H-bomb tests called off and signed a petition opposing the McCarran-Walter Immigration Act.

By this time, you may well be saying, "Why do you say such nasty things about these responsible people?"

The answer is simple – we didn't make the records for these SIECUS enthusiasts.

We are only reporting the facts, as Sergeant Friday would say.

How about Reinhold Neibuhr?

Yes, how about him? He signed the ad, for one thing, but he is also one of the champions in the Left-radical arsenal. Neibuhr is one of the better joiners, having belonged to, at last count, some 34 Communist front groups.

How did he find time to attend all those meetings?

He is a minister in the Evangelical synod of North America and has been a professor at the rabid radical Union Theological Seminary for the past 40 years and is presently professor emeritus.

He was a founder of the ADA – of which John Kennedy is reported to have observed, "I just don't understand that bunch," or something to that effect.

Neibuhr is also a resident member of the Council on Foreign Relations (CFR), frequently called the secret government of the United States.

Rabbi Roland Gittelson signed the ad. He belongs to 10 fronts and the Right Reverend Anson Stokes, who also signed, belongs or belonged to at least eight.

Author Mark Van Doren, who belonged to at least 10 fronts, signed the ad. He is best remembered for his son who was

193

once a TV luminary and who was caught up in a big quiz show cheating scandal some years ago.

A good example for the children.

Methodist Bishop John Lord, a member of 12 fronts, signed the ad, and also RALPH BUNCHE.

A whole book could be written about Bunche. He is also a member of 12 fronts and in 1954 he was awarded the Theodore Roosevelt Association medal. That so horrified Archibald Roosevelt, Teddie's son, that he fired off a lengthy letter of protest, listing Bunche's Communist ties.

It took 49 pages to complete the letter.

Bunche served with top Reds in organizing the National Negro Congress, cited as "Communist and subversive" by the government.

He was an official with the Institute of Pacific Relations, cited as the "major vehicle used by Communists to reorient American Far Eastern policies toward Communist objectives."

From 1935 to 1940, Bunche served as editorial advisor on a cited "Communist publication," *Science and Society.*

As soon as ALGER HISS was identified as a Communist agent by WHITTAKER CHAMBERS, Bunche jumped to his defense.

He should have.

Bunche served as personal secretary to Hiss during the infamous Dumbarton Oaks conference in 1944 when the framework for the United Nations was first set down.

In 1945 Bunche accompanied Hiss to the UN founding convention in San Francisco.

At a loyalty board hearing in Washington, two top ranking former members of the Communist Party — both of them negroes — swore they had known Bunche as a *Communist* when they were active in the Party. Shortly thereafter the handsome Manning Johnson died mysteriously in an auto crash. His co-testifier, Leonard Patterson, lived until 1968.

However, before his death Patterson toured the country, speaking against Communism and warning his fellow Ameri-

194

cans of their impending fate.

On May 31, 1954, the Communist Daily Worker came to the defense of Bunche and called the two negro witnesses "stool pigeons."

Well, a stool pigeon is a man who talks about something he knows!

Lest we bore the reader, we will simply name the rest of the ad signers and give the number of their Red front affiliations and a sketchy background.

Arthur Goldberg signed the ad. He was a member of at least four fronts.

Stuart Chase, member of countless extremist Left causes, signed.

Marriner Eccles, former chairman of the Federal Reserve Board and a Socialist economist, was a signer.

W.H. Ferry, former president of Ford Foundation's Fund for the Republic and a member of innumerable extremist Left groups also signed it.

Jerome Frank, professor of psychiatry at Johns Hopkins, a member of innumerable radical Left outfits, very pro-Red China and pro-North Vietnam, signed.

Brigadier General Hugh Hester, a member of six identified Red fronts, signed the ad.

Archibald MacLeish, a member of at least 38 fronts, probably the top front joiner in the nation, was a signatory.

Dr. Harold Urey, a member of 14 Red fronts, signed.

Robert C. Weaver, longtime government employee and a member of several Red fronts signed. When confronted with his Communist fronts by Congress, he claimed he had been "duped" into joining. Maybe he was "duped" into supporting SIECUS, too?

Lt. General James Gavin, an ardent 'recognize Red China' advocate, signed.

Senator Ernest Gruening has an 18 per cent conservative voting record in Congress and is one of the nation's leading Left radicals. He signed the ad.

Frederick Hovde, a member of the CFR, was a signatory, as was Floyd McKissick, leader of the revolutionary Congress on Racial Equality, CORE.

Robert McNamara, disastrous chairman of the board of the Ford Motor Company (the Edsel) and an even more disastrous Secretary of Defense is now the head of the World Bank. God help us!

He signed the pro-SIECUS ad.

Senator Lee Metcalf, with a lowly 7 per cent conservative voting record, and a rabid Left supporter, signed.

Hans Morgenthau, German-born member of the CFR and and ADA as well as the Atlantic Union (Leftist) said the Communist slaughter in Tibet was "part of Red China's traditional nationalist policies." He signed the ad.

Lewis Mumford, a member of at least 21 organizations cited subversive and/or Communist, signed. He received the Medal of Freedom from Lyndon in 1964.

Do you, dear reader, enjoy the thought that the nation's highest medal was given to one of the nation's leading Red front joiners?

General David Shoup, with a very anti-American Vietnam stand, has publicly stated we must coexist with Communism. He signed.

Bishop Donald Tippett of the Methodist Church, loves to have Communists speak in his churches and refuses to let anti-Communists appear. He is a good one to support sex instruction since he recently talked about the "advantages of adultery." He signed the ad.

Jerome Wiesner, a professor and former chairman of the Arms Control and Disarmament Committee, met secretly in Moscow with Soviet leaders, and reportedly presented plans to scrap our strategic defenses. The Communists were "quite reasonable," he said. Wiesner signed the ad.

In that mishmash of extremists we also find Dear Abby and Ann Landers, the two Freedman sisters, and, regrettably, one of my favorite actresses, Teresa Wright. I fell in love with her at the age of 13 or so.

Dr. Mary Calderone, who is defended by the above "responsible" people, claims she has a "covenant with youth."

However, we don't ever recall her stating exactly what group of young people she polled to find that out.

So long as she is surrounded by parasites of the educational establishment she is serene, confident and in her element. However, if a hostile question is thrown, she has been known to walk off the stage in a huff or to simply refuse to answer.

In Anaheim, and wherever there are those who embrace the SIECUS doctrine, the pro-sex educators dismiss all criticism with an airy wave of the hand and outraged cries of smear and John Birchism.

The sexologists appear to be driven by fear — driven by some powerful force — perhaps a deadly fear of their *Masters.*

Things went so well, for over a decade, that Mary Calderone could blithely declare in the pages of the California School Health Journal, in 1967, "Now the time for talking and planning is past."

The time had come, she said, for work, for pouring out a rash of sex education guidelines and materials and for serving as consultants on district family life committees.

And so it was done.

All across the land the obsessed harbingers of fleshly joys wandered, spreading their gospel according to Mary Calderone ahead of them, engulfing school after school.

One such place was Nashville, Tennessee, a place famed in storied legends of the Old South, a place steeped in the old fashioned gospel of the Bible Belt. One day the people of that city awoke to discover they were being beseiged and beguiled by the sexology missionaries.

Overnight they awoke, in the Spring of 1969, to find they

197

were on the verge of a complete SIECUS program, patterned after the Anaheim program.

Things might have been different if the residents had only known who was visiting their fair city.

Anaheim's Sally Williams was there, that's who!

In 1968 she came to Nashville as a paid consultant, and like a reverse tide, to Anaheim came Nashville's Margaret Kerr, a teacher and head of the sex education committee.

When their duplicity was finally exposed by the Nashville Banner, a general distribution daily and the state's largest newspaper, the sex promoters could only howl in frustration, "Misinformation, smear and smut have lowered our teacher's morale."

It probably did lower the morale of the sex promoters.

Their trial balloon had been punctured, nay, deflated by a gallant member of the Metro board named James Warren.

A critic of Metro government, which they have in Nashville, Warren became as equally incensed over sex education.

He did a little snooping around and discovered the board of education had sent two applications to the federal Office of Education in an attempt to secure funding for the Anaheim style program.

Those applications stand as a clear warning to parents over the United States.

The Nashville program was based on the premise that "the church and the home have not, and cannot, meet the needs of the times."

Therefore, moving forward from that false premise, the sexperts sought to design a program for the city that would later become a mandated program for all 152 districts in the state.

But Warren exposed their nasty little game, and in the process was supported by most of the citizens including the majority of his own Metro board.

There is no evidence that any other district asked the Nashville school board for any help in setting up sex instruction.

198

Yet, according to the applications sent to the Office of Education, the Nashville schools director clearly spelled out that this was a main reason why they wanted the money.

Subterfuge — thy name is sexologist.

Working clandestinely and in the dark, the documents were secretly prepared.

"The objective of the proposal," they read, "is to prepare a guide on family life and sex education in sufficient detail whereby a program of sex education would be available to all the schools of Tennessee."

The applications were signed by the school's director, John Harris, on June 21, 1968 and the application stated they wanted $34,195. Later they lowered the request to $20,416 in the second application.

Not only did the Nashville educators want to put in mandatory sex instruction from grades one through 12, but they wanted to include every school in the state.

SIECUS was listed on the application as a "new voluntary health agency," that would serve as the "number one agency to coordinate our efforts in planning and implementing a program in sex education and family life."

Right in step, the school board requested the federal government to provide additional funds of $1,324 to pay for three consultants.

The three consultants were to be Mary Calderone, Sally Williams, and Esther Schulz, all three SIECUS board members at the time.*

"The home and church have not, possibly cannot, meet the

---

*Dr. Melvin Anchell is a distinguished physician in Los Angeles and one time colleague of the famed Dr. Kinsey. Anchell recently wrote a reply to the President's Commission of Pornography. A portion of his reply reads, "The notion that school teachers presiding over coeducation sex classes can correctly develop a child's sexuality is not in accord with psychological findings. Nor, can the science of the mind defend the idea that

199

needs of the times as it related to sexuality as a part of one's being," the application stated.

That was typical sexologist talk.

Other sources of assistance were listed on the Nashville application. They were, "Child Study Association of America"; "The experience of Hinsdale, Illinois, which has a complete sex education program in its schools"; "Many of the major religious denominations who have developed or are working on sex education curricula," and "New developments in such cities as Anaheim; University City, Missouri; Washington, D.C. and the state of Illinois." There certainly were some new Anaheim developments — but none that would please the sexperts.

The 15 member advisory board in Nashville was given some interesting assignments, not the least of which was to "direct a public relations program in cooperation with the PTA."

Last of all, the guide was to be made available "for statewide use."

Nashville sexologists had clearly been caught with their pants down, or their dresses up, and they were rather embarrassed.

Among the "outstanding authorities" cited in the federal application was Dr. Mary Calderone, who recently stated, "Sex

---

providing children with knowledge of the sex, sex organs and reproduction will enable them to make a satisfactory sexual adjustment — much less prevent or cure maladjustments. Psychological disturbances do not result from a lack of such knowledge, either early or late in life. Paradoxically, detailed, public schooling in these matters is prone to produce the very abnormalities that proponents of current sex programs say they wish to prevent. Most contemporary youth are informed about the mechanics of mating and many have a medical understanding of gestation and how to deliver a baby. In my experience as a physician, with not an inconsiderable number of young patients, I find that the overly informed youth are the ones most likely to have sexual problems."

is not the prerogative of Christianity," and Isadore Rubin, editor of Sexology Magazine and an identified Communist.

Rubin was a logical choice. After all, he seems to have been in charge of book reviews for SIECUS, and in May 1969, reviewed a new sex education book ostensibly written by Sally Williams and Esther Schulz. Williams and Schulz, he said in glowing terms, "are two knowledgeable leaders in the field of sex education."

The text, he said, "adds a highly useful and practical guide for teachers and school administrators interested in developing a program of family life and sex education in their schools."

Rubin concludes, "It (book) includes sections on planning a program and preparing school personnel for it; the questions children ask; suggested content for primary grades through high school and effective teaching aids and techniques."

The book, he said, "is a highly important contribution to teachers."

And can you imagine – Sally Williams was ousted from her job and her sex education program was totally dumped just months after this glowing review came out.

Of course, around Anaheim there is some question as to whether Mrs. Williams really did much writing on the book. People who worked in the office with her insist she can't spell very well and her sentence structure leaves much to be desired, they say.

In addition to reviewing books for SIECUS, Rubin advises school systems and others on which sex education publications and books are most useful for their classes. Many of the SIECUS recommendations were high on the list for Nashville.

The Nashville story is not concluded, but it is typical of stories raging all over the United States.

Another typical city is Rochester, New York, but this time the sex program is in the Catholic schools.

Overnight the parents awoke to find the sexologists had taken over.

In the words of Mary Grooms, a columnist for a large

Rochester daily, "The material is so explicit that it is the envy of public educators. In fact, it is so anatomically and sexually explicit that some parents, especially fathers, are in a state of shock after seeing the syllabus."

But not Bishop Fulton Sheen, apparently, for that was his parish and he didn't seem to care a fig leaf about the whole controversy.

However, maybe his precipitous retirement from that post in 1969 might have been due to the uproar.

Mrs. Grooms added, "While the Catholic curriculum makes a few attempts at mentioning God here and there, a major objective is, according to the syllabus, to 'develop an understanding of and an objective attitude toward sex.' "

She added that if pictures were used to illustrate the things talked about they would be clearly pornographic.

Mrs. Grooms states, "In primitive societies, which modern sexologists hold up as examples for us to emulate, sex is free, frequent and open. It does not seem to occur to the sexologists that there may be a connection between a group's sexual habits and its accomplishments as a people."

Imagine that — a newspaper reporter had to tell the Catholic clergy and hierarchy about God and morals and all the rest of it.

In all the city, only one priest dared to raise his voice, and raise it he did — long, loud, and clear.

That priest was handsome and youthful Father John Nacca, pastor of St. Francis Assisi Church.

Out of over 100 church schools in the diocese, his was the only one where the diocesan sex program was forbidden.

"The program is dangerous," he thundered from his pulpit, "and has an appalling and needlessly detailed syllabus."

"Most parents," he added, "are not aware of the injustice perpretrated upon their children in some schools where they have to sit through nauseating, clinical, needlessly detailed information on sex organs, masturbation and prostitution.

"Those few who advocate this program think that by giving

these children all this tempting information they will not sin. That is as silly as saying that if you put an alcoholic in a liquor store he will cure himself of drinking."

"The sex education promoters," he said, "are crackpots — educators who experiment with immortal souls.

And yet again, in Rahway, a suburb of New York City, William Berko, 29 year old school board member blames SIE-CUS for what he calls the "amoral context" in which sex education is taught.

"Take a look at this stuff," he says, displaying a fistful of SIECUS pamphlets. That, he says, is why he took his children out of the public schools.

"In my church," he says, "children go to catechism to learn a fixed set of moral rules — to learn their faith, including the Church teaching on sex. I don't want them taught in school that this is just a matter of opinion."

He is referring to the kind of SIECUS materials that read, ". . . attempting to indoctrinate young people with a set of rigid rules and ready made formulas is doomed to failure in a period of transition and change."

In Poway, California, students were subjected to Sensitivity Training in class, involving intimate caresses by students. One boy goes into a trance and strikes his head against the wall. He is taken to the school nurse who says he is stunned because he did not have any breakfast. An hour later the boy is found ill in a restroom and is taken home by another student.

That boy had met the change agents.

A parent in Michigan writes us that she is amazed at the indifference exhibited by school administrators who are confronted with evidence that their schools are being used as spawning grounds for subversion and immorality.

She has encountered the change agents.

A college professor talks to students at Garden Grove High

School and tells them to forget their parents, church and community and to turn on with drugs.

He is a change agent.

In San Marino, California an assistant school superintendent militantly pushes sex education, despite the clearcut evidence that the public is mostly against it. Sex education goes down to defeat, but he promptly   renews the struggle.

He is a change agent.

In an Anaheim classroom, psychedelic lights and music are employed to help the students "psych out."

The district public relations man, Henry Davis, insists the setting is "a regular part of today's student mood."

Those students have met the change agents.

Paul Dearth, family life teacher in the Anaheim district receives the teacher-of-the-year award at Anaheim High School during a public schools week ceremony.

He had been under severe attack by parents in the district for his sex education classroom techniques.

The person presenting the award stated Dearth had been voted best teacher by his fellow faculty members.

Teachers in the school phone your author, angry and upset. They had not been consulted and they did not know anyone who had been consulted.

It turns out the award was bestowed by five teachers who had been chosen to make the award decision by the school principal.

The change agents were at work.

In Long Beach City College, five males, three professors and two students, address a group of 80 girls on the subject of "What Men Think of Women."

It turns into an orgiastic display of foul obscenities, suggestive and lewd remarks and an unbelievable psychological rape of the girls.

The dirtier the language becomes, the more the girls seem to enjoy it. The more viciously depraved the attacks upon them, the more the girls enjoy it. The more suggestive and

204

filthy the words, the louder the girls laugh.

Most of those girls are studying to be elementary school teachers.

Those girls have met the change agents.

That is how it operates — in your state, your town, your schools. And that is how it reaches down into your home and your family.

Take Jane Smith.

That's not her real name, but she lives in Orange County, California, and has lived there all her life.

A beautiful girl with great blue eyes and long blond hair, just two years ago Jane enrolled at a local state school at the age of 19. She entered with a low A grade point average and maintained a comparable grade point while at the school for several months.

Jane enrolled in a course under Professor Jones (not his real name) and soon found herself involved with the hippie group on campus led by Jones.

Her parents, particularly her father, were disturbed by the association, but forced themselves to accept it. They attributed their daughter's interest in the bizarre group as late maturation and excessive social concern fostered by her prior educational experiences.

Further, there was the attitude on the part of Jane that her teachers could do no wrong.

When her mother learned that Jones had arranged for a meeting place for his "handholding in candle light" disciples in a deserted attic of an old home on the campus, she was more than normally upset. She was beginning to question the professor's motives.

Soon after, Jane's parents — still trying to play along — entertained Jones and his strange friends in their home. The professor's wife informed Mrs. Smith that the age for alcoholic consumption should be lowered to 18.

During the evening, the hippie band went through their ritual of holding hands in a circle in candle light and engaging in intimate self criticism.

The ceremony was described by a witness, who was familiar with the technique, as "Sensitivity Training in the classic sense."

The Smiths, however, were still completely in the dark as to the nature of such training and the significance of the evening's activities escaped them.

About that time, Jane dropped out of school, and was convinced by a young male family friend that she should stop seeing the hippie clan.

This was a major undertaking. Jane's attachment to Jones and his band was almost a pathological addiction, due to the fact that her ego had been overstimulated by being rapidly advanced to leadership — in spite of (or perhaps because of) her naivete and immaturity.

Soon thereafter she informed her mother that she was pregnant — but that it was all right because God had instructed her to have, "for the love of God, a love experience with the group."

She said she was to have a child "for God."

Jane proceeded to broadcast her coming motherhood all over the neighborhood, to friends and relatives, and even made long distance calls to inform relatives out of the state.

She withdrew her savings and purchased a basinette in preparation for the arrival of her "God-child" which she claimed was sired "by the group."

It soon developed that she was not pregnant after all — and then her story changed.

Now she insisted she must take immediate steps to become pregnant, "but it is perfectly all right because I am responding to God's command in my heart."

Her parents just did not understand, she said, particularly her father. The fact that she MUST have sexual relations AGAIN with the GROUP was not sinful for her, she insisted,

206

because she had been divinely instructed. The child would not be conceived for love of man but for love of God.

No amount of Biblical confrontation would shake Jane loose from her insistent point of view.

The Smiths finally realized they were confronted with something far more menacing and frightening than teenage rebellion. At their insistance, Jane was admitted to the psychiatric ward at a Catholic hospital.

Jane was patronizing toward her parents at this point. She firmly insisted, however, that she was not sick. She insisted she must conform to God's wishes and commands that she become pregnant by the group.

Her insistence that the group take part was inconsequential, she said, only understood by herself, God and "this group who make love for the love of God."

At the hospital Jane was classed a paranoid and admitted for treatment but was shortly thereafter sent to UCLA Medical Center.

The Smiths became alarmed when they discovered the psychiatric ward at the center was filled with Hippie types, just like the ones she left behind at the college. They were also surprised, and horrified, to discover that several of her fellow patients were school teachers.

At the time of her hospitalization, Jane had received all A grades in two summer courses at a private college, a school unrelated to the one where the Sensitivity Training had been carried out.

Jane, the UCLA psychiatrist said, was schizophrenic. There followed a searing three months of non-commital prognosis by the attending physicians and little progress could be seen in Jane's condition.

Jane insisted on returning home – to the terror of the parents, who realized no progress had been made. However, the physician aided them with an important recommendation – that the parents place Jane under absolute discipline.

They were to tell her that any false move would promptly

207

put her back into the hospital. One wonders what would have been the case if the discipline had been applied BEFORE she started attending college.

There was some question as to whether or not she had unwittingly been exposed to LSD, but she steadfastly denied it. However, her symptoms were considered in keeping with LSD induced psychosis.

In any case, one who knows her well insists that Jane's condition stems exclusively from her association with Jones and the group.

The girl's immaturity could not withstand the amorality conveyed by the group. It was too contrary to her religious training and the moral standards of the home.

She therefore turned inward in order to escape from herself and her own conscience.

At the same time Jane was undergoing her experience at the college, Jones was leading a revolutionary, anarchistic group on the campus in addition to his hippie gang.

Jones is still teaching people at that state run institution. *Could he be teaching your daughter tomorrow?*

XII

BLASPHEMY

In 1948 a group of strange people met in crumbling Prodebrady Castle in Czechoslovakia. There, in those dank and dark rooms were representatives of UNESCO, and from the United States came some of the most radical people in the nation.

Out of that meeting came a series of booklets called "Towards a World Understanding," the blueprint for a totalitarian world of the very near future when America will be no more and this nation will be ruled by regional governors of a one world slave state.

Volume six of that series was called "The Influence of Home and Community on Children Under 13 Years of Age."

That booklet contains a series of research questions which indicate an intention to stimulate ultimate classroom expeditions into the field of sex education.

Some of the research questions in the booklet are: (1) Are there devices for limiting the size of the family? (2) What are the typical feelings of pregnant women? (3) What is the child told about where babies come from?

If those questions seem familiar, it is because those are the questions now being raised in thousands of once peaceful classrooms in this country nearly 20 years after the publication of the UNESCO series.

The series – and especially two of the booklets – is an attempt to arrive at a familial pattern that would be acceptable in a one world administration.

In one of the pamphlets, the blatant statement is made that all patriotism and feelings of nationalism must be destroyed.

Since the publication of those significant booklets, thousands of change agents in the mass media help lay down the proper line – as a working newsman, I can say that without fear of contradiction.

The UNESCO plan has indeed had its insidious effect upon the children of this land.

Parents are ridiculed by teachers, clergymen, psychologists and other so-called professionals, and are constantly told they are not capable of rearing their own children.

Children are encouraged on every hand to disrespect the views of their parents, and those parents are repeatedly referred to as outdated old relics of a dead era, outworn and unfit to cope with today's modern world.

And over the land wander the Child Seducers, garnering respect on every hand while seducing the young who are put into their care.

America now has the highest taxes and the lowest prestige, the highest crime and the lowest morality. It has the highest national debt and the lowest value of the dollar in its history. It has more restrictive laws and less personal freedom for its citizens. It has more crime and riots and less protection for the taxpayer who has to pick up the tab for all the destruction. There is less national pride and more dissension, and the price the American people have paid has been their liberty, their honor and over 275,000 American young men slaughtered or maimed in a hopeless, purposefully no-win war.

That is the state of the nation just 20 years after UNESCO began to make its awesome and frightening impact upon our educational, religious and political life.

Where does the nation go to from here?

Does the age for rape go down to eight years old? Will all our high schools have sex rooms, as was suggested by sexologists in Sweden? What next? Babylon? Rome? Carthage? Sodom and Gomorrah?

Or are we travelling the road of Socialist Germany, when Hitler used human sex farms for selective breeding and when some could finally get their libidinal satisfaction only through the sex acts of the Marquis de Sade?

Unspeakable sexual atrocities committed in Roman bacchanalia were not unlike the sadism flaunted daily in America be-for millions on television and in the movies.

Is this Rome — when America's leaders dine at sumptuous banquets while our cities burn?

Is this Rome — when America's political leaders vie for the favor of prostitutes and sexual degenerates?

Or could it be Nazi Germany?

Does it really matter?

They both stood for the same thing.

General William Dean, as he was released from his North Korean captors was told they would soon see him in America, because they would "corrupt one generation of your young people and then you will have nothing left with which to defend yourselves."

In a midwest school the children see a film that shows the alleged seven places on a woman's body where she can be sexually stimulated.

The children are nine years old.

In countless schools, mere infants learn all the latest contraceptive techniques, while being told they should not discuss it with their parents.

In other classes, children model sex organs out of clay and explicit descriptions of the sexual organs and their use is given to millions of little children in hundreds of schools.

In Anaheim, at one point, the obscene words for sexual acts and sexual anatomy were written on the blackboard, while the teacher drummed the clinical terms for the same things into the children's minds.

In Anaheim, the long respected concept of learning readiness was tossed out the window by the sexologists — so all 13 year olds learned the same thing and all 15 year olds and so forth. Never mind such important things as physical, mental and emotional maturity.

And the children all over this land see a film that tells them, "Once again, man is made in the image of MAN."

In the book, "He and She," the author tells the children, "A boy ought to be able to see a girl naked and enjoy her nakedness without any sense of guilt."

Religion, he adds, must have MAN as its center.

Children are led into a situational interpretation of every act and are made to be aware of "sexuality" in everything they do.

In the words of Governor Ronald Reagan, "They have taken prayer and Bible reading out of our schools and have substituted sex education."

"When a nation loses its morals," he said, "that nation is doomed to vanish from the face of the earth."

Promoters of sex classes have repeatedly been accused of using lies, deceit and duplicity to put in their programs.

Therefore, they cry, do away with all moral rules and let each man decide for himself — that is the new Freedom.

Stepping over the debris and the wreckage they have caused, the New Moralists tell us that we need thirteen years of their brand of family life education to solve the very problems they were instrumental in causing.

The narrator in the popular sex instruction film, "A Basis For Morality," makes it very clear: " . . . the old sanctions have gone . . . we don't believe the Bible . . . parents are out of date . . . the idea that woman should remain a virgin until marriage is nonsense."

An outfit that has heatedly promoted sex in the schools is the National Congress of Parents and Teachers.

Unfortunately, millions of good people belong to local units of the PTA without knowing anything about the national organization. It was captured by the Left, generations ago and is today the most powerful and effective single school voice for extremist views on educational innovations.

Take as an example, the May 1969 issue of the California PTA magazine. That issue carried two lead articles, "The Case for Sex Education" and "Can Parents and Teenagers Negotiate."

In both articles are found the hallmark of the PTA mother — the excessive permissiveness that has plunged both school and society into near chaos in our time.

All family difficulties should be "negotiated," they write. The author then proceeds to give a long list of differences young people have with their parents, including the conditions of school instruction, the quality of teachers, the lack of freedom to choose their own teachers, class groupings, the school schedule, the kind and amount of homework, the grading system and examinations.

How any responsible adult can expect a child of ten years old to dictate in these areas — or even to negotiate the matter — is simply incomprehensible.

But it is not incomprehensible to the PTA, because they are in the business of sowing confusion in homes.

All through the article there is the thinly disguised threat that parents better listen with bated breath to every word of wisdom emanating from the mouths of their offspring — or else.

Anyone who has been in the company of teenagers these days will discover that they are no smarter than any other group of teenagers in history. They might know a few more obscenities and use them more freely and they might know what it's like to fry their brains with drugs, but that doesn't make them any smarter.

They are, in a word, the "lippiest" generation in the history of the whole human race. Their mouths are never still, and much of what they say is pure prattle and errant nonsense.

But we are supposed to listen to them.

For instance, the PTA magazine quotes a Dr. Charles Keller, "Young people not only want to be listened to but they are worth listening to."

That pretty well tells you at what age level Dr. Keller was frozen.

And as always, in the article absolutely no blame for any of the youth problems is attached to the school. It is the parent, the parent and yet again the parent.

Never mind that the schools have the students for most of their waking hours.

Never mind that the schools have done more to shape the thinking of today's youth than any parents ever could.

Never mind that rebellion, subversion and downright treason are aided and abetted by thousands of teachers, with the help of their eager young charges.

However, the PTA writer makes us all feel better when he adds, as an afterthought, "Of course, few young persons expect to win every time."

Mighty decent of them.

In the article on sex instruction, the national president of the PTA sounds off as if she had made up her mind in the crib that sex instruction was the greatest thing since Eve knew her apples, and nothing under God's blue sky is going to change it.

True, her opening paragraph does give a limp left handed pinky to the parents who don't think sex instruction should be compulsory, but that is only to sucker in the gullible fish.

She succeeds admirably.

Sound education is basic to children, she says, and the PTA has long advocated it. Of course, she never gets around to telling us exactly what she means by "sound."

The sex instruction afficionados never do.

She makes the flat claim that early sex instruction in schools will not cause children to experiment. That, of course, is simply a dodge since there has NEVER been any scientific study to determine that.

She also claims that the sex classes will probably have the result of damping the young person's ardor.

A likely story. Apparently she knows nothing about the sexual fires that burn in the young man's breast.

"Have you outgrown Saviours, Gods and supernaturalism," reads a humanist advertisement in the New Republic. "Then welcome to the American Humanist Association . . . the humanist relies only upon himself and is concerned only with this life."

But how are they selling this bunko scheme to the schools?

In the classes, where else. Alice McCalls' book, "Toward Adulthood," for instance, contains a so-called morality chart drawn up by a self confessed humanist, and past president of the American Humanist Association, Dr. Lester Kirkendall.

That book is found in thousands of classrooms, including the eleventh grade at Rock Island (Illinois) High School.

Dr. Bryan Green of England narrated a film strip that is used all over the nation, in thousands of schools. "I am a convinced Humanist and not ashamed of it," he says in the film.

Is that why 50 per cent of all teenage marriages in America now take place with a pregnant bride? If the girl is under 18, she has an 80 per cent chance of being pregnant as she marches down the aisle.

All of history pulses with warning cries in America today. In "The Cause," a book published in 1953, the Spanish government set down its findings as to one of the root causes for the Communist takeover of Spain in the early 1930's.

On page 399 of that book we read, "The moral corruption and disintegration of family and social ties reigning throughout the Marxist zones during the civil war were a direct consequence of Communism, which acted as guide and beneficiary of the Popular Front, the latter simply serving it as a mask."

The book continues, "The sexual immorality existing at the very battle fronts caused alarm even among the Red military chiefs in view of the havoc certain disease caused among the military men."

Marriages were celebrated with ease, the book reports, and divorces were even easier to obtain. Some women had a dozen husbands at one time and collected military insurance from all of them when they were killed.

"Blasphemies and public scandals were every day events amongst the population and abortions were legalized and facilitated at public health centers," they added.

"Degradation among children," they write, "had been initiated by Communism during the pre-revolutionary period by means of an organization known as the Red Pioneers. Under the pretence of attending to their welfare, a multitude of children were separated from their families and sent to Soviet Russia, without hope of ever returning, in order to serve a soulless scheme of proselytism and propaganda."

When America's young people turn from the sin purging of Christianity they can only turn to a Charles Manson — a Messiah, Satan, Jesus, God — for without the sacrifice of Christ there is no remission of sin. That awful burden of sin and guilt will manifest itself more and more in sex, drugs and heinous slaughter as the pathetic and frightening zombies graduate with ever increasing tempo from our public schools and colleges.

And the whole hideous fabric will be held tenuously together by modern black magic, mysticism, sorcery, occultism and devil worship.

"It is better to have had a positive Wasserman test (for Syphillis) than never to have loved at all," said Dr. Eugene Schoenfeld, a medical doctor on the staff at UC, Berkeley.

A nice upstanding fellow, hey?

Schoenfeld was recently pictured in a newspaper, astride his motorcycle, wearing a dirty sweatshirt, long girlish hair waving in the breeze, while caressing his bare and dirty feet. He hardly looked very loveable — Wasserman positive or no.

Still, maybe Chris Lundberg, writing in the Santa Ana Register, summed it all up very well.

"Economically," he said, "state controlled education is inefficient; morally, it is an obscenity."

Elizabeth Patterson, who wrote "The God of the Machine," had a clear insight into the situation also.

"The most vindictive resentment may be expected from

216

the padagogic (teaching) profession for any suggestions that they should be dislodged from their dictatorial positions; it will be expressed mainly in epithets — such as reactionary," she wrote.

In Anaheim, Sam Campbell had a word to say about the battle put up by the professional sexologists who tried to take over the Anaheim High School District.

"We are happy to report," he said, "that the professional sexologists believe they have lost the battle to appropriate the bodies of the little children of America. In the past 10 days, by direct mail, they fired a salvo of disgusting material designed to incite the lusts of adults in order to gain community support for their sickening program for children. They also expected revolutionary benefits from articles in prestigious magazines. They successfully enlisted the support of the California Medical Association, over the heated protests of many physicians. One notable banking institution mailed out to its credit card holders a free magazine in which we counted ten specific obscenities. So, the professional sexologists put on a mighty, skillfully organized orchestration of both glamorized and crude pornography. But all this disgusting material succeeded in doing was to incite a groundswell of indignation."

Opponents of the sex classes have ample reason for making angry charges, since in case after case the true motives of the promoters have been revealed, only to have the sexologists streak off in another direction, beginning the charade all over again.

That is the case in the state of Illinois.

Unlike many states, Illinois has gone all out to aid school districts from the state level in the promotion, planning and implementation of the sex courses.

In a catalog issued by the state superintendent, Ray Page, the entire panoply of SIECUS names and materials is displayed for the benefit of local districts.

The superintendent ends his foreword to the catalog with, "It is hoped this publication will assist school districts in enhancing the total health education program and in turn the present and future health of the youth of Illinois."

Of course, that's the one state in the union that has abolished all sex laws pertaining to adults.

Readers of the catalog, familiar with the furor raised across the land by SIECUS people and materials, will be pardoned if they raise some questions about the superintendent's honesty or, perhaps, his good sense.

Some of the films included are: "Animal and Human Beginnings"; "Human Growth"; "A Basis for Sex Morality"(possibly the most blasphemous film ever made anywhere); "Sex, a Moral Dilemma"; "How Babies Are Made" (which shows chickens, dogs and people copulating); "About Girls and About Boys" and "A Young Man's Dilemma."

When the "Dilemma" film was shown in Simi Valley to 800 parents, the largest gathering of parents in the history of the town, it caused the angriest outburst ever witnessed by your author. There were practically no parents in that huge audience who were not clearly outraged.

One beautiful young matron stood and almost screamed at the sex instruction coordinator (or whatever name he went under), "How can you show that film to our children?"

She didn't get much of an answer, since the film had been shown to the children for two years without the parents knowing about it.

The Illinois catalog is replete with SIECUS board members, supporters and contributors.

Among them are Evelyn Duvall; Johnson and Masters*; Marion Lerrigo; Helen Southard; Lester Kirkendall; Judson

---

*Johnson and Masters — whose claim to fame is several hundred unmarried copulating couples they filmed in their laboratory in living color.

218

Landis; Helen Manley; Deryck Calderwood and Isadore Rubin.

Most of them are listed in the catalog more than once and Mary Calderone has six works listed.

SIECUS is prominently listed as a resource, along with the National Board of the YWCA; the NEA; the National Congress of the PTA; the Journal of School Health (which is loaded with SIECUS references); the SIECUS newsletter; the American School Health Association and Time-Life, which produce the notorious "How Babies Are Made" book.

In other words, if there is such a thing as a SIECUS program, Illinois has it, and yet local districts throughout the state consistently insist they have nothing but nice little local programs.

Actually, as thousands of parents have discovered, there is no such thing as a LOCAL program.

At the same time, the Roman Catholic Cana Conference Sex Education Pilot Project, 720 Rush Street, Chicago, put out their own syllabus called "Becoming a Person."

This is a wide ranging discussion of every single aspect of sex relations, yet nowhere is there a single mention of God, sin, religion, conscience or anything even remotely resembling a Christian standard.

In fact, the Catholic syllabus admits on its front cover that most of the material came from the American School Health Association. A Christian who weighs the Cana syllabus against Catholic beliefs can find no justification for much of the materials. It is a Godless approach to a sensitive subject.

An Evanston, Illinois mother is more intelligent than all the sexologists put together. She recently wrote the Chicago Tribune as follows.

"Joey, come up to the house this minute," shouts Mrs. Schmidt, across two back yards. "You'll be late again for your sex education class."

"Aw ma, not that stuff again," yells Joey. "The bases are loaded and I'm up to bat."

The Evanston mother continues, "Puberty does not an adolescent make, nor padded bra a teenager. Fortunately, most parents have a built in sense of timing. We recognize that Susie is ready for toilet training six months earlier than Nancy. Amy, we know, wants to read in kindergarten, while Jessie doesn't want to start until the first grade."

But who mentions sex education readiness?" she wonders. "The result is that one child can receive satisfying answers to urgent questions, while another is pulled into a classroom situation that bears no relationship to his immediate needs."

"It's still too early to predict a future of promiscuity or of frigidity, *but it's not too early to recognize nightmares, tension, confusion and fear,*" she said.

The Evanston mother then gave an example. Eddie's father, she says, was relieved when the school offered a course in sex education. It would take care of the problem of communication.

A year later, his face blazing, Eddie turned to his father and blurted, "You can't make me go to that class again. You can darn well talk to me yourself."

Even the most fumbling attempts on the part of the father meant more to Eddie than all the polished classrooms in the world. For, despite his attitude of indifference, what Eddie really wanted to know were his father's attitudes.

True, in some homes communication is nearly impossible — and we should be concerned about how to reach those parents — but we must never lose sight of the average child and his parents.

A typical example is found in a booklet published by the Group for the Advancement of Psychiatry, 1790 Broadway, New York, under the title, "Factors Used to Increase the Susceptibility of Individuals to Forceful Indoctrination: Observations and Experiments."

Published in 1956, the booklet with the jaw cracking title

220

describes a series of mind bending experiments by such people as Dr. Jack Vernon, Princeton; Dr. Melton Meltzer, former chief medical officer, Alcatraz; Dr. David Tyler, University of Puerto Rico; Dr. Edwin Weinstein, Walter Reed Army Institute, Washington, D.C.; Dr. Joseph Brozek, University of Minnesota and Dr. Harold Wolf, Cornell Medical College.

Without implying any ulterior motives to the participants of the seminar, it was nonetheless a terrifying glimpse into the ghastly world that must have seemed far away in 1956 but that is close upon us in 1970.

Dr. Vernon discussed the results of an experiment he conducted in the social and physical isolation of human beings.

He said he had conducted tests in "Sensory Shut Down or Sensory Deprivation," in which there was planned, drastic reduction in the amount and variability of the normal sensory stimuli.

Volunteers were put into a confinement cell, a floating room which was both sound and light proof, and which had 16 walls, between each of which was a five inch air space. It was, in effect, a floating room within a larger room.

The period of confinement within the dark and silent room was 48 hours, though the confinee could ask to be let out at any time. Only one did so during the course of the experiment.

Results of the confinement showed progressive mental deterioration, which slowly repaired itself after release, taking at least two days for the person to get back to normal.

The subjects, when released, engaged in much idle chatter, but one side effect was particularly interesting.

Vernon described this as "an inordinate number of four letter words" used by the guinea pigs.

In a book called "A Book About Me," published by Science Research Associates, an affiliate of the IBM Corporation, the zenith of change agentry is reached.

The author is Edith Jay, a professor at Wayne State University and formerly the head of guidance for the Santa Barbara, California schools.

A recent poll of medical students at Wayne State showed that nearly half were chronic users of drugs, according to a national press service.

Also, on the campus is the Merrill-Palmer Institute, a change agent factory, and three SIECUS board members live in the city of Detroit, where the school is located.

Mrs. Jay's book gives a series of pictures on each page under such captions as "Places I Have Been," "Rooms in Our House," "People Who Live in Our House," "Things We Have in Our House," "Where I Sleep," "Where I Eat and Play," "Things I Do at Home," "My Clothes," "Things I Play With at Home," "Things I Do By Myself," "People I See, Know and Like," "Foods I Like to Eat," "Things I Am Afraid Of," "What I Like About Sunday" and "My Playmates."

The child is then told to cross out all the pictures that do not apply to himself.

From that completed book the teacher has a perfect cross-profile of the child, his family, his home, his playmates and so forth — an incredible way of invading the privacy of children and their parents.

This kind of mind manipulating has been proceeding apace, especially since the end of World War II.

Of course, these experiments on the human psyche are important in relation to space travel — but the potential use under a ruthless dictatorship becomes readily apparent.

If anyone knows anything about the subject of the mind manipulators it is Dr. McDermon, the California Assistant Superintendent of Schools.

In Anaheim, McDermon talked about Secular Humanism and the problems in our public schools on February 6, 1970.

Having spent his entire adult life in the field of education, he did his master's degree work under the Grand Guru of the change agents, Dr. Carl Rogers.

McDermon, a dark and intense man, described his search for the plotters as "like trying to describe a spider's web when you are only looking at one thread, or trying to describe a crazy quilt pattern if you only see a square foot of it."

The campus turmoil and the anti-social manifestations of the young, today, he said, are due to something that has been going on inside. In other words, the public sees only the symptoms without ever finding out the nature of the disease.

The whole educational structure in America, he said, is infected with a religion known as Secular Humanism, another word for atheism. Though the California state education code specifically (under section 13136) calls for the teaching of morality and the fact that teacher candidates must submit evidence of good moral character, this is being ignored, today.

Why?

He had the answer for that too. Within the education profession, he said, the termites of the Humanists have been busily gnawing away. He gave several instances of how the ethical and moral codes in the public schools have been changing in the past decade or so.

Under section 13202, he said, the teacher can be suspended and his license to teach must be revoked for immoral and unprofessional conduct. Now the standards committee, made up of professional educators, is asking that the law be changed to read that the teacher "could be reinstated after a short suspension."

The problem is, he said, that while the law identified certain crimes based on immoral acts, the definition of immoral has changed . . . Therefore, it is almost impossible, according to some educators, to commit any act that is immoral — except to salute the flag, say a prayer or defend your country, perhaps.

And if you follow the reasons for these changes far enough, he said, you will find yourself standing on the steps of the United States Supreme Court.

Secular Humanism, he said, has penetrated deep into all the teacher training institutions of this land and the students are being brainwashed into believing that there is no such thing as a base act.

For instance, assault with intent to commit rape means automatic mandatory revocation of a credential in California. However, the credential is seldom lifted for that crime. Why? Because the educators have been putting pressure on the state office to make that particularly loathesome crime a minor issue and the teacher, they say, should be reinstated after a brief suspension.

Indecent exposure has always meant permanent and mandatory suspension, followed by revocation of the credential. Now the standards committee wants that changed to "subject to reinstatement."

Loitering in a public toilet for purposes of performing an immoral act used to mean mandatory revocation of the credential. The standards committee want to change that to read "temporary suspension."

As long ago as in the time of George Washington, said McDermon, the intellectual confrontation was gathering force between Secular Humanism and those who believe man is responsible to God.

Time Magazine summed up the definition of Humanism in it's August 9, 1962 issue as "those who believe in ethical non-religion, where the Supreme Being is man and prayer is a telephone conversation with no one at the other end."

The title of the article was: "The Supreme Being — Man."

"This confrontation in our schools must be recognized for what it is," said McDermon, "if we are to save the public schools."

And then the web spins ever tighter, as McDermon pointed out, that John Dewey disciple Scott Nearing was the architect of the United Nations Charter.

Except, he said, that the UN did not go quite as far as Nearing wanted them to go. He not only wanted one totalitarian, Socialist world, but he also wanted the United States to be the food basket for the rest of the world.

The UN thought that wasn't a very wise strategy at that point in their Marxist planning.

Nearing said that we must have a revolutionary class in America that will devote the next 40 years to bringing about a Marxist revolt in the schools and in the nation. Of course, that was years ago and Nearing's plans have basically come true.

"We must train these revolutionaries like we train doctors and dentists," said Nearing, "and in order to do this we must get into the colleges and the schools."

They have done just that.

Teachers, he said, must reach for power, and then he drew a perfect blueprint for converting our tax supported school system into Marxist institutions.

"Now," said McDermon, "because of the work of people like Carl Rogers, the professional educators have come to look upon schools as mental health centers or psychiatric clinics."

"I helped to write the book on sociodrama and psychodrama when I worked under Rogers," said McDermon, "so I know whereof I speak. I know the dangers."

Teachers, he said, are to become "facilitators," with the students being taken apart and reassembled like a jigsaw puzzle, made into "something better," in the words of Rogers.

And in the words of McDermon, "Better for what and for whom?"

"Now," said McDermon, "we are faced in Californis with the new Social Sciences Framework, and that scares me to death."

"It is nothing more nor less than self analysis bordering on psychoanalysis," he said, "where religion is omitted and humanism is glorified."

"Civics, history, geography and economics are to be drastically diminished," he added, "and the entire framework filled with the kind of self analysis advocated by Carl Rogers — the 'Who Am I and Who Are They' kind of thing."

The whole purpose of the new framework is to get the student to question his values, his history and his religion," said McDermon, "while he is led to believe he evolved from a lower animal."

The goals of the new framework, he said, coincide exactly with the goals set forth in 1933 by the Secular Humanists in their Humanist Manifesto.

And what is the result of all this? McDermon summed it up.

"Our heritage and our system of government doesn't have to be apologized for," he said, "provided it is given a voice in America's classrooms. But it is not given a voice, and it is being systematically shut off in most colleges and most high schools and most elementary schools. It has now reached the point where our children publicly refuse to salute the flag and pledge allegiance to this nation."

Of course McDermon is right — but he will probably be branded a right-wing extremist by the kooky, far-out radicals who have captured America's so-called public schools.

They are not public — not any longer.

They are the private hunting preserve of vicious and de-praved behaviorists who want to commit psychic rape upon your children.

XIII

TWENTY YEARS EARLY

Fred McPeake of Knoxville, Tennessee, found out that trying to deal with school people is like trying to find a sane man in an insane asylum.

McPeake's frustrating experience began when he became head of a local organization called Volunteers for Education.

Since sex education had reared its jaded head in the district, McPeake decided the best way to fight the problem would be to get hold of a district sex film, "Love and the Facts of Life," produced by Cathedral Films, and show it around to various service clubs and churches.

He therefore mailed out a letter on August 15, 1969, to program chairmen for various groups offering to show the film free of charge. He added that if the program time was limited he would show shorter films called "Having A Baby," "Who Am I?" and "Contraceptive Methods," all films owned by the district.

McPeake added, at the end of the letter – albeit with tongue firmly planted in cheek, "This public service assists interested parents and adults in having a meaningful opportunity to view this educational material. We do not discuss the merits of the material. We only provide the service for parents and adults to view the material."

That letter came about because the district superintendent refused to let the parents in town see the sex films. Apparently, what was good enough to show the kids was too much for their parents.

The request for the showing came from the Powell Republican Club and Mrs. Doyle, the superintendent, said she had a previous commitment (a usual dodge) and besides, the district policy didn't allow for such screenings.

Dr. Doyle said the board policy allowed showing to "interested groups but not to political groups."

227

So, McPeake got the films for his own organization, figuring he would make a little hay while the sun shone and while the controversy was still raging.

He made arrangements to have a showing in the W.N.O.X. auditorium.

Needless to say, the local educational establishment became very upset about this unexpected move.

An overflow crowd packed the W.N.O.X. auditorium to see the films, shown under the auspices of McPeake's group and the Concerned Church Leaders of Knox County.

Over 1,000 people were turned away from the auditorium which seats 1,200.

After the film the people were asked to submit their opinions of the film. Of the 839 who responded, 677 said they were opposed to showing the film in the public schools and only 132 were in favor, with 30 undecided.

The ministers all said they were against the films because they taught sex facts with no morality.

At that point McPeake wrote a letter to superintendent Doyle, requesting permission to appear at the next regular board meeting to "Make a request relative to the sex education program in the Knox County Schools."

He added his presentation would be brief and it would only take five minutes.

McPeake is a man of few words.

That really painted Mrs. Doyle into a corner. She fired back a letter on district stationery, "I have talked with Mr. Bailey, chairman of our board, concerning your request to appear before the board at the regular meeting. It is our opinion that there is no need at this time to have any further discussions.

"I am having a meeting with a group of Concerned Church Leaders at 9 a.m., September 30, 1969 at 400 W. Hill Avenue and I suggest you be free to attend this meeting. I would further suggest you submit your recommendations to me in writing; I, in turn, will present them to the staff for consideration as we continue to examine health and science curriculum materials."

On October 2, since McPeake couldn't get through to the board, he had a letter printed as an editorial in the Knoxville News Sentinel, stating that the board had denied permission for parents to see the films and that several groups of parents had requested such showing in vain. Therefore, he was calling upon the superintendent and the board to schedule showings in school auditoriums to give parents a meaningful opportunity to view the material.

"How can parents intelligently grant or withhold permission (for their children to take the sex classes) if they have not personally viewed the material in these films?" he asked.

About that time, Mrs. Doyle apparently threatened legal action to prevent McPeake's group from showing "Love and the Facts of Life" to interested adults.

McPeake fired off another letter to Mrs. Doyle.

"Replying to your expressed possibility of bringing legal action to prevent our showing of the filmstrip "Love and the Facts of Life" to interested parents, permit me to suggest that this could raise some interesting points of academic freedom and constitutional rights of free speech. If your considered judgement calls for legal procedure, may I suggest that you proceed."

By now, Mrs. Doyle was getting upset. She accused McPeake of being a lowdown Bircher, in the presence of an audience in the city. It didn't take long for her words to get back to McPeake.

He was smart enough to see that this was nothing but the usual dirty smear campaign opening up on him. He promptly sent her a letter.

"It has come to my attention that you have stated, in the presence of an audience, that I am a member of the John Birch Society and hold office in the organization. This is totally incorrect. I am not a member, never have been, nor do I plan to join. May I suggest you refrain from making such

229

statements not based on fact?"

The controversy still continues. However, we would be willing to put a little money on McPeake as the eventual winner in that little fracas.

In Orange County, where Anaheim is located, the Santa Ana Register carried a letter from a James Bass of Buena Park, located on the edge of the Anaheim Union High School District.

"So-called public schools are not public at all," he wrote. "They are government-run, tax-supported institutions of rebellion and pornography. Children do not learn radicalism and perversion at home. How many parents do you think would teach it to their children, much less let strangers do it?

"I don't mean just sexual perversion, but the perverting of all things causing the erosion of solid foundations for judging right and wrong, truth and error. Everything has to be some shade of grey in these tax-supported atheistic shrines of corruption."

Strong words? Not at all.

In Hawaii, the students in a particular junior high school were given an assignment during school hours. The assignment was to attend a movie then playing in the city of Honolulu.

What was the film?

The picture is one called "Paint Your Wagon" — which concerns itself with violence, hatred, fornication, drunken debauchery and what have you. It is hardly fit fare for those same children whose sex lives the school people are so concerned about.

In Orange County, the students were told to go and see the revolutionary, radical, hate America film called "Easy Rider." That film glorifies drugs and the drop-out, freak-out life and is possibly responsible for influencing more young people to turn into human vegetables than any other product of the mass media — while at the same time getting its stars

230

and producers very rich at your children's expense. The same assignment was made at Western High School in Torrance, California. Children not attending had their grades lowered.

Dorothy Binyon, a fighting mad mother from the State of Washington laid it right on the line in a speech delivered to the state school board on December 1, 1969.

"We submit one major task of education is to help students become mature citizens who are capable of distinguishing legitimate social values from intellectual garbage. We would expect educated men and women to understand some of the consequences of their actions. I wish to thank a vast number of educators in this state, and all who have had a part in bringing sex education and all other experimental programs to light. You have unwittingly been instrumental in awakening parents and citizens as to how far you have gone in prostituting the faith and trust placed in you by parents for many generations. For the first time in many years parents are taking a good hard look at just what is being taught in our public schools. You have revealed yourselves not to be the intelligent, moral, trustworthy people you profess to be. You have revealed yourselves to be the root cause of all the moral decay we see all around us. And no longer will you be able to ask, 'Don't you trust us?'

"My answer — and the answer of all those I represent — is, 'NO, we no longer trust you.' "

But the public schools are not alone in propagating the moral decadence, decay and death that Mrs. Binyon talks about.

The following are some excerpts from a text book, "Here and Now," used in Our Lady of Mercy High School, Middlebelt, Farmington, Michigan.

On page 139 the students read an account of a 19 year old cashier (male) as he views three girls who enter his store.

"She was a chunky kid, with a good tan and a sweet broad soft-looking can, with those two crescents of white just under it, where the sun never seems to hit . . . Still, with that prim look, she lifts a folded dollar bill out of the hollow at the cen-

231

ter of her nubbled pink top . . . I thought that was so cute. I crease the bill, tenderly, as you may imagine, it having just come from between the two smoothest scoops of vanilla I had ever known were there . . . "

What was the reaction of the so-called nun, Sister Camille, the principal, when she was asked why such a book was permitted in the 10th grade?

"These are the 1970's," she said, "and this sort of thing is all around the girls – you cannot hide it from them."

I suggest, rather, that Sister Camille was getting her own kicks in having her pink cheeked female charges read such rot.

That same story describes the 19 year old boy's opinion of adult women as follows:

"She's one of those cash-register-watchers, a witch about the age of fifty with rouge on her cheekbones and no eyebrows . . . and I know it made her day to trip me up . . . if she'd been born at the right time they'd have burned her at the stake."

He then described his view of the adult shoppers as follows:

"The sheep, pushing their carts down the aisle – the girls were walking against the traffic – were pretty hilarious. You could see them, when Queenie's white shoulders dawned on them, kind of jerk, or hop, or hiccup, but their eyes snapped back to their own baskets and on they pushed.

" 'Is it done?' asks the responsible married man, finding his voice. I forgot to say, he thinks he is going to be manager (of the store) some day, maybe in 1990, when it's called the Great Alexandrov and Petrooshki Tea Company or something."

The boy checker then ridicules the morals of society and the attitude of the older man who is the manager.

"Lengel's pretty dreary, teaches Sunday School and the rest. He comes over and says, 'Girls, this isn't the beach.' He repeated it. His repeating this struck me as funny, as if it had just occurred to him and he had been thinking all these years that the A&P was a great big sand dune and he was the head lifeguard. He concentrates on giving the girls that sad Sunday-

232

school-superintendent stare."

It would seem that Sister Camille believes that rather than raising the pig sty morals of the 1970's, she, as an educator, should bring the morals of her charges down to the pig sty level.

But if it is already that bad in Catholic parochial schools — imagine what is going on in the secular, atheistic public schools. If they do these things in the green tree, what will they do in the dry?

Well, for one thing, they are setting up SCHOOLS WITH-OUT FAILURE.

Dr. William Glasser, who did his psychiatric work among the dropouts from society at the Ventura School for (wayward) Girls, came to the conclusion that delinquency is caused because people fail in life, especially in school.

Starting with that premise, the logical conclusion is that no one will henceforth be flunked and everybody will be well adjusted.

The system is already in effect throughout the state of California, although they don't really call them Schools Without Failure. Buena Park, for instance, in so-called Conservative Orange County, installed the system in two elementary schools in February, 1970. More than 1,000 students will study under a system where they get no grades and no report cards.

One of the outfits pushing for this notion is called Educator Training Center, ETC, and the programming support is coming from two supposedly religious schools, Pepperdine College and Mount St. Mary's College.

Pepperdine College has managed to give the impression of being a conservative Christian school, while at the same time sponsoring some of the most ludicrous academic brainstorms in the country.

They are currently in the process of turning over their main Los Angeles site to urban studies, while building a magnificent new seaside campus just north of Malibu, California.

Pepperdine and Mt. St. Mary's conduct classes for ETC

233

and give credit – also without the teachers failing, we should add.

The MA course consists of nine units taken at ETC; three in the philosophy of Schools Without Failure; three in implementation and three in methodology of research.

Six more units are taken at random at either Pepperdine or St. Mary's and 15 units are given for a project phase in planning projects to institute changes in the schools.

Glasser states we are no longer in a "Survival Society," since the young people know they no longer have to worry about making a living as the government will take care of them. Therefore, he calls the present youthful generation the "Identity Society," when young people have nothing but leisure to search for their own identity.

One wonders, who will feed the "identity society" when those in the "survival society" are dead and no longer able to pay taxes?

It doesn't take much effort to discover the identity of most of today's aimless and wandering young people. An editor on the coast summed it up neatly when he said he spent about a year talking to young people, probing their minds and trying to discover what they are really like.

He discovered they were, in his words, "NOTHING. Their minds were *totally blank.*"

Glasser doesn't think that's so bad, especially since he is getting rich off the Reality Therapy he coined.

In fact, his office is in the same building that houses Dr. Melvin Anchell, who has little use for the Glasser notions.

Glasser's first little office has expanded, until he now runs a veritable factory.

Facts and knowledge are unimportant, says Glasser.

Well, that's all right, since they aren't getting much of either one in school these days, anyway.

"Memorization," he complains, "makes children feel there is a right memorized answer to every question."

Good grief. We can't even have right answers now, can we?

"If I were principal," he says, "I would say that no child could ever be evaluated in terms of grades or a rating on anything that was pure memory."

Schools should teach children that thinking is fun, he adds.

Well, if you haven't memorized anything, and you have no facts and no knowledge, what is there to think about?

There is no right or wrong from a moral point of view, Glasser insists, and the only criterion for behavior is in terms of social reality and the person's own desires.

That, of course, is a perfect definition of Humanism, which is what we have been saying through all the pages of this book.

Glasser admits you need a diploma to get a job, but he suggests that we can get around that simply by giving one (a diploma) to everybody, ipso facto.

His therapy is carried on in the classroom through the circle discussion method, where the children sit around and do three things – social problem solving, open ended discussion and conducting educational diagnostic meetings.

"All problems relative to the class as a group and to any individual in the class are eligible for discussion," he states, and in open ended meetings the children are encouraged to say anything that comes to mind. The teacher makes no value judgements of any kind and the children voice their opinions and conclusions in any way they see fit.

According to Glasser, "No one can fail in a class meeting, because one person's opinion is just as good as another's – there is no right or wrong. The only wrong, perhaps, is not to participate at all."

His approach is described as "psychotherapy," which leads to the inevitable conclusion that the children are to be treated as patients in a psycho ward – which the schools have apparently become anyway.

The children are encouraged constantly to solve all the needs of man without ever acknowledging the ultimate authority of God.

235

The Anaheim sex education experiment shocked and rocked the whole nation, from coast to coast, with over 2,000 Anaheim curriculum guides going out to over 2,000 school districts and Sally Williams flying hither and yon.

Still, despite Anaheim's infamy, the first sex instruction program to really get off the ground — or maybe off the bed — was the one that began in Chico, California in 1947.

Chico was an unlikely place for a sex instruction experiment, but then, the conspirators are unlikely people.

There was little to commend the place, in 1947. It was just a quiet little country town, with a small teacher's college and a beautiful little river and park meandering through the suburbs.

It was notable only for being the site of an Errol Flynn movie called "The Adventures of Robin Hood."

Maybe that was why they decided to put in sex instruction there. After all, Flynn was quite a roue in his day, we are told.

Through the auspices of the State Department of Education, the program that is now infamously known throughout the nation was launched on a sea of infamy, deceit, duplicity, stealth and chicanery.

One of the men who helped to launch it was Ralph Eckert, then a second rate employee of the department, but now a very big man on the campus of Long Beach State College — the campus famed for its nudie shows in class.

Eckert did not stage the nudie shows — but controversy seems to follow him wherever he goes.

Many of the plotting meetings were held at the old Chico Oaks Hotel, long since demolished but at that time a town landmark and a point of civic pride.

One of the participants was said to have remarked, "We are going to put sex education into every school district in the country before we are through."

Apparently the purpose was to use Chico as a base, a pilot

236

program, from which to spread to other towns and cities and states.

During one of the meetings, a slip of paper was distributed to the participants. On the paper it stated that school principals should sneak the program into their schools before the public caught on.

It is interesting that Dr. Lester Kirkendall should echo those same words about 20 years later at Anaheim's Charter House hotel.

The participants were also told to put only the best students into the classes, since they would be less likely to blab to their parents about what was being taught.

Last, they were told to enlist the aid of liberal clergymen, teachers, the local PTA councils (Kirkendall said the same thing) and liberal businessmen.

The Chico story is revealed in the 1947 hearings of the California Legislature Report of the Joint Fact Finding Committee on UnAmerican Activities. Members of the committee were Jack Tenny and Nelson Dilworth, as well as Hugh Burns and Frank Gordon, all Senators.

At the same time, the Grand Jury launched an investigation on request of the local American Legion post on the grounds that the materials used in the sex classes were obscene and subversive.

But the notes of both investigations fail to tell the story of the terror that went on in the town, directed at those who were trying to expose the machinations of the mind benders.

People were threatened with bodily harm — and some of the principals in the case are still, after twenty years, too terrified to talk about it.

Representing the Assembly on the joint committee were Randall Dickey, Fred Kraft, Harold Sawallisch and John Thompson.

A quote from the first page of the report will give you some idea of the modus operandi of the sex education promoters.

237

"During February in 1947," reads the report, "a delegation of World War II veterans called on the chairman of the committee and presented a petition, signed by nearly one hundred Chico residents, requesting an investigation of certain books used in connection with a course of study at Chico High School. The veterans committee presented the chairman with copies of the books in question."

A brief examination of the books disclosed the material to be "totally unfit" for school children of any age.

An investigator was sent to Chico and he found out enough so that a full investigation was launched on February 26, 1947.

After the committee had completed its hearings they concluded, "It is the considered opinion of the committee that the books in question strike at the sanctity of marriage, the family, and religion."

They then proceeded to discuss material from one of the books, "Your Marriage," by Norman Hines.

The following is a quote from page 11 of that textbook:

"You know the broad outline of that story: How religion and the state have forced maladjusted people to live together in Holy Wedlock, so that they might warp their own children in the same manner as they have been warped. You know, also, the hard, stiff fight that evolved against Holy DEAD-LOCK has required. You know where the state has all too often tried by law to make married people dating machines by conspiring against the people."

The committee then summarized various books.

According to the committee, the main text was "Marriage and Family Relations," by Robert Foster, published by Mc-Millan Company.

Other books were "Family Living in Our Schools," by Beulah Coon and Bess Koontz; "Coming of Age," by Esther Jones; "Psychology and Human Living" by M.E. Bennett; "Your Marriage," by Norman Hines and "Marriage for Moderns," by Henry Bowman.

Is the Bess Koontz referred to above the same Elizabeth

238

Koontz who is Nixon's appointee to the Women's Division of Labor, a SIECUS board member and former wheel in the NEA?

Anyhow, the committee then quoted from "Marriage and Family Relations," page 134, as follows, "Let us first recognize sex and human reproduction as physical functions belonging to the field of biology. As such, they have no ethical or social importance. They have no more moral quality than eating, breathing or sleeping."

That, of course, is precisely why the sex education foes are fighting these programs.

The kind of lying deceit that went on in Chico is evident in the fact that when the school district administrators were caught with their pants down, they promptly cut an entire chapter out of the book, "Marriage and Family Relationships" with razor blades.

That was the infamous chapter nine.

It was the chapter that started all the fuss when the course, called "Basic Twelve," was first started.

The committee then interviewed J. Partridge of Oroville, who was the county superintendent of schools at the time. He equivocated and tried to dodge every question that was asked by the committee members.

Over and over he squealed that the committee was "reading things out of context," the oldest dodge in the world.

An-obscenity-is-an-obscenity-is-an-obscenity, as the saying goes.

But he did give one particularly damning piece of evidence, in that he admitted the course was put into the school district without formal approval from the state board of education. He said he did so because he felt the "silence on the part of the board in regard to course material indicated they were in favor of it."

The committee then interviews Frederick Martin, the superintendent of the Chico City Schools.

Martin squirmed and hedged at every opportunity. He was a most unwilling witness, but on page 330 he is quoted as giving some rather interesting testimony concerning Dr. Eckert, who, by the way, is still defending SIECUS and sex instruction at every opportunity.

Question: *And that supplementary reading – why was that deletion made?*

Answer: *Because when we decided to not use this book or any of the other books that were sent to us as sample copies – and may I say these lists were sent by the state department of education (not the state board) – the man who heads up the work, Dr. Ralph Eckert, and the outline coming from them, we felt duty bound they should outline and study pretty carefully the list.*

Question: *Which you did?*

Answer: *We did, and when we found out all that this included, we found it did not belong in the high school, and we recommended that it not even be recommended to the board of education, and it was not . . .*

Question: *He (Dr. Ralph Eckert) came here and talked, didn't he?*

Answer: *Not publicly. He was here and worked with several people in the school department where this work was given.*

Question: *Didn't he make a press release?*

Answer: *That's right.*

Question: *Put an article in your paper approving this course?*

Answer: *That's right.*

That testimony, which linked Eckert to this early sex instruction effort, is particularly important in light of the committee's final summary on the last page of their report. Remember, Eckert APPROVED the course and the books, according to the superintendent.

"The committee finds that certain sex books, included in a proposed course in the Chico High School, follow or parallel the Communist Party line for the destruction of the moral fiber of American youth. Disrespect for parents, religion and law is subtly woven throughout the context of the books in question. The committee finds the books to be pornographic

in content, immoral in many respects and totally unfit for high school students."

And now, Ralph Eckert — the same Eckert — is the head of the sociology department at Long Beach State College. Readers can see by this what brand of ideology is best rewarded by your tax supported school system.

Do you enjoy getting kicked in the teeth?

After their findings — and that of the Grand Jury — were made public on a rainy winter evening, the sexologists packed up their sex books in haste and fled town. But their last words, as they left the Oaks Hotel, were, "We will be back one day, and when we return this program will be in every school in the United States because NOBODY can stop us."

And their predictions have come true, just twenty years from that abortive attempt.

Evelyn Burns became the scourge of the school board in general and Paul Cook in particular, in the early days of 1968.

Always she was in the fray, reading, visiting classes, viewing films, attending speeches by Cook and Williams, and looking up the backgrounds of the people who were promoting the sex programs.

Cook and Williams were on the horns of a dilemma. They were dying to get to the public in order to tell their story, but everywhere they went, Mrs. Burns was sure to follow.

Cook, avoiding Mrs. Burns for once, stood before a group of Republicans in the city of Yorba Linda one night giving his usual canned pitch that was beginning to sound like a broken record.

In the course of his speech he denied any explicit instructions were given in ways to perform the sex act, however it just so happened that Mrs. Eleanor Howe was in the audience with a textbook for the seventh grade, written by Sally Williams and Esther Schulz.

241

She couldn't get any of the brave men in the audience to read from the textbook. The chairman of the meeting finally volunteered to do so, if Cook continued to refuse the chore, all the while turning various shades of red.

"I won't talk to you, Mrs. Howe," Cook sputtered, but he finally gave in and did read the passage aloud.

It was later described by one of the audience members as a "blueprint for sexual intercourse."

XIV

DO YOUR OWN THING

Do-your-own-thing is the essence of the John Dewey philosophy. It is the philosophy of the tax supported schools in America today, and it is the philosophy of a whole generation of young people who have chosen to digress to the animal level in all their undertakings.

Around 1921 John Dewey went to Russia and played a very significant role in setting up the educational system under Communism.

Just ten years later, by 1931, the entire country was in total disarray and chaos. The young roved the streets of the cities in terror gangs, wolf packs of depraved and degenerate sub-humans.

Illegitimacy rates skyrocketed, and venereal disease became a raging inferno from Moscow to Stalingrad.

The entire nation was in danger of immediate and total collapse.

By 1931, the ruling hierarchy in Russia realized that no civilization, not even Communism, could survive the do-your-own-thing philosophy of John Dewey.

Stalin cracked down with a vengeance.

Thousands of young people were rounded up and shipped off to Siberia, where they died in the mines. Others were given the choice of conforming to society or being shot. It was a time of onerous suppression of dissent and do-your-own-thingism.

The Russian educational system was transformed overnight into a Spartan, Puritanical system, with no frills and with absolute, rigid discipline.

Communists learned their lesson — *and they also learned how best to destroy a civilized nation like the United States.* They have been working on that premise ever since.

And one of the programs best calculated to serve as the

243

vehicle for the change agents is the so-called family life and sex instruction programs now being installed in schools all across this land.

Dewey was smart enough to realize that the schools would be the vehicle to bring about the Fascist tyranny he dreamed about and worked to bring into being.

"They (the schools)," he said, "take an active part in determining the social order of the future . . . according as the teachers align themselves with the newer forces making for social control of economic forces."

And in Orange County, California, the state assistant superintendent of education, Collier McDermon, warned an audience in January, 1970, "If you think the Dewey philosophy of so-called progressive education is dead in our schools, you are deluding yourself."

"Teachers," said Dr. Jesse Newlon, a Dewey disciple, "can not be neutral in the struggle to bring on Socialism."

"Marxism will applaud the teachers who prepare in an organized way to build a better society," said the Marxist magazine Science and Society in the Fall of 1936.

And the NEA knows how to avoid the critics.

"There is need for professional solidarity in protesting all forms of censorship, suppression and attacks on education."

That's the kind of resistance the NEA was talking about in 1951 when they were beginning to realize that there were still a few people left in the United States who would stand up to the UNESCO dictated school policies of the NEA.

In Bulletin number 35 of the NEA entitled, "In Defense of Democracy," an NEA official, Harold Benjamin, declared that all those who opposed some wild and way out innovations of the Pasadena, California superintendent of schools were "the enemy."

The new policy found within the educational Grand Design has, as its basic philosophical tenet, the religion of Humanism and the teachers become directors (clinicians) of the student's behavioral pattern and attitudes instead of disseminators of knowledge.

Now, if the people of this country want their children to go to a psychiatric clinic every day, they would undoubtedly make the necessary arrangements. They most certainly have not authorized the transforming of their schools into mental hospitals.

The method through which the Grand Design is to bring about the desired attitude changes is found in Group Therapy.

That particular form of change agentry owes its impetus to Pavlovian psychology and the death of Freudian psycho-analysis, and the men responsible for sealing the Freudian coffin are Dr. J.L. Moreno and the late Kurt Lewin.

Moreno stated at one point, " . . . I was trying to plant the seeds of a creative revolution. The only way to get rid of the God syndrome is to act it out in class (role playing)."

Moreno told students at Long Beach State College on Feb-ruary 28, 1967 that Communism had failed in the Soviet Union because the Russians tried to organize it from the top down.

In America, he said, it must be organized differently — from the ground up and small groups (communes).

The Grand Design is defined beautifully in the Hawaii Master Plan for Education on pages 127 and 128.

"By 1985," they write chillingly, "it should be more ac-curate to term a teacher a learning clinician, for the schools will be clinics, whose purpose is to provide individualized edu-cational and psychological services to the student (patient)."

Under the Grand Design there are two parallels in develop-ment.

First, there is the formation of the Consortium Curriculum Project Council. Their goal will be to develop a superior sys-tem of planning and implementing (brainwashing) curriculum that will promote use of all personnel in decision making.

Second, the Grand Design includes the formation of a Citizen's Advisory Committee, which has as its stated goal discovering the processes through which the tax supported

245

schools might be improved.

All that may sound relatively innocuous, except that both the Consortium and the Citizen's group use the same three textbooks: "Taxonomy of Educational Objectives"; "The Teacher, Empiricist" and "Developing Attitudes Towards Learning."

Taxonomy, for those who have not heard the word before, has been described as a "revolutionary plan devised by the behavioral scientists consisting of a classification of educational objectives in behavioral form."

"What we are classifying is the INTENDED BEHAVIOR OF STUDENTS (emphasis ours)", writes the author of "Taxonomy of Educational Objectives."

He adds, "We are to classify the way in which individuals are to act, think, and feel as the result of participating in some particular unit of instruction."

Under that system, the teacher completes the following steps.

First, he would translate objectives into descriptions of behavior which will be displayed if objectives are achieved.

Second, he would identify the situations in which the presence or absence of behavior can be observed and recorded.

Third, establish an acceptable level of performance.

Fourth, apply criterian measures or administer a test.

Fifth, analyze the results and recycle the process in terms of the earlier stated objectives.

Of course, wherever the behaviorists are, the publishers of books and school materials are not far behind.

The 3M Company has, in fact, evolved an entire program for the schools that wraps up the behaviorist objectives into one neat little package.

Known as the conceptual framework, the 3M program covers kindergarten through the twelfth grades.

Health education is the generalized framework concept at the top level and within are found three key concepts called, "Growing and Developing," "Interacting" and "Decision

Making."

These are the unifying threads of the curriculum and are closely interrelated with the ten underlying concepts, the general student behavior and, finally, the behavioral objective.

Again, in the 3M program, as in Taxonomy, the student is to think, feel and act the way the teacher wishes.

In the 3M program, all behavioral changes and attitudes are based on the premise that man has three dimensions: physical, mental and social. Note the lack of any SPIRITUAL dimension. Thus the program is deliberately designed to produce good little humanists who will not believe in God.

The basic classroom technique of Taxonomy and of the 3M program is Sensitivity Training.

For instance, the teacher guide for the family life concept of the 3M program reads: "The field of health education is such that it cuts across and into practically every personal, familial and social human relationship in the life of each student."

That, of course, verifies exactly what the critics of these programs have been saying right along.

Since the teachers now get the students after their character has already been formed at home, it is somewhat more difficult for teachers to brainwash them. Therefore, the behaviorists now want to get their hands on them before the children reach the age of three.

Ideally, they would want to take the children away from their mothers as soon as they are born — except that it poses too many problems of logistics.

The tots will be brainwashed in mini-schools, pre-school classes and in the pre-primary continuum.

Mini-schools, the latest rave idea among the educators, are envisioned as places where the children will receive carefully designed experiences beginning at the age of three. Each mini-school would enroll around six or eight students, so they can receive maximum attention from the clinician in charge.

The pre-primary continuum is a new creation designed to

247

replace the contemporary kindergarten. This presupposes the child will spend one to four years preparing to perform well in the primary continuum.

In that regard, the pre-primary continuum will stress such extracurricular activity as educational travel; school camping; informal dramatics (sociodrama); intramural sports that stress mass participation and youthful service to the community.

Along the way, drugs will be introduced on an experimental basis, designed to improve the student's learning qualities.

For some of the children in urban areas there will be mandatory foster homes and boarding schools, so the children can *en masse* be taken out from under the influence of their parents.

The criteria for taking away the children will be many. One will be that the authorities deem the child "endangered by the sensory input with unsatisfactory social consequences in his home environment."

If the child can be taken away on that pretext, the reader can be sure these will not only be children from so-called "bad" homes in ghetto or slum areas. They could also take them away because the parents are deemed to have political views with which the authorities disagree.

In fact, such a thing happened in Northern California some time ago when a judge decided the boy's father was too "arty."

Of course, if you are dealing in mental health nonsense and turning your classrooms into perpetual freak out factories, what better way to do it than through an outfit called the School Health Association.

That's a nice, sterile sounding kind of name.

Can anything bad come out of the School Health Association, of all things? Doesn't the very sound of it conjure up visions of very proper types in white surgical gowns and nurses with no makeup on?

What on earth could be sinister about that?

Plenty.

Dr. Geoffrey Estey writes in a recent issue of the Journal

of School Health, "The teacher, perhaps more than the parent, knows what is best for him (the child)."

That unmitigated gall is followed with something even more startling. "Unfortunately, the myth of Puritan tradition that children are naturally bad, hence, require strict authority and stern discipline in order that they may develop properly, still generally prevails."

Too bad about that, it seems. Have to get rid of that nasty old degenerate Puritanism.

Dr. Estey is all uptight about Original Sin.

"This myth of Original Sin," he bleats, "among others, when coupled with pressures both in the family and school, tends to lead to an emphasis on faults and our inadequacies of behavior."

Inadequacies of behavior?

Has Estey visited juvenile hall lately and seen the depraved animals passing for human beings who now infest those kinds of places? Has he walked down Hollywood Boulevard and looked at the freaked out, depraved abominations who pass for human beings?

Estey was busy flailing away at Christianity in a talk he gave in, of all places, Red Czechoslovakia, at a meeting of the World Mental Health Federation on July 12, 1966.

Coupled with the School Health Association – and coupled is a good word for the obscenity – is the National Association of Independent Schools, believe it or not.

The NAIS is up to its groin in its involvement with SIECUS.

For instance, on March 3, 1967, the NAIS held a conference. The subject was "Planning a Program of Sex Education," and, lo and behold, the speaker was Mrs. SIECUS, herself, Dr. Mary Calderone.

The NAIS doesn't mess around with second raters – and now your children aren't even safe in many private schools.

"Sex education," Dr. Calderone told the gaping delegates, "is inevitable."

So is death – but most people put it off as long as possible.

249

She further opined that "Sex education is a constant under today's present social conditions."

"The best springboard for this kind of self-confrontation," she said, "are the series of SIECUS Discussion Guides and the April 1966, issue of General Social Issues.

"Nothing less will do as a starter," she added, "but still — they are only starters."

"Meet with the others in your communities," she told the NAIS delegates, "in order to defend or debate your convictions."

Yes, the delegates better get their stories straight before they get back to the old home town.

She then launched into her usual polemic for installing kindergarten through twelfth grade sex classes.

"Such plays as 'Hamlet' and 'An American Tragedy,' "she said, "should be used in English as spring boards for discussions about sex."

Come on, now, she has got to be kidding.

Oh, but she's not!

NAIS put out a booklet that included the Calderone remarks and the booklet was loaded with SIECUS names.

What are these people — CONSPIRATORS?

Just remember, YOU said it — I didn't.

For instance, the sexologists have come up with a film called "A Basis for Morality," which contains no morality at all — unless it is the morality espoused by Beelzebub.

In that film, God and Christ are blasphemed and religion is mocked.

Nice fare for your kids on a sunny spring day in English class, hey?

SIECUS board member and National Council of Churches high muck-a-muck William Genne writes for the Journal of the American College Health Association.

What could possibly be wrong with a college health group? Doesn't that conjure visions of healthy young athletes fighting it out on the gym floor?

250

Nope!

In the May 1967 issue of the Health Association's journal, Genne toe dances around the issue of sex education for college students.

"Just as we strive to free young people from the tyranny of the 'thou-shalt-not,' " he writes, "so we must strive to free them from the tyranny of the 'thou shalt.' "

Then, too, there is the matter of population *control* under the disguise of keeping the population down so we don't all starve to death.

For instance, in the American Review of World Health, published by M.H. Orr of the UN, we find the name of Dr. Mary S. Calderone listed as one of their patrons.

That's nice.

We also find the following organizations listed as supporters of the UN magazine: The American Heart Association; The American Hospital Association; the Coca-Cola Company; the CIBA Corporation; the Eastman Kodak Company; Geigy Chemical Corporation; Eli Lilly and Company; Merck and Company and Merck, Sharpe and Dohme; Minnesota Mining and Manufacturing; The National Foundation; National Tuberculosis Association; Parke, Davis and Company; Planned Parenthood Federation of America (of which Dr. Calderone is past president); G.D. Searle and Company; Shell Chemical Company; Smith, Kline and French Laboratories; Stauffer Chemical; Upjohn Company and the Warner-Chilcott Laboratories.

Birds of a feather — even moulting ones — do flock together.

Who are some of the individuals connected with this UN sponsored outfit? Well, the late Victor Reuther was one.

Dr. Mary Calderone is another, along with Bishop John Wesley Lord, peripatetic Red front joiner.

In addition to the organization and firms listed above, the magazine boasted the following list of supporters: The Foundation for International Child Health; Hadassah, the female arm of the B'nai B'rith; Hoffman-LaRoche; the Methodist

251

Board of Christian (?) Concern; The National Federation of Practical Nurses; the United Auto Workers (Walter Reuther); SIECUS; the United Cerebral Palsy Association; the United Nations Association of the US; the United States Committee for UNICEF and the World Rehabilitation Fund.

Other associated groups are: Associated Health Organizations of Akron, Ohio; Cleveland Health Museum; Duchess County Health Association; Iowa Division of the UN; Hawaii Public Health Association; Mount Vernon Chapter of the UN Association; Massachusetts Department of Public Health; Central Nassau (where Calderone lives) Medical Group; New England Health Education Associates; Greater New York Association of Industrial Nurses; New York League of Business and Professional Women; Ohio Tuberculosis and Health Association; the Oregon Division of the UN Associates; Patterson Department of Health; Philadelphia-Montgomery Tuberculosis Association; Presbyterian Office of International Affairs; Rochester and Monroe County Health Department; St. Andrews Episcopal Church Women of Ann Arbor; San Francisco Chapter of the UN Association; Santa Cruz Chapter of the UN Association; Southern California Committee for the (UN) WHO; Star-Rand Company; Tynek Corporation; UN Association of Central New York and Washington State Nurses Association.

All that long and tedious list of rare birds, busily fouling their own nest, is found in the "American Review of World Health" and are linked by that publication to world population control.

Another link in the control-the-people-through-controlling-the-population crowd is found in a magazine called "Population Challenge," which is available from the American Association for World Health, 777 United Nations Plaza, New York.

"Population Challenge" is a magazine devoted to glorifying a do-gooder American governmental operation called AID.

A wag referred to AID recently as AMERICANS INDEED?

The World Health Organization, for which Dr. Frank Calderone faithfully toiled, has offices in every single nation in

252

the world, large and small, including such choice spots as Gabon, Rwanda, Dehomey and – the United States.

The United States headquarters for WHO is a magnificent edifice built in Washington, D.C. on land turned over to the UN by our government and the building was constructed with funds from the W.K. Kellogg Foundation, Battle Creek, Michigan. How does that taste with your morning cereal?

Other headquarters are located in Delhi, Copenhagen, Manila and Brazzaville, all in fantastically beautiful buildings.

What kind of teachers are coming from the hands of the behaviorists who now control the nation's teacher training institutions?

They are like the teacher at Pioneer High School in Whittier, California who had some of his drama students put on a play for the local PTA on February 11, 1970. Replete with four-letter, unprintable obscenities, the play was entitled "Where's Lefty," and was notable for the way the name of Christ was blasphemously used. The play ends with the heroine dressed as a Communist Party worker who invited her fellow students to, "Unite Comrades." The play closed with all the students giving the clenched fist, Communist salute.

Or is it like the teacher in one town who had her little charges sitting around on the floor, covered with sheets, pretending they were bean sprouts?

Or is it the teacher in Garden Grove who told the students to give up their school, family, church and community and "turn on with drugs because that's where the scene is?"

Or is it the teacher in Anaheim who told her pupils that her favorite play was "Hair," which has music filled with four-letter, unprintable obscenities and actors urinating on the American flag?

Or is it like teachers all over the country who lead their students in marches, waving the Viet Cong flag and spitting on the American flag, while chanting for the overthrow of the government?

Or is it the teacher who conducted marathon Sensitivity

253

Training classes in the Long Beach motel that led to two students being permanently deranged?

Or is it the teachers who are, themselves, drug addicts?

Or is it the teachers in school after school who call on their students to rise up and overthrow the Constitution and destroy the capitalist system?

Thousands of such teachers, all over this land, make up the greatest internal subversive force in the history of any civilized nation.

Can this nation survive them? Can this nation survive its involvement with the United Nations?

For instance, in "Towards A World Understanding," Volume Seven, UNESCO writers state, "In order to produce a body of public opinion favorable to world cooperation, we must mould the minds of the future citizens of the world, directing them toward a geographical and hence, universal attitude. The teacher should prepare the child for membership in the world community."

They add, "The world of the future should be a world in which national sovereignty is utterly subordinated to international authority."

Dr. Bella V. Dodd, now deceased, was once the most powerful, resourceful and indefatigable commisar of the American Communist Party in the field of education.

Converted to Catholicism by Bishop Fulton Sheen, Dr. Dodd became an equally great champion of freedom.

In 1952 she told the United States Senate, "The Communist Party as a whole adopted a line of being for progressive education . . . (it) was eagerly seized upon and championed by the Comintern as the ideal system for limiting the ability of children in capitalistic societies to read, write or to think for themselves or to act for themselves, and so to cause them to depend upon the state for a guaranteed livelihood and for the protection against the hazards caused by their inadequate training for the battle of life."

A perfect example of how the traitorous forces work is detailed in a book called "Education or Indoctrination" by Mary Allen. It is the story of what happened in Pasadena in 1948 when the parents awoke to find out they were being subverted along with their children.

These are her words, and the truth of her words has been bourne out by our own investigation on the scene twenty years later.

"In 1948, the planners of the new or modern education launched a full-scale invasion of the schools in Pasadena under the leadership of the new superintendent, Willard Goslin. There seems little doubt that the city was the testing ground for the whole nation.

"The reader has had little or no opportunity to get the true facts. From coast to coast a distorted version of what happened in Pasadena has been circulated. Wherever people have resisted the modern trends in education, they have been propagandized with stories of vicious attacks upon the public schools. Pasadena has been held up as exhibit A. Practically all the material that has been written concerning the Pasadena controversy has indicated strongly that the people opposing Goslin's modern education were undermining the public schools and thereby were traitors to America.

"Let us examine the facts. What were these people defending? What were they opposing?

"The people in Pasadena were defending the American way of life as provided in the Constitution and the Bill of Rights. As parents, under the Constitution they exercised their right to state the kind of education they wanted for their children. Since they felt that the traditional form of education provided greater literacy, more inquisitive minds in their children and better discipline, parents sought to protect this form of education against annihilation. They urged the teaching of com-

255

petition, American history and the basic fundamentals. They defended free enterprise and capitalism because it had provided the best system yet known to man.

"In order to defend their beliefs, it was necessary for the people in Pasadena to oppose the socialistic trends thrust upon them. When they saw the axe swing at their concept of democracy, saw the blows strike the individual, watched them gather momentum toward collectivism, and learned they had to be re-educated in their concepts of democracy, they rebelled. Loose interpretation of the constitution, the use of textbooks (such as the Building America series) which had been declared unfit for California schools by the state board of education, the hiring of radical left-wing thinkers to augment the school program, and constant pressure to eliminate the majority vote in favor of the consensus of opinion, all contrary to the security of the American way of life, frightened the people. It appeared to them that not only democracy but also the public schools were in danger, and therefore they protested loudly.

"It was clear then, as it is today, that the majority of the people did not want the program of education that Goslin advocated. However, when citizens protested, they were ignored. As their voices grew louder, they were criticized. Every conceivable weapon was used to drown the voice of the people. Anyone who openly opposed the school administration was promptly denounced. Finally, when the people in Pasadena knew that their voices would not be heard, when they learned that they must accept something they did not want, they turned to one defense that the Constitution provided for them.

"On June 2, 1950, the voices of more than 22,000 people were heard. In the secrecy of the election booth they stamped their disapproval, and the Goslin administration was defeated by a vote of two to one. Five months later, Willard Goslin was asked to resign.

"The Pasadena story should have ended with his resignation. It didn't. Just as the city was beginning to emerge from the horrors of the confusion that prevailed during Goslin's administration, Pasadena was thrown into a new and larger battle arena. Radio broadcasts denounced Goslin's opposition. Book reviewers warned of the danger of such forces as those who overthrew the superintendent. Speakers blasted the 'Fascist' attempts to take over the schools. Educators pointed the finger of blame at the 'race haters.' Teachers were warned to be on guard against those who attacked progressive education. Analysts defined the hard core of Goslin's opposition as malcontents, reactionaries, those whose children did not do well in school, super-patriots, tax haters, race haters, the over-zealous and the over-ambitious.

"Unfortunately, such propaganda was widely distributed. It created a fear of a danger that does not exist and clouded a very real danger and silenced many fine people who were working for better education.

"Pasadena learned it was impossible to resist the trend in education. After they forced Goslin's resignation, the National Commission for the Defense of Democracy through Education, an adjunct of the National Education Association, sent a squad of inspectors into the field of battle (Pasadena) to seek out the forces behind the opposition to Goslin. The educators' plans for extending democracy were throttled by such activity, they said. Free, democratic public schools were being confined in a strait jacket because certain groups refused to pay for necessary improvements, they protested.

"Thus, the citizens of Pasadena found that instead of being heralded as the standard bearers for good education, they were being condemned as attackers of the public schools.

"In another report of the NEA Defense Committee, Dr. Harold Benjamin branded Goslin's opposition as the 'enemy'. On July 3, 1950, Dr. Benjamin, chairman of the Defense Committee, addressed the NEA on the subject, 'Report on the Enemy.' According to him, anyone who voted against a school tax, who opposed the modern trends, who believed in the 3 R's, who recognized the dangers of socialism or who was

257

embued with patriotism was the enemy. In short, the enemy was anyone who did not have views coinciding with his own and that of the Defense Committee."

Benjamin then unleased some vitriolic and acerbic comments about the nature of the "enemy" he was talking about.

"He comes under many disguises," said Benjamin. "He has a lot of aliases . . . Sometimes he dresses in the fancy uniform of the super-patriot . . . Sometimes this enemy drapes himself in the mantle of religious orthodoxy, breathing pious expressions of opposition to sin along with lies about public education. The enemy in this campaign against the public schools is also sometimes a cool calculating military adventurer."

Benjamin's speech was replete with lies, including his charge that one Allen A. Zoll, who he described as a fascist anti-Semite, was behind Goslin's ouster.

Nothing could be further from the truth – but the paranoic educators are not deterred by such things as telling the truth.

Benjamin then announced that the tiny minority of extremists he represented would finish their seizure of America's schools.

"The enemy in this campaign," he said, "is stronger than he looks. If we get our combat team ready, however, get the information it needs for its decisions swiftly and accurately before it, even a stronger enemy than this one would make hardly more than a ripple in the smoothness of our advance."

This miniscule group of power mad tyrants have been zealously working ever since and the American people have suffered defeat after defeat, simply because, unorganized, the people were no match for the tight organization of the child destroyers.

The campaign of the educator's combat teams is aimed at millions of America's little children, who have no soldiers to defend them.

It is aimed at your child and it is aimed at you.

Benjamin and his NEA cohorts were well read and well prepared for the battle.

258

In 1934 Norman Woelfel gave them their blueprint in the following words:

" . . . a united front of radically inclined educators (is needed to) form their defensive lines under the banner of basic convictions, ally themselves with all other social groups of similar orientation among the people and fight heroically against whatever forces elect to lay down the gauge to do battle."

In the city of San Luis Obispo, California a battle has shaped up that is as titanic in its own way as the one in Pasadena twenty years before.

That is the battle over sex education in the tax supported schools.

Led by Janet Becker, a soft spoken opponent of radicalism and institutionalized crackpotism, Mrs. Becker and her committee slapped a law suit against the school board to stop them from proceeding with their sex program.

After $6,000 and 12 months had passed, the suit is still pending in Superior Court.

But the battle continues, led by Mrs. Becker and such people as Lila Ervin, who spends days and weeks and months researching and getting at the facts.

On February 2, 1970, Mrs. Becker stood before the school board and pilloried them for allowing the showing of a particular film strip that was so outlandish as to stagger any mature adult.

The board listened with dumb ears.

According to Mrs. Becker, the film strip will be available for grades 10 and 12. It is called, "Values for Teenagers: The Choice is Yours."

Having listened to the dialogue and viewed that filmstrip myself, I am inclined to agree with Mrs. Becker that it poses a clear and present danger of corrupting the young — and even

259

the old for that matter.

Perhaps, since our conclusions are the same, arrived at independently, it is as well that we use Mrs. Becker's words in describing this film.

"I am well aware of the positive appearing aspects of the filmstrip in question. It's in color; it's up-to-date; the clothing and hairstyles are modern; the kids like that kind of music; it appears to be impromptu; it's fast moving and we've all been programmed to believe teenagers think this way and therefore we tend to accept it without question. Also, it seems to commend individuality; appears to present many different young people (this is done by changing frames more frequently than voices).

"First, in part one of the film, the narrator attempts to qualify the content; in effect, it is a denial of responsibility for the content, and the film's obvious bias.

"From there, the film presents a barrage of complaints and gripes which imply the following: teens are all confused; pressure is great and almost unbearable; it isn't easy to be a teenager; you can't always tell what's right and what's wrong; lots of adults are hypocrites, maybe even parents; parents lie, smoke, drink, drink, drink, and drive too fast. Parents haven't much to offer the teenager and don't know what they are doing. The world is moving too fast, but SOME manage to cope with it. Some even try to make it better. Model yourself after someone you admire; follow a leader; but not the government or parents. Parents are mixed up, too busy to pay attention and TOO INVOLVED WITH TEENAGERS ACTIVITIES AND THE TEENAGER HIMSELF TO BE RATIONAL. Parent's values are all wrong; adults are dishonest; fun things are all illegal; parents don't give reasons for things; all adults are dishonest; cheating is necessary because of pressure; competition is negative; fear and hopelessness result from the threat of the bomb and all it signifies; it's a difficult world, a difficult time and teenagers get confused."

Mrs. Becker adds, "Part Two of the film tells the viewer

that decisions are hard; it is a big responsibility and something teenagers must do alone; teenagers are lost; they can't believe who is right, parents, adults or society; teens turn to their peers and pick a leader to follow; the group represents security, but you cannot be an individual in a group; the group, like society, is negative; groups can be coercive like parents, adults and society; clubs organized to do something are good; sororities and fraternities are not good; competition is bad and leads to cheating and corruption; the worst pressure of all is from friends and they won't let you be yourself, either; teenagers have a choice, and they can do anything they want and be anything they want. The narration ends with the speaker telling the young people that parents, adults and society are not to be trusted. Religion is never mentioned. Even friends cannot be believed, and only the teenager can establish his own value system. They must be his own, and in the film, the concept of good values is not gone into in any way."

When I viewed this film, in the process of doing some research for a newspaper article, I discovered it leaves the young people on an island with absolutely no point of reference, except his own feelings, his wants and a great deal of distrust for all authority, as well as the feeling that life is a terrible place filled with fear, hard times and nothing but trouble.

At no time is the young person told that the civilized world is full of choices that must be made daily, choices that might be good for us but might go against the grain of our natural desires.

'The Choice is Yours' is a do-your-own-thing philosophy in a slick package.

In addition, there are at least seven aspects of the film that are vital to Sensitivity Training.

First, the dialogue is constantly critical of SELF, parents, adults, and of society, of groups in general and groups in particular, of friends and of the law.

Second, the film sets the stage for confessing in a public place (classroom) to acts of an illegal or immoral nature.

"I've cheated . . . "

It tells how some people justify an epicurean philosophy and then the young person in the film admits that she, too, is horrified by thoughts of the bomb and all it entails. One boy in the film admits to having been out drinking beer with the other boys, which is illegal for a minor, thus setting a further negative example.

Third, the narrator serves as the trainer or group leader. The film makes a significant point that the narrator is SYMPATHETIC rather than EMPATHETIC, which is an important distinction. The Sensitivity trainer is always SYMPATHETIC and never empathetic, in order to draw out the criticism from the person. In the film, the trainer takes the young viewer from self criticism to hopelessness to distrust.

He then tells the youngster that he has been given the difficult job in a difficult world of establishing his values. He plants firmly in the young person's mind the fact that there is no place to turn except INWARD. The 'do your own thing' philosophy is extolled by the trainer by indirection.

Fourth, all of the dialogue is highly emotional and based on gut feeling throughout. No facts are presented − only opinions, and no logic is used. It has no constructive academic content.

Fifth, the individual is isolated. This is necessary in Sensitivity Training sessions, in order for the individual to become dependent upon the trainer and, by transference, upon the group.

Sixth, the shifting of personal responsibility is done by leaving no doubt as to where the responsibility lies. The next step is to eliminate all guilt feelings by eliminating right from wrong.

Last, the film is designed to level off everyone. This is done through presenting parents as no better guide than anyone else. All persons are presented as equal in importance or in lack of importance. All people are negative influences.

Absolutely no constructive conclusions are reached in the

film strip and it is a mental trip to nowhere.

If the generation gap was ever to be widened, this film would do it by instructing the minor that all choices are his without any help from anyone else.

Particularly destructive is this aspect of the film, since parents, under the law, are responsible for the minor's actions – not the school or teachers.

Competition, the narration states, is a "pressure producing" social ill.

Since readers may question the conclusions drawn above, we are reproducing some of the actual dialogue from the film.

Narrator: *The program you are about to see concerns teenagers. In it a number of them speak out about pressures and problems they face every day. They are real people and not actors. They are neither typical nor atypical. They are simply individuals expressing themselves. You may not agree with what you hear. You may not have any friends who feel this way. But, we hope you will discuss these comments when the film is over. Perhaps you will have an opinion of your own.*

Girl: *Well, I think teenagers are very confused about the world, I mean its terribly confusing when you're growing up, particularly when you're trying to find yourself in an adult world and you have so many things to choose from . . . your parents may think one way, friends may think another way, and their parents some way else, and you don't really know where to turn to.*

Boy: *Well, for myself, I always find myself in a constant confusion of what I'm here for, y'know. The pressure today is so great, and I always find myself asking myself, 'What am I doing here? What's my purpose? Where am I going?' or sometimes I think it's no use – uh – y'know. I'm just in a sort of confused state of mind about what I'm going to do.*

Narrator: *It isn't easy to be a teenager. You can't always tell what's right and what's wrong.*

Other comments from young people include such remarks as "Your parents tell you never to lie . . . and then you find

263

out they lie to you and they don't want you to drink and then they come home boozed . . ."

"Smoking and drinking, y'know, telling your kids not to smoke and drink, meanwhile they're smoking and drinking. All that stuff. Don't drive fast, don't drive after you had a drink, and parents do it all the time."

"There's conflict between the way he is told to act and the way he sees people around him acting in the adult world . . . mixing the teenager up."

"Things are progressing way too fast for people . . . that's the whole problem. We're progressing way too fast technologically and we're not progressing socially or mentally . . . "

"I worked for Project Headstart . . . and it was one of the most thrilling things I have ever done . . . "

"Kids . . . don't know where to go. They need a guide and a leader. Parents aren't good examples, because they say — well, they aren't good guides. Who are you going to turn to?"

And on and on and on.

After viewing this film, the viewer is left with the distinct impression that there isn't a single young person in the world who is coping with his problems and adjusting to life.

Millions of young people will view this film — and others just like it — in thousands of classrooms all over America.

And then you wonder why the young people appear to be alienated from parents, friends and family? You wonder why they have no faith in their own ability? You wonder why they are turning to drugs to cop out? You wonder why a whole generation of young people is on a freaked out do-your-own-thing trip?

YOU NEED WONDER NO LONGER!

XV

TWO YOUNG MEN

We'll call this boy Rick, though that is not his real name. He lives in a city noted for its fine school buildings, its great bands and its marvelous athletic teams.

Rick looks like the All-American kid. Husky; blond hair; bright blue, rather enormous eyes fringed by lashes that would make any girl jealous. He is six feet tall, as straight as a willow tree and has strong white teeth that flash when he smiles, which is often − NOW.

Rick, you see, is an ex-high school athletic star − and he is an ex-addict.

It started in his Sophomore year in high school.

Already active in sports, he was brought up in a family that believed in wholesome recreation and in all the finer things in life.

Rick was turned onto Marijuana by a classmate at his high school.

The long road straight down to the pit of hell had begun for him.

By the time he was a junior in high school he was taking LSD − sometimes as often as four or five times a week.

He was living two lives.

On the one hand he was the campus hero. He was popular, admired, with fancy clothes, his own car and adulation for being the school track star.

On the other hand, he was a furtive user of drugs, who was in a daze most of the time.

Rick was the only boy on the team who used drugs regularly, and he used them constantly, even during training.

His drug using friends were the football players, many of whom were considered to be some of the outstanding football

265

stars in the state.

Yet, they were on drugs – living the same kind of double life as Rick.

But let Rick tell it in his own words.

"It was a bummer, man," he says, "and I was so strung out towards the last I didn't even know where I was most of the time. I finally went into convulsions from the LSD, and my nerves are still shot from it."

Somewhere along the line, Rick became a pusher.

"I was supporting a pill habit, too," he said, "and I was pushing everything in sight. Man, I knew one guy who was making $17,000 a month, just pushing drugs."

"Around Christmas last year," continued Rick, "a bunch of my football playing friends and myself decided to go on up to the Lake because we knew there was going to be a big party. We had a couple cans of Reds (pills) and all the way up we tried to see which one could take the most. I had around six but by that time my habit was so big that it didn't bother me much. Some of the other guys had 10 each. Well, we got up to the party and it was jumping, with kids all over the place and most of them on drugs. We couldn't find a place to sleep, there, so we went over to the other side of the lake where I knew there was a cabin we could stay in. We broke in when we got there, but by that time we had picked up a couple hitchhikers, so there were five of us.

"All the way to the cabin the guys were gobbling 'Reds' like animals, whole handfuls at a time. Man, it was something else.

"We were all strung out when we got there – so three of the guys decided to go down to town to see if they could find some chicks and bring them back to the cabin.

"John (not his real name) and I went into the bedroom and just went out unconscious on the bed.

"When I woke up I was choking and strangling. The room was full of smoke and John was sitting up, gasping for breath right along with me. But we were both still wasted on Reds

266

and our reflexes were shot. I tried to drag him to the door, but I couldn't make it with him.

"I didn't realize that two of the other guys had come back to the cabin and were asleep inside the cabin. By the time I got outside, there was a big explosion and the whole place went up like a ball of flame. The three of them were burned to death.

"Fortunately for one of the hitchhikers, he had stayed in the car at the bottom of the hill and was passed out during the entire nightmare."

Did the death of Rick's football star friends turn him around?

Not at all.

He kept right on taking drugs, until finally he came to the realization that he was destroying himself and something had to be done. He turned to God for help — and found it. Now he works with Teen Challenge, trying to help other young people.

What does all this have to do with the tax supported school system?

Plenty.

The tax supported school system has become a center for the drug traffic, a center for the distribution, sale and use of every drug known to man.

Pushers frequent the campuses — and are often found to be student leaders.

Rick seems to have an insight.

"It all began around the time of the Beatles popularity," he said. "The kids started imitating them — clothes, hair, the whole bit. The mass media played its part in turning on the kids and so did the Madison Avenue advertising men. And then there is the schools. If anybody is to be blamed for turning out the kids who are on drugs, I suppose I would have to say the school was as much to blame as anything."

But HOW are the schools to blame?

For the past several decades — but particularly in the last

267

ten years — the tax supported school system has become the center for revolution and subversion. Part of that subversive process is drugs.

Rick says it well.

"My brother is due to graduate from a state college this year," he says, "and man, that's a bummer. I've been on that campus. I've seen the drug scene there. Everybody's on drugs — and that's no lie. My own brother's on drugs and he's going to be a teacher next year in the public schools. The public colleges are their own world — they sit inside there and take their drugs and laugh at the world outside. They are a law unto themselves. Only, when they graduate they take the drugs with them — into the classrooms, into the law courts, into the business world. Why, one of my biggest drug using friends is studying to be a dentist at a junior college and he is going to be a hooked dentist when he gets out of there."

By now you are probably wondering, is there nothing good about the tax supported school system?

The answer is obvious — and hardly needs any space allotted to it. There are thousands of good — and heartbroken — teachers in America's school system and many of them have taken the trouble to write us and phone in to us to cry on our shoulders about the tragic situation they are faced with in their classrooms. Hardly a day passes that we don't hear from at least a half dozen.

There are thousands of good students — though their ranks grow smaller with increased momentum every passing day.

There are hundreds of good courses, offered by conscientious teachers, courses designed to help young people face life realistically.

But all that is like the most beautiful chocolate cake in the world, lovely to look at and great to taste — except that it is as dangerous as a booby trap and laced with a lethal dose of arsenic.

The tax supported school system is beautiful to look at. Magnificent buildings. Colorful marching bands. Cheering

268

crowds at football games. Great musical ensembles. Marvelous laboratories. Well-equipped libraries.

But all that is only the frosting on the arsenic loaded cake.

The conspirators and those who are actively working to destroy this nation are using the tax supported school system as their number one vehicle. As a matter of fact, they could not bring this nation to its knees unless they had the tax supported school system to work through.

If they didn't have the so-called public schools, they would have to invent them.

Listen to the National Education Association in its Forecast 70.

"As nonschool preschool programs begin to operate, educators will assume a formal reponsibility for children when they reach two years old. Biochemical and psychological mediation of learning is likely to increase. Drugs will be introduced experimentally to improve the learning qualities such as personality, concentration and memory. The application of Biochemical research findings, heretofore centered in infra-human subjects, such as fish, could be a source of conspicuous controversy when children become the objects of experimentation . . . the teacher role will more accurately be termed a learning clinician. Schools are becoming clinics, whose purpose is to provide individual psychological treatment for the student."

And in the Hawaii Master Plan for education we read: "Schools will be swept into a whole new area of collaboration with bio-chemists and psychologists . . . and this will be a source of conspicuous controversy when children become the objects of such experimentation . . . there will be considerable protest on the part of parents when children are subjected to these drugs, and this parental protest must be overcome . . . Ribonucleic acid will become a useful tool in dealing with children. That is a substance found in human cells that is responsible for storing information in the brain . . . the schools will be asked to share the tasks of the home in rearing the

269

child and to assume larger responsibility for developing youth, especially in regard to social work."

Let a Vancouver, Washington mother tell you about her introduction to the world of drugs.

"I awoke suddenly, loud yells ringing in my ears. The noise seemed to come from our basement, and my first reaction was anger.

"Our 17-year old son had gone to a party Friday night and hadn't come home yet when I went to bed; from all the racket, it sounded as though he'd brought 10 friends home with him. I pulled on my housecoat, peering down into the basement stairs. But it was dark and quiet down there. I hesitated, puzzled.

"And then a blood curdling shriek filled the air — and a wierd sing song chant began *'Blood, blood, blood. Kill, kill, kill.'* I dashed to the front of the house, opening the living room door.

"A dark haired boy sat on the porch, his back leaning against our front door so that, when I pulled it open, he almost fell into the room. An unearthly scream came from his lips as he rolled to one side.

" 'What's the matter? Are you hurt?' I asked, but the boy didn't hear me. He looked up at me, half-rose and lunged through our door, almost knocking me down.

" 'Tommy,' I gasped, my mind refusing to believe my eyes. He was a friend of my son's, and we knew him well. For the last two years he'd been at our house constantly. But this Tommy looked like a wild person, strange. His eyes darted unseeing, and his trousers and undershorts were pulled down around his knees.

" 'Tommy,' I said senselessly, aware that my daughter had come down the stairs to stand there watching, 'Pull up your pants.'

270

"He lunged at me again and I jumped back. He crouched on the floor, ready to spring, that sing-song chant coming from his lips, spouting obscenities in a musical cadence. My daughter peered at him, her eyes wide and frightened.

"Suddenly he sat down on the floor, yanked off his boots, and began ripping off his trousers and his shorts. He waved his shorts in the air in one hand, repeating over and over again, 'Dirty underwear, dirty underwear.'

" 'Tommy,' I said again, but he didn't seem to recognize me.

"And then suddenly I knew!

" 'Get your dad,' I cried to my daughter, and she dashed up to the bedroom to wake her father. I watched, stupefied, while the boy shredded his clothes.

"Then suddenly he spied a ball-point pen on the table. He lurched across the room to grab it, sat down on the floor and began stabbing viciously at his naked genitals.

" 'Rupture, rupture, rupture,' he chanted, and I was almost numb with disbelief.

" 'Help,' I screamed at my husband, 'He's going to hurt himself,' and almost without thought, I closed in to kick the pen from his hand. The pen flew across the room and his hand closed around my ankle. As I jerked away, he leaped toward me again — and I ran, terrified.

"As my husband came into the room, Tommy had once more gotten to his feet and began tearing at his clothes, four-letter words streaming from his lips. He threw his jacket across the room, tore off his shirt and danced nakedly around. Funny, I remember thinking, how I told him to pull up his pants — and now his nakedness seems unimportant.

" 'Call the police,' my husband said.

"As I dialed the operator, Tommy had flopped back down on the floor and was methodically and violently banging his head as hard as he could — whack, whack, whack — on the floor. The telephone operator got the police station for me, and for a second Tommy lapsed into silence, his eyes darting

271

frantically around the room.

"As I stammered out our address, though, he once again started gouging viciously at his legs, his genitals, his stomach, screaming, 'Hate, hate, hate.' His fingernails drew blood, but each time my husband got close, trying to stop him from scratching at himself, he would lunge as though he were going to attack my husband.

"The police were there in a short time, since they were just around the corner. Numerous reports had been called in because of Tommy's screaming outside, and the police had been looking for him. They immediately radioed for an ambulance, and then came into the house.

" 'What'd he take?' one asked, but we didn't have any answers.

" 'Looks like LSD,' said the other.

" 'Brutality,' Tommy screamed at them. 'You're going to take me and kill me.'

"He doubled up in a ball on the floor, but then, when no one bothered him, he returned to his preoccupations with ripping his skin apart, as he'd ripped the clothes from his body.

"When it became obvious he was going to hurt himself if not stopped, the police finally handcuffed him — but it took three grown men to hold him down to get the handcuffs on, and even this didn't stop his self-mutilation. He just used the handcuffs as a weapon on himself.

"The chanted obscenities went on and on and on. In one breath he screamed that he had seen God and in the next breath he was crying about blood and guts and killing. We stood there transfixed, staring, horror-stricken by the hatred and violence and self-destruction.

"We didn't interfere, except to stop him when his gouging of himself became too bad. As long as we kept our distance, it was as though he was in the room all alone, oblivious to his audience.

"There was a skirmish when he began to draw blood on his body. He bounced from the davenport and collapsed again on the floor.

" 'What did you take, son?' the policeman asked, and Tommy's sing-song began again, changing to, 'Acid and speed, acid and speed, acid and speed.'

" 'Where did you get it?' And the chanting stopped.

"*Silence. Code of the wild.*

"For a moment Tommy seemed almost normal as he said, 'I won't tell.' Then he rocketed back into his LSD world, where we couldn't follow, pounding his head on the floor. After what seemed to be forever, the ambulance came to take him to the hospital.

" 'Why do they do it?' my husband said sadly.

" 'Looking for seventh heaven,' the policeman said, 'But it looks like that kid found seventh hell.'

"The night wasn't over. My daughter, who had watched from the top of the stairs, was hysterical. My son, who had cowered outside in the darkness, afraid to come in, finally sat in the dining room, sobbing, his head in his hands.

" 'Why? Why did it happen, Mom?'

" 'LSD' I said simply.

" 'But I never believed what grownups said about it,' he sobbed. 'We've taken it before, and no one ever acted the way Tommy did tonight. I thought bad trips were just a bunch of junk grownups made up to scare kids.'

"His father and I sat and stared at each other, completely at a loss to know what to say.

"We hadn't known he had been using drugs; visions of our son thrashing around on the floor like Tommy went through our heads. And our son had been informed. We made sure he knew what these drugs were and what they could do.

"If the kids won't believe us when we tell them what will happen — well, what is there to say?

"The night wasn't over for Tommy either. The ambulance driver stopped back at the house to talk to the policemen after he'd taken the boy to the hospital.

" 'Wow,' he said, 'you thought he was bad here. When we

got him to the hospital, that kid really flipped.'

"And after the horror we had been through, no stretch of my imagination could picture any way that he could have been worse at the hospital.

"The night wasn't over for the policemen either.

" 'Well,' said one of them, 'that's the third one tonight. If experience is any judge, there'll be at least two more.'

Remember this mother's words — *"If the kids won't believe us when we tell them what will happen — well, what is there to say?"*

Your children are in deadly peril.

As the Hawaii Master Plan makes clear: "Much more power must be given students in the educational process."

The plan then adds that the school should totally *restructure* the students of Hawaii (and all over America) in regard to their VALUES, THEIR ATTITUDES TOWARD THEMSELVES AND OTHERS: THEIR ATTITUDES TOWARD THEIR HOME, SCHOOL, PARENTS, STATE AND IN THE RE-SHAPING OF THE CHILD'S RELIGIOUS BELIEFS.

"The schools of the past have stressed stability, fixed habits, memorization of facts and development of specific tools," they say. "In the future, the schools should stress the development of attitudes appropriate to change and a commitment to flexibility and reason."

The state, they add, "should look in to the feasibility of institutionalizing sensitivity and encounter training."

Your children are now under the control of humanists and men and women of amoral principles who are determined to reproduce themselves in your children and the kind of inner rebellion that leads to the nightmare hell of drugs and death, paved with the one world philosophy of socialism and humanism.

The foundation was laid in the tax supported schools by

274

the John Dewey disciples in the 1930's. It was reinforced by the directives of UNESCO in the 1950's and maintained by the social scientists in the 1960's.

In the words of Arlo Guthrie, son of the Communist Woody Guthrie, and young hero of millions of America's young people: "What's reality?"

Millions of American young people are finding Arlo Guthrie's reality in drugs, degradation and stupifying escape from life.

The tax supported schools, especially in the social sciences, have taught your children to engage in so-called "discipline of responsible dissent," which, to the young, means *no discipline at all.*

The schools are programming your children to be selected subjects that meet the criterion of the social scientist, with selected teachers, preconditioned to the mold of the master social scientist. And the end result is the super social scientist who is destined to control and perpetrate the new social order.

Parents all across America live in fear.

They fear their own tax supported school system.

They fear their children's teacher.

They fear the textbooks.

They fear their own children.

And is it any wonder?

Mrs. Joseph Bean, the wife of a Glendale, California school district trustee summed it up in a blistering speech she delivered before her husband's board in the early part of 1970.

"The traditional philosophy of education," she said, "recognizes that there are absolutes, eternal truths, immutable truths, and that the school is vitally interested and instrumental in transmitting these absolutes to our young.

"Without official recognition and without official adoption," she adds, "a new philosophy has largely replaced the official one in this country's schools. This philosophy is behaviorism and holds that man is not responsible for his actions,

275

that he is a victim of his environment and not accountable for his acts. Behaviorism is the predominant scientific and social philosophy of our age."

And of course, this courageous wife of an even more courageous school board member and prominent physician was absolutely right.

Under the behavioristic philosophy, little if any emphasis is placed on systematic subject matter instruction. For instance, the California state curriculum commission's new social studies framework would eliminate all textbooks. They changed the name from social studies to the Social Sciences in the process.

Using the inquiry method, which the framework requires, entire sections of mankind's history are ignored and great gaps will appear in the child's education — and all on purpose.

Traditionally, as Mrs. Bean pointed out in her talk, education has accomplished one main function. That is, to transmit the values of the past to the future. Values of the family, with its morality, religion and ethical standards have been passed on to the children, first by the home and then by the school and community at large.

That value system, of course, is the accumulated value structure of 2,000 years of western civilization.

It is the yardstick through which the youngster is able to determine what is right and wrong, what is proper or improper, what is acceptable and unacceptable, what is healthy or harmful. It will remain with him as his yardstick for judgement and decision making as an adult.

But now, in the tax supported schools, the intent of the social sciences is to make the child uncomfortably aware of the societal breakdown we are now going through and to train him to concentrate all his youthful energy upon the social-action arena of conflict.

The marked lessening of emphasis on academic achievement has born fruit in our own time. It has resulted in rootless, spineless, fuzzy headed young people with no character

276

and even less in the way of morals. It has resulted in an alley cat mentality on the part of the boys and female rabbit mentality on the part of the girls.

Now the achiever is embarrassed to show his ability, so the capable student will often underachieve in order to show he is not different from the rest of the herd.

This is an unnatural condition in this society — a flinching from success.

It has rewarded the average or mediocre student with peer popularity and approval, paving the way for even more problems in the unnatural condition of his identity image.

So it is that the youngsters of America find it easy — and desirable — to identify with the mediocre in music, clothes and outlandish behavior.

It has dirtied all our existence.

So it becomes, to the Hippies, "hostile vibrations in the Haight Ashbury," and it became blood and horror and death for Sharon Tate and her friends.

For the young, stripped of all standards and values out of the past, are left but hollow shells — waiting to be filled with consumate evil.

Black masses are held in the hills above the Sunset Strip — and Governor Ronald Reagan warns that the nation is on the brink of going the way of Rome, to dust and ashes.

For instead of emphasizing the development of the individual, the new philosophy seeks to develop the group-man, which is an internal contradiction in itself. A man is a significant unit of the human race and a group can neither act nor think and a class of students cannot think.

Only individual people can think.

The purpose is to destroy in the mind of the child the value system with which he arrived at school.

And not alone in the schools, according to Ventura County CCC chairman Gloria Stott.

On February 13, 1970 a bus load of 70 teenagers from upper middle class white neighborhoods in Los Angeles were

277

taken to Camarillo Mental Hospital to spend 72 hours in sensitivity and group encounter.

The purpose? Allegedly to help them to communicate with each other and to help them become more sensitive.

The real purpose? *To make well minds sick.*

Students from the University of Southern California were signed up to lead these mentally well students into the nightmare world of the behaviorists.

And the parents of these helpless teenagers cooperated!

However, to get back to what is actually being done in the school.

Having destroyed for the student his value system, the class is then expected to determine standards by group consensus. This is now popularly known as situation ethics (Joseph Fletcher), fun morality (playboy) or the New Morality.

The student, with his yardstick taken away from him, now relies upon the decisions of the group for his values, his morals and his behavior. This changes from day to day, since, according to the behaviorists, truth is not permanent.

It changes from day to day to suit the needs of man. It embraces no absolutes.

Still you say, the teachers are always talking about the person doing his own thing. How can he do his own thing if he acts with the group?

Simple.

They mean that everyone is to do his own thing in the atmosphere of pluralism, and this wipes out the development of behavioral standards. Such lip service has nothing whatever to do with individual development but rather with damaging the student. It creates an atmosphere within which the student acts in isolation of the moral code which he inherited. This results not only in harm to himself but, by the same measure, in harm to society.

The Behavioral Scientist develops the theory and writes voluminous tomes on his theory, adapting it for the classroom.

His books are those studied by the college students who

will one day be teachers. The teachers will then transport that behaviorist knowledge into your child's classroom.

During the past few years, almost everything published in the field of education has been in the area of behaviorism, the new philosophy. Truth is redefined as a "social good."

If an idea or a fact does not serve the public welfare or the social good, it is discounted. All past thinking and moral judgements are dismissed. The preparation for those living in the society envisioned by the behaviorists and the teachers must no longer aim toward creating a freely chosen moral agent — but instead it must emphasize the directing of the individual to the social good.

The difference between the old and the new education is important. Where the old is initiated, the new merely conditions and programs. The old dealt with its pupils as grown birds deal with young birds when they teach them to fly. The new deals with the child more as the poultry keeper deals with the young chickens — making them thus and thus for purposes of which the birds know nothing. In a word, the old was a kind of propagation — men transmitting manhood to men.

The new is merely propaganda.

By and large the behaviorists are Humanists, that is, they hold that man is his own god, and that truth, as the essence of social good, must be manipulated to support the current popular social theory. To this overmantling philosophy of Humanism is owed the devastating success of behaviorism.

Eagerly the innovations of the behavioral scientists are taken up by the classroom teachers. Very little basic research is conducted, these days, in education itself. Rather, whatever the behaviorists set forth is accepted and implemented by educators in the absence of their own research.

Is it any wonder that millions of America's youth have become hippies, yippies, yahoos, drug addicts, alcoholics and just plain sick degenerates?

The schools, together with their compatriots in the press, the movies, the radio and TV, the recording industry and the

279

court system, have brought this nightmare upon America.

In fact, the total breakdown around us is so staggering and complete that a sane man is quite incapable of putting it all together into one schematic whole.

The mind boggles — and refuses to accept it all in one piece.

George Roche, one of the most brilliant minds in education, states that departure from tradition, morality and even from human thought — which seems far advanced in theory — has scarcely begun in practice. *The most sweeping and damaging changes to our society still lie ahead* — unless God intervenes — or parents begin to assert themselves once more.

Mrs. Bean prepared the following chart, which clearly shows the two opposing philosophies, the old and the new. A mere glimpse at the chart will show exactly where we have been, where we are today and where we are going.

It is not a pleasant prospect.

OPPOSING PHILOSOPHIES IN EDUCATION

TRADITIONAL	NEW (BEHAVIORISTIC)
Instruction in subject matter (organized and systematic) – knowledge.	Little systematic subject matter.
Instruction in skills.	Less emphasis on skills.
Individual development to the greatest potential.	Group-man – destruction of the individual.
Value system for judgement making as an adult.	Standards by group consensus/Situation ethics.
Absolutes – eternal verities. Truth.	Embraces no absolutes, no eternal verities, no constant truths.
There is a GOD who is the final authority.	Man is his own god and is the final authority.
Man is a fallen creature, sinful, in need of redemption.	Man never fell and so-called sins are only myths.
Morality is based on the Natural Law of God.	Morality is doing what the group wants and acting interpersonally.
Man is responsible for his actions.	Man is not responsible for his actions.

And from all this comes madness. From it comes the Zodiac, stalking a frightened and frightening San Francisco, where suicides now rank the highest in all the world, a city best described as Sodom by the Bay.

"I like killing people," the Zodiac writes, "because it is more fun than killing wild game in the forest . . . because man is the most dangerous animal of all. To kill something gives me the most thrilling experience . . . the best part of it is when I die I will be reborn in paradise, and all that I have killed will become my slaves. I will not give you my name because you will try to slow down or stop my collecting of slaves for my afterlife . . . "

And his note is filled with misspelled words and no punctuation at all.

Madness has come out from the asylum and now infests the streets and the homes of America.

Where once the mentally ill were locked away, for the protection of society, now, thanks to the behaviorists and their followers in the mass media, the mad are glorified, deified and made rock and roll record artists so the teenagers can spend millions buying their records.

Jerry Farber, a so-called teacher at Cal State Los Angeles, writes an article entitled "The Student As Nigger," replete with unspeakable epithets, blasphemies and obscenities.

He ends up being guest lecturer at San Diego State College — and all on YOUR money.

Further, foul writing Farber is currently "assisting with some of the student problems at San Diego State."

Isadore (SIECUS) Rubin complained bitterly in a book entitled "Sex Education and the Teenager," published by Diablo Press, "In California, a high school teacher is suspended from his classroom because he asked his students to fill out a questionaire on their sex life . . . the community has not yet decided whether it wants a broad and meaningful program of sex education or merely a narrow program."

To which one woman replied that it was none of the

teacher's damn business vis a vis the student's sex life – unless he or she is some kind of voyeur who gets his kicks that way.

Dr. Lester Kirkendall cries out, "Humanistic liberalism believes that morality must be judged not on the basis of inflexible absolute, but on the basis of the consequences of an act upon the broad interpersonal relationships of people."

Oh, is that so?

Let's listen to behaviorist Paul Goodman, writing in the same book.

"All of our troubles in this area (sex) are the troubles of society. The young are confused because we live in a bad world. Our main duty is to change that world."

Agreed.

It is a bad world, but the behaviorists are steadily making it even worse.

Sexologist Ben Ard, in the same book, agrees with Goodman.

" . . . Insofar as young people have accepted the advice from adults to do as I do and be as I am, and have actually done as their parents and teachers have done, we have perpetrated one of the world's sickest cultures as far as sex is concerned."

Ard wants to do away with the "moralistic judgements" about sex.

"We need to avoid the sanctimonious, saccharine, sacred sentimental approach to sex education which has been with us so long . . . we need to get away from sex education that emphasizes the reproductive, repressive, religious approach. We must change the underlying value assumptions from those of our traditional, moralistic sex codes to a more rational, pluralistic sex ethic."

Do you still doubt that the sexologists are trying to get their grubby hands on the bodies of your children?

Well, it you do doubt it, read on.

At the University of Minnesota, a rather incredible creature named Gerhard Neubeck teaches a course called "Human Sexual Behavior."

Young people just like yours attend this class.

In his class no word is forbidden and no question is too hot to handle. The professor quotes from the poetry (erotica) of e.e. cummings; Bertrand Russell's autobiography and John Updike's sex novel, "Couples." He also quotes freely from the lascivious Johnson and Masters study, wherein several hundred unmarried couples copulated in front of sound movie cameras.

Neubeck also reads such things as a long description of sexual intercourse written by a degenerate in her thirties, telling her reactions after having sexual intercourse. The passage is both explicit and intense as she describes the whole matrix of love making – sounds and all.

Is that the kind of exposure you want for your children? If so, you have some hangups of your own, as Freud would say.

Then we have another sex teacher, Alan (SIECUS) Guttmacher.

"All we ask of our young generation," he says, "is a feeling of sexual responsibility."

He was talking to a class of 10th and 11th graders.

In a saner day he would have not only been run out of town, but he would undoubtedly have suffered a little violence at the hands of outraged parents on the way. Now he is given honors and awards and teaches the teachers who will be teaching your children.

Oh, but he has a sense of morality!

"Don't enter premarital sex lightly," he tells the youngsters, who by that time can probably hardly wait to get out to the back seat of their old man's car. "Enter it after deep and searching thought. If in doubt – don't."

By now you are probably saying to yourself, "Has the whole world gone mad?"

Nearly, but not quite.

Oh yes, Guttmacher adds, "You must not exploit a sexual partner . . . premarital sex should be entered into as a faithful episode . . . choose your mate carefully and remain faithful at the time."

284

The young people must fornicate with fidelity, otherwise it is immoral.

"But please," he begs, "You must use effective controls." And how about the parents of these young people?

"To most parents this will sound alarming," he clucks.

He then sums it all up. "It is rather simple. Premarital sex is all right if you are in love and faithful — for awhile, and if you can't be good, be careful. *Parents who feel these principles are wrong cannot and should not look to the schools for decisive help.*" (Emphasis ours.)

These days, you are an old fogy if you can't remember wanting to see your mother and father cavorting about in the altogether.

The sexologists would say you have sex hangups.

We would say *they* are sick.

285

XVI

STRANGE VOICES

There are those who claim that without today's tax-supported school, the average young man or woman would have no possibility of obtaining an education.

This is simply untrue.

Mass education was very much a fact long before the idea of universal education became a plank in the Communist Manifesto.

Compulsory support of schools is nothing more or less than slavery, pure and simple, and is not defensible from an ethical point of view.

What about this fiction that most children would be ignorant if we did not have tax supported schools?

In 19th Century England, the truly revolutionary mass educational experiments were not brought about by the government but through efforts of dedicated individuals.

For instance, in 1796, a Quaker named Joseph Lancaster opened a school in London. His students were the ragged and impoverished children of factory workers, miners and even orphans.

Citizens were astounded to find out that these pathetic lumps of clay were able to read and write in a very short time. By the time he reached the age of 21, Lancaster had opened a number of schools, all in temporary buildings.

He decided the time had come for a permanent home, and over the entrance of his school went the words: "All that will may send their children and have them freely educated; and those who do not wish to have education for nothing may pay as they wish."

It has been said that Lancaster was incredibly able to teach 10,000 children AT ONCE. This was done by teaching fundamentals to a few of the older boys, and then letting them teach the others. It really worked, with some children learning

286

to read in a matter of weeks.

There were monitors for reading, writing, spelling and arithmetic and others ruled papers, graded papers and gave examinations to the children. The children were promoted as soon as they had mastered a particular feat.

As a result of his success, donations from rich and famous began to flow into Lancaster's projects. He also received a yearly contribution from the Royal Family, starting in 1801.

DeWitt Clinton, in America, imitated much of Lancaster's educational theories when he opened his own New York Free School Society.

However, some religious groups criticized Lancaster for not taking more of an interest in religion, and this criticism turned out to be good because they promptly began their own schools.

John Stuart Mill stated, " . . . we can ourselves speak decidedly as to the rapid progress which the love of education makes among the lower orders in England. Even around London . . . there is hardly a village that has not something of a school; and not many children of either sex who are not taught more or less, reading and writing. We have met families in which, for weeks, not an article of sustenance but potatoes had been used — yet for every child the hard earned sum was provided to send them to school."

In other words, much to the surprise of some, the poor were only too eager to finance their own education at great personal sacrifice.

However all this blooming-of-the-rose of education was to come to a halt, when education became a political issue. The English, in 1833, began to offer government assistance to the private schools and this was gradually increased until the schools were almost all totally under the control of government.

Meanwhile in America, state involvement in the field of education began much earlier, in Massachusetts, with the Puritan leaders passing compulsory education laws as far back as 1643.

287

However, the amount of governmental intervention was minimal until the start of the 19th Century in most parts of the colonies and in the young states.

At the turn of the century, private schools were burgeoning all over, and church schools were commonplace and found in every town of any size. As we have mentioned, DeWitt Clinton, in 1805, founded his Free School Society.

New York State has the dubious honor of starting the first real state school system in 1812. However, it is interesting to note that the superintendent of education for the state said that when the government schools were organized nearly all of the children in the state were already being educated.

The report of 1821 showed that of the 380,000 children of school age in the state (between five and 16), 342,479 were already attending school privately.

In other words, universal education was already a fact in New York before the intervention of the state.

Since the private, voluntary schools could not compete with the tax-subsidized schools for money, by the middle of the 19th Century the private schools were in a declining state which has continued to the present time. DeWitt Clinton's Free School Society held out until 1853 when it finally merged with the New York City system.

Thus it was that the state purposely destroyed private and voluntary schooling in favor of a compulsory, tax-supported system that the politicians could control.

The question is, can a bad tree bring forth good fruit?

First, consider one Havelock Ellis, the man who long ago promulgated sex education philosophy through his major work *Studies in the Physiology of Sex* (seven volumes, 1897-1928). The work has been banned on obscenity charges, according to the book, *Keynes at Harvard* by Dobbs. Today the Ellis book is literally a Bible of sexual studies in our colleges and universities.

288

Ellis was a psychopath, yet he is hailed in our halls of academe as the "Father of Social Psychology."

In Isaac Goldberg's book on *Havelock Ellis* and in Halroyd's *Lytton Strachey, vol. 1,* there are accounts of Freud's close association with Ellis.

Ellis made his depraved and degenerate leftist friends think that everything they did was perfectly normal. This is found in *Lytton Strachey*, which is a collection of writings. The writers were the friends of Ellis, a group of perverts and sado-masochists who had a deliberate policy of corrupting the young.

According to the *Encyclopedia Britannica,* 13th edition, vol. 9, pages 890-91 and 323-34, this same group of degenerates practiced buying small boys from their parents in the Mediterranean area and crudely castrating them in order to make them effeminate.

Many of the boys died of infection. They were sold into slavery by parents who were poor, ignorant and superstitious. Ellis, the man who fathered much of the present day philosophy of sex education now used in public and private schools was involved in these activities.

John Maynard Keynes, father of our modern deficit spending economic policy was part of that same group. (See *Lytton Strachey,* vol. 1 and 2, or the revised *Keynes at Harvard.*)

In the book, *Sage of Sex,* by Calder-Marshall, pages 20-39, Ellis is said to have driven his wife into insanity by forcing her into lesbianism against her will. The mental collapse occurred after he wrote to her and told her he was having a bizarre and abnormal sexual relationship with Margaret Sanger.

And who is Margaret Sanger? She was the mother of planned parenthood, and was the moving force behind planned parenthood for many years in this nation and abroad.

In fact, she formed the *Planned Parenthood Association* and the *International Planned Parenthood Association,* out of which grew the infamous Swedish Sex Education program.

Dr. Mary Calderone, the mother of modern day sex instruction was the medical head of Planned Parenthood prior to taking on her present job as executive director of SIECUS.

This then, is the part of school sex instruction that the sexologists never tell parents about.

Too, it is a part that many local school board members, administrators and teachers do not know about.

Now that you know that this is the foundation for your school's sex instruction program, are you still in favor of it? If so — what does that say about you?

Sometime during 1968 a story came out of Flint, Michigan to the effect that a gym teacher had disrobed before her class and had conducted herself in an improper manner.

That story was repeated throughout the nation, with various embellishments being added as it went along.

Paul Cook, in his speeches, denies the incident took place as claimed — and insists that the teacher used a screen for changing into various costumes.

Paul Cook was wrong.

These are the facts.

At Bentley Junior High School, in Flint, a teacher came into her eighth grade gym class, dressed in skirt, loafers, panties, bra and blouse.

She announced she was going to show these young girls how they acted. She then pulled herself up on the stage, turning and twisting, her skirt slipping up and showing her thighs. Then she started undressing in front of the girls, on the stage.

When the teacher was down to her panties and bra, she asked if she stimulated any of them, and stated if not, they were abnormal.

She pointed to one girl and said, "Do I stimulate you?"

The girl replied sarcastically, "I'm sure one girl stimulates another girl."

The teacher then put on hip huggers and informed her class that they were sexier with a wide belt than with a narrow belt and that the color orange was a sexy color.

She kept asking the students if they were sexually stimulated when they showed their legs. The teacher then gave them a list of words to put their own definitions to, such as vagina, penis, emission, intercourse, masturbation and climax. It was a list about 85 words long.

She also asked her students if they ever had a desire to go to bed with their fathers or brothers and if they didn't (have the desire) they were abnormal.

The teacher also asked the students if they could imagine her and another teacher (male) in bed together dressed as she was at the time – in a bikini.

He was her fiance.

In one of the letters submitted to the board at the time, the parents of four children made the following charges:

"On April 17, 1968, a Miss ————, physical education teacher at Bentley Junior High School conducted a supposed sex education class in school.

"This class, held throughout the day, was nothing but filthy, lurid, off-beat trash. Not only did she strip to her underwear in the presence of the girls, but also inquired of them, with the removal of each piece of clothing, whether or not she was stimulating them.

"She informed them how certain male teachers in the building stimulate her because of their hairy chests and legs and because they wear Jade East cologne.

"She told the girls they were abnormal if they have no urge to go to bed with their fathers or brothers and she said they could be stimulated by shaving their own legs. She then demonstrated what she called a stimulating walk.

"After going through this part of the class, she presented the girls with a list of 85 words and asked them to write their own definitions of such words as coitus, masturbation, virgin, penis, ejaculation and nocturnal emission.

"On April 19, 1968, a meeting of 40 or 50 mothers and the teacher in question was held at the school. The principal re-

291

fused to sit in on the meeting. However, one of the board members was present. She heard Miss ———— admit to every charge and she denied nothing. With every question put to her by a mother she said she wanted the girls to 'identify.' What she meant by that we have never figured out. I fully believe she is a very sick woman and should be relieved of her job. The effect has been far-reaching among the girls and boys of the building.

"I also feel that the principal, Mr. Charles Heidtke, failed in his duty as her superior by allowing this class to be taught by her. She informed the mothers that she has a *problem* that Mr. Heidtke knows about and that ONLY IN THE FALL DID SHE BECOME A WOMAN.

"Since this incident, she has become very unkind to the girls and shows definite mental strain. I believe it would be in the best interest of herself if she were removed from the teaching staff.

"Our board refuses to take any action against either Miss ———— or Mr. Heidtke, even though the incidents have been proved. Surely we as moral parents, trying to rear moral children, should have our efforts rewarded. God knows, with our children seeing and hearing of crime and immorality all around them, they don't need it taught to them in the classroom."

The spokeswoman for the protesting parents was Rose Henry.

Instead of facing the issue squarely, the board members upbraided the parents for publicizing the event and then proceeded to whitewash the entire thing, stating they found insufficient evidence to dismiss the teacher or her supervisor.

The entire story was carried in the Flint Daily Journal on several occasions.

Yet, despite this evidence of impropriety in the classroom, Cook used this incident time and again, in speech after speech, to attempt to descredit those opposed to school sex instruction.

He usually began by informing his audience that the anti-sex instruction forces use unfair and slanderous attacks. Then

292

he gave the Flint case as a clear cut example of how parents take a perfectly innocent case, (she was only changing her clothes behind a screen, he insists) making the school district look bad in the process.

There is a man in California, supported by the taxpayers, who has become the International spokesman for violence, and revolution. His name is Herbert Marcuse, and he is a "professor" of philosophy at the tax supported University of California at San Diego.

A foreigner (German) by birth, in 1917 Marcuse was allegedly a member of a lunatic left outfit calling itself the Sparticists, named after the slave who led a revolt in Rome. This particularly leftist group was so far out that Lenin was forced to write a book denouncing them as unfit maniacs who had no right to involve themselves in his revolution.

Anyhow, when Hitler came to power, Marcuse fled to the sanctuary of the United States and went to work for Intelligence in our State Department.

Hitler's gain was our loss.

Marcuse has become the aged darling of millions of American young people, preaching a doctrine that says, in effect, give young people all the degenerate sex and drugs they want and they will destroy the country for us.

His books, extolling the virtues of sex, drugs and revolution are among the most popular books on hundreds of campuses, and are usually on sale right next to the capitalist cash register.

In June, 1968, the pro-Red Students for a Democratic Society (SDS) met in convention at Michigan State University. With the red flag of Communism and the black flag of Anarchy displayed prominently in the student union, they extolled the person of Marcuse as their patron saint and invoked his philosophy as guide and goal.

At the same time, his latest literary garbage was being

293

hailed in European student centers, and was being promoted under the slogan: "Marx, the God; Marcuse, the Prophet; Mao, the Sword."

Marcuse is the feeble, tottering old leader of a new breed of Roman barbarians who have latched upon our tax supported schools like buzzards and vultures on the dead.

Trained and primed by men such as Marcuse, they are ready to destroy the very institutions that have given them shelter from the wrath of the tax paying public.

Their goal is senseless destruction and they have only one platform: destroy America and the capitalist system and let anarchy reign.

They are for eliminating all moral and ethical values, and attack the society that is stupid enough to support them in the sanctuary of the tax supported campus.

They send their barbaric hordes into every trickle and rivulet of the mainstream of America, there to undermine its very foundations with every tactic known to advocates of sedition and treason.

Meanwhile from campus, press, pulpit and the halls of government they anesthetize the public against what they are attempting to do, crying that this is only "student unrest, change and academic freedom."

As the SDS was teaching its delegates how to make Molotov cocktails at Michigan State, the American Legion in San Diego was trying to get Marcuse fired, since his is an age so advanced that he is past retirement. The Legion rightly accused him of corrupting the morals of the students and using the reflected prestige of his university status to serve the cause of violence, murder, revolution and totalitarian repression of all views but his own.

However, fellow radicals on the faculty (in the majority on the campus) were able to wrap the phoney mantle of "academic freedom" around the doddering old man's frame.

With a kind of sad indignation, Marcuse denied all, but his books are a living indictment and brand him a liar.

294

Marcuse, the obscure German-Jewish scholar who fled Hitler's Germany has come a long way — and not just geographically.

At the end of World War II, when our government's romance with the Russians cooled slightly, Marcuse submerged and nothing was heard from him until he surfaced in 1955 at Brandeis University as professor of politics. He began a 14 year series of writing characterized primarily for their hatred of America.

During that period of time he established three basic double-think reversals of logical reality which bore considerable relationship to Plato's "Cave Allegory," — the illusion is reality and the reality is illusion.

First, in his book, "One Dimensional Man," published in 1964, he indicated that the *hope* of world revolution was remote because man is not actually repressed by the poverty talked about by Marx. Instead, mankind is repressed and oppressed by the great consumer wealth that technological society has provided.

The second double-think reversal took place in a book called "Repressive Tolerance," written in 1965. He said in that book that present day concepts of individual freedom are only a mirage-like device by which the power structures (capitalists) actually regress the "free society" which is found *only* on the *left*. In the name of *Freedom,* therefore, *the left must suppress the right and the center.*

In other words, the center and the right should be allowed *no* freedom of speech, with thought or action in the name of freedom for the left, only.

In the third double-think gambit, Marcuse wrote a book called "Essay on Liberation" in 1969. Here he reverses classical Marxism — that man will emerge as a totally transformed, new free man only after the proletariat has overthrown the state. In the Marcusean philosophy, a "new man" must be created as a possible alternative to the existing corrupt and obscene man. The elimination of the existing state apparatus,

295

followed by an idealistic utopia, is a prominent part of the program.

All three of these "double-think" reversals are mirrored in the beliefs and actions of the New Left barbarians.

According to William Thompson, associate professor of history at Pierce College, Los Angeles, whose investigation of Marcusean thought resulted in the above analysis, "Marcuse substitutes for Marx's proletariat an amorphous group of social and political outcasts – the exploited, the so-called intelligentsia and the colored races. These elements are the necessary vanguard seeking changes in all other men by serving as 'catalysts of rebellion in the majorities.' The vanguard must surrender totally to Freudian (sexual) frenzy. Those who belong to it must go totally radical, negative and regressive in every physical and psychological aspect. The assault upon the masses must be completely without restraint."

Thompson, who is correct in his analysis, states "The commitment to a total sexual-sensual existence must be absolute – devoid of all moral disciplines of the conventional society. The carriers must literally infect the masses with Marcuse's liberation concept. The masses are insane and only the Marcuseans (degenerates) are sane."

It becomes obvious why students and their teachers are so eager to adopt the Marcusean doctrine, because it allows them nobility and great reward for a hedonistic degenerate descent into the blackest depths of moral depravity.

So it is that a Marquis de Sade becomes the vanguard of the great new world of tomorrow.

The Marcuseans believe that any act against God, man or society is justifiable in pursuit of the "new man," who according to Thompson, "as a living temple of obscenity will still be pristine pure by the Marcusean standard."

According to Marcuse, this hedonistic dogma is not harmful. Millions of students read his books and thousands of them sit at his feet in the tax-supported classroom.

Dozens of his proteges are now teaching in the tax sup-

296

ported schools at all levels. Is it any wonder that degeneracy is the hall mark of learning in thousands of schools in this country?

In May, 1968, Marcuse journeyed to Europe to personally congratulate the two student leaders of the bloody uprisings in Germany and France, Red Rudy Dutschke and Cohn-Bendit.

He bubbled — "The Sorbonne — fantastic."

In Rome, with Cohn-Bendit, he ordered the entire audience to rise to its feet while they all sang the Communist *Internationale*. Stopping off in Paris, he chummed with the Red murderers from North Vietnam and attended a UNESCO symposium in praise of Karl Marx.

Marcuse appeared on the platform with the Black racist, H. Rap Brown, in New York in 1968, even though he writes that he believes racists should be deprived of free speech and assembly.

Apparently, that applies only to white racists or negro racists who are anti-Communist. Marcuse, at the same time, bragged that his philosophy had caused the riots at Columbia, the Sorbonne and Berlin.

It is, in the words of Thompson, "too late to deal with Marcuse on campus. Because of his age, God may soon work His will."

What his followers say and do outside the campus is practically beyond control, because the Supreme Court is extremely tolerant toward sedition, treason and criminal anarchy of all kinds. In fact, Justice William O. Douglas recently wrote a book advocating violent revolution to overthrow the government.

Marcuse has dug the grave for the American way of life — and the tax supported school system is going to be the graveyard.

And one month after the above remarks on Marcuse were written, his star pupil, Angela Davis, was sought throughout the western world on charges of flight to avoid prosecution for

297

murder and kidnapping.

The case is a simple one. Miss Davis — the object of paens of praise in a new book on sex education by Mary Breasted — is accused of supplying the guns with which a judge and others were murdered in San Rafael, California.

Of course, the dead judge might have had himself partially to blame for his own death. In a fit of permissiveness, he banished all guns from the courthouse, stating that gun toting policemen are a bad image to the public.

Meanwhile, Angela Davis was described by the FBI as "presumed to be armed and dangerous."

Mary Breasted had been in Anaheim for several days — driving around in a beat up old model flivver — when I first encountered her in the celebrity suite at the Grand Hotel.

She was there to cover a showing of the film, Pavlov's Children, she said, for an article that she was writing on sex education — and she looked quite ill at ease.

Her lack of poise, I thought at the time, was probably due to the fact that she looked so poor — strangely out of place in the glittering environs of Anaheim's plushiest hostelry.

Still, Eleanor Howe, Lillian Drake (who had produced the film) and others were so busy with the hundreds of people who streamed into an adjoining suite for three days to see continuous showings of the film that they forgot to ask her for her credentials.

In the next few weeks, Miss Breasted managed to intrude herself into the homes of most of the people who had been working night and day for months to bring some kind of sanity back into Anaheim's tax supported school system.

Too tired to spend time on anyone, nonetheless they spent hours entertaining her, feeding her and telling her all about themselves and about their feelings, hopes and dreams.

A thin woman with the scars of past acne on her face, Miss

298

Breasted, it turned out, was the star reporter for the Village Voice, an underground paper that makes the Los Angeles Free Press seem like a publication put out by the Women's Christian Temperance Union.

Having just arrived back in Anaheim from an exhausting two week speaking trip through the Northwest, I was hardly in a mood for long interviews. However, nothing would do, Miss Breasted insisted, but that she talk to me since her investigation would not be complete without talking to the reporter who had been so deeply involved.

That sounded reasonable, so I suggested we visit a local place for lunch that is known for its chili — exactly the same recipe used at Chasen's in Hollywood, reportedly.

Miss Breasted was very nervous. Her closely bitten fingernails gripped her tape recorder as if it offered her some kind of security.

"What is she so nervous about?" I wondered, getting the creepy feeling that she was glancing over her shoulder to see who was following her.

But, when the steaming bowls of chili arrived, her nervousness seemed to vanish as she plowed into the plate's contents.

For myself, I started answering her questions in a relatively disinterested manner, thinking of all the work that was piled up on my desk back at the office.

About half way through the interview — which turned out to be argumentative, since Miss Breasted kept interrupting my train of thought to argue vehemently about one point or another — the nagging doubt about her intentions at the back of my mind suddenly jumped out at me.

Miss Breasted didn't get too much straight information out of me thereafter.

However, ignoring her personal attributes, or lack of them, it is perhaps more important to consider her philosophical motivations.

Miss Breasted, you see, was no novice at attacking middle ground Americans. She had in fact, a long history of extremist

299

associations, all tilted very far to the left – and she admittedly moved in avante garde circles where the vast majority of Americans could not follow, not even in their wildest imaginations.

The mere fact that she was later to thank Wesley McCune, who she admitted was a "muckraker," for his help in writing the book, will give the reader some idea of what she was up to in Anaheim and why she attempted to vociferously – to the point of sheer boredom —— make a hero out of Hank Davis.

Wesley McCune, at the same time, is affiliated with Group Research, Inc., generally known throughout America for its frequent and highly financed attacks upon anyone whose political affiliations are slightly to the right of Mao Tse Tung. Hence President Nixon, Dr. Max Rafferty, Ronald Reagan and Vice President Spiro Agnew are, in the eyes of Wesley McCune, Right Wing Extremists.

They are also Right Wing Extremists in the eyes of Miss Breasted.

Miss Breasted finally left Anaheim, after interviewing everyone in sight, and apparently fled back to the security of Greenwich Village, where she proceeded to work on a book that was to appear in August, 1970.

Her literary baby was delivered to Sam Campbell's desk on August 11, and caused a tumult of merriment in the Anaheim Bulletin office.

Naturally, everyone even remotely connected with the Anaheim struggle was eager to see what, if anything, Miss Breasted had to say about them.

Sam Campbell was wounded to the quick when he discovered that Miss Breasted thought him hopelessly out of date for liking Lawrence Welk, Spiro Agnew (at times) and for believing in the Second Coming of Jesus Christ.

But then, when everyone had settled back down at their typewriters, we read the volume carefully.

By the time the last page was reached, we were actually feeling sorry for the author, realizing that her expressed desire to

300

write novels had apparently conquered her non-fiction objectivity.

Miss Breasted's very expensive book is replete with countless errors of fact, omissions and distortions.

Perhaps her most unfortunate attacks are reserved for two opponents during the sex instruction battle, Paul Dearth and Eleanor Howe.

Dearth, who is actually a pretty nice fellow, was literally pilloried by Miss Breasted, who was offended by the ostentatious manner in which he lives and who, it becomes apparent, felt sexually threatened by him.

A handsome fellow, Dearth apparently became something of a sex symbol to the very much uptight Miss Breasted, who admitted in the foreword to her book that she became very nervous around men who seemed somehow threateningly virile.

Miss Breasted seemed to turn all her hungup sexual fantasies upon poor Dearth.

The sex instruction battlers of Anaheim had not, presumably, done anything to personally harm Miss Breasted — and yet her polemic reads like a one-woman crusade against those who have personally maligned her.

It is a strange and distorted glass through which Miss Breasted is gazing — but that distortion is no more acute than is the distorted *milieu* in which she moves and lives and hates.

In trying desperately to dig up some dirt on the background of the Anaheim sex education opponents, Miss Breasted ends up with sly innuendoes, as for instance, her false intimation that Mrs. Pippenger was not legally married simply because Jan thought it was none of her business.

She did the same thing in garbling my own background, purposely or otherwise.

Miss Breasted was extremely kind to another Davis — Angela, of UCLA Communist professor fame. As a matter of fact, Miss Davis is treated with awe and wonder by Miss

301

Breasted.

It must have been rather embarrassing to the publishers to realize that her book was released the very week that Angela Davis was being sought by the police on a warrant charging her with murder and kidnapping.

It was terribly ungallant of Miss Davis to repay the kindness shown her by Miss Breasted in this callous manner.

Other heroes of Miss Breasted, according to her book, are Herbert Marcuse – who advocates using sex and drugs to prime young people for revolt against the Establishment and Mr. Paul Cook, the former Anaheim school superintendent.

Aside from all the unfortunate errors in her book, perhaps the saddest omission is the fact that the committee members who fought the sex education battle in Anaheim were not all that upset individually with teachers and others who were involved in teaching or promoting sex education.

It was not a personality issue – and it was not a matter of assassinating characters – since the sex instruction opponents were interested in issues and in philosophies behind the movement.

Noticeably missing in her book are interviews with teachers in Anaheim – or anywhere else, for that matter. She would have found, as we have, that a majority of teachers in Anaheim were on the side of the Citizen's Committee.

On August 4, 1970, Jim Townsend received a letter in the mail from a prominent Orange County teacher. That letter put the lie to everything that Mary Breasted tried to say.

The teacher congratulated Townsend on the "exceptional newspaper" that he edited called "The Educator," adding that he is "performing a public service long needed."

Teachers, she wrote, "cannot wait to get their hands on each new Educator . . . and they rant and rave, stating that you are out to destroy public education."

302

"The real truth is, what they really mean is that you are giving the public facts they never had before, and as you know, facts are one thing radical teachers and administrators cannot stand to have made public," she wrote.

She adds that it is "absolutely essential" that his voice continue to be heard across the nation, for "nothing will make the leftwing educators happier than to see your voice stilled."

The teacher adds she personally knows of a dozen teachers who have begun to wonder about the innovative programs in their district after reading the paper, and adds that at least three teachers had "switched over to the conservative side from reading your paper. So please don't give up."

"May I thank you and Mrs. Howe, John Steinbacher and Sam Campbell for the fight you are putting up for all of us," she concluded.

Miss Breasted could never understand such honesty.

A second letter came to the Anaheim Bulletin from another teacher in the local district. Assuring us that she was entirely in sympathy with the Bulletin's stand on most issues, she added that at a recent dinner in her home, a "leading educator" in the county had voiced the opinion that "Steinbacher, Campbell and Townsend ought to get an award for what they have done for the children of Anaheim."

And that reminds me of the secretary for the district who reported to the committee that Mrs. Williams, at one point during the controversy, "came storming into the office, cursing and banging doors in outraged anger, and kicked a wastebasket clear across the room, papers flying everywhere."

And surprisingly, for one who claimed to be such a meticulous writer, Miss Breasted spelled Jan Pippenger's name wrong throughout her entire book.

Another glaring error is made when she states the film star, John Carradine, narrated several Fact Records. He only narrated one of them (#17), and he also narrated "The Child Seducers" for American-United.*

In the end, one can only feel sorry for the frightened Breasteds of this world, whose philosophy she sums up herself on the last page in a quote from Albert Szent-Gyorgyi.

"I would share with my classmates rejection of the whole world as it is — all of it. Is there any point in studying and work? Fornication — at least that is something good. What else is there to do? Fornicate and take drugs against this terrible strain of idiots who govern the world . . . "

Miss Breasted fights nameless paranoic fears on nearly every page of her book — nameless terrors that must keep her awake nights worrying about the Right Wing Conspiracy led by such Right Wing Extremists as Reagan, Rafferty, Agnew, the Republican Party, and of course, lower echelon plotters such as your author.

There is a plot and a conspiracy, she shrieks in defense of Angela Davis — wanted on a federal charge of murder and kidnapping.

To her, Miss Davis is the complete woman, the "very beautiful" Negro who is after all, only a Communist being systematically attacked by all those paranoid anti-Communists who see something of a threat in Miss Davis.

Talking about her long suffering alter ego, Miss Breasted writes, "Angela Davis was a very beautiful black woman who had gotten the Regents all in a flap by proudly flaunting the fact that she was a bona fide Communist . . . so there was photogenic Angela, the latest living outrage to the local (Anaheim) anti-Communists."

Miss Breasted then goes on to a spirited defense of the Hippies, Yippies, Black Panthers "with their gleaming guns and proud postures."

---

*The Child Seducers, 33-1/3 rpm — Script by John Steinbacher. Available from Educator Publications at $5.00. Mary Breasted called the record "The greatest indictment of 20th Century America ever written — a masterpiece."

But of course — with her alter ego Angela sought for murder and kidnapping — Miss Breasted would probably admire all those gleaming guns, in the correct hands.

Most of all, Miss Breasted admired Angela because she "spoke in a gentle voice and didn't swear on camera."

The Child Seducers come in many shapes and sizes — and they are found in all walks of life, a veritable seething underground determined to pervert, distort and eventually destroy the American home and with it the institutions that have made the United States the world's most uniquely successful experiment.

George Paules of Parsippany is a parent who ran across the blandishments of the Child Seducers.

Paules, an armored vehicle commander in the Second World War, is a fighter now, on another and perhaps more important front — the home front.

The war time history of Paules reads like exciting fiction, from battling through seven major engagements to a so-called suicide mission assigned by the legendary General Patton, a suicide mission he and his small crew miraculously survived.

Then came the Korean War, and further service to his country aboard United States Naval vessels and work as an observer for Naval Intelligence.

"I live in a beautiful 10-room house that fronts a beautiful lake," he recently wrote, "in a rotten town corrupted by public officials that I have described in previous letters. They have tried to drive me out of town for two years. I send my two children to private Christian schools to protect them from the perversion and corruption extant in the tax supported schools. Yet, I am forced to pay exhorbitant taxes, of which more than 70 per cent subsidizes our tax supported school system which corrupts our children with impunity, turns out 75 per cent of its high school students as drug addicts, according to a 16-year

305

old girl addict who was turned in by her mother, and pays $100,000 per year to a bureaucrat of a superintendent, his self-appointed sex expert who is in charge of curriculum and instruction, an assistant superintendent in charge of personnel who opposed sex instruction until he was promoted to assistant superintendent and a convicted sex offender who is now the superintendent's administrative assistant."

But there is a whole lot more to the horror that is the tax supported school system of Parsippany than the story of one incredibly brave man who dares to stand up against official and unspeakable corruption that can only be whispered about in the shadows.

John Kucek, handsome young resident of Parsippany, came face to face with the hellish forces of darkness that spread sticky tentacles across the school system and the town, itself, when he was sued for divorce by his wife.

The following is an official abstract of an incredible exchange between John Kucek and the court of the Juvenile and Domestic Relations Court, Morristown, New Jersey, next door to the town of Parsippany.

Juvenile and Domestic Relations Court
of the County of Morris
An Abstract of Stenographic Transcript of Testimony
Before: HONORABLE BERTRAM POLOW
Morris County Court House, Morristown, N.J.
BARBARA KUCEK, Plaintiff
vs
JOHN KUCEK, Defendant
Heard: May 19, 1970
Appearances: Irving Youngelson, Esq., for Plaintiff

The Court: *You must support the children.*
Mr. Kucek: *Well, I offered fifty dollars ($50.00) a week your honor.*
The Court: *You're willing to pay $50.00 a week?*
Mr. Youngelson: *...He's the controller of a large company and*

makes twenty thousand dollars a year, and we're asking fifty dollars a week for each child. They are twelve and eleven respectively. The condition that he offered . . . was that these children be permitted to be sent by him to a private school instead of going to the public school in Parsippany . . . He says, in effect, that the public school system is communistic and all this sort of thing.

The Court: *Everybody is entitled to their opinion . . . Now, what's wrong with sending your children to private school, if he wants to pay the fifty dollars in addition to paying for the school?*

Mr. Youngelson: *This school is a school that is not approved by the plaintiff, wife. It's the Christian School in Dover.*

The Court: *Is that true, Mr. Kucek? Was that your condition?*

Mr. K: *Yes, sir, your honor. I'm very much concerned about the education of my children. Not only their academic education but their moral training. I'm willing to send them to any private school . . .*

The Court: *What's wrong with the Parsippany school?*

Mr. K: *. . . that meets the approval of you, the court, and myself. What's wrong with the Parsippany schools, for one thing, I have found that private schools are academically superior to public schools. The school in question, The American Christian School in Succasunna averages two years above public schools academically.*

The Court: *Well, are your children particularly gifted or unusual?*

Mr. K: *Yes, they are, your honor. They . . . well, at least in my opinion they are. And I am able and willing to provide a good education for them, and I'll do anything that's necessary in order to accomplish this.*

The Court: *. . . But, I'm not going to take all that into consideration, I'm only interested in how much you should pay for support.*

Mr. K: *Your honor, I'll furnish any amount that I possibly can in order to see that these children get a decent education . . .*

The Court: *Now, are you telling me that your moral scruples prevent your paying or that you can't afford to pay? I would like to know which?*

Mr. K: *Well, I think I can afford to pay.*

The Court: *How much? Can you afford to pay a hundred dollars a week?*

Mr. K: *With a struggle I can, and again, it would have to do with whether or not they went to a private school and received proper instruction. I would, even if I couldn't afford it with my present job, I'd even get another job or do whatever I could in order to see that these children receive a proper education . . .*

The Court: *What denomination are you?*

Mr. K: *Christian.*

The Court: *Well, now that's a broad, general –*

Mr. K: *No, sir.*

The Court: *–denomination, isn't it?*

Mr. K: *No, not within the context of the Bible it isn't. No, no sir, it's very confining.*

The Court: *Well, isn't your wife a Christian?*

Mr. K: *No, sir.*

The Court: *Then you don't belong to any particular sect within the Christian church?*

Mr. K: *Well, I do. I attend a Baptist church, however, the denomination is not significant your honor. Its distinction is Christianity.*

The Court: *Is this what has come between you and your wife?*

Mr. K: *Well, possibly your honor, yes. I only became a Christian last year.*

The Court: *What were you before that?*

Mr. K: *Well, about the same as her and most others, a nominal Christian or an atheist, agnostic, various–*

The Court: *Is it conceivable to you Mr. Kucek, that perhaps you're wrong? And, perhaps that you're the bigot in this situation?*

Mr. K: *Your honor, if I'm wrong then the Bible is wrong and*

308

I'll stand behind the Bible.

The Court: *The Bible as you see it, as you interpret it, isn't that right?*

Mr. K: *Well, no, as every Christian interprets it your honor.*

The Court: *Is it possible that there are any other faiths, that we're following besides yours?*

Mr. K: *Well, there are many faiths, yes.*

The Court: *And yours is the only true one, is that it?*

Mr. K: *According to the Bible, yes.*

The Court: *All right, I can see that it would be useless and fruitless to pursue this any further. Sir, as far as I'm concerned, I'm convinced that you are the one, who is* **bigoted,** *who is* **narrow** *and who is* **uninformed.** *You're the one who needs help. I have no doubt about that. Now, I would suggest that if anybody is driving your family apart, it is you. And, that you're the one who needs help and I suggest you see a psychiatrist.*

Mr. K: *Yes, sir, except I cannot make any payments until these children are in a private school.*

The Court: *Well, you're going to be in the County Jail, sir. You are not going to set the conditions, I am.*

Mr. K: *And if you think that putting me in jail is going to solve this problem then you're wrong too.*

The Court: *No, the only problem it will solve will be to convince you that you're going to comply with the order of the Court.*

Mr. K: *I can't if I don't have a job your honor.*

The Court: *Well, you have a job.*

Mr. K: *I won't have if I go to jail your honor.*

The Court: *This man needs help and you and I are going to try to help him, Mr. Youngelson.*

Mr. K: *Even if it kills me, right your honor?*

As this book goes to press, word comes from John Kucek that he is "in flight, because the Marxist-liberal atmosphere

309

in New Jersey sickens me, so I am traveling for health reasons."

Kucek, for daring to stand up against the child seducers lost one wife, two daughters, a $20,000 a year job, a $40,000 home ($30,000 equity), an automobile, a house full of furniture and two white German shepherd dogs.

Evidence has also come to us concerning the corrupt situation in the city of Parsippany, information so damning that much of it cannot be published here, even though the evidence will stand up in any court of law.

However, some of that damaging testimony and information should be recorded here – as a warning to parents all over America and in order to put the truth in print for all the world to see.

John Sheehy, Parsippany's assistant superintendent of schools and self-styled sex expert has close links with SIECUS and Montclair State College's sex training director, Dr. Charity Burden. We have 40 pages of documentation showing how Sheehy invades surrounding school districts with his sex curriculum, to the disgust of the teachers, and barges in on teacher discussion groups, pushing his curriculum and his sex philosophy.

One teacher in another district stood up to Sheehy, engaging him in debate and forced him to publicly admit his program could be damaging to children.

Then we have a Negro educator, Joseph Darden, who instructs teachers in his specialty, sex education, at Newark State College.

Teachers have written down statements – which are on file – to the effect that Darden advocated "gutter language" or the use of profanities and vulgarism both in the classroom and between teachers.

In October, 1969, Darden appeared before an audience in East Orange, N.J. where he spoke on a panel and said, "Man created God in his own image."

Then there is the strange case of educator Joseph Ford and a sex scandal in Parsippany.

Ford is the co-author of Sheehy's sex curriculum, the original and all the revised versions.

He is also a convicted sex offender, who performed his acts of sexual perversion in the presence of small children. After Ford was convicted, fined and placed on a year's probation as a sex offender guilty of "lewd and lascivious conduct" by Boonton, N.J. magistrate Roy Gensen, Parsippany's school board president, Betty Minor — who is employed as a guidance counselor by the district — promoted him to the post of administrative assistant to Parsippany's school superintendent George Oldham, after allowing him to resign as principal of Lake Hiawatha School.

Then there is the wierd case of the school psychologist in Margate, N.J. who blew his brains out with a gun after police charged him with sexual molestation of a young school boy.

That case was widely reported in the Parsippany press, though the Ford story only ran in an out-of-town newspaper, conveniently.

Last we have the case of a school superintendent in adjacent Hanover, also pushing Sheehy's sex program, who was arrested by local police with a gun in his car, purportedly on the way to kill a rival resident in a fight over a girlfriend.

His school board decided not to press charges because "the incident did not occur on school property."

And what happened to George Paules when he tried to tell his fellow citizens about all these things?

At the very first meeting where he dared to stand and voice his objections to the sex program, he was approached by a school sycophant who told him to move out of town if he didn't like the schools.

Subsequently, Paules family was subjected to unbelievable harassment and intimidation, threatening phone calls that seemed to coincide with school board meetings he attended.

The calls were reported to the police and the telephone company and the following month Paules was sued for libel by the district.

311

Paules' attorney told him that the school board attorney — illegally retained after the New Jersey State School Board ruled he could not be used for that purpose — frankly admitted to him (Paules' attorney) that the suit's purpose was to silence Paules.

The other purpose of the suit, obviously, was to influence the 1969 school board elections.

If Paules would be a good boy and remain silent, he said, the suit would be dropped quietly.

In addition, school personnel told Paules that if he took the whole matter into court — after the board finally dropped the suit — that they would call in "NEA lawyers who would discredit me, producing false witnesses, false documents and, if all else failed, commit me."

Paules' eight year old daughter was assaulted by the teenage daughter of a school board member, who tried to push her into a ditch right in front of her own house in broad daylight.

Mrs. Paules thereupon came to her daughter's defense and was arrested for battery and assault against a juvenile, with the complaint signed by the teenager's father.

When the judge heard Paules' side and the transparently obvious lies of the plaintiff's witnesses, he dismissed the case.

But the harassement continues. The very night Paules corresponded with me — in October, 1970 — his house was pelted with rotten eggs.

"My wife says let's move out of this sick town." said Paules, "and I suppose that is the idea . . . "

All over America, similar outrages are being carried on under the disguise of protecting the corrupt and degenerate tax supported school system.

XVII

CHILD SEDUCERS

As I drove my car across the California border the usual Oregon rain was falling — the kind of rain the natives call "Oregon mist." It was September, 1969.

Drops of water oozed between the window and the top of my convertible, plopping noisily on my left leg like a friendly welcoming committee.

The steady tatoo of drops seemed to beat out a message I translated into, "Welcome home, welcome home, welcome home."

And home it was, for I had spent a happy boyhood along the Oregon coast.

Roseburg was just up the highway, around a few hilly bends in the road, the town I romped and played in as a child.

After Roseburg, and a big crowd at the fairgrounds, I aimed the car toward Eugene, home of the bustling University of Oregon.

Again, a surprisingly large crowd turned out at the courthouse that night to hear me.

The next morning it was raining harder than ever as I drove toward Portland. Now the drops didn't seem so friendly. They were cold and forbidding.

"Damned convertible," I muttered, *"Never buy another one; brand new and leaks like a seive. They can send a rocket to the moon,"* I thought, *"but they can't make a lousy leakproof convertible."*

All the while the drops seemed to say, *"You fool, you fool, you fool."*

I was getting colder and angrier and I couldn't shake off the unpleasant feeling that had come over me during the twenty-four hours I had spent in Eugene.

Maybe it was the sight of hundreds of incredibly filthy hippies who thronged up and down the principle thoroughfare — most of them students at the University.

Maybe it was the block long line — mostly youngsters — that lounged in front of the theater where "I Am Curious - Yellow" was playing.

Or maybe it was the casual words dropped here and there by people — like the man at the gas station.

I had mentioned Arthur Fleming to him in idle chatter, the name of the long time president of the University and former head of the Department of Health, Education and Welfare.

The man's eyes had narrowed and his lips drew back in a razor straight line.

"Thank God he's left," he said, reminding me that Fleming had recently transferred to the Presbyterian college in Minnesota.

On arriving at the Minnesota campus, Fleming had promptly complained in a speech that students were not violent enough to suit him.

However the man at the gas station didn't know that the man who replaced Fleming had come from San Jose State College, where he had opened the flood gates to the revolution and encouraged the kind of permissiveness that led to full scale riots and intimidation of conservative faculty members.

(Interestingly enough, San Jose college students were reportedly in the vanguard of those who attacked the automobile carrying President Richard Nixon, Governor Ronald Reagan and Senator George Murphy during the 1970 election campaign.)

The sexologists were very busy in Eugene; I had suspected that was the case. After all, the Ellis Brown Trust, one of the earliest sexology promotion outfits, had an office on the campus and the president of the University was, under terms of the trust, an honorary administrator. The school had a vested interest, I thought.

Eugene, as could have been predicted, was on the verge of installing a complete sex education program despite strong opposition from many citizens.

314

Fear was the name of the Eugene game — just as it was in every town in the country where the sexologists were at work — fear and panic on the part of parents who could not quite understand what was happening to their children and to themselves.

The battle of Eugene, we realized, had only begun, for when the effects of the sex program became apparent, thousands of others would join the original dissenters — but would it be too late to save the children?

Just down the highway a few miles lay the sprawling campus of the State University, formerly called Oregon State College, in the farming region of Corvallis.

How many of these farmers knew what went on behind the walls of that school in the name of sociology?

Would the farmers believe it if you told them?

Oregon State, after all, had been the center for the activities of Lester Kirkendall for many years.

It was still raining when I drove into Portland, Oregon. But, it was like coming home.

It was twenty years since I had lived there, and I was not prepared for the changes that had taken place — the new freeway cutting through the heart of town, the magnificent coliseum where once the old Portland Auditorium had stood, the rows of new houses on the outskirts.

But the smells were the same — from the mighty Columbia River and from paper factories that still spewed chemicals into the air that smelled exactly like rotten eggs; and the acrid sweet smell of burning sawdust from the lumber mills.

Wheeling the car over the ancient Burnside bridge, I made my way through a cacophony of cars and trucks toward the heart of the city. Skid row hadn't changed much. The old Apostolic Faith Church was still there; its huge neon sign informing the passing throngs "Jesus, Light of the World," but where the huge Multnomah Hotel had stood there was a collection of new buildings.

Finally I turned onto Broadway, the great theatre street

that winds for two miles through the heart of the city. The movie palaces — most of them — were still there, bringing back memories of youthful escapades when I cut classes at nearby Pacific University to sit before the screens of the Broadway or the enormous old Paramount.

Time had made few changes — except that cocktail bars were scattered in profusion up and down the street.

At the hotel two attractive women were waiting in the lobby to greet me, Doris Wood and Mary Kangas.

It was warm and peaceful inside the lobby, lights sparkling against brass fixtures and the sound of laughter and music from the cocktail lounge.

The women had arranged for a press conference, and had paid for the room, themselves. Unfortunately, the local liberal paper, the Oregonian-Journal, didn't see fit to cooperate, despite the fact that Mrs. Kangas was a prominent member of the governor's committee that was looking into the family life and sex education courses in the state.

Still, a local TV station was there, and a handsome young Negro greeted the two women as if they were old friends — which apparently they were.

I felt half apologetic about the missing press. This was one of the few times that a local newspaper had ignored one of their own colleagues of the fourth estate.

Again there was that almost indefinable sense of fear, but not from the two women. They looked as if they were quite capable of handling themselves in any kind of a scrap.

But the conservatives in the city, it seemed, were badly divided — fighting among themselves when they should have been keeping their eye on the enemy. That wasn't unusual since it is the nature of conservatives to be independent.

Then came the radio station, and an hour interview on a telephone talk show that stretched into two hours and then into three hours and then into nearly four hours.

The conservatives of Portland, starved for news from the "outside world," were deluging the station with telephone

316

calls. Over and over came the woeful tale of a lack of representation for their point of view in any of the mass media.

Portland, a notoriously liberal union town, had gotten even more liberal since the days when I made its streets my playground.

The conservatives literally felt they had their backs to the wall, fighting not only their own battle but fighting the battle for the rest of us as well.

That night, at the Coliseum, a capacity crowd jammed the largest meeting room in the place — a rip roaring, enthusiastic crowd that had come to hear one of their champions speak for them.

I hardly felt up to the task — filled with too many mixed emotions and memories of that beautiful city. My duty, as I saw it at that moment, was to call for a unification of their forces, and so I did, to thundering applause.

On my way back to Anaheim, the unrelenting rain followed me into California.

It seemed to be trying to give me another message as it splattered frantically into the front seat. Suddenly, as if some supernatural voice was talking to me, I thought back to the night before in Portland; of the four hour broadcast, the throng that attended my lecture, and the newspaper that gave me the cold shoulder.

That had been a home town for me, for awhile; why not make every hamlet, village and city my HOMETOWN?

Why not inform everyone of this fire breathing dragon that would incinerate morals, fidelity, religious beliefs and patriotism; that would deprive us of our constitutional rights to Life, Liberty and the Pursuit of Happiness and sell us down the river into the clutches of the Communists. Why not tell them about the sex education quagmire, the child seducers and the change artists?

Surely in every community there are people like Sam Campbell, Jim Townsend, Eleanor Howe, Jan Pippenger, Evelyn Burns and the rest of the antagonists who fought the battle

317

and won.

Even though their local newspapers ignore the issue for fear of losing a few dollars in advertising, these people must be informed.

That would be my goal.

They must be made aware of their enemies, and how to ferret them out and destroy them.

They must become aware of the facts that the parents in Anaheim discovered to their horror.

Parents in Anaheim who investigated the sex instruction program discovered that their schools were even worse than they had imagined.

They discovered subversion at the very heart of the educational structure, and at every level.

Subversion in this context is meant the downgrading of patriotism and the allegiance the normal child feels toward his country.

They found the system emphasizing the negative and minimizing the strengths and accomplishments of our system of government.

They found teachers downgrading the potentialities of the free enterprise system that has given six per cent of the world's population most of the world's wealth.

They discovered the schools were minimizing the ability of individual Americans and individual institutions.

They found the schools pitting child against parent and class (of people) against class.

They found the schools were blaming all evil on one class of people and attributing all virtue to another class.

They discovered the schools were branding capitalism as the enemy of the people and an implacable foe of human rights, as incapable of social conscience and hostile to change.

They found their schools teaching that the only solution to our problems is found in some kind of totalitarian system best described as COMMUNAZI.

They found the schools were filled with agents who were

318

teaching that Socialism was an ideal form of life.

They discovered the schools teaching that a planned collectivist economy and the welfare state are ideals to be reached at all costs.

They found the schools had taken to themselves the job of "social reconstruction," a task that was not theirs in the first place and a task the taxpayers never delegated to the schools.

They found the schools reaching for absolute power through national and local teacher organizations, and they discovered the teachers were being encouraged to grasp for power without having to account to the taxpayers for their activities.

Last, they found their children were being indoctrinated into a one world philosophy, with tax supported schools serving as the prime promoter of supranational sovereignty or world government — eradicating, beginning with kindergarten, all love of country and loyalty for America.

In the name of so-called progressive education and academic freedom, the educators were attributing supreme virtues to the new and unproved, to an attitude of cynical skepticism and cynical distrust of human motives and impulses.

A significant segment of the educational community has been proclaiming for at least the past 25 years that it is the right and duty of educators to undertake the remolding of society.

That wasn't new, since Dewey had been talking about that decades before.

But now it takes on a new sense of urgency and haste.

The movement found advocacy, expression and implementation through policies promulgated by the National Education Association, through thousands of books and journals, through indoctrination of fledgling teachers in colleges and at educational conferences.

What, then, were their basic premises?

First, capitalism and free enterprise were dead or dying, doomed to extinction. In their place would rise the new Socialist state.

Second, they insisted the school must assume the leading role to bring about the collapse of capitalism.

Third, the child must be conditioned to fit into that total world order.

And they succeeded – frighteningly – and to a very great degree.

Fourth, they called for a revision of the educational system and the philosophy and the curriculum in order to rapidly advance their cause.

Fifth, many teachers embraced the anti-American syndrome that this change to a Fascist state could only come about by class conflict and violence. Hence, the children were to be programmed into becoming the front line cannonfodder for the coming inevitable conflict.

Sixth, recognizing there will be some kind of opposition to their juggernaut in the tax supported schools, they proposed various steps to power, designed to help the administrators and educators deal with the opposition and smash all resistance to their tyranny.

Seventh, since teachers were to play the vital role as change agents, it was important for the schools to know where the teachers stood in the political/economic/social order.

Following World War II, the notion was engendered for radical change, and stated over and over in countless educational journals. Countless conferences were held to get the teachers to go along with them. Later, those same people extended their call for a Fascist state in America to embrace the whole world.

The NEA, of course, was leading the whole parade into collectivism and most parents paid them no heed.

On July 6, 1951, the NEA, expecting resistance to their tyrannical ideas, passed a resolution in San Francisco that called for a crushing of all opposition. That was actually an echo from the thirtieth yearbook of the American Association of School Administrators.

"Public education in America is under its heaviest attack in

320

history," they stormed, thereupon setting up a straw man. "This attack is not aimed at improving free education but in destroying it."

Now, in the first place there is no such thing as a free education, just as there's no such thing as a free lunch. Second, there was hardly much of a furor, since most Americans were sound asleep and snoring loudly.

Sam Campbell outlined a strategy to cope with the realities the sexologists now face.

"Well, we have a word for the professional sexologists. Gentlemen, you are finished. You have been outgeneraled. You chose the point of decision, but you met there a power that is greater than your own. You do not understand that power, but now at least you respect it. Curious? Read Ephesians 6:17. That is what is beating the sexologists."

"Letters pour into the Anaheim Bulletin from all parts of the nation," Campbell continued. "They pour in at an unprecedented rate. They come from anguished parents. They are requests for information on how to fight this gruesome monster that is reaching out through the hereto greatly trusted tax supported school system, to throw its ancient, evil, lustful arms around the little children of this land.

"This is a war. It rages in every state and every city. We have on our desk pleas from Calgary, Canada, and a news story of strange events transpiring in West Germany. The sexologists launched this war. Apparently, they have been able to rope in some very sensible people. For awhile they thought everything was going their way. The signal was 'full throttle ahead.' By mid year, 1967, it was as if some powerful person at some central place had pushed a button and the whole apparatus began to function.

"These worshippers of Baal did not know one thing. They did not know they were being watched. They did not know they were being infiltrated. They did not know that careful records were being kept. Now they are puzzled. They are puzzled that their private consultations are no longer private.

321

They are puzzled that their most secret meetings are uncovered. They dare not whisper for fear that what is hidden will be shouted from the housetops.

"The object of war is to meet the enemy with superior power at the points of decision. The sexologists are meeting a superior power. They do not know where it comes from. They have not learned that God-fearing people are the most powerful force on earth. They do not understand such power. We have it from their own lips. From a communique distributed through the wretched sexologist cabal at the Sacramento level, we get this word: 'This group (the sex education opponents), estimated to be no more than 10 per cent of the school community, seems to be motivated by dynamics considerably deeper than the rational level. My own prognosis is that there will be a long delay which may prove fatal to our project . . . ' "

That scripture verse from Ephesians, coming down the centuries, does indeed sound the death knell, in time, for all those who conspire to poison the wells of knowledge and seduce the bodies of America's children.

"And take unto you the helmet of salvation," it reads, "and the sword of the spirit — which is the Word of God."

In Anaheim — as in other towns and cities across the nation — groups of young people are beginning to come to grips with the empty void left by the behaviorists. They are turning to God.

God may be dead in America's tax supported schools, but he is very much alive in such youth oriented programs as Teen Challenge, Campus Crusade for Christ, the Catholic Youth Organization (CYO) and so forth.

And in these organizations, the answers are found in the plain old fashioned way — through a search for the eternal verities.

It may be that if this republic is to be saved from total chaos and internal destruction, that salvation will come from just such organizational leadership.

It will surely not come from the behavioral science laboratories and the tax supported schools, both of which are contributing to the problem rather than helping to solve it.

Yes, in Anaheim there are a few people who really care.

Among those people are the members of the board of the Citizen's Committee of California, Inc. Unsung and unheralded – their names never mentioned in the furor that erupted over the sex instruction program – they form, nonetheless, a solid core of responsible and dedicated citizens that make it possible for the committee to carry on many of its functions.

Orange County's most popular children's dentist, Dr. James Garry, is one whose quiet strength was always there when it was needed most. His background reads like a Horatio Alger success story.

Garry was a bombardier in the Eighth Air Force during World War II and is a former prisoner of war. He is active in the American Legion and the Disabled American Veterans as well as being the president of the Fullerton chapter of the California Republican Assembly. Garry is also the vice president of the Freedom Forum in Orange County and belongs to the American Association of Dentists.

The past president of the Orange County Dental Staff, Garry is popular and highly admired among his fellow professionals, and he belongs to at least six of the leading professional dental societies in the nation.

Another unsung hero in the continuing war over better education is the Citizen's Committee board member William Jolissaint, public relations man for Karl Karcher Enterprises and a devout Roman Catholic. A member of the Fatima Crusade, Jolissaint spent much time in prayer for the success of the committee's endeavors. Who can tell how much his faith helped?

Jolissaint sings in the St. Boniface Church Choir in Anaheim and is one of the Ambassadors for the Anaheim Chamber of Commerce.

William Krebs, a true intellectual, is a solid rock of dependable self assurance when times get rough. He is a good one to have in your corner when the storms are raging.

An engineer for a principle aerospace company, Krebs has been for many years a major wheel horse in Orange County Republican politics. It is Bill Krebs who helps run the precinct operations in the Anaheim area during elections. Krebs is a past president of the Anaheim area Republican Assembly and still serves as a member of the board of directors.

With a brilliant background in history, Krebs is able to sort out the trivial from the significant and to put current social problems into the perspective of time and eternity.

Meanwhile, Dr. William Kott — popular Anaheim dentist — has taken a leave of absence from the Citizen's Committee board to attend school in San Francisco in order to get an advanced doctorate in orthodontics.

One of the first distinguished Anaheim men to serve on the board, Kott's counsel was always eagerly sought by committee state chairman, Jim Townsend.

On the other hand, Kott's impassioned way of verbalizing his ideas became the bane and scourge of Anaheim leftists.

Up and down the state of California there are Citizen's Committee chairmen, each doing their part in a synchronized whole that works with amazing smoothness and agility.

There is none of the usual bureaucratic nonsense attached to the committee's operations.

Townsend has a way of slicing through the trivia and going to the heart of the matter, while his board members and supporters are well schooled in the need to keep their eye on the goal. It is this single mindedness that makes it possible for the committee to win triumph after triumph on the California scene.

In Anaheim, the Citizen's Committee members — subjected to unbelievable calumny by certain school forces — found their position on sex education vindicated when enrollment in the drastically curtailed new sex course dropped to only one-fifth the enrollment of the year before. The public had listened, had

324

weighed the issues and had taken a stand.

For nearly two years the mail poured into the committee's Fullerton offices, from every city and state in the nation and even from foreign countries. Visits by reporters from such prestigious newspapers as the Christian Science Monitor became almost a daily occurrence.

Reporters for such magazines as the Reader's Digest came to Townsend's office for materials for stories on sex education, while television and radio stations vied with each other in sending out reporters to cover the ongoing struggle.

Thousands of pieces of mail went out from the committee offices, across the land, educating other citizens in far away places to the nature of the school programs they were opposing.

Most of that vast distribution was paid for by the committee, with little assistance from those who were requesting the material.

Finally, in the spring of 1969, Townsend inaugurated his own monthly newspaper, "The Educator." *

The advent of the newspaper opened up a whole new can of worms and broadened the scope of those who were fighting the behaviorists.

Newsmen in Orange County gave freely of their time and talent to write for the paper and to prepare it for the press.

And it didn't take long for the enemy to take notice. In the February, 1970 issue of Psychology Today, the editors blasted The Educator as the biggest single threat to the behaviorist's programs.

The Educator is "terrorizing the parents" of America, the magazine cried, implying that the Citizen's Committee of California was the single most effective force in fighting school sex education and Sensitivity Training.

Of course, there is no direct connection between The Edu-

---

*The Educator, published at 1110 S. Pomona Avenue, Fullerton, California. $6 per year.

325

cator and the Citizen's Committee — but the enemy knew that the committee's voice had been increased a thousand fold by the advent of the newspaper, which goes to every corner of the United States.

The Citizen's Committee had fulfilled its pledge. When the sex issue first broke, Townsend growled that he would not be happy until the sex program in Anaheim — that had spread around the nation — was demolished, as an example to school boards everywhere. The program isn't quite demolished — but the people who were instrumental in setting it up are no longer in positions of power and the program is drastically revised.

As one voice, parents cry the same emphatic refrain: "We will regain our rightful place as preceptors of our children's moral attitudes."

And if the tax supported system does not listen to them, if the professional educators and their behaviorist cohorts do not cease their willful seduction of the young, these same people will, one day soon, padlock the school house doors.

If that happens, a whole generation yet unborn will call them blessed, for they will have preserved freedom.

For they know that they are not wrestling against only flesh and blood. They are wrestling against principalities, against powers, against spiritual wickedness in high places. They are battling the dark forces of this world.

These parents are obeying a spiritual injunction. They are putting on the armor of God — so they can stand against evil in their own day. And when they have done all they can, with the help of their fellow citizens and the help of God, they will still be standing, unafraid and taller than ever before.

For this they know — evil seducers shall become worse and worse, deceiving others and being deceived. False prophets of false gods will arise, deceiving the very elect.

In the words of a famous priest, "Today there is no land that offers an escape. Today we are surrounded by Communists. They border our nation north of Alaska; they poise their lethal weapons on the shores of Cuba; they dominate the con-

326

tinent of Asia; they flex their muscles in every European country; they hail Castro throughout South America and number at least 50 million adherents and sympathizers from Minnesota to Florida, from New York to Los Angeles.

"In a sense, we are trapped not only physically but ideologically. There is no room for God or Christ in most of our universities. But there is ample room for Karl Marx and his progeny. Catholics are not even safe religiously inside the walls of the once great Catholic University, once the bastion of our faith.

"Whither then can Protestant or Catholic or Jew seek refuge and safety in a nation where the Red menace has risen so rapidly that it overshadows the entire earth?

"Whither, then, can Americans flee to escape the holocaust that all but blind men see?

"Either stand and fight — and die, if needs be — or learn to bend your stiff neck and stiffer knees to grovel at the feet of our conquerors."

The Mother of God spoke to the world at Fatima, and her words ring down the corridors of time to our day.

"There will be a kind of false peace before the advent of the anti-Christ. Man's only thoughts will be upon diversions and amusements. The wicked will indulge in all sin, but the children of the Holy Church, the children of the faith, my sincere followers, will wax strong in the love of God and in the virtues that are most dear to me. Happy the humble souls that are guided by the Holy Ghost. I will fight with them until they have reached the end of the age.

"For a time the Church will be delivered to great persecutions. That will be the hour of darkness, and the Church will experience a great crisis. The powerful officials of the State and the Church will be suppressed and done away with, and all law and order as well as justice. There will be murder and hate and envy and deceit, with no love or regard for one's country or family.

"Lucifer, with a very great number of demons, will be un-

327

chained from Hell. By degrees they shall abolish the faith, even among persons consecrated to God. They shall bind them in such manner that, without very special graces, these persons shall imbibe the spirit of those wicked angels.

" . . . for a time the Church will be exposed to very great persecutions. This shall be the time of darkness . . .

"I address a pressing appeal to the earth. I call upon the true disciples of the living God, who reigns in the heavens; I call upon the true imitators of Christ made man, the only true Saviour of mankind.

"Go ye forth and manifest yourselves as my children. I am with you and within you, so your faith may be a light which illumines you in these unhappy days and that your zeal may make you long for the glory and the honor of the Most High. *Fight, ye children of light; combat, ye small bands that can see, for this is the time of times, the end of ends.*

"Together with the anti-Christ, the demons will work false miracles in the earth and air. Voices will be heard in the air. Then men will desert religion and become worse. Men will let themselves be deceived, because they refused to adore the real Christ who lived bodily among them.

" . . . The whole world shall be struck with terror, and many will allow themselves to be seduced, because they have not believed the true Christ living among them. The sun becomes dark. Faith only shall survive. So the time! The abyss opens! Behold the king of kings of darkness! *Behold the beast with his subjects . . .* "

So the battle is that of the temporal versus the spiritual, of the anti-Christ versus the Lord of Heaven and Earth.

One small battleground in this titanic struggle is the tax supported school system of the United States. The children are the prize in this clash of wills and of purposes. Their bodies and their souls hang in the balance.

With God and His Son locked out of America's school rooms, the battle for the souls of the young must be joined in adult circles, before school boards and before administrators

328

and teachers.

Satan reigns in the classrooms of this land — for no child can utter an audible prayer to Almighty God without running risk of censure.

The anti-Christ is working in very human ways to seal the bondage of the free.

We know that in the end God will win the battle.

Meanwhile, he tells us to put on His whole armor, that we may be able to stand in this evil day — and having done all we can, to stand with our backs against the gate, sword in hand, the sword of the Spirit.

Christ the King has issued His call to arms.

Will you obey Him?

ADDENDUM TO THIRD PRINTING – March, 1971

Non-teaching professionals in the fields of social work, sociology, psychology and psychiatry have literally taken over America's school system. Most of the innovations that have caused angry reactions on the part of parents and some teachers have been brought into the districts by outsiders, people who are not teachers, are not credentialed to teach and who have no business interjecting their ideas into the classroom.

Teachers have passively allowed this bizarre thing to happen, while they have spent much of their time fighting the people who have been trying to warn them that their own profession of education is being subverted by non-educators who have attached themselves to the public schools for that purpose.

For instance, I was present on March 15, 1971 at the Anaheim Convention Center when Sally Williams told delegates to a meeting of the California Medical Association that the main purpose of the Anaheim sex instruction program was to cause behavioral changes in children and alter their attitudes.

That, of course, was what the Citizen's Committee had claimed all along.

Mrs. Williams said, "It became evident that the parents simply were not ready to allow a shift in control (of the morals, attitudes and behavior of their children) from them (the parents) to the schools."

She lamented the fact and suggested that the behavioral scientists must work on ways to overcome this parent resistance by changing adult attitudes.

Dr. Tom Robinson, a Newport Beach physician, agreed with Mrs. Williams, and added, "Most students come to school with a structured value system from their parents (and) the most propagandizing high school cannot undo it."

However, Robinson saw a ray of hope in brainwashing the students into a new ethic – or a new non-ethic.

"To the extent they (the teachers) can create questions in the child's mind relative to other value systems," he said, "that is fine, but we must admit that we stir up anxieties in parents (who have) rigid value systems."

In other words, Mrs. Williams – one of the nation's leading sex instructors – and Robinson, who supports such programs, were saying that the ethics and moral attitudes the child brings to school from home are too rigid and traditional – and the child must be exposed to "other value systems" in order to break down his resistance to change.

JOHN STEINBACHER

EPILOGUE

The brilliant F.A. Hayek said much the same thing we have said in this book in his masterful "Counter-Revolution of Science: Studies of the Abuse of Reason" published by Collier-MacMillan, Ltd., London.

On page 92 and 93 Hayek writes: "It may indeed prove to be far the most difficult and not the least important task for human reason rationally to comprehend its own limitations. It is essential for the growth of reason that as individuals we should bow to forces and obey principles which we cannot hope to fully understand, yet on which the advance and even the preservation of civilization depends. Historically this has been achieved by the influence of the various religious creeds and by traditions and superstitions which made men submit to those forces by an appeal to his emotions rather than to his reason. *The most dangerous stage in the growth of civilization may well be that in which man has come to regard all these beliefs as superstitions and refused to accept or to submit to anything which he does not rationally understand.* The rationalist whose reason is not sufficient to teach him those limitations of the powers of conscious reason, and who despises all the institutions and customs which have not been consciously designed, *would thus become the destroyer of the civilization built upon them.* This may well prove a hurdle which man will repeatedly reach, only to be thrown back into barbarism.

" . . . Common acceptance of formal rules is indeed the only alternative to direction by a single will man has yet discovered. The general acceptance of such a body of rules is no less important because they have not been rationally constructed. It is at least doubtful whether it would be possible in this way to construct a new moral code that would have any chance of acceptance. But so long as we have not succeeded in doing so, any general refusal to accept existing moral codes merely

331

because their expediency has not been rationally demonstrated is to destroy one of the roots of our civilization."

Perhaps Spencer said it all in the following few words, "There is a principle which is proof against all argument . . . and which cannot fail to keep a man in everlasting stupidity and ignorance. That principle is condemnation without investigation."

After three years of investigation, I can claim to be somewhat removed from the man of whom Spencer speaks.

I can hope the reader will go and do likewise, for the scriptures tell me in eloquent simplicity how children are to be reared and how families are to be maintained.

In the sixth chapter of Ephesians, Paul writes, "Children, obey your parents in the Lord, for this is right. Honor thy father and thy mother; which is the first commandment with promise; that it may be well with thee, and thou mayest live long on the earth. And ye father, provoke not your children to wrath, but bring them up in the nurture and admonition of the Lord."

Yet, if the educational establishment has its way, neither children nor fathers will be able to obey this injunction of God.

In the words of Congressman John G. Schmitz, "The would-be totalitarians have already turned many of our schools into boiling cauldrons of crisis and strife. We dare not let them extend their turmoil into lives of two and three year old children who are utterly defenseless against it."

When all is said and done, will the parents of America awake from their sleep long enough to protect the defenseless little ones who are now on the front line of the ideological struggle for their minds, souls and bodies?

Or will they sacrifice their children for expediency, pleasure and apathy, earning Christ's condemnation for those who harm his little ones.

"Woe unto that man who would harm one of these my little ones. It were far better for him that a millstone were placed around his neck and he were dropped into the depths

332

of the sea."

What an awesome responsibility then, for the parents and teachers of America – *a frightening responsibility.*

Yet, when parents and teachers alike determine to assume the burden for educating for freedom instead of indoctrinating for totalitarianism, things will begin to happen.

Again the children of America will sing the songs of childhood, and play the games of youth in a springtime world of joy and heartfelt fulfillment.

They will be allowed to function as children while they are still young – and they will be protected by their parents from individuals and movements that would seduce them into perversion, darkness and spiritual death.

For if the children of America are seduced into the ways of treason, drugs, crime and immorality, *parents* will only have themselves to blame – for not knowing what is going on in that neighborhood schoolroom.

And if parents stand idly by while their children are lost to all reason, they will not be held blameless before the Creator of us all.

APPENDIX ONE

July 6, 1970
REMARKS DELIVERED BY COLLIN E. COOPER, M.D., TO A LA CANADA UNIFIED SCHOOL DISTRICT REVIEW COMMITTEE, CONVENED TO CONSIDER A REQUEST FOR RECONSIDERATION OF THE *SHES* HEALTH EDUCATION CURRICULUM

On May 21, 1970, a letter written by me appeared in the Ledger. I did not write the editorial headline giving a caption to this letter and so take no responsibility for it. I take full responsibility for the contents of the letter. Its pertinence to the entire question of the SHES health education curriculum make it a good starting point. Few who have talked to me about that letter have shown any real understanding of it. The most common mistake to date is the allegation that I was claiming there were dirty pictures to be shown to the district's pupils or that sex education was to be taught. Neither was even hinted at by my letter. What was said was extremely important and pertinent to the reason for which you are all gathered here today.

The Sex Information and Education Council of the United States (SIECUS) was incorporated in May of 1964. The School Health Education Study (SHES) was put together in 1960 and ensconsed in the headquarters of the NEA by the fall of 1961. Most of the people who later spun off and incorporated SIECUS were involved with SHES from the very beginning. In fact, the original printing of the basic document, 1967, was far more explicit about the direct ties between SHES and SIECUS. Why these references were deleted for the second printing of March 1968 is a question this committee should ponder. The currently available basic document still goes to the trouble to thank two members of the board of SIECUS for their very special help, Mary S. Calderone and Wallace

334

Fulton. To me, the overriding question is, that if the philosophy of what was later to be identified with SIECUS could be harbored in the bosom of SHES from the very beginning, later incorporated as the sex education part of Concept 6 of the SHES curriculum, and eventually to mold the entire curriculum through the premeditated overlap and integration of all the concepts by this philosophy, how could our district even consider this curriculum? From 1965 on, many communities in this country, one as close as Alhambra, found themselves fighting what they called SIECUS, i.e., its philosophy and the natural outgrowth of that philosophy, the terribly inappropriate classroom material. What they didn't find out until later was that they were really fighting one of the first two concepts of SHES to be tried out, Concept 6! Can this pagan ethic which is now branded as SIECUS, and really the so-called "new morality," only exist in just one concept and not affect the total curriculum? The answer is a resounding no! The basic document brags repeatedly about the thorough saturation and interrelationship of *all* the Concepts by means of this philosophy. SIECUS, as an approach to sex education, is simply a specific expression of the very general philosophy of Humanism, with its rejection of absolutes, worship of man as the supreme-being, and its resorting to situation ethics for its moral code. From this point of view, since SHES *has* adopted this view of life, the curriculum must be junked before it ever gets started in this district!

For the purpose of this talk I am going to state briefly what is an extremely important and fully documented point. The book HEALTH EDUCATION: A CONCEPTUAL APPROACH TO CURRICULUM DESIGN, and called the basic document by all those concerned with this curriculum, is an important and authoritative book in the field of education and deals in its own words with "basic education issues." All the material in the curriculum is derived from and dependent on the basic document, as *any* reading of the introduction to *every* Teaching-Learning Guide will corroborate!

Conceptualized education, whether it be in the field of health or social studies, is designed to carry out and teach to the child a specific philosophy which is anti-Christian. The total content of these presentations will demonstrate this beyond a shadow of a doubt! In addition, the SHES curriculum is open to criticism by looking at the specifics of the classroom materials and the thoughts developed in the In-Service Workshop. But, because of the premeditated and intended interrelatedness of the curriculum, its overall philosophy *must* be understood before touching, much less adopting, the curriculum! This is done by reading and studying the basic document.

Since the curriculum is alleged by its proponents to teach about health, its philosophy of and definition of health should be examined. This is referred to in the basic document as "the dimensions of health" and then renamed "subconcepts." These specifically interrelate all the ten major Concepts. They are "physical, mental and social." After playing the variations on this for several pages, the whole idea is summed up by their words, "physical status, mental well-being, and social awareness." This is then called "man's total self." The full implications of this are staggering but it should be perfectly obvious to this committee that the SHES total man has no spiritual dimension. This should be abundantly clear to those of you on this committee who are familiar with the YMCA Triad of Mind, Body and Spirit! In my opinion, this curriculum should be thrown out on this basis alone! While there are those who would argue that public schools are forbidden to teach for Christ, I have not yet met anyone willing to say that they must teach for the anti-Christ! This is not a health education curriculum teaching the basic facts about health and disease as our district's educational policy puts it; it is a philosophical system. It is in point of fact a humanistic philosophy, which *is* a religion by a decision of the U.S. Supreme Court.

A second set of tenets which bind the curriculum together are called Key Concepts. These are listed as "growing and developing, interacting, and decision making." These particular words and this type of thinking permeate the writing of the educationists and they repeatedly refer to man as the decision-making animal. The basic document states that decision making is what separates man from the animals! This is totally false as far as the science of animal behavior is concerned and yet this scientifically false idea is the basis for an interrelationship of all of this curriculum's aspects!

This behavioristic-mechanistic approach to man is best seen in Concept 5 and was quite well revealed in even the rapid exposure that the transparencies were given in on June 9th! The basic document summarizes Concept 5 with a final sentence which has been the subject of endless books — "Man is, in essence, not apart from environment." In buying this, we have committed ourselves to an anti-Christian view of life. This first appeared in modern form in the early 19th Century and was proposed by the men who were later known as the fountainhead of socialism! In my view, and that of the last 2,000 years of man's experience, what makes man unique is his constant need for and seeking of God. God the creator becomes God the father in the successful completion of this search, and that is the truth which is the source of what we call Western civilization! If we are to acquiesce to the denial of our school district's right to teach the *correct* philosophical system, we must not instead teach a philosophical system which *denies* God! This so-called curriculum teaches this philosophy, not an organized discipline of knowledge!

Dr. Gus T. Dalis is of crucial importance to this whole discussion and deserves mention here. As one of the writers of this curriculum, he is one of eight chosen from the entire country! When you consider that the SHES group was based on the East Coast, picking a man from Los Angeles to be on the Writing Group is of even more significance! He is also the co-author of a book, HEALTH INSTRUCTION: THEORY INTO PRACTICE, which is credited by SHES with translating taxonomy's goals for general education into this health cur-

337

riculum. This is of singular importance and can only be fully appreciated by reading *how* the educationists have awaited such a development for the past decade! Finally, Dr. Dalis is in Europe, where part of his time will be spent at a conference on the social studies curriculum. He will be teaching a workshop on educational techniques. Anyone who heard his presentation for Inquiry can be sure that this will be a major topic.

Of all the systems for inducing a specific classroom environment in which to teach children, this is the most evil. Inquiry's theoretical basis and its practical application best exemplify the total philosophy of the educationists for the 1970's. It *is* called for in the SHES curriculum and all so-called conceptualized curriculums. It has received the most publicity in relation to the "new social studies" but is definitely not limited to this. All the anticipated new curriculums, which will be conceptual in form, run on the inquiry method. SHES is *no* exception.

The goal of the inquirists is to develop children who "think like social scientists." By any acceptable definition of the scientific method there has never been such a thing as a social scientist! Real scientific investigation is conducted by a mature man whose own character is committed to a system of absolutes as a secure frame of reference on which to build future knowledge. This is not possible when dealing with the totally immature and untrained minds of children.

The clue phrase having reference to the inquiry method and which appears several times in the basic document is "critical thinking." You should be aware that this exact phrase appears repeatedly in educational jargon. When a question is raised about its meaning, the counter-question is posed, "Are you against critical thinking?" This rejoiner evades the point. Critical thinking, if an honest definition be applied, is a perfectly acceptable approach to many subjects at the post-graduate level and beyond. Critical thinking, so-called, and forms of inquiry, are used in law schools to examine and learn about areas in the law and their application. The principle of scien-

338

tific investigation frequently uses the kind of critical thinking about which the layman thinks he knows the definition. Not accepting the obvious answer, seeking alternative explanations, and testing them until true and reproducible results are found, is a way of life to the good scientist. This is done by mature minds, in narrow areas of intellectual endeavor. What is being proposed by the inquirists is that such highly sophisticated and very difficult-to-master-and-use techniques be taught to children starting in kindergarten or before, if the behaviorists have their way. (This is a setting in which so-called critical thinking is foreign and even dangerous to the normal maturation of the child's mind.)

The Center for the Study of Instruction, and its Director Paul Brandwein, are the best contemporary and representative examples of thinking and writing in this area. For a further exposition on the matter of both the Center and Brandwein, you will find material in the pamphlet to guide your study. The most thorough-going discussion of Inquiry in a relatively short space can be found in the foreword, or explanation to the teachers, of the new social studies curriculum written by the Center and published by Harcourt, Brace and World. This is a conceptualized curriculum and as such teaches no discipline or body of organized knowledge. Since this textual series is being considered by the State of California for adoption, it is available in the Glendale Library for study. The ideas being communicated by these people are not the rantings of some educational offshoot or nut! These are the very current and mainstream educational ideas and the ones upon which the curricular revolution of the 1970's is being built. All the references to basic educational theory and practice are the same whether you read Brandwein or the basic document!

One of the fundamental premises upon which Inquiry is built is founded on what educationists call the "values continuum." This concept views all values as existing on a spectrum of continuum. They may vary by shades of gray from one end to the other of the spectrum but it is important to remember

339

that neither end is labelled either good or bad! No value judgement is ever made in inquiry and the teacher is forcefully condemned if she attempts this in the classroom! This idea then as a generality has been applied in the approach to Concept 9 and fully developed there.

In this approach to knowledge, there are no absolutes. "The sad fact emerged that rules were often set by an authority (the parent) and were not subject to appeal" is Brandwein's lament when a child comes to the classroom with fixed notions. The child is quickly brought to the realization through the use of Inquiry that there are many other possible positions to take on any subject, and what is more evil is that these various positions are stated to all be equally valid! "After role-playing, a values discussion should follow which must be open-ended. If the teacher feels there is only one possible solution, then the discussion is not a values-seeking one but a preaching for conformity." This preaching for conformity is roundly condemned!

The Center for the Study of Instruction sponsored a series of articles in TODAY'S EDUCATION. The one in the May 1969 issue was entitled, INQUIRY. For the authors, the following quote registers approval of Inquiry. For me it is a strong reason why any curriculum based on or utilizing Inquiry in any form must not be used in our district! "For the students, the most important result of learning through inquiry is a change in attitudes toward knowledge. As they engage in the dialogue of inquiry, they begin to view knowledge as tentative rather than absolute, and they consider all knowledge claims as being subject to revision and confirmation." The observers to the In-Service Workshop clearly saw Inquiry advocated, its importance emphasized, and the intention to use this method in our district stressed. No surprise, SHES is useless without it!

The ultimate result of the anti-Christian position held by the educationist today is summarized in Brandwein's words when he says, " . . . the child begins to see each person as of

340

supreme moral worth." The full meaning of this idea boggles the imagination! To understand what is being said here does not require straining at or twisting the meaning of words. All the writings of the educationists, mainstream educational thinking, repeat this idea endlessly. The child is being led to see a totally false view of life. He is to believe that each person regardless of what he does or says or stands for, is equally worthwhile. Thus, their views must be accepted as equally valid with all other views on all matters. There is no right or wrong until the group has sifted through all the possible choices of all these equally valid positions and has come up with a consensus which is the right thing for that time and place. THERE ARE NO ABSOLUTES! But, more importantly, Brandwein imputes to every person equal and supreme moral worth! This denies the possibility of any absolute moral standard or morality of any higher origin than man himself. This is what the educationists affirm over and over again, and this is the point of Inquiry, no matter how you slice it or excuse it! Any doctrine of absolute good and evil is denied as is the possibility of anything called sin. Furthermore, guilt, which of course must arise if you actually believe that there is sin and drives you to repent for your sins, is flatly called a "destructive emotion." This is one strong reason why teachers using inquiry are so constantly told they must not make value judgements in the classroom. To do so would imply that some students were wrong and others right and therefore evoke guilt which is supposedly destructive in the student's life, but more importantly, destroys the inquiry environment! For this culmination of Humanism I refer you to the Humanist Manifesto, reprinted in its entirety in the excellent Klotz Report submitted to the State Board of Education in 1969.*

---

*"The American family structure produces mentally ill children." Israel Ehrenburg (alias Ashley Montagu), SIECUS board member, during a speech to 1,000 home economics teachers at the Anaheim Convention Center, Nov. 9, 1970.

341

The total effect of group dynamics, sensitivity training, inquiry method, or as Brandwein euphemistically puts it, "the skill of interdependence," is to degrade the family as the God-ordained unit upon which to build a healthy society. Nothing good is said about the family by the Educationists, nothing good is said about the family in the Workshop. The child, when he returns to the classroom, is purged of any handicap to his "scientific thinking" which he may have picked up from his family, is taught to unlearn absolutes, and his thinking is reshaped to conform to the group opinion!

SHES, as with all conceptualized curricula, teaches no body of organized knowledge or any discipline of study. The curriculum is totally non-graded and this is intentional. This approach to health education as an integral part of the implementation of this curriculum in our district was re-affirmed in our Workshop and is characteristic of conceptualized education.

This brings us to the subject of "testing and evaluation." These words are used continually in relation to this curriculum. Unwary parents, equipped with the standard and long-accepted definitions of these words, assume that this means such procedures will be used to determine whether or not the curriculum is worth continuing at all after a probationary period. This is not so!! Testing and evaluation is used to determine whether the teachers are performing up to standard and whether or not the students are achieving the objectives assigned, without actually grading them, but not with the idea in mind of junking the curriculum. Only to retrain the teacher

(Footnote continued from page 341)
Also speaking was Elizabeth Koontz, SIECUS board member, former president of the NEA and President Nixon's choice to head the Division of Women's Labor of HEW. These two SIECUS members were invited to speak by the very same Department of Education that outlawed SIECUS materials as unfit for California school children.

or recycle the student. It is by the so-called testing and evaluation that the curriculum's monitors can determine if the teacher is effectively using the intended sensitivity training — group dynamics — inquiry approach to bring the students efficiently to the designated objectives. While the pattern of lay and professional "committees" appointed by the district's administrative staff to "look into health education" has been repeated in district after district, it has been in reality the educationist who has urged the use of these curricula and guided them to adoption. Only when parents, concerned about the sanctity of the family relationship, knowledgeable about the importance of maintaining individuality, and convinced that only truth should be taught in our educational institutions, have become aroused and incensed, has a conceptualized curriculum been removed!

[The following remarks were addressed by Dr. Cooper to the La Canada School Board on July 18, 1970, just two weeks after the previous remarks were made. It shows how the enemy consistently works to confuse the issues and to deliberately misconstrue what is said.]

It has come to my attention through recent public statements, that my remarks to the committee on July 6, 1970, are already being misconstrued. Perhaps this is due in part to their brevity which was necessitated by the time limit imposed.

The misconstruction which has come to my attention is in the area of "critical thinking." I do not believe that critical thinking as used by the inquirists applies to mathematical problem solving nor to the investigation used in the physical sciences. It is absurdly ridiculous to contend, as has now been done publicly, that I am critical of or against such problem solving techniques in such courses! The inquirists are advocating teaching all children a way of thinking which denies to the child the right to refer to any absolute standard, or use any rule as an objective measurement by which to decide whether the group opinion, which is highly prized by the inquirist, is

343

correct or not.

The group arrived at the solution, and there is no other standard!

"Because man is a social animal," says the inquirist, children should learn to turn to the group to validate their value judgements. The inquirists propose that all children, of all ages, in all subjects (and they, in fact, plan to do away with such subject matter) use that approach to all knowledge which says that everything is literally relative! This, to the inquirist, is critical thinking. I disagree with this most emphatically! I do not wish the review committee to be deceived that I think anything else.

I resent the inquirists' taking the idea of problem solving using the guidance of absolutes, and perverting this to mean the opposite, i.e., no absolutes allowed in anything, and call it critical thinking! This is not critical thinking, it is garbage. It is in fact, the end result of the Humanists' perversion of traditional education.

APPENDIX TWO

Dr. Joseph Bean is a physician and a distinguished member of the Glendale, California school board. In that role, he has repeatedly spoken out on many of the issues covered in this book

In the following critique, Dr. Bean masterfully dissects the goals and aims of the social planners who are operating through the social studies programs to bring about a One World, collectivized society.

No more damning testimony can be found anywhere in the field of literature than this classic study.

To parents all over America, Dr. Bean's words come as a clear warning of a present danger so great that it threatens the entire fabric of western civilization. Ignoring his findings will be at our own peril.

Further, ignoring the roots of this disastrous situation — principally the National Education Association — will spell the end of America as we have always known it.

The time is short — the stakes are your children!

WHAT ARE THE SOCIAL STUDIES?
by Dr. Joseph Bean

Presented to Legislators and Interested Citizens
in Sacramento, California, September 22, 1970

In education today, curriculum is where the action is. We are hearing less and less about financing. There is a common assumption the federal government will take care of that, if we fail to do so at the local level. At any rate, the excitement today is in the classroom and involves a new rash of innovations upon which our schools are being structured. To keep up with the innovations, one has to run fast just to stand still. In fact, by running fast, it is still impossible to keep up.

The most significant of these innovations involve the social studies in California, and it is information on this department of our curriculum which I wish to share with you. When new devices are proposed, this information may serve you in good stead.

Firstly, let us define two terms. *Social sciences* are compartmentalized bodies of knowledge including history, geography, sociology, anthropology, and political science. Each represents a specific discipline of study. *Social studies* are courses of study which cut across the boundaries of the various social science disciplines and deal with the problems of living in the present day. Social studies, at any grade level, consist of several problems which currently confront man. Supporting material is drawn from each of the social science disciplines which relates to the particular subject being studied, or problem being studied. History is not taught as such — specific historical incidents are utilized only when they have a bearing on the problem.

Authors, in their social studies textbooks, and especially in their forewords to these books, enumerate the purposes of social studies. Some of these aims we will now mention briefly,

346

in the language of the authors:

1. The important work of the social studies at the early elementary level is necessarily directed toward aiding the student to unlearn what he already knows. His attitudes toward the major social issues confronting us are biased by his family, his community, and his church. The social studies frequently involves unsettling of his convictions, to be followed by the attempt to get him to view questions as open which he may have considered as already closed, and to guide him in acquiring a new perspective.

2. The most important social issue facing man today is the creation of a world political mechanism which views man as comprising a world community. In modern times there has been no more potent social force than that of nationalism. A nation is described as a cult within world society. Allegiance to a nation is the biggest stumbling block to creation of international government. National boundaries and the concept of sovereignty must be abolished. The quickest way to abolish nation-states and their sovereignty is to condition the young to another and broader allegiance. Opinion favorable to international government will be developed in the social studies in the elementary school.

3. From the first day of school the child must learn to view man in his totality, with common physical needs (food and shelter), and common physical characteristics. Their likenesses are far more significant than their differences. The differences between peoples over the globe are very superficial. Mankind must be viewed as a global phenomenon, and the artificiality of political boundaries (nations) is detrimental to the provision for each human of his share of the world's abundance.

These three statements are typical of those found in social studies textbooks.

347

A look at the early history of social studies will take us back to 1905 when John Dewey had become the dominant voice in the training of candidates for doctoral degrees in education. At Harvard and at Columbia University, Dewey's philosophy of education was being implemented, a philosophy which came to be known as progressive education.

Dewey was a national socialist, promoting 100% state control and ownership of property and of all means of production, whether capital, natural resources, or labor. He called it collectivism. We call it collectivism today.

In 1905 he began chapters in our universities of an organization called the Intercollegiate Socialist Society, whose purpose was to promote an intelligent interest in collectivism among college men and women. The Society gained considerable strength, not only in members, but in the quality of mind which it attracted. Many of the best minds of the country were in the movement. Among the Society's first officers and promoters were Jack London, Clarence Darrow, Upton Sinclair, Walter Lippmann, and W.E.B. DuBois. Eminent thinkers from England working with Dewey for collectivizing the United States were Bertrand Russell, George Orwell, George Bernard Shaw, and later Sir Julian Huxley.

In 1921 the Society changed its name to League for Industrial Democracy, and announced the purpose of "education for a new social order based on production for use and not for profit." By the mid-thirties there were 125 college chapters, and in 1941 Dewey served as president. The further announced purpose was to place its members in the pulpit, in the leadership of labor unions, in both political parties, in the classroom as teachers, and in the fields of textbook writing and revision in order to gain control of these facets of American life. The League, begun in 1921, had succeeded beyond their expectations by the mid-thirties, in all of these fields.

Early in the century Dewey had formed the Progressive Education Association, and in 1915 the American Association of University Professors.

348

With this bit of background on a few of the men and organizations playing a part in our unfolding educational scene let us look at their work in developing what we call the social studies.

From 1908 Dewey and his colleagues began in earnest to develop the means for promoting their drive toward collectivism within the schools. Their chief device was to develop social studies for the classroom. All subjects in the curriculum were to be utilized for their purpose, but social studies were to carry the chief burden for the conversion.

By the 1930's the political climate was more suitable for their work and the decade from 1932 to 1942 saw a spate of writings, speeches, symposia, conventions, conferences, and frenzied organizational activity on the subject. That decade saw the initiation of social studies departments in public school curriculum in several important local school systems in the country. By the forties social studies had moved in to the elementary schools, and the mentors of the device felt it necessary to write a handbook for elementary school teachers explaining to them the nature and purpose of social studies, and how best to approach the teaching of the subject.

The handbook, Social Studies for Children, 1944, is most instructive, and delineates with considerable precision how the school is to determine the child's social development — i.e. the child's progression toward a position from which he will accept the collectivist viewpoint as his own.

From the decade of 1932-42, let us listen to the country's outstanding educators talk about their aim for America through the schools, and through social studies in particular.

Dr. George S. Counts, professor of education at Columbia University, speaking to the Progressive Education Association in 1932, proposes creation of a 100% controlled collectivist society and says:

This cultural revolution possesses a single mighty integrating principle — the building of a new society in which there will be neither rich nor poor ... in which a

349

condition of essential equality will unite all races and nations into one brotherhood . . . A devotion to the common good . . . penetrates and colors every aspect of the cultural life of the country . . .

The achievement of this goal would seem to require fundamental changes in the economic system. Historic capitalism, with its deification of the principle of selfishness, its reliance upon the forces of competition, its placing of property above human rights, and its exaltation of the profit motive, will either have to be replaced altogether, or so radically changed in form and spirit that its identity will be completely lost. To accomplish this we need a coordinated, planned, and socialized economy . . . If the machine is to serve all, and serve all equally, it cannot be the property of the few . . . natural resources and all important forms of capital will have to be collectively owned.

As a result of this speech, the Progressive Education Association formed a Committee on Social and Economic Problems, making Dr. Counts its chairman. In 1933 the Committee issued "A Call to the Teachers of the Nation" which stated:

Clearly, if democracy is to survive . . . it must be dissociated from its individualistic connections and be rephrased in terms of the collectivist reality. In the highly integrated social order of the twentieth century individual men cannot own and operate the means of production as they did at the time of the founding of the nation.

In a long report of the Commission on Social Studies, published by the American Historical Association in 1932, the statement is made:

There is a notable waning of the once widespread popular faith in economic individualism, and leaders in public affairs, supported by a growing mass of the population, are demanding the introduction into economy of ever wider measures of planning and control.

Cumulative evidence supports the conclusion that, in

the United States as in other countries, the age of individualism and laissez-faire in economy and government is closing and that a new age of collectivism is emerging . . . in which individual property rights will be abridged.

The American Association of School Administrators of the NEA stated in a report in 1934 by Dr. Willard Givens, Superintendent of Oakland, California:

This report comes directly from the thinking of more than one thousand superintendents.

A dying laissez-faire must be completely destroyed and all of us including the owners, must be subjected to a large degree of social control.

He went on to state that the Association was entering into a nationwide campaign to nationalize industries, banks, and other aspects of the economy so they could be used as a unified national system in the interest of the people.

Sixty of the country's leading educators joined to make a statement on the subject in the collectivist monthly called the 'Social Frontier:'

For the American people the age of individualism in economy is closing and the age of collectivism is opening. We support it. Our commitment to collectivism is beyond recall.

In 1935 these same sixty men stated:

The mistaken notion that freedom is identical with the institutions of property and profit should not be allowed to go unchallenged . . . Only state ownership and state control of the means of production can secure freedom.

If regimentation is the result of informed leadership of the nation, then such regimentation is not regimentation at all; it is rather humanization, liberalization, and socialization.

The central theme of those pushing for collectivization was simply this: Production must be for use, not for profit. In other words, production of goods and services is for the con-

351

sumer to make his life more abundant — production must be completely separated from the idea of profit.

In the publication "Progressive Education," Jesse Newlon of Columbia University said:

> To effect a more equitable distribution of the national income, a curb must be put upon the operation of the profit motive. The making of profit can no longer be regarded as the aim of production. Production must be primarily for use. To accomplish this, we must make fundamental changes in our form of government.

Dr. Harold Rugg, professor of Columbia University, Teachers College, stated:

> We must teach in the schools that a completely state-owned and operated economy must be developed.

And many, many more such statements marked that decade in education.

There can be no question of a teacher's right to accept and, as a citizen, to promote outside the classroom a premise that capitalism will or should be replaced by collectivist socialism. It is something else, however, when teachers become agents and advocates of collectivism before the involuntary audience of their students. And it is something further that public education be the agency and medium for the accomplishment of the purpose.

It was in 1933 and '34 that the Dewey oriented educators took as their prime goal that 'the school take an active part in helping to build the new social order.' The literature is replete with articles urging *indoctrination and propagandizing* of the student for collectivism. These exact words were used.

It was this type of thinking which gave birth to the social studies, and with this in mind, let us look at what social studies have accomplished.

The curriculum planners for social studies worked from several basic tenets. Social studies must

1. be freed from traditional American morality
2. face squarely and courageously every social issue

352

3. come to grips with life in all its stark reality
4. establish a theory of social or state control over the entire life of the nation
5. pursue creating collectivism for our nation

In the early thirties the NEA stepped up its activity to collectivize the country. It urged the teachers to reach for power, and to place themselves in the position of being able to write the curriculum. The social studies curriculum would determine the attitudes, ideals, and behavior of the coming generation.

The social studies program must promote the development of the new social order rather than the development of the individual. The individual must be subordinated to social ends. Emphasis must be placed on the development of the social or state needs rather than the acquisitive impulses. The social studies fostered a disposition which made the pupil intolerant of the economic institutions and beliefs of the American people, institutions deeply rooted in popular prejudice.

The tasks facing the educators then were:
1. Write textbooks integrating the social sciences into the social studies.
2. Persuade state school board when possible to adopt the social studies as a substitute for the traditional subject disciplines of history, geography, economics, civics, etc.
3. When unable to sell the social studies to state boards of education, at least rewrite the texts to substitute the philosophy of collectivism for free enterprise.

On the subject of textbook revision, the principal supervisor of the elementary schools in Winston-Salem, N.C., stated:

It fairly staggers one to consider the tremendous task ahead in revision of our existing textbooks if they are to be of any use at all in a collectivist society. Hardly a public school textbook now in use but is saturated with the profit psychology. Arithmetics are permeated with profit and loss, gain, making money. Even geographies are replete with production for gain. And as for histories!

It was in the thirties that the term *uncoerced persuasion*

came into use as the chief means of altering traditional attitudes of the students. Since that time the burden of the editorial content of nearly all professional educational journals has been the pursuit of effecting the above described social change in this country, chiefly through the social studies.

During and immediately following World War II, the emphasis on creating a new economic and social order in this country was expanded to include the entire globe. Not only was the United States to be 100% collectivized, the whole world would be better off as a global collective. To achieve collectivism for the entire world, a political mechanism for the world would be necessary. This political mechanism would be a global government which would remove national sovereignty of all countries. The social studies was, of course, just the vehicle for eliciting the support of the coming Americans for such a venture. If the social studies could orient the 44 million children in the United States (many more million today) to the new order, it would be no trick at all to carry the remainder of the world into a global government to establish collectivism for all men.

One brief quote, representative of many thousands, by the social studies wing of education in the early fifties is this:

The chief aim of education today should be the preparation of children and adolescents to participate consciously and actively in the building of a world government. This preparation should include the formation and the development of psychological attitudes favorable to the construction, maintenance, and advancement of the new world government.

The social studies men assigned themselves the task of rewriting history for our classrooms and prophesied that after the establishment of a world government, a world authority would determine the content of history books for all peoples. The bibliographies of new history books are an unabashed array of works referred to by the social studies men as writings of the radical thinkers.

In the teaching of geography, the lessons "act as a corrective to exaggerated nationalism and mistaken chauvinism." Geography is not taught as such, as in the past, but in the presentation of a social studies lesson, the teacher will draw upon those facts of social geography which will enable her to build new concepts of global thinking. Geography is used to break down the isolation of national identity in the mind of the child, and develop instead a world sense. *"Geography teaching can and should train children more thoroughly by giving them a world outlook and making them citizens of the world,"* (1951, Toward World Understanding).

In 1951 the social scientists planned to use *conservation* as an ideal topic around which to generate enthusiasm for oneness of the world. *This was the incipiency of the present ecology phase of the protest movement.*

The social planners state that attitudes brought to school by the child which are harmful to building world citizenship are corrected whenever possible and replaced with the 'proper' attitudes simply by the wise use of geography in the classroom. The teaching of geography must have an international purpose.

In 1952 and '53 aroused public opinion against this abuse of the public schools put quite a crimp in the actions and statements of the social studies planners. Many individuals and organizations went underground at that time, and did not surface again until the Supreme Court of the United States, itself populated mostly with social planners, removed such laws as would curtail the collectivists. When they did resurface in the 60's, college curriculum in the social sciences had been almost completely replaced by curriculum programs espousing only the collectivist aim. Charles Luckman, chairman of the board for state colleges in California for two terms, was able to say in 1966 that 64% of our college students preferred collectivism to capitalism. He spoke eloquently against continued abuse of our tax-supported institutions of higher learning.

By the 60's the social studies people had also come a long way toward revamping the courses at the junior high and high

355

school levels, and during this period this movement came very much into the open.

We could not talk about social studies in California without giving the state curriculum commission its full due. When it is time to adopt new textbooks, the curriculum commission brings in an array of newly published textbooks to the State Board of Education. The commission recommends the adoption of certain of the books. The Board meeting is attended by a couple of hundred educators eager to see the new books adopted, without revision. They sit breathing down the Board's neck during the meeting at which the public hearing is held on the proposed books. The whole procedure serves, it seems to many observers, as an intimidating influence on the Board. The free-enterprisers, those lay people who come to speak against adoption of this type of text, are roundly ridiculed and dismissed with contempt by the professionals sitting in the audience.

From the time social studies was originated in the thirties, the theorists have had trouble with many of the classroom teachers. The teachers continue to think of social studies largely as a body of received wisdom that students must 'learn,' and have taught in what might be called a 'content-stuffing' style. To make social studies more effective in altering children's attitudes and behavior, much attention is being given today to re-training teachers to handle the subject in an 'improved' fashion.

The social studies are 'problem' oriented. That is, current social problems and issues, all emotionally laden, make up the entire subject-matter. The students, through classroom discussion and through searching for data on their own, bring together the thought of current writers, politicians, and officials on the subject. In gathering data, the class reads publications such as newsweeklies, Life and Look magazines, and newspaper articles. Most of the recommended sources for data are hardly ones to recommend to a student who needs information and not bias. After the data is collected, it is evaluated

356

and conclusions are drawn. The student will discard his old values, confirm them, or gain new ones. It is this very ridding the student of his old values and the substitution of new ones that is bothering most parents today. In the literature of one large Southern California district, the social studies approach is to "present controversial issues which consistently challenge students' values and encourage them to form new convictions and values of their own." This is typical of many school districts.*

In California social studies classes today, in junior and senior high schools, the problems around which the curriculum is built are those issues associated with the protest movement. The protest movement, begun in 1954, has had several passing

---

*Even utter failure is heavily rewarded among the ranks of the schoolmen – if their ideology is all right.

For instance, Robert Jenkins, former superintendent of the San Francisco Unified School District, recently resigned to work as president of the M.W. Sullivan Preschool Center Co.

That company is an affiliate of the company that published the Sullivan Readers, a series of books that has come under fire nationally for teaching violence, disrespect for law and order and so forth.

Jenkins resigned however, just before the results of his one year pilot program – using the Sullivan Readers – were made public in San Francisco.

The results, according to the highly liberal San Francisco Chronicle of Nov. 7 were "complete and utter failure."

The students in the third grade dropped five months behind their peers in regular classes and those in the sixth grade fell five months behind.

That didn't daunt Jenkins. He now states that the Sullivan Reader fiasco is going to be exported to every town and hamlet in the nation through his preschool centers.

He will, said Jenkins, give the preschool children "the same kind of success and achievement" as achieved in San Francisco.

phases, beginning with civil rights as the cause celebre. Racial equality consumed several years and gave way to the poverty phase. After poverty came the free speech and academic freedom putsch, then the anti-war phase, followed by ecology and women's liberation. If a person is an astute observer of the world scene, he can predict the next couple of phases with reasonable accuracy.

In the social studies classes in our secondary schools the student is politicized, prepared for political and social action. Social studies is considered the primadonna of the curriculum today, because of its capacity to move the student into predetermined attitudes and action.

When we hear educators crying out for relevant education, what do they mean? Let us take the definition of the educators themselves: education to be relevant must have to do with the identification of the student with the pressing social issues of the day. The classroom must be used to discuss and form conclusions about the country's ills, and these issues are usually ghetto blight, poverty, the war in Vietnam, changing the social and economic order, academic freedom, ecology, etc. The issues considered closely parallel the fads in the protest movement.

The current big aim of social studies is to eliminate textbooks and let the students research the problems for themselves. This approach in the new social studies is called inquiry. The teaching of content is very *out*; the use of outside source data and class consensus on the problems is very *in*. An article in the NEA Journal recently stated that the teacher merely acts as a planner and manager of the inquiry by the students. She keeps attendance records and maintains reasonable order. She praises and encourages the student but never commands or criticizes. She emphasizes that the values of the students must be publicly defensible. I submit that this is an unexcused abuse of privacy and an intellectual enslavement which will surpass our deepest fears. The student must view knowledge as tentative rather than absolute, and knowledge is subject to

358

continuous revision. All issues studied must concern the student's personal problems or current social problems. No one is to be viewed as an authority on any subject — the student reads what he will and then makes up his own mind, in the critical light of his peers. This from the NEA.

Social studies are concerned not with what the child learns in terms of the knowledge he gains, but with what attitudes he develops. It further is concerned with what action grows out of those attitudes. How the student feels and acts is the special province of the social studies. One statement of the social studies people which sums up this matter is "primary school still tends to function as if it were an institution for the abolition of illiteracy."

The social studies people want increased use of camps, both social and educational, sensitivity training for destruction of values so that the student can determine his values by group consensus, political action including demonstrations and other forms of dissent, the inclusion of students on school boards, abolition of grades or marks to report academic performance, flexible scheduling of classes so as to remove traditional community controls and channels, resource centers to provide all those Life, Look, Newsweek, and Council of Foreign Relations Quarterly magazines, resource centers to which the students can go to spend upward of half their school day, and many, many more innovations. In fact, one would be pressed at the moment to indicate one current innovation in education that is not the work of the social studies people, aided and abetted by the behavioral scientists.

We have cried out for years for innovation in education to close the gap between our technological advance and our cultural advance. May it be made clear that today the innovations are hitting faster than we can keep up with them. It is overwhelming. Yes, we wanted innovations, but not the kind we are getting. There has been a paucity of research by education itself in the way education can be improved. The innovations we are getting are coming from behavioral scientists, by and large. Today, not just in social studies, but in all curriculum, the thrust is away from development of skills, away from acquiring knowledge, away from developing the individual for his own sake.

Since World War II a vast body of literature in education has been produced, mostly written in what we call educationese. This type of double-talk came into wide usage in the fifties, and only by learning the language can you hope to understand everything you want to know about education today. It is nowhere more evident than in the literature of the social studies curriculum.

The result of instruction given our children in social studies classes is evident in rejection of family standards of morality and ethics, and in the student protests, demands, riots, destruction of property and destruction of life which we see today. The process of instruction sensitizes students to drop out with hippies, turn on with the hopheads, or tear down with the revolutionaries.

The State Board of Education has designated its meeting in October for the final adoption of new textbooks in social studies for kindergarten through fourth grade. Under instruction from the Board, the books have been under revision for three months to remove those lines or paragraphs which heavy-handedly sensitize the child toward the goals of a new society. However, it is the philosophy of the books which is damaging. If 90% of the text were eliminated, the philosophy would remain. The California Senate has stated on occasions past that if 5% of the content of a textbook is devoted to a damaging philosophy, the book is just as harmful as if the entire content were so geared.

We need to remove social studies from the curriculum of our schools; securing partial revision of textbooks is a step which only picks at the symptom — the entire disease must be eradicated. We need to return to the teaching of the separate subject fields of history, geography, economics, political science, etc.

360

APPENDIX THREE

STATEMENT OF JAMES M. PARSONS, M.D.
on behalf of
SEX INFORMATION & EDUCATION COUNCIL OF PHYSICIANS (SIECOP)
concerning the report of the Commission
on OBSCENITY AND PORNOGRAPHY

Introduction

The Sex Information and Education Council of Physicians (SIECOP) was organized as a nonprofit corporation in California in 1969. The medical doctors affiliated with SIECOP are accredited physicians and surgeons in good standing with their colleagues, and are engaged in family practice and other medical specialties. SIECOP has both East Coast and West Coast offices, competent legal Counsel, and General Members throughout the U.S.

Since SIECOP has been primarily concerned with the subject known as "sex education" and has conducted extensive research into the subject, the Hon. Charles H. Keating, Jr., Member of the Presidential Commission on Obscenity and Pornography, has requested that SIECOP make an evaluation of the Commission's advocacy of "sex education" as a possible alternative to the legal control of obscenity and pornography.

Therefore, this STATEMENT is submitted, with its documentation. Also, a Select Research Committee of SIECOP has been designated, to expand and fully document the thesis of this research into a POSITION PAPER which will soon be published as a public service.

SEX EDUCATION: BACKGROUND & DEFINITION

While the term "sex education" is popularly believed to mean classroom instruction in human biology and reproduction, sexual hygiene and the dangers of venereal diseases, it plainly does not. Actually, the promoters of sex education refer contemptuously to such courses as "plumbing" courses.

One can understand the term sex education only by reference to publications of the sex educators, who have organized themselves into such groups as the E.C. Brown Trust Foundation, SEXOLOGY (magazine), the Sex Information and Educational Council of the U.S., the Planned Parenthood-World Population group, the American Association of Sex Educators and Counselors, the American Humanist Association, certain Humanist groups which refer to themselves by names such as "Ethical Union" or "Ethical Culture" – and others.

While the above listing of corporations may appear formidable to the casual observer, it is to be noted that a *small coterie of individuals* accounts for the total number of corporations listed above. For example, Lester Kirkendall, an active proponent of sex education in the U.S. and abroad, figures prominently in most of the above listed organizations, by his writings; moreover, he is an Editor of SEXOLOGY, a Board Member of SIECUS, serves in a similar capacity with the American Association of Sex Educators and Counselors (a SIECUS offshoot), is a member of the Editorial Advisory Board of THE HUMANIST, which is published by the American Humanist Association, writes on occasion for the E.C. Brown Trust Foundation – *et cetera* . . .

Although SIECUS may claim that public opinion polls show approval of sex education, it is a fact that the personalities which promote the concept of sex education are not generally trusted.* The open orientation toward the religion of Humanism which is manifested by those prominent in the sex education movement has alerted many parents to examine sex education curricula, only to find with dismay that Humanism is being taught to their children, as part of sex education. Also,

---

*Dr. Esther Schulz was co-author of the late unlamented Anaheim sex instruction program.

In the first week of September 1969, she manned a SIECUS booth for the Congress of Religious Instruction, a meeting sponsored by the Catholic Churches of Louisiana.

She received an invitation to attend from the Diocese of

despite the denials of SIECUS' Dr. Calderone in PLAYBOY magazine, sensitivity training is an integral part of sex education. All sex education curriculum guides inspected thus far by SIECOP bear the telltale vocabulary of sensitivity training: "role-playing" - "encounter group" - etc. Of course, one should expect sensitivity training in any activity sponsored by Humanists, since *American Humanist Association recruiting literature lists as one of the Humanist objectives "developing practical means of improving encounter and human potential groups"* (or, sensitivity training).

LaFayette and was told to "come quietly."

The person extending the invitation told her the Congress would be closed to the public, that the "Birchers and far-rightists are so absorbed in their fight against integration right now, they won't know SIECUS is here."

When asked if it was not true that the state legislature had banned sex instruction from all tax supported schools, Dr. Schulz said, "Oh, it's only for this year," accompanied by joyful laughter.

She laughed again when asked what would happen if the legislature voted the same way in 1970.

"Oh it won't," she said, "that's all under control. Besides, the commissioner of education will have the sole responsibility for the approval of the curriculum."

Since there is no commissioner in the state, her questioner was curious.

Dr. Schulz replied that the commissioner would be hired by the education committee appointed by the governor and would be an experienced educator.

"All experienced educators are aware of the importance of sex education," she said.

She went on to say that the state board of education would be stripped of most of its duties.

What does all that mean? Looked at in the context of the ideas and programs being pushed by the behaviorists, it simply

363

We are now ready to define and describe accurately what is called sex education. The objective and dispassionate student of sex education and SIECUS-consulted curriculum guides will discern:

(1) Sensitivity training;
(2) Indoctrination in Humanism;
(3) Kindergarten through Twelfth Grade stimulation of school children with sexual materials (such as sex books, line drawings, audio-visual aids, film strips and motion pictures).

PORNOGRAPHY – DEFINITIONS & COMPARISONS

SIECOP is perfectly willing to accept that definition of pornography which has been advanced by Drs. Eberhard and Phyllis Kronhausen in their book, *Pornography and the Law,* Ballantine Books, 1961, page 18: "In pornography (hard core obscenity), the main purpose is to stimulate erotic response in

---

adds up to the following:

The Governor of Louisiana now appoints the members of the coordinating council for higher education, recently created by constitutional amendment to oversee curriculum at the college level.

The members of this board are appointed, not elected, and could overrule both the state board of education and the local school boards if the state legislature gave them power to set curriculum.

This would mean nationalizing and federalizing the entire school system in Louisiana under HEW (Health, Education and Welfare), thereby losing state and local control, and losing all control of the children's destiny by the parents and taxpayers.

Since the board is appointed, not elected, parents would have no control over them. Hence, the board could not be removed by the voters and they would be, in all reality, the UNTOUCHABLES.

364

the reader. And that is all."

SIECOP accepts the Kronhausens' definition of pornography with full knowledge that certain works of the Kronhausens are now offered for sale by *Evergreen Review,* published by Mr. Barney Rosset, a well known pornographer. Mr. Rosset was featured in the *Saturday Evening Post* article of January 25, 1969, "How to Publish 'Dirty' Books for Fun and Profit."

At the present time, when even the learned Justices of the United States Supreme Court seem confused as to the meaning of pornography and reluctant to pass judgment, it is a fact that Barney Rosset's publications fall into the clear category of pornography by common consensus.

Reason for emphasis of the preceding sentences is as follows:

(1) To show that SIECOP wholeheartedly accepts the definition of the pornographers themselves for purposes of its discussion;

(2) To point out that pornography exists, and that perhaps the best clue to its prompt recognition is the willingness of the purveyor of pornography to label his wares accurately by advertising them as obscenity and/or pornography.

The laws of the United States are under attack as regards pornography; however, it is submitted that a measure of legal risk still exists for any pornographer who openly advertises his presence as such. Therefore, pornographic materials which are advertised as such must be regarded as pornographic. SIECOP has noted that the California corporation ELYSIUM, Inc. is in the business of pornography by publication of its magazines, such as *New Living, Sundisk, Nude Living, Ankh, Jaybird,* etc.

Evergreen Review has run advertisements which offer *Ankh* Magazine, and the display ad itself contains the words "obscenity and pornography" both as a description of the offering, and an inducement to purchase. ELYSIUM, Inc. magazines are at least as pornographic as *Evergreen Review*, bearing in mind "the main purpose is to stimulate erotic response in the reader." Moreover, the ELYSIUM, Inc. publication (Ankh magazine) is

365

openly advertised as "obscenity and pornography."

Therefore, for the purpose of this communication, the publications of the ELYSIUM, Inc. will be accepted as definitive examples of "hard core" pornography. Also, the goals of ELYSIUM, Inc. as printed in its magazines will be considered and evaluated.

If an accurate assessment can be made of the Commission's opinion that sex education offers a positive alternative to the legal control of pornography, such assessment must be made by a systematic comparison of the underlying philosophies and objectives of the two competing alternatives. *Stated differently, sex education can offer a positive alternative to pornography but only if its basic philosophies and objectives are sufficiently at variance with those of pornography so that sex education in schools will be perceived by students as significantly different from pornographic influences.*

Since the Sex Information and Education Council of the United States is the prime mover behind what is called sex education, it is most pertinent that the philosophies and objectives of SIECUS be compared to the philosophies and objectives of a purveyor of pornography such as ELYSIUM, Inc.

The following paragraphs are direct comparisons, made between the objectives of these organizations, drawing our information from the printed ELYSIUM Institute Goals and SIECUS Study Guide No. 1, entitled "Sex Education."

Comparison of Goals

(1) ELYSIUM, Inc.

To inform the individual of how he can acquire adequate knowledge of his own physical, mental and emotional developmental processes . . .

SIECUS

To provide for the individual and adequate knowledge of his own physical, mental and emotional maturation processes as related to sex.

(2) ELYSIUM, Inc.

To alleviate and ultimately to help banish guilt or shame

366

relating to the naked body, to help banish fears and anxieties relating to individual sexual development . . .

SIECUS

To eliminate fears and anxieties relative to individual sexual development and adjustments.

(3) ELYSIUM, Inc.

To instill recognition and appreciation of the positive benefits that wholesome human relations can bring to individual and family living.

SIECUS

To provide an appreciation of the positive satisfaction that wholesome human relations can bring in both individual and family living.

The ELYSIUM, Inc. goals have been compared with the objectives of sex education with an attorney; he states that it is not possible that the two documents could have been written independently. In other words, either the pornographers of ELYSIUM, Inc. *are* the sex educators of SIECUS, or else one group has been "cribbing" from the other. *In any event, the philosophies and objectives of the pornographers of ELYSIUM, Inc. and of the sex educators of SIECUS are practically identical, as can be seen by the preceding comparison of their stated objectives.* A more complete comparison of the goals of these apparently separate corporations will serve only to prove more conclusively that these people hold substantially the same philosophies and objectives.

Therefore, it is questionable as to the motives of those of the Presidential Commission who have seen fit to recommend sex education as a positive alternative to legal control of pornography. It is believed that the Presidential Commission cannot be so ignorant as to make such a recommendation without complete research. If the Commission's research were complete, the members would have noticed carefully that the philosophies and objectives of so-called opposing concepts, pornography and sex education — as represented respectively

367

by ELYSIUM, Inc. and SIECUS – are actually identical in every essential respect.

How can sex education offer an "alternative" to pornography when the printed objectives of the one are but verbatim transcripts, or else crude paraphrases, of the other? This is an *alternative*?

The Commission should also notice the Elysium Institute Directory, which lists those groups with which ELYSIUM, Inc. maintains "an exchange of information and courtesies." Therein will be found Humanist organizations, pornographers, and sensitivity training centers – and always SIECUS.

Since the Commission apparently sees little if any harm in pornography, the following facts are offered for its information:

(1) Wherever the International Planned Parenthood Federation is firmly ensconced, as in Sweden and Denmark, all laws against pornography are systematically weakened and ultimately destroyed.

(2) It is instructive to note that in Sweden, the National Society for Sex Education (founded by Elise Ottesen-Jensen, who was also a founder of the International Planned Parenthood Federation) was able to legalize homosexuality and zoophilia in 1944, two years before sex education went into the schools. Sex education includes education in the perversions, including homosexuality and zoophilia (sexual intercourse with animals).

(3) Sex education becomes the main vocation of the Planned Parenthood people once the laws against pornography are materially weakened, and it is promoted as a "defense against pornography."

(4) Those who doubt that SIECUS is promoting homosexuality and zoophilia here in the United States should read BOYS AND SEX, by Wardell Pomeroy, SIECUS Board Member.

(5) After some 20 years of sex education in Sweden, the following results were seen:

    (a) Sweden had the highest venereal disease rate in

the world. (WHO statistics.)

(b)   Promiscuity was so rampant that marriage no longer was respected; family life disintegrated; girls who were 15 years old could be prescribed The Pill without parental knowledge or consent.   SEX & SOCIETY IN SWEDEN, Birgitta Linner, Pantheon Press.

(c)   Sweden's large population of sexual perverts found spokesmen to declare that perversions were normal, that even pedophiliacs had a right to indulge their perversion, and that perverts should be accorded the courtesy of being referred to as members of an "erotic minority group." THE EROTIC MINORITIES, Lars Ullerstam, Grove Press, Inc., 1964.

(d)   In early 1964, the Swedish National Government was formally petitioned by prominent physicians and educators to bring an end to the sex education experiment which had caused "an unnatural over-sexualization of the rising generation."

Shortly after the reaction within Sweden against the results of sex education, Dr. Mary Calderone incorporated SIECUS in Delaware (April 29, 1964). Formerly, she had served as Medical Director of Planned Parenthood of U.S. from the year 1953, when the first annual meeting of the International Planned Parenthood Federation was held in Stockholm.

The Presidential Commission should note that all plans for the incorporation of SIECUS had been laid well in advance. The laws against pornography in the U.S. had been weakened by repeated assaults in high courts which appealed to "civil liberties" and were decided in favor of pornographers because certain judges (as Mr. Abe Fortas) had achieved advantageous position. The prominent pornographer, Barney Rosset, was coming into his own, and was to make a fortune selling pornography. The pornography which was available was a good excuse for sex education to "defend against pornography."

But the promoters of sex education had made extra preparations. A corporation called ELYSIUM, Inc. had been formed

369

in California on February 24, 1961, and was already busy flooding the U.S. with pornography.

With the aid of a public relations campaign of fantastic scope and brilliance conducted by one of the nation's highest priced "image maker" firms, Ruder & Finn, Inc., SIECUS did well for awhile, but two fatal mistakes were made.

Lester Kirkendall, who wrote SIECUS Study Guide No. 1, made a monumental mistake when he wrote out the "Objectives of Sex Education" because he too obviously copies them from the "ELYSIUM INSTITUTE Goals."

But the really big mistake, and the one which the Commission will not be able to surmount, is their own draft report recommending sex education as an "alternative" to pornography, which prompted the diligent search by SIECOP for a statement of philosophies and objectives of pornographers that led straight to the "ELYSIUM INSTITUTE Goals" — which are the same as those of sex education.

When this STATEMENT is received by the Hon. Charles H. Keating, Jr., Member of the Presidential Commission, with its documentation, for the inspection of those Members of the Commission who have signed up on the *farcical notion that sex education is a "defense" against pornography or some kind of "alternative" to it, it will be apparent that such a justification for sex education is forever checkmated.*

The Commission's draft report itself is evidence that a gigantic fraud is being perpetrated upon the American people.

The evidence in SIECOP's files shows that the *group responsible for this colossal hoax called sex education is the American Civil Liberties Union.* In some manner, Dean Lockhart — a member of ACLU — was made Chairman of the Commission. In turn he hired Paul Bender, of ACLU. Afterward legal control of pornography was forgotten and the trend of the Commission was toward the so-called "alternative" of sex education, which would be to the direct benefit of Planned Parenthood-World Population and SIECUS. The attorney for both mentioned organizations, Harriet Pilpel, has been a National

370

Director of ACLU since 1962. Harriet Pilpel's law firm, Greenbaum, Wolff & Ernst, handled the original incorporation of SIECUS, and Harriet Pilpel served on the SIECUS Board of Directors.

It has been noted that SIECUS-consulted sex education curriculum guides advocate Humanism. The definitive book behind Humanism is THE PHILOSOPHY OF HUMANISM, by Corliss Lamont, who was for 20 years a National Director of ACLU. The "Ethical Culture" and "Ethical Union" Humanist groups are mentioned in Lamont's book. The membership of the sex educators in Humanist, Ethical Culture and Ethical Union groups has been mentioned already, but it is instructive indeed to investigate the members of Harriet Pilpel's law firm for members of Humanist, Ethical Culture and Ethical Union groups. It will be found that this law firm (Greenbaum, Wolff & Ernst) is stacked with Humanists, and it is a veritable "gilded nest" for high officials of the American Civil Liberties Union.

Any intelligent person who examines the multitude of names and interlocking organizations behind *sex education, Humanism, and pornography* in the United States will be convinced that *this movement called sex education is but the stalking horse of an international pornography cartel.*

Pornography is their excuse for sex education, their "image maker" public relations justification for getting the pornography onto transparencies and into the classroom as a "defense" against printed pornography. A child can walk away from a newsstand or throw away erotic mail, but if he walks out of his classroom he becomes a truant. Sex education is the slick pornographer's way to "play both ends against the middle" while matters steadily deteriorate until a nation gets itself into the sad shape of Sweden, at which point the Planned Parenthood pied pipers pack up their gear and move into another country where they aren't so well known.

Pornography is not only harmful to individuals, it can haul down entire nations. And the ACLU's lawyers know this better

371

than anyone. Moreover, if ACLU would have us believe that sex education is a "defense" against pornography, then let ACLU explain why those countries which have accepted sex education (e.g., Sweden, Denmark) have ended up with more pornography than ever.

The Commission's draft report uses the tentative endorsement of sex education given by the American Medical Association as a bolster to their arguments. Before the Commission's final draft is written committing A.M.A. to sex education, it is suggested that the Board of Trustees of A.M.A. be asked the following questions:

(1) Was the A.M.A.'s general membership polled in order to arrive at an endorsement of sex education?

(2) Since sensitivity training was warned against editorially in the Journal of A.M.A., how can A.M.A. endorse sex education — which includes sensitivity training?

(3) Is it compatible with medical ethics to use the image of ethical physicians to promote a secular religion in public schools — especially when that promotion is done surreptitiously?

This would be fair to A.M.A.'s Board of Trustees since it would allow them to bail out of the Commission's report right now, and let the ACLU run its own sideshow without soiling the white coats of the ethical physicians of the nation.

A complete POSITION PAPER, soon to be published by SIECOP, will recommend legal controls for pornography via two means:

(1) enactment into law of acceptable definitions, and enforcement of the law, and

(2) constitutional amendment allowing the judgement of local juries in pornography cases to be respected, and without appellate review.

As for sexual instruction in schools, SIECOP is now preparing a curriculum guide that will be proper and adequate. It will not include sensitivity training or Humanism.

James M. Parsons, M.D., President of SIECOP

READER'S BIBLIOGRAPHY FOR RESEARCH

The conscientious reader, who is not about to accept second hand what he can learn on his own, may want to research the question that we have raised in this book. If so, the following list of materials and publications, with a brief description of the contents, will give the reader a pattern to follow. It is suggested the material, if at all possible, be studied in the order in which it is listed here.

1. SIECUS NEWSLETTER, Vol. 3, No. 1, Spring, 1961. This newsletter is by Frances Breed and Dr. Mary Calderone and deals specifically with ways to involve the community in sex education. Miss Breed is a divorcee and prolific contributor to sex education manuals, etc. Note specifically, in this newsletter, page 1 at the top of the third column regarding "political levels," and on page 2 a discussion involving Esther Schulz and Anaheim's Sally R. Williams, now a nurse in the district after having been demoted to the position in the spring, 1969. Miss Williams was "suddenly" discovered to have no teaching credential, after preparing teacher's manuals on sex education and running the entire family life program for four years.

2. SIECUS STUDY GUIDE, No. 1, Sex Education, page 6: "Few parents or teachers are adequately informed or sufficiently secure to engage in free and open dialogue with youth on the subject of sex, especially when questions of standards, personal behavior and development of moral values arise."

In the first place, this quote spells out clearly the danger of the SIECUS brand of sex education, when they arbitrarily set themselves up as arbiters of moral behavior (situation ethics) and pass judgement upon parents who by and large are doing a fair job, or at least are doing as good a job as any stranger in a classroom.

Note too, that on page 11 of that study guide we find sensitivity training recommended. They also talk about the need

373

to RE-EDUCATE and RECONSTRUCT the adolescent who, they claim, has received a whole set of WRONG attitudes and ideas about sex.

This kind of emotional engineering should of course, be reserved for skilled psychiatrists and then only for sick minds.

And then, we find their most consistent doctrine set forth on page 15 of the study guide when they state, "Sex education must be thought of as being education — not moral indoctrination."

3. NATIONAL COUNCIL OF CHURCHES: INTERFAITH STATEMENT ON SEX EDUCATION.

This booklet was published by William Genne's favorite outfit, the Commission on Marriage and the Family of the NCC, a commission on which Genne serves. It can be obtained from the NCC at 475 Riverside Drive, New York City. On page 3 the author states, "School can integrate sound sexual information and attitudes with total education which the child receives in social studies, civics, literature, history, home economics and the biological and behavioral sciences."

So there you have it. Any parent who thinks he can keep his or her child from being forced into a sex class can readily see that the purpose is to put it into every class so it cannot be avoided. The mind manipulators leave nothing to chance.

4. AMERICAN EDUCATION MAGAZINE, United States Office of Education, November, 1966, Document number FSS .233:33046.

This document is available from the Government Printing Office at fifteen cents.

"If you tell 5-year olds that this (sexual intercourse) is the way fathers and mothers reaffirm their love for each other, and that they can choose when they will have a baby (contraception) you are teaching responsible parenthood, responsible sexuality, right in the kindergarten."

Can the reader believe that? They are talking about mere

infants, remember. How about the Catholic belief that will not permit the use of contraceptives? Does that make Catholics second class citizens? Or are they determined to stamp out that Catholic doctrine by catching a whole generation when it is five years old and reorienting this thinking?

There is also an inference on the last page that school sex education will prevent such things as premarital pregnancies, venereal disease, teenage weddings and so forth. This is, of course, totally unsubstantiated and rubbish, as the Swedish disaster has proven.

Anyone who doubts for one minute that the Federal Government is not the major force behind school sex education need only read this government document.

5. THE REVOLUTION IN SEX EDUCATION by Helen Southard (This is available from SIECUS.)

The attempt to level out the sexes is graphically described in the booklet as follows: "It is important in the early school years to discourage boy-girl competition based on relative values of activities preferred by one sex or the other. Activities should not be labeled exclusively as boys or girls."

It would seem this attempt to blur the sexes is diametrically opposite to one of SIECUS' stated goals, which is to (supposedly) enhance awareness of one's own sexual being as male or female. How can you both enhance male and female awareness and at the same time suppress it in the young at the most impressionable age?

6. SIECUS NEWSLETTER, Vol. 4, No. 2, December, 1968, page 2:

This sheet documents clearly the relationship between sex education and sensitivity training. Note book review on page 5 "Self-Love" and others.

7. SIECUS NEWSLETTER, Vol. 4, No. 3, February, 1969, page 2:

375

"Not only is it unnecessary to have a society that insists sex relations should be the way of cementing families together and producing more and more children, but we're also approaching the period when you don't need sex in the normal sense of the word at all to produce children."

8. HOW TO USE SOCIODRAMA: National Council for the Social Studies, a department of the NEA.
    How To Do It Series No. 20 – 35¢, page 3:
"Role-playing is more than an exercise. It can be used to teach social skills and desirable attitudes and to promote the learning of behavior patterns necessary for good citizenship as well as for individual success in social life." There seems to be an open question as to whose behaviour patterns and desirable attitudes will be taught, and as such this would appear to be an infringement on family privacy and possibly on personal moral values. However, role-playing and sociodrama is widely used as a part of Family Life (Sex) Education.

9. SEX EDUCATION AND THE VERY YOUNG CHILD, by Mary S. Calderone, PTA Magazine, Reprint available from SIECUS.
Advocates telling 3-year olds the facts of intercourse.

10. JOURNAL OF RELIGION AND HEALTH, July, 1967. Reprint available from SIECUS.
Article discusses the influence of Behavioral Scientists on sex-education, teacher-training and planning.

11. CALLED TO RESPONSIBLE FREEDOM, National Council of Churches, (Meaning of Sex in the Christian Life).
States that a man who loves God and his neighbor DOESN'T NEED ANY LAW OR RULES to tell him what to do; that one is not bound by rules of behavior.

12. TRANSITION IN SEX VALUES – IMPLICATIONS FOR THE EDUCATION OF ADOLESCENTS, Isadore Rubin, Journal of Marriage and The Family, reprint 5/65 available from SIECUS, 20¢:
Describes several theories of sexuality and their advocates. Note page 186-87. Also, "What the educator must do is not provide ready-made formulas and prepackaged values, but provide knowledge, insight and values on the basis of whatever the adolescent may choose for himself." This free choice indicates no need of parental guidance.

13. SIECUS NEWSLETTER, Vol. 2, No. 5, Winter, 1967. "The Office of Education of the Department of HEW provided almost all the necessary funds for a SIECUS working conference in Washington during December, 1966."

14. SIECUS NEWSLETTER, Vol. 4, No. 1, October, 1968. SEX & THE RELIGIOUS / MORAL DILEMMA:
Quoting Father Thomas Wassmer, "All morality, properly understood, is situational, is aware of the increasing importance placed upon circumstances, motives, historical evolution, approach that all behaviour is relative and there is no such thing as a fixed moral value."

15. DISTRICT ATTORNEY WILLIAM CAHN of Nassau County, New York, has admitted that Dr. F.A. Calderone, husband of Dr. Mary Calderone of SIECUS, who deplores the onslaught of sex in media in speeches across the nation, permits "girlie burlesque shows" at the theatre he owns, the Mineola.

16. PHILIP HAUSER, Director of Population Research and Training Center, University of Chicago, in speaking to the Child Welfare League stated that Government must assume many traditional functions of the family and that the

family should play an increasingly minor role. Request a copy of his speech from the University.

17. An interesting book on Student unrest is obtainable from the Fire and Police Research Association of Los Angeles, Committee on Public Education, 3354 Glendale Blvd., Los Angeles, 90039.

18. SEX EDUCATION IN SCHOOLS: Education USA Special Report, National School Publications Relations Association, NEA, $3.00.
Lists programs throughout country and much information advocating sex education. Interesting to note the play given to premarital pregnancy, promiscuity, v.d., etc., and inference that sex education will clear this (contrary to what SIECUS members such as Kirkendall say).

19. STATE OF ILLINOIS POLICY STATEMENT ON FAMILY LIFE & SEX EDUCATION, Office of the Superintendent of Public Instruction, Springfield, Illinois.
"It is desirable that appropriate instruction be included on topics such as petting, premarital chastity vs. premarital sexual intercourse (infers that pros of premarital relations will be also promoted and children left to their own decisions) masturbation, VD, pornography and obscenity, dangers of the world population explosion and selected legal aspects of sexual behavior."

20. SEX EDUCATION IN SCHOOL (See No. 18) page 12; The best way to obtain public support, says Lester A. Kirkendall, professor of family life at Oregon St. University (and board member of SIECUS) is through the school's normal relations with the public. And the more the sex education curriculum can be INTERWOVEN INTO THE NORMAL SCHOOL PROGRAM the less it is apt to be singled out as unusual or threatening.

378

In this connection, Kirkendall suggests a useful strategy. Most schools teach something about sex education, even if it is only reproduction information in biology classes or love between the sexes in English literature courses. He believes that any school district wanting to develop a more formal or comprehensive approach is fully warranted in saying that it is EXPANDING AND IMPROVING rather than 'starting' a sex education program. THE PUBLIC, he points out, IS LESS FEARFUL OF EXPANDING THAN OF INNOVATING ANYTHING. (Emphasis ours.)

Page 14: Quoting Mary Calderone of SIECUS: "There are no authorities – believe me – in this field. It is ironic that the best people to advise on how to give sound, adequate reproductive and sex education to children 10 years old and younger are probably those who have just left that stage themselves." (Thus she admits there are no authorities and suggests that other children are the best authorities, while still insisting the schools are the ONLY authorities qualified to teach sex education.)

Page 17: "If, however, school administrators feel that the issue of parental permission CANNOT BE BYPASSED, we favor MAKING IT NECESSARY FOR THE PARENTS WHO OBJECT TO WRITE THE SCHOOL to this effect. Putting the responsibility on the parents will probably encourage them to give serious thought to the matter before they make a formal request."

Page 17: "Most kindergartners and 1st graders are quite aware of differences between male and female, are 'giggly' and self-conscious when references are made to parts of the body. On trips with his mother, the child has seen pregnant women and wondered why they were so fat. But the answers he got may have been helpful, foolish, harsh or even dishonest." Once again parents are denigrated.

21. SEXUALITY AND SEXUAL LEARNING IN THE

CHILD, John H. Gagnon, Psychiatry Journal reprint available from SIECUS, No. 017, 50¢.
Quoting Freud, page 228: "We can have analogous experiences, I think, when we give children sexual enlightenment. I am far from maintaining that this is a harmful or unnecessary thing to do, but it is clear that the PROPHYLACTIC EFFECT OF THIS LIBERAL MEASURE HAS BEEN GREATLY OVEREMPHASIZED." (Emphasis ours.)

22.   SEX IN THE 60's, TIME/LIFE BOOKS, 1968, page 101: Kirkendall of Oregon State (and SIECUS), who has been working on sex education since 1928, DECRIES THE TENDENCY OF PARENTS TO LOOK ON SEX EDUCATION AS "DISASTER INSURANCE." "The old threats of pregnancy, venereal disease and community disapproval no longer carry the weight they once did," according to Kirkendall. It would be more practical, Kirkendall thinks, to teach them contraception.

23.   SEX EDUCATION RESOURCE UNIT, Grades 5, 6 or 7: American Association for Health, Physical Education and Recreation, of the NEA, page 1:
"Isolated lectures and artificial divisions of the class by sex are not in harmony with sound education." (This advocation of teaching in mixed classes has been accepted by most Family Life programs throughout the nation.)

24.   QUESTIONS PARENTS ASK ABOUT SEX EDUCATION, by James W. Maddock, Director of Family Life Education, Association for Family Living, Chicago Tribune Magazine, 7/28/68:
"No longer can the family naively pretend to hand down intact a set of 'rules to live by' which will guide the young through all situations." "Sex education is not moral indoctrination." (Emphasis HIS).

380

25. NATIONAL ELEMENTARY PRINCIPAL, November, 1968, NEA, $1.00.
Entire Issue on Sex Education — should be read cover to cover! Suggests extensive use of sensitivity training. "Problems of Implementing a New Health Education Curriculum. As a behavioral science it relies heavily upon psychology . . . " (Mental therapy by untrained teachers??)

26. POLICY STATEMENT ON FAMILY LIFE AND SEX EDUCATION, Office of Superintendent, State of Ill., Springfield.
Should be read cover to cover — includes statements to effect that we must not wait for qualified teachers; there is NO provision for removing child from program; sex education is concerned with basic issues related to sexual conduct which have moral, ethical and religious implications. (The mild suggestion is made that schools should not infringe on religious principles, if possible.) It suggests that older children can take sex information home TO EDUCATE THEIR PARENTS.

27. HEALTH EDUCATION PROGRAM FOR TELEVISION, School District of Kansas City, Missouri, 1211 McGee Street, Kansas City — for 7th and 8th grades:
Includes telecasts on such things as understanding mental illness, medical self-help and shock; radioactive fallout and shelters. Recommends books: HUMAN GROWTH, LOVE AND SEX IN PLAIN LANGUAGE, MOVING INTO MANHOOD.

28. GETTING STARTED. A Pioneer Program in health guidance and sex education, Glen Cove Public Schools, New York, $1.00.
Includes a K-4 program which is most interesting. *Detailed instructions are given on how to take kindergartners together to visit boys bathroom and view photographs of nude children.*

29. SCHOOL HEALTH EDUCATION STUDY (SHES) Cur-

riculum Materials, 3M, St. Paul, Minn. Catalog is free. Concept 6, Level III, Catalog No. 4362.

"The Human Reproduction Systems" contains transparencies with disturbingly *graphic drawings of reproductive organs, and overlays of erection of standing male facing female in position for insertion.* Used in Minnesota junior high schools.

30. **EXCERPTS FROM SEX EDUCATION AND FAMILY LIFE, Prepared for Catholic Schools by the Committee on Sex Education, Diocese of Rochester, N.Y.**

K-8 program includes trips to boys' bathrooms.

31. **BECOMING A PERSON, Sex Education Pilot Project, Cana Conference of Chicago Archdiocese, 720 N. Rush Street, Chicago.**

Includes *bathroom trips*, suggests "discourage baby terms, slang terms and possible dirty words picked up from family and siblings." Complete K-8 program.

32. **RESOURCE UNIT FOR FAMILY LIFE EDUCATION, Grade 5, Field Test Copy, Chicago, Illinois Board of Education, 228 N. La Salle Street.**

Includes role-playing, problem-box in classroom for discussion of problems with parents and siblings; molding uterus in clay; test of pupil's sex knowledge; questions in the back cover all sorts of intimate subjects, including sexual aberations.

33. **APPROACHING ADULTHOOD, NEA/AMA 1960, for 16-20 year olds (used with 14 year olds in Chicago — used throughout the nation.)**

In Chicago a class skipped the chapters on biology and went directly to those on dating, petting, etc., page 26: "Some arguments commonly offered in favor of engaging in premarital relations are 1) that one no longer needs to worry about becoming pregnant because new contraceptive knowledge is available, and 2) that there is now no need to fear contracting

382

a venereal disease because new drugs have made these diseases nothing to fear."

34.   GUIDE TO SEXOLOGY, Paperback Library, 95¢.
Test in back of this book was administered verbatim to a high school class in Loara High School, Anaheim, California in 1967. Book is published by editors of Sexology Magazine, includes articles by Kirkendall, Genne, Rubin and others of SIECUS. Subjects cover all forms of sexual aberation and maladjustment. Biographies of contributors in back of book list one as a practicing transvestite and another as a male prostitute.

35.   LOVE & SEX IN PLAIN LANGUAGE, Eric Johnson, *Bantam Pathfinder*, 60¢.
Advocated by State of Illinois for 7th graders. Used throughout country in public and parochial programs, description of movement in coitus, ejaculation, vaginal contraction, orgasm, encourages masturbation, give complete description of all forms of contraception, etc.

36.   LOVE & THE FACTS OF LIFE, Evelyn Duvall*(of SIECUS), published by Association Press, N.Y. (National Board of YMCA) in pocketbook 95¢.
Recommended by State of Illinois for 7th graders and used throughout the nation in public and parochial programs, it has chapters on Falling in Love with a Married Man (or Woman); sterilization; prostitution; v.d.; sex fantasies; What's the Harm in Petting? etc. "If you awaken after a date with a feeling of happiness and joy of living, if you find yourself eagerly looking forward to seeing your date again, if you like being together, sharing all sorts of things with each other, it probably means your physical love-making is appropriate." (Page 232.)

---

*Listed by HCUA as having signed letter to President Truman requesting clemency for the atom bomb traitors, Julius and Ethel Rosenberg.

"A married woman has already proved her appeal to at least the one man who married her. She has learned how to love and be loved, to relax into some of the fullness of woman's role in the interplay of the sexes that is mutually satisfying to both." (Page 66.) "A man may be married and yet not have all his emotional needs within the marriage." (Page 64.) "The married man is often more tender, more gentle, more courteous, more expressive of his affection with women." (Page 63.) "Passion alone can be painful. It usually has an element of hurting in it. Lovers may want to bite and crush each other when speaking in these accents of love." (Page 26.)

37. TIME OF YOUR LIFE, Teacher's Manual, grades 4, 5, 6. *Bay Region Instructional Television for Education,* 590 Hamilton St., Redwood City, Calif. $1.75 + postage. JUST SOLD to National Center for School and College Television for national distribution on *educational television.* Has been shown throughout California, and in Hawaii.

This teacher's manual is impossible to describe and the prurient aspects of it would take several pages to describe. The first several chapters involve sensitivity training. Chapters on sex include description of ejaculation as three or four squirts of a water pistol; illustrate circumcision with a baggy sweater sleeve; describe frequency of intercourse at various ages *up to 80 years*; show animation of foreskin pushed back and forth on penis; graphics of penis spurting semen; head-on view of vagina; describe all details of erection including feel, and smell of semen; encourages masturbation; encourages girls to look at themselves "down there" and describes "a very sensitive bump" they may not know they have. SINCE THIS CAN NOW BE BEAMED ON EDUCATION TV ANYWHERE IN THE COUNTRY, WE STRONGLY URGE YOU TO OBTAIN THIS TEACHERS' MANUAL FOR YOURSELF AND READ IT CAREFULLY.

38. SEX KNOWLEDGE INVENTORY — Form X Revised,

Family Life Publications, Box 6725, Durham, N.C., used in *San Mateo County, Calif. Grades 9-12.*

Includes detailed questioning of sex act, stimulation of clitoris, positions of intercourse, birth control, masturbation, size of organs, etc.

39. HOW BABIES ARE MADE. Slides for K-3rd grade, used nationally, written up in national news media. Available from Abby Press, St. Meinrad, Indiana, 47577, $12.98 including postage.

Includes pictures of paper-sculptures showing animals mating, and a couple in bed under sheet, indicating that mommy and daddy are doing what the dogs and chickens did.

40. Miscellaneous textbooks in use throughout the nation (and filmstrips):

    A Baby is Born
    A Story About You
    Attaining Manhood (And Womanhood)
    Basis for Sexual Morality (filmstrip)
    Boy to Man (film)
    Choosing Your Goals — Lyons and Carnahan
    Concordia Series — K-3rd
    Day Life Begins (film)
    Especially for Boys (Girls) - (film)
    Fertilization and Birth (film)
    First Nine Months of Life
    For Youth to Know — Laidlaw
    Growing Up
    Getting Along with Parents
    Girl to Woman (film)
    How We Are Born - Follett (primary)
    Human Reproduction - Part D (Eye Gate House, Jamaica, N.Y.)
    HE and SHE - Barnes, Penguin
    How Life Begins

385

Happy Little Hamsters (film)
Helping Children Understand Sex - SRA
Helping Boys and Girls Understand Their Sex Roles
    - SRA
HUMAN GROWTH - Wexler (film)
Human Growth and Reproduction (Laidlaw)
Human and Animal Beginnings (film)
The Human Story - Scott Foresman
Love and Sex - Eric Johnson
Life Begins - Eye Gate House Film
Life Can Be Sexual - Witt
Man and Woman - Follett (primary)
Modern Sex Education
Phoebe (film on situation ethics)
Our Family Works Together (2nd grade film)
Plain White Envelope (film on cheating)
Sex: A Moral Dilemma for Teenagers (filmstrip)
Story of Growing Up - record
The Game - (An unbelievable film about seduction
    of a virgin)
Take the High Road - Concordia series
Wonderfully Made - Concordia series

41. WHAT PARENTS SHOULD KNOW ABOUT SEX
     EDUCATION IN THE SCHOOLS, No. 051-02066,
     NEA, 1201 16th St. NW, Washington, D.C. 20036.
     35/$1.00.

"For the most part adults have abandoned the weighty responsibility of teaching children and youth about sex and its proper
role in human relationships. The School has emerged as the
agency best equipped to help young people learn to live com-
fortably with the evolving sexual ethic of the adult world."

   "Traditionally sex education has been a function of the
home or of the church. Is it now a proper function of the
schools? Yes, because all the evidence shows that most children are not receiving adequate sex education at home,in

386

church, or elsewhere. The schools can provide a body of accurate knowledge about sex that most parents seem unable or unwilling to give their children."

"Much sex education can be given as a normal part of class work in Biology, and Chemistry - in Economics and Civics courses - in Literature, History and Social Studies. To be of real value, they must be incorporated in a well-coordinated, continuing health education program for all students, beginning in the kindergarten."

"Probably *in the beginning* schools will get further if they allow the child of any parents who seriously object to the program to be excused from it." (Emphasis ours.)

QUOTATIONS FROM SIECUS PERSONNEL AND PUBLICATIONS

SIECUS BROCHURE, 1967-68, page 5: "It is not the job of any voluntary health organization which SIECUS is, to make moral judgements; SIECUS can be neither for nor against illegitimacy, premarital sex — nor any other manifestation of human sexual phenomena."

SIECUS STUDY GUIDE No. 5, page 15: "The choice of a premarital sexual standard is a personal moral choice, and no amount of facts or trends can 'prove' scientifically that one ought to choose a particular standard. Thus, the individual is in a sense 'free.' "

READER'S DIGEST, June 1968, page 81: Kirkendall: "And if present trends continue, premarital intercourse will almost certainly increase. The need for sex education, therefore, is that much greater."

Ibid, page 80: "Most people have the vague hope that it will somehow cure half the world's ills — reduce casual sex experience, cut down on illegitimate births, eliminate venereal disease. To be perfectly blunt about it, we have no way of knowing that sex education will solve any problems."

Ibid, page 83: "There's no way that you can proceed with-

387

out some risk. You have to admit that there are people teaching in schools who have sexual problems of their own they haven't worked through — quite frankly, we don't have adequate training facilities right now."

SEX AND THE TEENAGER — A symposium, Quotation by Isadore Rubin,* page 70: "For the community to ask the sex educator to take on the responsibility of cutting down on illegitimacy or on venereal disease is to ask him to undertake a task that is foredoomed to failure."

SEXOLOGY MAGAZINE: (Editor Rubin was treasurer of SIECUS; Parent Guidance Editor Kirkendall is a founder of SEICUS; numerous contributors to SEXOLOGY are, or were once, on the board of directors of SIECUS, or are recommended by them.)

April, 1968, page 624, Article by David Mace, past president of SIECUS: "The simple fact is that through most of our history in Western Christendom we have based our standards of sexual behavior on premises that are now totally insupportable — on the folklore of the ancient Hebrews and on the musings of medieval monks, concepts that are simply obsolete."

June, 1968, page 773, Comment by Dr. Albert Ellis: "I certainly agree that if we are ever to become at all rational about our system of dating and marriage, the double standard will have to go. However, it seems to me that one of the main ways of getting rid of the standard is to encourage premarital sex relations today."

April, 1968, Editorial, Isadore Rubin: "It is high time that we cleanse every trace of dirt from the word contraception. We should begin to teach our young people — at home, in school and elsewhere — that the more immoral kind of teenage behavior is not sex relations before marriage, but carelessly bringing a child into the world before one is mature enough to care for it."

*Deceased.

388

PHI DELTA KAPPAN, May 1968, Vol. XLIX, No. 9: The Pill, The Sexual Revolution and the Schools, by Ashley Montagu, page 483. "Spelled out in practical terms, what this means is that our schools must become institutes for the teaching of human responsibility, with this as the primary purpose of education, and instruction in the three 'R's' as purely secondary to this main purpose."

REDBOOK, Sept. 1967, page 140: "(the students) most of all share their feelings about parents, brothers, sisters, one another and themselves." . . . "Family relationships are discussed at length, and the children naturally refer to their home experiences with parents who seem unfair, spoiled younger sisters, and older brothers who are bullies."

POST, June 29, 1968, page 27, Dr. Mary Calderone: "Everything that science knows about sex and sexuality our children must have access to . . . We must give full information."

McCALLS, Jan. 1968, page 116: "Methods of illegal abortion. Instruments used by amateur abortionists include the following: crochet hooks, nail files, knitting needles, wires, wire coat hangers, combs, plastic bottles, hair pins, turkey quills, nut picks. These instruments often puncture the uterus or its surrounding tissues, causing serious damage that may lead to tragedy." (Quoting from the teaching manual of a public high school.)

TIME, June 9, 1968, On Teaching Children About Sex, page 37: "Teachers try to make the subject matter as specific as possible — especially in the elementary grades where they assign children to model the male and female genitals in clay."

McCALLS, op cit, page 117: "A group of 50 high school juniors and seniors, boys and girls, watched a visiting lecturer apply a contraceptive to a life sized plastic phalus."

389

FAMILY LIFE AND SEX EDUCATION PAMPHLETS AND CURRICULUM GUIDES
(The following are recommended by NEA)

SEX IN THE '60's — Time-Life Books, Rockefeller Center, N.Y. $1.00.

EDUCATING ACTIVIST YOUTH: A CHALLENGE TO RE-SEARCH — California Teachers Association proceedings of 20th Annual State Conference on Education Research, 1705 Murchison Drive, Burlingame, California.

SEX EDUCATION AND THE SCHOOLS — Harper and Row, 49 E. 33rd Street, New York $4.50

A CURRICULUM GUIDE IN SEX EDUCATION — Helen Manley, State Publishing Co., St. Louis, Mo. $1.75

FAMILY LIFE AND SEX EDUCATION IN THE ELEMEN-TARY SCHOOL — Manley, Dept. of Elem/Kg/Nurs. Ed. NEA, 1201 16th St., NW., Washington, D.C. $1.00

SCHOOL HEALTH EDUCATION STUDY, INC. (SHES) — Health Education: A Conceptual approach to Curriculum Design, 3M, St. Paul, Minn. $8.95 (A catalog is available free)

JOURNAL OF SCHOOL HEALTH, May 1967.

JOURNAL OF HEALTH, PHYSICAL EDUCATION, RECRE-ATION, September 1966.

CHILDREN MAGAZINE (H.E.W.), July 1967.

SATURDAY EVENING POST, June 29, 1968.

WASHINGTON POST, October 8, 1967.

JOURNAL OF MARRIAGE AND THE FAMILY, May 1967

PHI DELTA KAPPAN, September 1968.

WHAT PARENTS SHOULD KNOW ABOUT SEX EDUCA-TION IN THE SCHOOLS, NEA pamphlet 35/$1.00.

CURRICULUM GUIDES AND POLICIES

ANAHEIM UNION HIGH SCHOOL (California) P.O. Box 3520, $10.00 — Family Life and Sex Education, Course Outline, Grades 7 - 12. (Out of print.)

BALTIMORE CITY PUBLIC SCHOOLS, 2519 N. Charles St., Baltimore, Md. — 3 pamphlets on Sex Ed. resources, and K - 6 and 7 - 12 guides, 50¢ each.

FAYETTE COUNTY PUBLIC SCHOOLS, 400 Lafayette Dr., Lexington, Ky. Elementary and Junior and High Schools resources guides, $3.00 each.

FLINT COMMUNITY SCHOOLS, 806 W. 6th Ave., Flint, Michigan — Sex Ed. Guide for Teachers, $1.00.

KANSAS CITY SCHOOL DIST. TELEVISION — 7th Grade Health — Board of Edu. Bldg., Kansas City, Mo., free.

KEOKUK COMMUNITY SCHOOL DISTRICT, 228 Middle Road, Keokuk, Iowa — Marriage and Family Living, and Personal Adjustment — 50¢ each.

MARYLAND STATE DEPT. OF EDUCATION — Principles and Guidelines, 301 E. Preston, Baltimore, Maryland.

MICHIGAN STATE BOARD OF EDUCATION — Planning PL and SE, Lansing, Michigan. Also: Planning for Sex Education.

NATIONAL ASSOC. OF INDEPENDENT SCHOOLS — Planning a Program of Sex Education, 50¢.

N.C. DEPT. OF PUBLIC INSTRUCTION — Sex Edu. Policy Statement, Raleigh, North Carolina.

OHIO DEPT. OF EDUCATION — The School and Sex Edu., Ohio Depts. Bldg., Rm. 606, Columbus, Ohio.

SAN DIEGO SCHOOLS, 4100 Normal Street, San Diego, Calif. "Growing Up." $1.25

UNIVERSITY CITY, 725 Kingsland Ave., University City, Mo., Family Living and Sexuality, Curriculum Outlines K - 6, $2.00. Also: Planning '68 Curriculum, $2.00.

SOURCES OF ADDITIONAL INFORMATION:

Audio Visual:
  Health Guidance in Family Living and Sex Edu. - Glenn Educational Films, Inc., P.O. Box 371, Monsey, N.Y.
  Kentucky State Board of Health, Mental Health, Films used at Teacher's Workshops.
  YMCA: Sex Education, Let's Get Going - 600 Lexington Ave., New York.
  Society for Visual Education, 1345 Diversey Parkway, Chicago, Illinois.
  Guidance Association, Box 5, Pleasantville, N.Y. "Sex: A Moral Dilemma for Teenagers."
Handling all SIECUS recommended audio-visual materials plus study guides:
  Henk Newenhouse, Inc., 1825 Willow Road, Northfield, Illinois 60093.
Curriculum and Policy Guides:
  GETTING STARTED – Glen Cove Publ., Glen Cove, N.Y. $1.00.
  FL and SE, K - 6, Louisville, Kentucky Public Schools, 506 Hill Street. $2.00. Also: FL and SE Resource Unit $1.00.
  Moorestown Township (N.J.) Publ. Schools, K - 6 Personal Growth Prog. n/c George Baker School, Maple Ave.
  N.J. State Dept. of Edu., Guidelines, 225 W. State Street, Trenton, N.J., 50¢.
  N.Y. City Publ. Schools – FL including SE – Bd. of Edu., 110 Livingston St., Brooklyn, N.Y., $3.00.
  Sex Education GIRL SCOUTING – and Resources Related to Sex Edu., Girl Scouts of America, 830 Third Ave., N.Y., 1967.
  U.S. DEPT. HEW – Bibliography on Family Life – NO LONGER AVAILABLE.
  Washington State Office of Public Instruction Bibliography, Olympia, Washington.

PUBLICATIONS WHICH MIGHT BE OF INTEREST

1. "Unfinished Stories for Use in the Classroom," from NEA Journal, 75¢. Situation ethics, peer/group decisions.
2. "Understanding Intergroup Relations," Association of Classroom Teachers, NEA, No. 21.
3. "Normal Adolescence," Group for the Advancement of Psychiatry, No. 68, 419 Park Ave. S., N.Y. 10016. $1.50.
4. "A Book About Me," by Science Research Associates, Chicago, 259 E. Erie. No. 5-1521. Picture-book (workbook) for primary grades to help teacher assess full and intimate family information. Send to SRA for their catalog.
5. "Goodbye to the Birds and Bees," An Approach by Dr. Mary Calderone, American Education Magazine, HEW Office of Edu., November 1966.
6. "Group Processes in Elementary and Secondary Schools," Association of Classroom Teachers, NEA No. 19.
7. Symposium No. 3, "Factors used to increase the susceptibility of individuals to forceful indoctrination: Observations and Experiments," Group for the Advancement of Psychiatry, December 1956.
8. Symposium No. 9, "Pavlovian Conditioning and American Psychiatry," G.A.P. 1964.
9. "Branded Child" by Edward Van Allen, Reportorial Press, P.O. Box 182, Mineola PO, Mineola, Long Isl., N.Y.
10. "Summerhill: A Radical Approach to Child Rearing, " A.S. Neil, Hart Publishing Co., N.Y.
11. "Sense Relaxation," by Bernard Gunther, paperback $2.95.
12. "Sex and Society in Sweden," Birgitta Linner, Pantheon press (introduction by Kirkendall of SIECUS).
13. SIECUS Study Guides as follows:
    No. 1.   Sex Education - Lester Kirkendall
    No. 2.   Homosexuality - Isadore Rubin
    No. 3.   Masturbation - Warren R. Johnson

No. 4. Characteristics of Male and Female Sexual Responses - Wardell Pomeroy

No. 5. Sexual Relations During Pregnancy and the Post-Delivery Period, - Leon Israel/Isadore Rubin

No. 6. Premarital Sexual Standards - Ira L. Reiss

No. 7. Film Resources for Sex Education

No. 8. Sexuality and the Life Cycle - Kirkendall/Rubin

We strongly recommend that you obtain the SIECUS catalog.

14. "Sex Education, USA," Guidance Assoc./Harcourt, Brace and World/SIECUS $1.00.

SENSITIVITY TRAINING
PUBLICATIONS WHICH MIGHT BE OF INTEREST

1. Issues in Human Relations Training," Nat'l. Training Lab., NEA 1962.

2. "The Dynamics of Planned Change," Lippid, Watson, Westly — Harcourt, Brace and World, 1958.

3. "Science and Human Behavior," Skinner; McMillan Co., N.Y. 1965.

4. "Self-Renewal: The Individual and the Innovative Society," John W. Gardner, Harper and Row, N.Y. 1965.

5. "T-Group Theory and Laboratory Method," Bradford, Gibb, Benne and Berenson.

6. "Some Applications of Behaviour Research," Likert, UNESCO 1957.

7. "Education for Freedom and World Understanding," U.S. Dept. of HEW, March 1962.

8. "Guidance and Counseling in Groups," NEA Journal, October 1966.

9. "Sensitivity Training in the Classroom," NEA Journal, January 1967.

10. "Concepts for Social Change," Cooperative Project for Education Development, National Training Labs, NEA.

11. "Concepts of Community Psychiatry, A Framework for Training," HEW and National Institute of Mental Health.

12. "National Elementary Principal," Vol. XLVII, No. 2, November 1968, NEA, $1.00.

BIBLIOGRAPHY

Saturday Evening Post, June 19, 1968, "Sex Invades the Schoolroom."

"Sex and the Teenager" symposium. Quoted by Rubin.

Reader's Digest, June 1968, page 81; June 1968, page 83.

Anaheim's Teachers Guide for Sex Education and Family Life. (Note: In this guide, the ways in which the child can be made contemptuous of his own family are clearly set forth.)

SIECUS: various newsletters.

SIECUS – Study Guide No. 1, page 8.

"Sex Edu. and the Schools," page 17.

Innumerable articles from the Anaheim Bulletin.

McCalls, January 1968, "Sex Education."

VALUATOR – CTA Magazine, Spring 1968, "Symposium of Sex Education."

"A Classroom Approach to Human Sexuality," by Esther Schulz and Sally Williams. (This is particularly important, since Williams, coordinator for sex edu. in Anaheim and a SIECUS board member outlines her concepts for all the world to see. But, beware the double talk.)

Herald-Examiner, "Chilling Aspect," Henry Taylor, May 7, '68.

See various copies of SEXOLOGY Magazine.

"Professor Comments on Sex," Anaheim Bulletin, 3/13/68.

See the various articles by John Steinbacher in the October, November and December 1968 issues of the Bulletin.

American Baby Magazine, April 1968, "Sex Education."

Phi Delta Kappan, May 1968, "The Pill, the Sex Revolution and the Schools," by Montagu.

"Knowing Your Sexual Needs," Anchell, Melvin. MUST reading.

TEEN Magazine, May 1968, "Sex and Dating."

Phi Delta Kappan, May 1968, "Putting Sex Back Into Sex Education."

"A Parent Looks at Sex Education," Richards, Barbara, 14641 Charloma Dr., Santa Ana, California.

Battle for the Mind, by Wm. W. Sargant, Doubleday, 1957.

Sensitivity Training, Church League of America, 422 N. Prospect St., Wheaton, Ill., October 1968. 50¢.

Inhibitions Thrown to the Winds, Life Magazine, July 12, '68.

The Great Group Binge, E.L. Hoover, West Sect., L.A. Times, January 1967.

2000 A.D., A Symposium, Carl Rogers, Alan Watts, Herman Kahn, ORACLE Newspaper, Vol. 1, No. 12; 1371 Haight St., San Francisco, Calif. 94117.

Issues in Human Relations Training, Irving Weschler and E.H. Schein, National Training Laboratories of the National Education Association, 1962.

The Dynamics of Planned Change, Lippitt, Watson, Westly — Harcourt, Brace and World, Inc. 1958.

Science and Human Behavior, B.F. Skinner — McMillan Co., New York, 1965.

Self-Renewal: The Individual and the Innovative Society by John W. Gardner — Harper and Row, N.Y. 1965.

Introduction to Western Behavioral Sciences Institute by Richard Farson, Mimeo.

T-Group Theory and Laboratory Method by Bradford, Givv, Benne & Berenson.

Examining Sensitivity Training and the Laboratory Method by James M. Hardy, Executive and Richard L. Batchelder, Associate, Research & Development Division, Nat'l. Board of YMCA. May 1968 issue of: Forum of the Association of Secretaries of the YMCA.

Sensitivity Training, The Trojan Horse by Marie Heller Paul, California Educators, Associated, Box 1129, Long Beach, California 90801, 25¢.

Brainwashing in the High School and Collectivism on Campus, by E.M. Root.

Education for Survival in the Struggle Against Communism, Senate Document 93, 87th Congress. (Supt. of Documents, Gov't. Printing Office, Washington, D.C. 35¢.)

Guidance and Counseling in Groups, article from NEA Journal,

October 1966.

Sensitivity Training in the Classroom, article from NEA Journal, January 1967.

Change In School Systems, National Training Labs of the NEA.

Peer Analysis, A Way to Help Adolescents, Dr. Allen Hassen, California Teacher's Asso. Journal, January 1958.

Sensitivity Training for Students, Berkeley Unified School District Inter-Group Education Project.

Concepts for Social Change, Watson, Goodwin. Published for Cooperative Project for Edu. Development, NTL of NEA.

Education in Ecstasy, Leonard, George; editor, Look Magazine. Three part series, Sept. 17, Oct. 1 and Oct. 15, 1968.

To Deceive the Elect-Cursillo, DeTar; Athanasius Press, Reno, Nevada.

How, Sister Gertrude Donnelly, Catholic Action, Notre Dame, Indiana.

Conversing with God, Rinker, Zondervan Publishers.

Communicating Love Through Prayer, Rinker, Zondervan.

The Church Executive, Price; Lloyd, Merrill and Johnson, 1967.

Church and Group Mania, Methodist Laymen, Box 323, North Hollywood, Calif.

Taste of New Wine, Miller; Word Book Publishers.

In Every War But One, Kinead, W.W. Norton Co., N.Y. 1959.

Brain Washing and the Men Who Defied It, Hunter; Pyramid Books, 1962.

Brainwashing in Red China, Hunter, Edward.

The Guerrilla and How to Fight Him, Lt. Col. T. Greene, Marine Corps Assoc. 1962. Includes article by Viet Cong General No Nguyen Giap, who decimated the French at Dienbienphu. The article is from Giap's book, "People's War, People's Army: The Vietcong Manual for Underdeveloped Countries," Praeger, 1962. (This is the publisher that put out the book, Oh! Sex Education, by Mary Breasted, in August 1970. The book was allegedly about the Anaheim sex education battle, but was really a book of character assassination that had nothing to do with the Anaheim

397

struggle. Those reading that book would know nothing about what really transpired in Anaheim.)

In the Presence of Mine Enemies, Clifford, John; Norton 1963.

Red China's Fighting Hordes, Lt. Col. Robert Rigg, Military Service Publishing Company 1952. This is the most definitive book on People's Liberation Army movements yet.

Quotations from Chairman Mao, Chapter 1, The Communist Party; Chapter 10, Leadership of Party Committees; and, Chapter 27, Criticism and Self Criticism.

Rape of the Mind, J.A.M. Meerloo, M.D., World Publishers 1956.

Thought Reform and Psychology of Totalism, Lifton, R.J., M.D.; Norton, 1961.

Communist Persuasion, Father Winance, Kennedy Press, 1959.

New Minds and New Men, Thomas Woody, MacMillan Company, 1932, the definitive story of the effects of the Dewey philosophy upon Soviet education, written by a Dewey follower.

Conduct of Inquiry: Kaplan, Abraham, Chandler Publishing Co., San Francisco. (A study of the contributions of behaviorism to education, written by one of the behaviorists.)

Readings in the Foundations of Education: Several volumes, Teacher's College, Columbia University, New York. Volume One is dedicated to Deweyphile William Heard Kilpatrick. Some of the most radical of the Dewey philosophers are found in this series of books including Harry Elmer Barnes; John Childs; John Dewey, himself; George Counts; I.L. Kandel; Boyd Bode; R. Bruce Raup; Ruth Benedict; William Graham Sumner; Randolph Bourne; Karl Mannheim; Alfred North Whitehead; Margaret Mead; Maxwell Stewart; Stuart Chase; Adolf Berle; Gardiner Means; John McVicker; N.S. Popov (head of Soviet education and a Kremlin agent); Florence Greenhoe; C.E.M. Joad; Maurice Leven; Harold Moulton; Clark Warburton; J.A. Hobson; Edmund de S. Brunner; Jeremy Bentham; James Warbasse; Ellis Cowling; Benson Landis.

INDEX

399

SIECUS Board Members — Past and Present

Robert L. Arnstein, M.D.
David Ausubel, M.D.
Alan Bell
Jessie Bernard, Ph.D.
George Packer Berry
Clark Blackburn
June Bricker, Ph.D.
Calfred Broderick, Ph.D.
Rev. Thomas Brown, D.D.
Mary Bunting
Vivian Cadden
Mary Calderone, M.D.
George Chamis
Catherine Chilman, Ph.D.
Cornelia Christenson
Harold T. Christensen, Ph.D.
William Graham Cole
William Darity, Ph.D.
Rev. Foster Doan
Lester Doniger
Evelyn Duvall
Asgusto Esquibel, M.D.
Moye Freymann, M.D.
Isao Fujimoto, M.D.
Wallace Fulton
John Gagnon
Evelyn Gendel, M.D.
Rev. William Genne
Ketayun Gould, Ph.D.
Father George Hagmaier, CSP
Reuben Hill
Joseph Himes

Father Walter Imbiorski
Warren Johnson
Richard Kay
Lester Kirkendall
Rabbi Bernard Kligfield
Sophia Kleegman
Elizabeth Koontz
Robert Laidlaw
Winn Laidlaw
Bernard Lander
G. Milton La Riviere
E. James Liberman, M.D.
Harold Lief, M.D.
David Mace
J. Noel Macy
Frederick Margolis, M.D.
William Masters, M.D.
Luigi Mastronianni, M.D.
Jane Mayer
John Money, Ph.D.
W. Ray Montgomery
Emily Mudd, Ph.D.
John Mudd, M.D.
Ethel Nash
Dean Morrison
Jerome Nathanson
James Peterson
William Peltz, M.D.
Harriet Pilpel
Wardell Pomeroy, Ph.D.
Ira Reiss
John Rock

400

SIECUS Board Members — Past and Present (con'd.)

Lloyd Rigler
Virgil Rogers
Isadore Rubin (deceased)
Aaron Rutledge
William Saltonstall
Rabbi Jeshaia, Schnitzer, M.D.
Gilbert Schimmel
Ralph Slovenko, Ph.D.
Helen Southard
Judge Juanita Kidd Stout
Mette Strong

Wilhelmina Thomas
Father John Thomas, SJ
Earl Ubell
Paul Vahanian
Joseph Van Vleck
Preston Valien
Clark Vincent
Bennetta Washington
Sally Williams
Leontine Young

SEXOLOGY MAGAZINE STAFF

(Asterisks denote SIECUS affiliation)

Hugo Gernsback, Editor in Chief
Harvey Gernsback, Publisher
*Isadore Rubin, Editor (deceased)
*LeMon Clark, Quest Dept.
*Lester Kirkendall, Parent Guidance
Philip Reichert
Mary Gernsback
Leonard Gross
Joseph Riazzo
Harry Benjamin
Bertina Baer
Madeon Gernsback
G. Aliquo
Jose DePoo

Consultant Board
Harry Benjamin
*LeMon Clark
*William Genne
*Lester Kirkendall
*Ashley Montagu
*Wardell Pomeroy
Philip Reichert
*Aaron Rutledge
Emilio Servadio
Walter Stokes

401

AMERICAN ASSOCIATION OF SEX EDUCATORS AND COUNSELORS

(Asterisks denote SIECUS Board or Staff Members)

Warren Johnson*
Jed Pearson*
Tom McGinnis
Edith Nash
Susan Roth
Nancy Berliner
John Chandler
Elizabeth Nichols
Marjorie Schumacher
Florence Yohalem
Morton Yohalem
Wilbur Cohen
Elizabeth Koontz*
Mrs. Bruce Eckman
Rabbi Balfour Brickner*
Ruth Chaskel
LeMon Clark*
Samuel Dodek
Louise Erlbeck
Bruce Fretz
Rev. William Genne*
W.F. Gains
Elizabeth Goodman
Eleanor Hamilton
Robert Harper
Richard Hey

P.K. Houdek
Gertrude Hunter
Lester Kirkendall*
Sophia Kleegman*
Harold Lief*
Gary London
Dorothy Lyons
Monsignor Thomas Lyons
David Mace*
Beryce MacLennon
Rev. James McHugh
Isadore Rubin*
Gerhard Neubeck
Ruth Newman
James Peterson
Roland Scott
Walter Stokes
Doris Terry
Marion Tucker
LuVerne Walker
Matthew Whitehead
Cecilia Wood
Mary Young
Donald Young
Rosalie Blasky

ONE FINAL PAGE

The story in this book has ended — but it has only begun for millions of America's children and their embattled parents.

Perversion and distortion of The Child Seducers will accelerate — and parents must continue to resist in every way they know how.

For myself, I will continue to aid parents with the articles exposing the machinations of the educational hucksters and charlatans in the pages of the daily *Anaheim Bulletin*, in my column, School and Family, and in the national monthly newspaper, *The Educator*.

The Educator picks up where this book leaves off, chronicling the every day activities of The Child Seducers and laying down the battle line for parents to follow all over America. With approximately 60 per cent of each edition devoted to education, *The Educator* will continue to be an ever growing force in the nation — and I will play a part, with your continuing help and encouragement.

If you do not already subscribe to *The Educator*, may I suggest you need to do so, in order to keep abreast of what is happening in the field of education in YOUR town and throughout the United States and Canada.

At just $6 for 12 issues, *The Educator* is one of the great bargains in the field of publishing — and it is so vital that I wish I could personally buy a subscription for everyone who has read this book.

Since I obviously cannot do that, may I suggest that you send your order for a year's subscription today to *The Educator*, 1110 S. Pomona Avenue, Fullerton, Calif. 92632 — Phone (714) 871-2950.

For those who want to subscribe to the daily *Anaheim Bulletin*, which carries my School and Family column, send $9 for three month's payment in advance to the Bulletin at 232 S. Lemon Avenue, Anaheim, California 92805.

Do yourself and your children a favor, and subscribe to one or both of these papers, today. **JOHN STEINBACHER**

MURDER ABOLITION MOVEMENT GROWING

Hon. John R. Rarick of Louisiana
in the House of Representatives — Monday, March 8, 1971

Mr. RARICK, Mr. Speaker, in recent years many controversial legislative proposals, extending from the extreme to the sublime, have been enacted into law not only by the Congress but by State and local legislative bodies. But never did I think that a measure legalizing the murder of innocents would be made a law. Yet, that is what has occurred in New York, California, Hawaii, and in some other States. I am referring to laws permitting abortion as a right.

The right to life is declared by the word of God in the Holy Bible and is also proclaimed in our Declaration of Independence and Constitution.

A constituent recently sent me a newspaper which is largely devoted to a discussion of the abortion problem. The newspaper is called the Educator, of Fullerton, Calif., and is edited by Mr. James Townsend. The Educator is an excellent newspaper in that it promotes morality, patriotism, free enterprise, constitutional government—those ideas, concepts, and practices which have made America strong spiritually as well as materially.

It is encouraging to know that Right-to-Life units are being formed across the Nation and to learn about what concerned mothers are doing to protect the rights of the unborn.

The articles on abortion are most enlightening. I urge that they be widely read.

I insert articles from the Educator following my remarks:

THE CHILD SEDUCERS
by John Steinbacher $7.95

For bulk rates, write to: **Educator Publications, Inc.
1110 S. Pomona Avenue, Fullerton, California 92632**